Honoré de Balzac

Ursule Mirouet and Other Stories

Honoré de Balzac

Ursule Mirouet and Other Stories

ISBN/EAN: 9783744751179

Printed in Europe, USA, Canada, Australia, Japan

Cover: Foto ©Thomas Meinert / pixelio.de

More available books at **www.hansebooks.com**

Ursule Mirouët

AND OTHER STORIES

TRANSLATED BY

CLARA BELL

WITH A PREFACE BY

GEORGE SAINTSBURY

.

PHILADELPHIA

THE GEBBIE PUBLISHING CO., Ltd.

1898

CONTENTS

LIST OF ILLUSTRATIONS

Drawn by D. Murray-Smith.

PREFACE.

"URSULE MIROUËT," dedicated by Balzac to his niece, Sophie Surville, and avowedly written "in the fear of the young person," or, as the author more elegantly puts it, "in uncompromising respect of the noble principles of a pious education," exposes itself by the very fact to two different sorts of prejudice. It is sure to be cried up by one set of judges as "wholesome," and to be cried down by another as "goody."

The latter charge is certainly unfair, for Balzac has by no means written the book in rose-pink and sky-blue only, nor has he been afraid to show things more or less as they are. Nevertheless, it is difficult not to admit that evidences of restraint and convention do exist. Ursule—even more than Eugénie, who becomes a person on at least two occasions, her struggle with her father, and her *revanche* over her cousin—is a thing of shreds and patches, an ideal being in whom that mysterious "candor," to which the French attach such excessive value in a girl, and which they make such haste to do away with altogether in a woman, seems to shut out all positive individuality. She is very nice; but she is not very human.

Nor can the machinery of dreams, hypnotism, Swedenborgianism, and what not, which Balzac, following out one of his well-known manias, chose to work into the book, be said to add very largely to its verisimilitude. It contrasts too sharply with the extremely prosaic, if not always very probable, details of Minoret-Levrault's theft of the will, and of the jealousy of the heirs, which it is interesting to contrast with Dickens' management of the same subject in "Great

Expectations." How far this combination is artistically possible or advisable is a question of abstract criticism into which we need not enter. I think it does not require much argument to prove that Balzac has not, as a matter of fact, quite shown the possibility or the desirableness here. I do not know in the work of a man of genius a more striking instance of the wisdom of the principle, *Nec Deus intersit*, to which, in our day, Horace would certainly have given the form, " Keep the supernatural in fiction out, unless you can't manage with the natural."

However, even this may be a question of opinion; and it is at least worth while to point out that in this book Balzac has anticipated, very curiously and interestingly, a large class of English fiction of a later day, which, in its turn, has been imitated in France. The whole scheme, indeed, of " Ursule Mirouët," by no means owing only to its respect of the young person, though doubtless partly owing to this, is far more that of an English novel than of a French. The absence of the usual " triangle," and of all courtship of married women, together with the difficulty (which a Frenchman even now, to some extent, experiences, and experienced much more in Balzac's days), of making very much of " honest " love scenes between man and maid, put Balzac's always fertile invention upon hunting out and setting to work other sources of interest, which, with the possible exception of the dream-and-vision part of the book, he has, as a rule, engineered very happily. Even the love affair between Ursule and Savinien de Portenduère is not to be contemptuously spoken of; and the figure of Savinien is very pleasantly touched. It is to be noted that even Balzac's favorite heroes of unprincipled convention—Marsay, Rastignac, and the rest—exhibit themselves less theatrically in their dealings with the youthful Vicomte than in almost any other of their numerous appearances. Marsay's theory of debt may be amusingly and advantageously contrasted with the opposite, but in a certain sense complementary, remarks of George Warrington on the same subject in "Pendennis." Madame de Portenduère, too, is good, and not overdone.

On the cabals against Ursule opinions may perhaps differ. It is not easy to say that anything is improbable in the case of a stupid malefactor like Minoret-Levrault; and *odisse quem læseris* is an eternal verity. Still, one would rather have been inclined to suppose that the postmaster, having been so completely successful in his theft, would instinctively feel that it was wiser to let Ursule alone. The malignity of Goupil, too, seems a little overdone, and the whole character of this agreeable lawyer's clerk again presents *mutatis mutandis* something of the eccentric extravagance of Dickens, between whom and Balzac the parallel is perpetually fascinating, because of its constant intermixture of likenesses and contrasts.

But the comic personages generally must be said to be very good. They are not overdone, as the great English novelist just referred to would probably have overdone them; indeed, Balzac has been distinctly sober and sparing in the delineation of their "humors." Dickens certainly, and most English novelists probably, would have been tempted to bring much more to the front poor Madame Crémière's linguistic peculiarities. These will remind everybody of Mrs. Malaprop, though they are more like a historical but much less famous example, the "Lingo Grande," which Southey in divers letters to Grosvenor Bedford puts into the mouth of his sister-in-law, Mrs. Coleridge. The doctor, the magistrate, the curé, the public prosecutor, and all the powers that be play their parts well, and more than a mere good word is deserved by Désiré Minoret, to whom Balzac has been rather cruel.

The doctor himself is a more problematical character. His conversion smacks a little of the stage; and it certainly might seem that such an experienced personage, well aware of the ferocity of the fortune-hunters who surrounded him,

would have taken rather more pains to put the future of Ursule
out of danger by lodging a duplicate will somewhere, or
availing himself of some of the devices in which French law,
even under the Code Napoléon, is nearly as fertile as English.
But the testamentary unreason of mankind is a sufficiently
well-authenticated fact to justify Balzac.

Altogether, the book, if not exactly in the first-class for
power, takes high rank for variety of interest and for the
peculiar character of its scheme. It has no duplicate in its
author's work, and we could not spare it. " Ursule Mirouët"
first appeared in a newspaper, *Le Messager*, in the issues of
August 25 to September 23 inclusive; and when next year it
was published in two volumes by Souverain, it had, as it had
in the periodical, twenty-one chapters with headings. Yet
another year, and it lost these chapters, and all divisions
except the two part-headings of " The Heirs in Alarm " and
" The Minoret Property," and took place in the third edition
of the "Scènes de La Vie de Province," and the first of the
" Comédie " generally.

The three short stories which follow the title story are each
quite characteristic of the author's style and manner. The
various descriptions of the heroine in " Madame Firmiani "
have a point and sparkle which are almost peculiar to the not
quite mature works of men of genius, and the actual story
has a lightness which perhaps would have disappeared if
Balzac had handled it at greater length. " A Forsaken
Woman " partakes more of the character of an anecdote than
that of a story; yet, withal, the account of the first meeting
of Madame de Beauséant and M. de Nueil is positively good;
and the introduction, with its sketch of what Balzac knew or
dreamed to be society, has the merit of most of his overtures.
" The Imaginary Mistress " may be called somewhat fantastic,
and the final trait, whether false or not to nature, will pro-
voke some critics. But the devotion of Paz is exactly one
of those things which suited Balzac best, and which he could

handle most effectively. "Madame Firmiani" was first published in the *Revue de Paris* for February, 1832; then became a "Conte Philosophique," and still in the same year a "Scène de la Vie Parisienne." It was in the 1842 collection that it took up its abode in the "Scènes de la Vie Privée." "A Forsaken Woman" appeared in the same periodical in September of the same year, was a "Scène de la Vie de Province" next year, and was shifted to the "Vie Privée" when the "Comédie" was first arranged. "The Imaginary Mistress" made its appearance about the same period, and took position in the "Scènes de la Vie Privée.

G. S.

URSULE MIROUËT

To Mademoiselle Sophie Surville.

*It is a real pleasure, my dear niece, to dedicate to
you a book of which the subject and the details have
gained the approbation—so difficult to secure—of a
young girl to whom the world is yet unknown, and
who will make no compromise with the high principles
derived from a pious education.   You young girls are
a public to be dreaded; you ought never to be suffered
to read any book less pure than your own pure souls,
and you are forbidden certain books, just as you are not
allowed to see society as it really is.   Is it not enough,
then, to make a writer proud, to know that he has
satisfied you?   Heaven grant that affection may not
have misled you!   Who can say?   The future only,
which you, I hope, will see, though he may not, who is
your uncle*

DE BALZAC.

I.

THE HEIRS IN ALARM.

As you enter Nemours coming from Paris, you cross the
canal of the Loing, whose banks form a rural rampart to the
pretty little town, and afford many picturesque walks.   Since
1830, unfortunately, many houses have been built beyond the
bridge.   If this suburb increases, the aspect of the town will
lose much of its attractive originality.

But in 1829 the country on each side of the road lay open,

*(1)

and the postmaster, a tall, burly man of about sixty, as he sat
on the highest point of the bridge one fine morning, could
command a view of what he would have called a ribbon-road.

The month of September was lavishing its wealth. The
atmosphere quivered with heat above the grass and stones,
not a cloud flecked the ethereal blue, of which the vivid trans-
parency was uniform to the very horizon, showing the extreme
rarity of the air. Indeed, Minoret-Levrault, the postmaster
in question, was obliged to shade his eyes with his hand not
to be quite dazzled. Out of patience with waiting, he looked
now at the lovely meadows spreading away to the right, where
his after-crop was growing apace, and now at the densely
wooded hills to the left, stretching from Nemours to Bouron.
And in the valley of the Loing, where the noises on the road
came back echoed from the hill, he could hear the gallop of
his own horses and the cracking of his postillions' whips.

Could any one but a postmaster get out of patience with
gazing at a field full of cattle, such as Paul Potter painted,
under a sky worthy of Raphael, by a canal overhung with
trees, like a picture by Hobbema? Any one who knows
Nemours, knows that nature there is as beautiful as art, whose
mission it is to spiritualize nature; the landscape there has
ideas, and suggests thoughts.

Still, on seeing Minoret-Levrault, an artist would have left
his place to sketch this country townsman; he was so original
by sheer force of being common. Combine all the characteristics of the brute and you get Caliban, who certainly is a
great creation. Where matter predominates, sentiment ends.
The postmaster, a living proof of this axiom, had one of
those countenances in which the student finds it hard to discern the soul through the violent purple hues of the coarsely
developed flesh. His little gored blue cap, with a peak, fitted
closely to a head so huge as to prove that Gall's science of
phrenology has not yet dealt with the exceptions to his rules.
The shining gray hair, which formed a fringe to the cap,

showed that white hairs may be the result of other causes than overworked brains or severe grief. His large ears were almost bursting round the edges from the fulness of too abundant blood, which seemed ready to spurt out after the smallest exertion. His complexion showed purple blotches under a brown pigment, the result of constant exposure to the sun. His gray eyes, restless and deep set, hidden under two black bushes of eyebrow, were like the eyes of the Kalmucks seen in Paris in 1815; if they glistened now and then, it could only be under the influence of a covetous idea. His nose, squat at the base, took a sudden turn up like the foot of a kettle. Thick lips harmonized with an almost disgusting double chin, rough with the stubble of a beard shaved scarcely twice a week, which rubbed a dirty necktie into a state of worn string; a very short neck, in rolls of fat, and puffy cheeks, completed this image of stupid strength, such as sculptors give to their caryatides. Minoret-Levrault was like one of those statues, with the difference, however, that they support something, while he had quite enough to do to support himself.

You will meet with many an Atlas like him. The man's torso was a huge block, a bull standing on his hind legs. Powerful arms terminated in thick, hard hands, broad and strong, apt at wielding the whip, the reins, and the pitchfork, hands which were no joke in the eyes of his postillions. The enormous stomach of this giant rested on legs as thick as the body of a full-grown man, and feet like an elephant's. Rage was no doubt rare in this man, but when it broke out it would be terrible, apoplectic. Though he was violent and incapable of reflection, the man had done nothing to justify the sinister threats of his appearance. When any one trembled before the giant, his post-boys would say, " Oh, he's not a bad fellow ! "

The " Master " of Nemours, to make use of an abbreviation common in many countries, wore a shooting jacket of bottle-green velveteen, trousers of striped green duck, and a vast yellow mohair waistcoat. In the waistcoat pocket an enormous snuff-box was evident, outlined by a black ring. That a snub nose argues a big snuff-box is a rule almost without exception.

Minoret-Levrault, as a son of the Revolution, and a spectator of the Empire, had never concerned himself with politics; as to his religious opinions, he had never set foot in a church but to be married; as to his principles in domestic life, they were contained in the Civil Code. He thought everything permissible that was not forbidden or indictable by law. He had never read anything but the local newspaper and some manuals relating to his business. He was regarded as a skillful agriculturist, but his knowledge was purely empirical.

In Minoret-Levrault, then, the mind did not give the lie to the body. He spoke rarely, and before delivering himself he always took a pinch of snuff to gain time to find, not ideas, but words. If he had been talkative, he would have seemed a failure.

When you think that this sort of elephant, without a trunk and without intelligence, was called Minoret-Levrault, must you not recognize, with Sterne, the occult power of names, which sometimes mask and sometimes label the character of their owners? In spite of these conspicuous disadvantages, in thirty-six years, the Revolution helping, he had made a fortune of thirty thousand francs a year in meadow-land, arable land, and woods.

Though Minoret, who had shares in the Nemours Messageries Company and an interest in the Gatinais Company at Paris, was still hard at work, it was not so much from habit as for the sake of his only son, for whom he wished to prepare handsome prospects. This son, who, in the peasants' phraseology, had become a gentleman, had just ended his studies for the law, and on the reopening of the courts was to be

sworn as a qualified attorney. Monsieur and Madame
Minoret-Levrault—for behind the colossus a woman is evident, a wife, without whom such a fortune would have been
impossible—had left their son free to choose his career, as a
notary at Paris, as public prosecutor in some country town,
as receiver-general, stockbroker, or postmaster. What fancy
might he not allow himself, to what profession might he not
aspire, as the son of a man of whom it was said from Montargis to Essonne, " Father Minoret does not know how much
he has ? "

This idea had received fresh confirmation when, four years
since, after selling his inn, Minoret built himself a splendid
house and stables, and removed the posting business from the
High Street to the river-side. The new buildings had cost
two hundred thousand francs, which gossip doubled for thirty
miles round. The posting-stage at Nemours required a great
number of horses; it worked as far as Fontainebleau on the
Paris side, and beyond the roads to Montargis and Montereau;
the relays were long, and the sandy soil about Montargis
justified the imaginary third horse, which is always paid for
and never seen. A man of Minoret's build and of Minoret's
wealth, at the head of such a concern, might well be called
without abuse of words the Master of Nemours. Though he
never gave a thought to God or the devil, and was a practical
materialist—as he was a practical agriculturist, a practical
egoist, a practical miser—Minoret had hitherto enjoyed un-
mixed happiness, if a merely material existence may be
regarded as happy. On seeing the pad of flesh which covered
the man's top vertebræ and pressed on his occiput, and
especially on hearing his shrill, thin voice, which contrasted
ludicrously with his bull-neck, a physiologist would have
understood at once why this great, coarse, burly countryman
adored his only son, and perhaps why he had so long awaited
his birth—as the name given to the child, Désiré, sufficiently
indicated. In short, if love, as betraying a rich physical

nature, is the promise of great things in a man, philosophers will understand the causes of Minoret's failure.

His wife, whom the son happily resembled, vied with his father in spoiling the boy. No child's nature could hold out against such idolatry. And, indeed, Désiré, who knew the extent of his power, was clever enough to draw on his mother's savings-box and dip his hand in his father's purse, making each of his fond parents believe that he had not applied to the other. Désiré, who played at Nemours a far more grateful part than that of a prince in his father's capital, had indulged all his fancies at Paris just as he did in his little native town, and had spent more than twelve thousand francs a year. But then, for this money, he had acquired ideas which would never have come into his head at Nemours; he had cast his provincial skin, he had learned the power of money, and had seen that the legal profession was a means of rising in the world. During the last year he had spent ten thousand francs more by forming intimacies with artists, journalists, and their mistresses.

A somewhat alarming confidential letter might have accounted, in case of need, for the postmaster's anxious lookout, a letter in which his son asked his sanction for a marriage; but Madame Minoret-Levrault, fully occupied in preparing a sumptuous meal in honor of the success and the return of the fully-fledged lawyer, had sent her husband out on the road, desiring him to ride forward if he saw no signs of the diligence. The diligence by which this only son was to arrive usually reached Nemours at about five in the morning, and it was now striking nine! What could cause such a delay? Had there been an upset? Was Désiré alive? Had he even broken a leg?

Three volleys of cracking whips rattle out, rending the air like the report of firearms; the red waistcoats of the post-boys are just in sight, ten horses neigh at once! The master takes off his cap and waves it; and he is seen. The best mounted of the postillions, who is returning with two dappled gray post-horses, touches up the beast he is riding, outstripping five sturdy diligence horses, and the Minorets of the stable, three carriage horses, and comes up to the master.

" Have you seen the ' Ducler?' ' "

On the high-roads all the coaches have names—fantastical enough : they are spoken of as the " Caillard," the " Ducler " (the diligence between Nemours and Paris), the "Grand-Bureau." Every new company's coach is the " Rival." At the time when the Lecomtes ran coaches, their vehicles were known as the " Comtesses."

" The ' Caillard ' did not overtake the ' Comtesse,' but the ' Grand-Bureau' caught her skirts, anyhow ! The ' Caillard ' and the 'Grand-Bureau' have done for the ' Françaises ' "—the coaches of the Messageries Françaises or royal mails. If you see a post-boy going fit to split, and refusing a glass of wine, question the guard ; he will cock his nose and stare into space, and reply, " The Rival is ahead ! " " And we cannot even see her ! " adds the postillion. " The wretch ! he has not given his passengers time to eat ! " " As if he had any ! " retorts the guard. " Whip up Polignac ! " All the worst horses are called Polignac. These are the standing jokes and subjects of conversation between the postillions and the guards on the top of the coaches. In France every profession has its own slang.

" Did you see inside the ' Ducler?' ' "

" Monsieur Désiré ? " says the postillion, interrupting his master. " Why, you must have heard us ! Our whips gave due notice of her. We made sure you would be on the road."

" Why is the diligence four hours late ? "

" The tire of one of the wheels came off between Essonne and Ponthierry. But there was no accident ; Cabirolle fortunately discovered it as we were going up the hill."

At this instant a woman in her Sunday best—for the bells of all the churches of Nemours were summoning the inhab-

itants to mid-day mass—a woman of about six-and-thirty, addressed the postmaster.

"Well, cousin," said she, "you would not believe me!
Our uncle is in the High Street with Ursule, and they are
going to mass."

In spite of the license of modern romance in the matter of
local coloring, it is impossible to carry realism so far as to
repeat the horrible abuse, mingled with oaths, which this news,
so undramatic as it would seem, brought from the wide mouth
of Minoret-Levrault; his thin voice became a hiss, and his
face had the appearance which the country-folk ingeniously
refer to as "sunstroke."

"Are you certain?" he asked after his first explosion of
rage.

The postillions as they went by touched three hats to the
master, who seemed neither to see nor hear them. Instead
of waiting for his son, Minoret-Levrault returned up the High
Street with his cousin.

"Did I not always tell you so?" she went on. "When
Doctor Minoret has fallen into his dotage, that sanctimonious
little slut will make a bigot of him; and as those who rule
the mind rule the purse, she will get all our money."

"But, Madame Massin," said the postmaster, quite confounded.

"Oh, yes!" cried Madame Massin, interrupting her cousin,
"you will say as Massin does: 'Is a girl of fifteen likely to
invent and execute such a plot? To make a man of eighty-
three, who never set foot in a church excepting to be married,
give up all his opinions? A man who has such a horror of
priests that he did not even go to the parish church with the
child the day of her first communion.' But, I say, if Doctor
Minoret has such a horror of priests, why, for the last fifteen
years, has he spent almost every evening of the week with the
Abbé Chaperon? The old hypocrite never fails to give Ursule
twenty francs to pay for a taper when she presents the wafer

for the mass. Why, do you not remember the gift Ursule made to the church as a thank-offering to the curé for having prepared her for her first communion? She spent all her money on it, and her godfather gave it back to her doubled. You men pay no heed to anything! When I heard all these details: 'Put away your baskets,' said I, 'the grapes are not for you!' A rich uncle does not behave in that way to a little hussy he has picked out of the gutter unless he means something by it."

"Pooh! cousin," replied the postmaster, "the good man is escorting her as far as the church by mere chance. It is a fine day, and he is going to take a walk."

"I tell you, cousin, our uncle has a prayer-book in his hand; and he looks so smug! However, you will see!"

"They have been playing a very sly game," observed the burly postmaster, "for old Bougival told me that there never was any religious discussion between the doctor and the Abbé Chaperon. Besides, the vicar of Nemours is the best man on earth; he would give his last shirt to a beggar; he is incapable of a mean action, and to filch an inheritance is a——"

"It is robbery!" said Madame Massin.

"It is worse!" cried Minoret-Levrault, exasperated by his voluble cousin's remark.

"I know," she went on, "that the Abbé Chaperon, though he is a priest, is an honest man. But he is capable of anything for the poor. He must have undermined Uncle Minoret, and the doctor has fallen into bigotry. We were easy in our minds, and now he is perverted. A man who never believed in anything, and who had principles! Oh, we are all done for! My husband is dreadfully upset."

Madame Massin, whose speeches were so many arrows that stung her stout cousin, made him walk as briskly as herself in spite of his size, to the great amazement of the people who were going to mass. She wanted to catch up with Uncle Minoret and show him to the postmaster.

On the Gatinais side of Nemours the town is commanded
by a hill, along the base of which the river Loing flows, and
the road runs to Montargis.   The church, on which time has
cast a rich mantle of gray, for it was certainly rebuilt in the
fourteenth century by the Guises, in whose honor Nemours
gave its name to a duchy and peerage, stands at the end of
the town beyond a large archway, as in a frame.   For buildings, as for men, position is everything.   Shaded by trees
and shown to advantage by a neat little square, this lonely
church has quite an imposing effect.   As they came out on to
the square, the postmaster could see his uncle giving his arm
to the young girl they had called Ursule, each carrying a
prayer-book, and just entering the church.   The old man
took off his hat in the porch, and his perfectly white head,
like a summit covered with snow, shone in the soft gloom of
the great doorway.

" Well, Minoret, what do you say to your uncle's conversion ? " cried the tax-receiver of Nemours, whose name was
Crémière.

" What do you expect me to say? " replied the postmaster,
offering him a pinch of snuff.

" Well answered, Father Levrault.   You cannot say what
you think, if a certain learned writer was correct in saying
that a man must necessarily think his words before he can
speak his thought," mischievously exclaimed a young man
who had just come up, and who played in Nemours the part
of Mephistopheles in " Faust."

This rascally fellow, named Goupil, was head clerk to Monsieur Crémière-Dionis, the notary of the town.   Notwithstanding the antecedents of an almost crapulous career, Dionis
had taken Goupil into his office when absolute destitution
hindered him from remaining any longer at Paris, where the
clerk had spent all the money left him by his father, a well-to-
do farmer, who meant him to become a notary.   Only to see
Goupil was enough to tell you that he had made haste to enjoy

life; for, to procure himself pleasure, he must have paid dearly for it. Though very short, the clerk, at seven-and-twenty, had a form as burly as that of any man of forty. Short, thin legs, a broad face with a mottled, muddy skin, like the sky before a storm, and a bald forehead, gave emphasis to this strange figure. His face looked as if it belonged to a hunchback, whose hump was an internal deformity. A peculiarity of this sour, pale face confirmed the notion of this invisible malformation. His nose, hooked and twisted, as is often the case with hunchbacks, had a crossway slope from right to left, instead of dividing the face down the middle. His mouth, pinched at the corners—the sardonic mouth—was always eager for irony. His thin, reddish hair fell in dank locks, showing the head through here and there. His great hands and clumsy wrists, at the end of overlong arms, were like talons, and very seldom clean. Goupil wore shoes only fit to be thrown into the dust-heap, and rusty-black, spun-silk stockings; his black coat and trousers, rubbed perfectly threadbare, and almost greasy with dirt; his abject waistcoats, with buttons from which the mould had slipped out; the old bandana he wore as a cravat—every part of his dress proclaimed the cynical misery to which his passions condemned him.

This aggregate of sinister details was completed by a pair of goat's eyes, the iris set in yellow rings, at once lascivious and cowardly. No man in Nemours was more feared or more respectfully treated than Goupil. Strong in pretensions which his ugliness allowed, he had the detestable wit that is peculiar to persons who take every liberty, and he made use of it to be revenged for the mortifications of his permanent jealousy. He rhymed satirical couplets such as are sung at the Carnival, he got up farcical demonstrations, and himself wrote almost the whole of the local newspaper gossip. Dionis, a keen, false nature, and therefore a timid one, kept Goupil as much out of fear as on account of his intelligence and his thorough

knowledge of family interests in the neighborhood.   But the
master so little trusted the clerk that he managed his accounts
himself, did not allow him to lodge at his house, and never
employed him on any confidential or delicate business. · The
clerk flattered his master, never showing the resentment he
felt at this conduct ; and he watched Madame Dionis with an
eye to revenge.   He had a quick intelligence, and worked
well and easily.

   "Oh you!   You are laughing already at our misfortunes,"
said the postmaster to the clerk, who was rubbing his hands.

   As Goupil basely flattered every passion of Désiré's, who for
the last five years had made him his companion, the postmaster
treated him cavalierly enough, never suspecting what a horrible
store of evil feeling was accumulating at the bottom of
Goupil's heart at each fresh thrust.   The clerk having come
to the conclusion that he, more than any one, needed money,
and knowing himself to be superior to all the good townsfolk
of Nemours, aimed at making a fortune, and counted on
Désiré's friendship to procure for him one of the three good
openings in the place—the registrarship of the law courts, the
business of one of the ushers, or that of Dionis.   So he
patiently endured the postmaster's hectoring and Madame
Minoret-Levrault's disdain, and played an ignominious part
to oblige Désiré, who, for these two years past, had left him
to console the Ariadnes he abandoned at the end of the vacation.   Thus, Goupil ate the crumbs of the suppers he had
prepared.

   "If I had been the old fool's nephew, he should not have
made God my co-heir," retorted the clerk, with a hideous
grin that showed his wide-set and threatening black teeth.

   At this moment Massin-Levrault, junior, the justice's
registrar, came up with his wife, and with him was Madame
Crémière, the tax-receiver's wife.   This man, one of the
crudest natives of the little town, had a face like a Tartar,
small, round eyes like sloes under a sloping forehead, crinkled

hair, an oily skin, large flat ears, a mouth almost without lips, and a thin beard. His manners had the merciless smoothness of the usurer whose dealings are based on fixed principles. He spoke like a man who has lost his voice. To complete the picture, he made his wife and his eldest daughter write out the copies of verdicts.

Madame Crémière was a very fat woman, doubtfully fair, with a thickly freckled complexion ; she wore her gowns too tight, was great friends with Madame Dionis, and passed as well informed because she read novels. This lady of finance of the lowest type, full of pretensions to elegance and culture, was awaiting her uncle's fortune to assume "a certain style," to decorate her drawing-room, and "receive" her fellow-townsfolk; for her husband refused to allow her clockwork lamps, lithographs, and the trifles she saw in the notary's wife's drawing-room. She was excessively afraid of Goupil, who was always on the watch to repeat her *capsulingies**—this was her way of saying *lapsus linguæ*. One day Madame Dionis said to her that she did not know what water to use for her teeth.

"Try gum water," said she.

By this time most of old Doctor Minoret's collateral relations had assembled in the church square, and the importance of the event which had agitated them was so universally understood, that the groups of peasants, men and women, armed with red umbrellas and clad in the bright hues which make them so picturesque on fête-days as they tramp the roads, all had their eyes turned on the doctor's presumptive heirs. In those little towns, which hold a middle rank between the larger villages and the great cities, people who do not attend mass linger in the square. They discuss business.

At Nemours the hour of mass is also that of a weekly money-market, to which come the residents in the scattered

* Madame Crémière's "capsulingies" are impossible to translate ; an equivalent is all that can be attempted.

houses from a mile and a half round. This accounts for the mutual understanding of the peasants as against the masters, on the price of produce in relation to labor.

"And how would you have hindered it?" said the master to Goupil.

"I would have made myself as indispensable to him as the air he breathes. But you did not know how to manage him to begin with. An inheritance needs as much looking after as a pretty woman, and for lack of care both may slip through your fingers. If my master's wife were here, she would tell you how accurate the comparison is," he added.

"But Monsieur Bongrand has just told me we need not be uneasy," said the justice's registrar.

"Oh! there are several ways of saying that," replied Goupil, with a laugh. "I should have liked to hear your cunning justice say that! Why, if there were nothing more to be done; if I, like him—for he lives at your uncle's—knew that the game was up, I should say with him, 'Don't be at all uneasy.'"

And as he spoke the words, Goupil smiled in such a comical way, and gave them so plain a meaning, that the inheritors at once suspected the registrar of having been taken in by the justice's cunning. The receiver of taxes, a fat little man, as insignificant as a tax-collector must be, and as witless as a clever wife could wish, demolished his co-heir Massin with: "Didn't I tell you so?"

As double-dealers always ascribe their own duplicity to others, Massin looked askance at the justice of the peace, who was at this moment standing near the church with a former client, the Marquis du Rouvre.

"If only I were sure of it!" said he.

"You could nullify the protection he extends to the Marquis du Rouvre, who is within the power of the law, and liable to imprisonment; he is deluging him with advice at this moment," said Goupil, insinuating an idea of revenge to the registrar. "But draw it mild with your chief; he is very wide awake; he must have some influence over your uncle, and may yet be able to prevent his leaving everything to the church."

"Pooh! we shall not die of it," said Minoret-Levrault, opening his huge snuff-box.

"You will not live by it either," replied Goupil, making the two women shiver; for they, more rapidly than their husbands, interpreted as privation the loss of the inheritance on which they had counted for comfort. "But we will drown this little grievance in floods of champagne, in honor of Désiré's return, won't we, *gros père ?* " he added, tapping the colossus in the stomach, and thus inviting himself for fear of being forgotten.

Before going any farther, the precise reader will perhaps be glad to have here a sort of preamble in the form of a pedigree, which indeed is very necessary to define the degrees of relationship in which the old man, so suddenly converted, stood to the three fathers of families or their wives. These intermarriages of kindred race in provincial life may be the subject of more than one instructive reflection.

At Nemours there are not more than three or four noble families, of no great rank or fame; among them, at the time of our story, shone that of the Portenduères. These exclusive families visit the nobility who possess lands and châteaux in the neighboring country—the D'Aiglemonts, for instance, owners of the fine estate of Saint-Lange, and the Marquis du Rouvre, on whose property, eaten up with mortgages, the townsfolk kept a greedy eye. The nobility who live in the towns have no wealth. Madame de Portenduère's whole estate consisted of a farm, yielding four thousand seven hundred francs a year, and her house in the town. In the opposite scale to this miniature Faubourg St. Germain are half a score of rich citizens, retired millers and tradespeople, in short, a miniature middle class, below whom struggle the small shopkeepers, the laboring class, and the peasants. This middle class affords here, as in the Swiss cantons and other small communities, the curious phenomenon of the dispersal of a few families native to the soil, perhaps ancient Gaulish clans, settling on a district, pervading it, and making all the inhabitants cousins. At the time of Louis XI., the period when the third estate at last took the by-names they were known by as permanent surnames, some of which presently mingled with those of the feudal class, the citizens of Nemours were all Minoret, Massin, Levrault, or Crémière. By Louis XIII.'s time these four families had given rise to Massin-Crémière, Levrault-Massin, Massin-Minoret, Minoret-Minoret, Crémière-Levrault, Levrault-Minoret-Massin, Massin-Levrault, Minoret-Massin, Massin-Massin, and Crémière-Massin ; all further diversified by " junior " and " eldest son ; " or by Crémière-François, Levrault-Jacques, and Jean-Minoret, enough to madden a Father Anselme, if the populace ever needed a genealogist.

The changes in this domestic kaleidoscope with four separate elements were so complicated by births and marriages, that the pedigree of the citizens of Nemours would have puzzled even the compilers of the "Almanac de Gotha," notwithstanding the atomic science with which they work out the zigzags of German alliances. For a long time the Minorets held the tanneries, the Crémières were the millers, the Massins went into business, the Levraults remained farmers.

Happily for the country, these four stocks struck out rather than round the trunk, or threw out suckers by the expatriation of sons who sought a living elsewhere : there are Minorets, cutlers, at Melun, Levraults at Montargis, Massins at Orleans, and Crémières who have grown rich at Paris. Very various are the destinies of these bees that have swarmed outside the native hive. Rich Massins employ laboring Massins, just as there are German princes in the service of Austria or Prussia. In the same department may be seen a Minoret millionaire protected by a Minoret soldier with the same blood in their veins ; but having only their names in common, these four shuttles had unceasingly woven a human web, of which each piece turned out a gown or a clout, the finest lawn or the coarsest lining. The same blood throbbed in their head, feet, or heart, in toiling hands, damaged lungs, or a brow big with genius. The heads of the clan faithfully clung to the little town where the ties of relationship could be re-laxed or tightened, as the results of this community of names might dictate.

In every country, with a change of names, you will find the same fact ; but bereft of the poetry with which feudality had invested it, and which Sir Walter Scott has reproduced with so much talent.

Look a little higher, and study humanity in history. All the noble families of the eleventh century, now almost all extinct excepting the royal race of Capet, must have co-oper-ated towards the birth of a Rohan, a Montmorency, a Bauffremont, a Mortemart of the present day ; at last, all would coexist in the blood of the humblest man of really gentle birth. In other words, every citizen is cousin to other citizens,.every noble is cousin to other nobles. As we are told in the sublime page of Biblical genealogy, in a thousand years the three families of Shem, Ham, and Japhet could people the whole earth. A family can become a nation ; and, unfortunately, a nation may become one single family. To prove this we have only to apply to a family pedigree—in which the ancestors multiply backwards in geometrical pro-gression—the sum worked out by the sage who invented the game of chess. He claimed, as his reward from the Persian king, an ear of corn for the first square on the board, two for the second, and so on, doubling the number every time, and proved that the whole kingdom could not pay it. This net-work of the nobility entangled in the network of the middle

2

class, this antagonism of blood—the one class protected by rigid traditions, the other by the active endurance of labor and the craft of trade instincts—brought about the Revolution of 1789. The two strains, almost united, are to be seen to-day face to face with collaterals bereft of their inheritance. What will they do? Our political future is big with the reply.

The family of the man who, in Louis XV.'s time, was the representative Minoret, was so large, that one of the five— the very Minoret whose coming to church was making such a sensation—went to seek his fortune in Paris, and appeared in his native town only at long intervals, whither he came, no doubt, to acquire his share of the inheritance at the death of his grandparents. After suffering a great deal, as all young men must who are gifted with a strong will and desire a place in the brilliant world of Paris, this son of the Minorets made a career more splendid perhaps than he had dreamed of at the beginning; for he devoted himself to medicine, one of the professions in which both talent and good-luck are needed, and good-luck even more than talent. Supported by Dupont (of Nemours), brought by a happy chance into contact with the Abbé Morellet (whom Voltaire nicknamed *Mords les*), and patronized by the encyclopedists, Doctor Minoret attached himself with fanatical devotion to the great physician Bordeu, Diderot's friend. D'Alembert, Helvétius, Baron d'Holbach, and Grimm, to whom he was a mere boy, ended, no doubt, like Bordeu, by taking an interest in Minoret, who in 1777 had a fine connection among the deists, encyclopedists, sensualists, materialists—call them as you will—the wealthy philosophers of that day. Though he was very little of a quack, he invented a famous remedy, Lelièvre's balsam, which was cried up in the *Mercure de France*, and which was permanently advertised on the last page of that paper, the encyclopedists' organ. The apothecary Lelièvre, a clever man of business, discerned a success where Dr. Minoret had seen nothing more than a preparation to be included in the pharmacopœia; he honestly divided the profits with the doctor, who was Rouelle's pupil in chemistry, as he was Bordeu's in medicine. It would have needed less to make him a materialist.

In 1778, when Rousseau's "Nouvelle Héloïse" was the rage, and men sometimes married for love, he married the daughter of Valentin Mirouët, the famous harpsichord player, herself a fine musician, but weakly and delicate, who died during the Revolution. Minoret was intimate with Robespierre, to whom he had once caused a gold medal to be awarded for a dissertation on these questions: "What is the origin of the opinion by which part of the shame attaching to the disgraceful punishment of a guilty man is reflected on all his family? Is this opinion generally useful or mischievous? And supposing it to be mischievous, by what means can we avert the disastrous results?" The Academy of Arts and Sciences at Metz, to which Minoret belonged, must still have the original copy of this discourse. Although, thanks to this friendship, the doctor's wife had nothing to fear, she lived in such dread of being sent to the scaffold that this invincible terror aggravated an aneurism due to a too sensitive nature. In spite of all the precautions a man could take who idolized his wife, Ursule met the truck full of condemned victims, and among them, as it happened, Madame Roland. The spectacle caused her death. Minoret, who had spoiled his Ursule, and refused her nothing, so that she had led a life of extravagant luxury, at her death found himself almost a poor man. Robespierre appointed him first physician to a hospital.

Although the name of Minoret had been somewhat famous during the vehement discussions to which mesmerism had given rise, a fame which had recalled him now and then to his relations' memory, the Revolution was so powerful a solvent, and broke up so many family connections, that in 1813 no one at

Nemours knew even of Doctor Minoret's existence, when an unexpected meeting suggested to him the idea of returning, as hares do, to die in his form.

In traveling through France, where the eye is so soon fatigued by the monotony of the wide plains, who has not known the delightful sensation of discerning, from the top of a hill where the road turns or descends, and where he expected to see a dull landscape, a green valley watered by a stream, and a little town sheltered under a cliff, like a hive in the hollow of an old willow-tree? As he hears the postillion's cry of "Come up!" while he walks at his horse's side, the traveler shakes off sleep, and admires as a dream within a dream some lovely scene which is to the stranger what a fine passage in a book is to the reader—a brilliant idea of nature. This is the effect produced by the sudden view of Nemours on the road from Burgundy. It is seen from the height in an amphitheatre of naked rocks, gray, white and black, like those which are scattered throughout the forest of Fontainebleau; and from among them shoot up solitary trees, standing out against the sky, and giving a rural aspect to this sort of tumble-down rampart. This is the end of the long wooded slope which rises from Nemours to Bouron, sheltering the road on one side. At the foot of these cliffs spreads a meadow-land, through which the Loing flows, in level pools ending in little waterfalls. This exquisite tract of country, cut through by the Montargis road, is like an elaborate opera scene, the effects seem so carefully worked up, and brought out in strong contrasts.

One morning the doctor, who had been sent for by a rich invalid in Burgundy, and who was hastening back to Paris, not having mentioned at the last change of horses which road he wished to take, was unwittingly brought through Nemours, and between two naps saw once more the landscape familiar to his childhood. The doctor had by this time lost many of his old friends. The disciple of the Encyclopedia had lived

to see La Harpe a convert, had buried Lebrun-Pindare, and
Marie-Joseph de Chénier, and Morellet, and Madame Helvétius. He had seen the *quasi* overthrow of Voltaire under the
attacks of Geoffroy, Fréron's successor. Hence he was thinking of retiring. And when the post-chaise stopped at the top
of the High Street of Nemours, his good feeling prompted
him to inquire after his family. Minoret-Levrault himself
came out to see the doctor, who recognized in the postmaster
his eldest brother's son. This nephew introduced as his
wife the only daughter of old Levrault-Crémière, who, twelve
years ago, had left her the posting business and the handsomest inn in Nemours.

"Well, nephew," said the doctor, "and have I any other
heirs?"

"My Aunt Minoret, your sister, married a Massin-Massin."

"Yes, the intendant at Saint-Lange."

"She died a widow, leaving one daughter, who has lately
married a Crémière-Crémière, a very nice fellow, who so far
has no appointment."

"To be sure; she is my own niece. Now, as my brother
at sea died unmarried, and Captain Minoret was killed at
Monte-Legino, and I am here, that is an end of my father's
family. Have I any relations on my mother's side? She
was a Jean-Massin-Levrault."

"Of the Jean-Massin-Levraults," replied Minoret-Levrault,
"only one daughter survived, who married Monsieur Cré-
mière-Levrault-Dionis, a dealer in corn and forage, who died
on the scaffold. His wife died of a broken heart, and quite
ruined, leaving one girl, married to a Levrault-Minoret, a
farmer at Montereau, who is doing well; and their daughter
has just married a Massin-Levrault, a notary's clerk at Montargis, where his father is a locksmith."

"So I have no lack of inheritors," said the doctor cheerfully,
and he determined to walk round Nemours in his nephew's
company.

The Loing meanders through the town, fringed with ter-
raced gardens and neat houses that look as if happiness should
inhabit there rather than elsewhere. When the doctor turned
out of the High Street into the Rue des Bourgeois, Minoret-
Levrault pointed out the property of Monsieur Levrault, a
rich ironmaster at Paris, who, he said, was lately dead.

" There, uncle," said he, " is a pretty house to be sold,
with a beautiful garden down to the river."

" Let us go in," said the doctor, seeing a house at the farther side of a paved courtyard, shut in by the walls of houses
on either side, hidden by clumps of trees and climbing plants.

" It is built on cellars," said the doctor as he went in, up
a high outside stairway, decorated with blue and white earthenware pots in which the geraniums were still in bloom. The
house, like most provincial residences, was pierced by a passage down the middle, leading from the courtyard to the garden ; to the right was a single sitting-room with four windows,
two to the yard, and two to the garden ; but Levrault-Levrault
had turned one of these into an entrance to a long conservatory built of brick, leading from the room to the river, where
it ended in a hideous Chinese summer-house.

" Very good ! " said the doctor.   " By roofing and flooring this conservatory I could make a place for my books, and
turn that amazing piece of architecture into a pretty little
study."

On the other side of the passage, looking on to the garden,
was a dining-room, decorated in imitation of lacquer, with a
black background and green and gold flowers ; this was
divided from the kitchen by the staircase. A little pantry
behind the lower flight led from the dining-room to the
kitchen, which had barred windows looking out on the courtyard. On the first floor were two sets of rooms, and above
that wainscoted attics, quite habitable. After a brief inspec-
tion of this house, which was covered with green vine-trellis
from top to bottom, on the courtyard front as well as on the

garden side, with a terrace to the river edged with earthenware flower-vases, the doctor remarked—

"Levrault-Levrault must have spent a good deal here!"

"Oh, his weight in gold!" replied Minoret-Levrault.
"He had a passion for flowers—such folly! 'What profit
do they bring?' as my wife says. As you see, a painter came
from Paris to paint his corridor with flowers in fresco. He
put in whole plate mirrors everywhere. The ceilings were
done up with cornices that cost six francs a foot. In the
dining-room the floor is of the finest inlay—such folly! The
house is not worth a penny the more for it."

"Well, nephew, buy it for me. Let me know when it is
settled; here is my address. The rest my lawyer will attend
to. Who lives opposite?" he asked as they went out into the
street.

"Some *émigrés*," said the postmaster; "a Chevalier de
Portenduère."

When the house was bought, the distinguished physician,
instead of coming to live in it, wrote orders to his nephew to
let it. Levrault's Folly was taken by the notary of Nemours,
who sold his business to Dionis his head clerk, and who died
two years after, leaving the doctor burthened with a house to
let just at the time when Napoleon's fate was being sealed in
the neighborhood. The doctor's heirs, somewhat taken in,
had at first supposed his wish to return to be a rich man's
whim, and were in despair when, as they imagined, he had
ties in Paris which kept him there, and would rob them of
his leavings. However, Minoret-Levrault's wife seized this
opportunity of writing to the doctor. The old man replied
that as soon as peace should be signed, the roads cleared of
soldiers, and communications free once more, he meant to
live at Nemours. He made his appearance there with two of
his clients, the architect to the hospital, and an upholsterer
who undertook the repairs, the rearrangement of the rooms,
and the removal of his furniture. Madame Minoret-Levrault

proposed to him as caretaker the cook of the departed notary, and this he agreed to.

When the heirs learned that their uncle, or great-uncle Minoret, was really going to live at Nemours, their families were seized by an absorbing but almost legitimate curiosity, in spite of the political events which just then more especially agitated the district of the Gatinais and Brie. Was their uncle rich? Was he economical or extravagant? Would he leave a fine fortune or nothing at all? Had he invested in annuities? All this they at last came to know, but with infinite difficulty, and by means of much backstairs spying.

After the death of his wife Ursule Mirouët, from 1789 to 1813, the doctor, who in 1805 had been appointed consulting physician to the Emperor, must have made a great deal of money, but no one knew how much; he lived very simply, with no expenses beyond a carriage by the year, and a splendid apartment; he never entertained, and almost always dined out. His housekeeper, furious at not being asked to go with him to Nemours, told Zélie Levrault, the postmaster's wife, that to her knowledge he had fourteen thousand francs a year in consols. Now, after practicing for twenty years in a profession which such appointments as head physician to a hospital, as physician to the Emperor, and as member of the institute could not fail to have made lucrative, these fourteen thousand francs a year as dividends on repeated investments argued no more than a hundred and sixty thousand francs in savings! And to have laid by no more than eight thousand francs a year, the doctor must have had many vices or virtues to indulge. Still, neither the housekeeper, nor Zélie, nor any one else could divine the secret of so small a fortune. Minoret, who was greatly regretted in his own neighborhood, was one of the most liberal benefactors in Paris, and, like Larrey, kept his acts of benevolence a profound secret.

So it was with the liveliest satisfaction that his heirs watched the arrival of their uncle's handsome furniture and extensive

library, and knew him to be an officer of the Legion of
Honor, and made Chevalier of the Order of Saint-Michael by
the King, in consequence, perhaps, of his retirement, which
made way for some favorite.   But the architect, the painters,
and the upholsterers had finished everything in the most comfortable fashion, and still the doctor came not.   Madame Minoret-Levrault, who watched the upholsterer and the architect as
though her own property were at stake, discovered, through
the inadvertence of a young man sent to put the books in
order, that the doctor had in his care an orphan named
Ursule.   This news caused strange dismay in the town of
Nemours.   At last the old man came home in about the
middle of January, 1815, and settled down without any fuss,
bringing with him a little girl of ten months and her nurse.

"Ursule cannot be his daughter; he is seventy-one years
old!" cried the alarmed expectants.

"Whoever she may be, she will give us plenty of bother,"
said Madame Massin.

The doctor's reception of his grandniece on the mother's
side was cold enough; her husband had just bought the place
of registrar to the justice of the peace, and they were the first
to venture on any allusion to the difficulties of their position.
Massin and his wife were not rich.   Massin's father, an iron-
worker at Montargis, had been obliged to compound with his
creditors, and worked now, at the age of sixty-seven, as hard
as a young man; he would have nothing to leave.   Madame
Massin's father, Levrault-Minoret, had lately died at Montereau of grief at the results of the fighting—his farmhouse
burnt down, his fields destroyed, and his cattle killed and eaten.

"We shall get nothing out of your great-uncle," said
Massin to his wife, who was expecting her second baby.

But the doctor secretly gave them ten thousand francs, with
which the registrar, as the friend of the notary and of the
usher of Nemours, had begun money-lending; and he made
the peasants pay such usurious interest that, at this later day,

Goupil knew him to possess about eighty thousand francs of unconfessed capital.

As to his other niece, the doctor, by his influence in Paris, procured the post of receiver of public moneys at Nemours for Crémière, and advanced the necessary security. Though Minoret-Levrault wanted nothing, Zélie, very jealous of her uncle's liberality to his two nieces, came to see him with her son, then ten years old, whom she was about to send to school in Paris, where, as she said, education was very costly. As physician to Monsieur de Fontanes, the doctor obtained a half-scholarship at the College of Louis le Grand for his grand-nephew, who was placed in the fourth class.

Crémière, Massin, and Minoret-Levrault, all three very common men, were condemned beyond appeal by the doctor during the first two or three months, while they were trying to circumvent their future prospects rather than himself. Persons who act by instinct have this disadvantage as compared with those who have ideas—they are more easily seen through. The inspirations of instinct are too elementary, and appeal too directly to the eye, not to be detected at once; while to penetrate ideas, the devices of the mind, equal intelligence is needed on both sides.

Having thus purchased the gratitude of his heirs, and to some extent stopped their mouths, the wily doctor alleged his occupations, his habits, and the care he gave to little Ursule, so as not to receive their visits, without, however, shutting his door to them : "He liked to dine alone; he went to bed and rose late; he had come back to his native place to enjoy repose and solitude." These whims in an old man seemed natural enough, and his expectant heirs were satisfied to pay him a weekly visit on Sundays between one and four, to which he vainly tried to put a stop by saying—

"Only come to see me when you want me."

The doctor, though he did not refuse his advice in serious cases, especially among the poor, would not become physician to the little asylum at Nemours, and declared that he would no longer practice.

"I have killed enough people!" said he, laughing, to the Curé Chaperon, who, knowing his benevolence, pleaded for the poor.

"He is quite an oddity."

This verdict on Doctor Minoret was the harmless revenge of wounded vanity, for the physician formed a little society for himself of persons who deserve to be contrasted with the heirs. Now, those of the town magnates who thought themselves worthy to swell the court circle of a man wearing the black ribbon of Saint Michael, nourished a ferment of jealousy against the doctor and his privileged friends which, unhappily, was not impotent.

By a singularity which can only be explained by the saying that "extremes meet," the materialist doctor and the priest of Nemours very soon were friends. The old man was very fond of backgammon, the favorite game of the clergy, and the abbé was a match for the physician. This game thus became the first bond between them. Then Minoret was charitable, and the curé of Nemours was the Fénelon of the Gatinais. They were both men of varied information; thus, in all Nemours, the man of God was the only man who could understand the atheist. In order to discuss any matter, two men must understand each other to begin with. What pleasure is there in saying sharp things to any one who does not feel them? The doctor and the priest had too much good taste, and had seen too much good company, not to observe its rules; they could therefore carry on the little warfare that is so necessary to conversation. Each hated the other's opinions, but they esteemed each other's character. If such contrasts and such sympathies are not the essential elements of intimacy, must we not despair of society, since, especially in France, some antagonism is indispensable to it? Contrariety of characters, not antagonism of opinions, is what gives rise to antipathies. So the Abbé Chaperon was the doctor's first friend at Nemours, and this friendship endured unfalteringly to the last.

This priest, now sixty years of age, had been curé of Nemours ever since the re-establishment of Catholic worship. He had refused promotion to be vicar-general of his diocese out of attachment to his flock. If those who were indifferent to religion thought the better of him for it, the faithful loved him all the more. Thus venerated by his flock, and esteemed by the community, the curé did good without inquiring too closely as to the religious views of those who were unfortunate. His own dwelling, scarcely supplied with furniture enough for the strictest necessities of life, was as cold and bare as a miser's hovel. Avarice and charity betray themselves by similar results; does not charity lay up in heaven the treasure that the miser hoards on earth? The Abbé Chaperon took his servant to task for every expense, more severely than Gobseck ever scolded his—if, indeed, that notorious Jew ever had a servant. The good priest often sold his silver shoe-buckles and breeches-buckles to give the money to some poor wretch he had found destitute. On seeing him come out of church with the tongues of his knee-straps pulled through the buttonholes, the devout ladies of the town would trot off to look for the cure's buckles at the one jeweler's and watchmaker's shop in Nemours, and reproach their pastor as they restored them to him. He never bought himself linen or clothes, and wore them till they were dropping to pieces. His underclothing, thick with darns, fretted his skin like a hair-shirt. Then Madame de Portenduère, or some other good soul, plotted with his houskeeper to replace his old shirts or cloth clothes by new ones while he slept; and the priest did not always immediately perceive the exchange. He dined off pewter, with iron forks and spoons; when, on great occasions, he had to receive his subordinate clergy and other curés, a duty that falls on the head of a district, he borrowed silver and table-linen from his friend the atheist.

"My plate is working out its salvation," the doctor would say.

His good deeds, which were sooner or later found out, and which he always reinforced with spiritual comfort, were carried out with sublime simplicity. And such a life was all the more meritorious because the abbé was full of erudition, as vast as it was various, and a man of superior abilities. In him refinement and elegance, the inseparable attributes of simplicity, added charm to elocution worthy of a prelate. His manners, his character, and his conduct gave to his society the exquisite flavor of all that is at once candid and subtle in a lofty intellect. Enjoying pleasantry, in a drawing-room he was never the priest. Until Doctor Minoret's arrival, this worthy man left his light under a bushel without a regret; but he no doubt liked him the better for calling it into play.

Possessed of a fairly good library and two thousand francs a year when he came to Nemours, in 1829, the curé had nothing left but the income from his church, and that he gave away almost entirely year by year. A man of good judgment in delicate affairs or in misfortune, more than one of those who never went to church in search of consolation went to the priest's house in quest of advice. An anecdote will suffice to complete this portrait of a character. Certain peasants, seldom it is true, but bad folks at any rate, said they were in danger of imprisonment for debt, or had themselves sued falsely, to stimulate the abbé's beneficence. They deceived their wives; and the women, seeing themselves threatened with eviction and their cows seized, by their innocent tears deceived the poor curé, who would find the seven or eight hundred francs demanded, which the peasants would spend on a little plot of ground. When some pious persons, church-wardens, pointed out the fraud, begging the curé to consult them for the future, that he might not be the victim of greed, he replied—

" Perhaps those men would have committed some crime to get their acre of land, and is it not a form of good to hinder evil ? ''

The reader may perhaps find pleasure in this sketch of a figure, remarkable because science and literature had entered that heart and that capable brain without corrupting them in any way.

At sixty years of age the Abbé Chaperon's hair was perfectly white, so keenly was he alive to the sufferings of others, and so deeply had the events of the Revolution affected him. Twice imprisoned for having twice refused to take certain oaths, he had twice (to use his own expression) said his *In manus.* He was of middle height, neither stout nor thin. His face, deeply furrowed, hollow-cheeked, and colorless, attracted the eye at once by the perfect calm of the lines and the purity of its outline, which looked as if fringed with light. There is a mysterious kind of radiance from the face of a perfectly chaste man. Brown eyes, with bright pupils, gave life to irregular features, under a powerful forehead. His gaze exercised a dominion that may be explained by its sweetness, which did not exclude strength. The arches of his brows were like deep vaults, shadowed by thick gray eyebrows, which frightened no one. As he had lost many teeth, his mouth was shapeless, and his cheeks were hollow ; but this ruin was not without charm, and his kindly wrinkles seemed always to be smiling at you.

He walked with difficulty, having very tender feet, without being gouty ; so in all weathers he wore soft calf-skin shoes. He thought trousers unsuitable to a priest, and always appeared in stout, black, worsted stockings, knitted by his housekeeper, and black cloth knee-breeches. He did not go out in his priest's gown, but in a brown overcoat and the three-cornered hat he had always bravely worn, even in the

worst times. This fine and noble old man, whose face was
always beautified by the serenity of a blameless soul, was
destined to have so great an influence on men and things in
this narrative that it was necessary to go to the sources of his
authority.

Minoret took in three papers—one liberal, one ministerial,
and one ultra — some periodical magazines and scientific
journals, of which the accumulation swelled his library.
These journals, the encyclopedist, and his books were an
attraction to a retired captain of the Royal Swedish Regiment,
Monsieur de Jordy, a gentleman, a Voltairean, and an old
bachelor, who lived on sixteen hundred francs a year, partly
pension and partly an annuity. After reading the papers for
some days, through the intervention of the curé, M. de Jordy
thought it becoming to call and thank the doctor. From his
very first visit the old captain, formerly a professor in the
military college, won the doctor's good graces, and the visit
was promptly returned.

Monsieur de Jordy, a lean, dry little man, but tormented
by blood to the head, though he had a very pale face, was
striking-looking by reason of a fine forehead, like Charles
XII., over which his hair was cropped short like that of the
soldier-king. His blue eyes, which would make one think
"Love has passed that way," though they were deeply sad,
were interesting at first sight, for their gaze betrayed remembrance; but on this point he kept his own secret so completely that his old friends never detected him in any allusion
to his past life, nor ever heard one of the exclamations which
are sometimes called forth by a similarity in misfortune. He
hid the painful mystery of his past under philosophical gaiety;
but when he thought himself alone, his movements, weighted
by a slowness evidently deliberate rather than senile, bore
witness to an ever-present painful thought. The abbé, indeed, had called him "The Christian without knowing it."

Always wearing a blue cloth suit, his somewhat stiff demeanor and his style of dress betrayed old habits of military discipline. His voice, soft and musical, spoke to the soul. His fine hands, and the shape of his face, recalling that of the Comte d'Artois, by showing how handsome he must have been in his youth, made the mystery of his life even more impenetrable. It was impossible not to wonder what was the disaster that had stricken a man so handsome, with courage, grace, learning, and all the most delightful qualities of heart which had formerly been united in his person. Monsieur de Jordy always shuddered at the name of Robespierre. He used a great deal of snuff, but, strange to say, he gave it up for little Ursule, who at first showed a dislike to him in consequence of this habit. Whenever he saw the child, the captain would gaze at her with lingering, almost passionate looks. He was so devoted to her games, and took so much interest in her, that this affection drew still tighter his tie to the doctor, who, on his part, never dared say to the old bachelor—

"Have you, too, lost children?"

There are beings, good and patient as he was, who go through life with a bitter memory in their hearts, and a smile, at once tender and sorrowful, on their lips, bearing in them the answer to the riddle, but never allowing it to be guessed —out of pride, or scorn, or perhaps revenge—having none but God to trust in or to comfort them. At Nemours, whither, like the doctor, he had come to die in peace, Monsieur de Jordy visited nobody but the curé, who was always at the service of his parishioners, and Madame de Portenduère, who went to bed at nine o'clock. Thus he, weary of the struggle, had at last taken to going to bed early too, notwithstanding the thorns that stuffed his pillow. Thus it was a happy chance for the doctor, as well as for the captain, to meet a man who had known the same society, who spoke the same language, with whom he could exchange ideas, and who went to bed late. When once Monsieur de Jordy, the Abbé Chaperon,

and Minoret had spent an evening together, they found it so
pleasant that the priest and the soldier came in every evening
at nine o'clock, when, little Ursule being in bed, the old man
was free.   And they all three sat talking till midnight, or one
o'clock.

Before long the trio became a quartette.   Another man,
who knew life well, and who had acquired in his profession
that large-mindedness, learning, accumulated observation,
shrewdness, and power of conversation which the soldier, the
physician, and the priest had gained in dealing with souls,
with diseases, and with teaching—the judge of the district,
Monsieur Bongrand—got wind of the pleasures of these evenings, and made himself acquainted with the doctor.

Before being appointed a justice at Nemours, Monsieur Bongrand had for ten years been attorney at Melun, where he
himself had pleaded in court, as is usual (in France) in towns
where there is no bar.   At the age of forty-five he found
himself a widower ; but feeling too active to do nothing, he
had applied for the appointment as justice of the peace at
Nemours, which had fallen vacant some months before the
doctor's arrival.   The keeper of the seals is always glad to
find a practical lawyer, and particularly a well-to-do man, to
hold these important posts.   Monsieur Bongrand lived very
simply at Nemours on his salary of fifteen hundred francs, and
could thus devote the rest of his income to his son, who was
studying for the bar at Paris, and at the same time working
up legal procedure under Derville, the famous attorney.

The elder Bongrand was a good deal like a retired brigadier ;
his was a face, not naturally pale, but washed out, where business, disappointment, and disgust had left their marks ; it was
wrinkled by much thought, and also by the pinched look of
a man who is constantly forced not to say all he thinks ; but
it was often illuminated by the smiles peculiar to men who, by
turns, believe everything or believe nothing, who are accustomed to see and hear everything without surprise, to sound

3

the depths which self-interest reveals at the bottom of men's hearts. Under his hair, which was faded rather than gray, and brushed in smooth waves on his head, rose a sagacious brow, its yellow tint harmonizing with that of his thin locks. His face, being rather short, gave him some resemblance to a fox, all the more so because his nose was short and sharp. As he spoke, his wide mouth, like that of all great talkers, sputtered out a spray of white foam-stars, which made his conversation so showery that Goupil used to say, maliciously : "You want an umbrella while you listen to him," or, "The justice of the peace rains decisions."

His eyes seemed keen behind his spectacles, but if he took them off his expression was dulled, and he looked stupid. Though lively, and even jovial, by his manner he gave himself rather too much the airs of a man of importance. His hands were almost always in his trousers' pockets, and he only took them out to settle his spectacles on his nose with a sort of mocking gesture, preliminary to some acute remark or clinching argument. These movements, with his loquacity and his innocent pretentiousness, betrayed the country lawyer; but such slight defects were merely superficial; he made up for them by an acquired geniality, which an exact moralist might define as the indulgence inherent in superiority. And if he had somewhat the look of a fox, he was also supposed to be extremely wily, without being dishonest. His cunning was the exercise of perspicacity. Do we not call folks cunning who can foresee results, and avoid the snares laid for them? The lawyer was fond of whist, a game which the doctor and the captain played, and which the priest soon learned to play with equal proficiency.

This little party created an oasis for themselves in Minoret's drawing-room. The Nemours town doctor, who was not deficient in education or manners, and who respected Minoret as an ornament to the profession, was also admitted ; but his business and fatigues, which compelled him to go to bed early that he might rise betimes, hindered him from being so regular a visitor as the doctor's three friends were.

The meetings of these five superior men, who alone in all the town had enough general culture to understand each other, accounts for Minoret's aversion for his heirs; though he might have to leave them his fortune, he could not admit them to his society. Whether the postmaster, the registrar, and the receiver understood this distinction, or were reassured by their uncle's loyal nature and benefactions, they ceased at any rate to call on him, to his very great satisfaction.

The four old players of whist and backgammon had, within seven or eight months of the doctor's settling at Nemours, formed a compact and exclusive little circle, which came to each of them as a sort of autumnal brotherhood, quite unlooked for, and therefore all the sweeter and more enjoyable. This family party of choice spirits found in Ursule a child whom each could adopt after his manner: the priest thought of her soul, the lawyer made himself her protector, the soldier promised himself that he would be her tutor; as for Minoret, he was father, mother, and doctor in one.

After acclimatizing himself, as it were, the old man fell into habits of life, regulated as it must be in all provincial towns. With Ursule as an excuse, he never received any one in the morning, and asked nobody to dinner; his friends could join him at six o'clock, and remain with him till midnight. The first comers found newspapers on the drawing-room table, and read while waiting for the others, or sometimes went to meet the doctor if he were out walking. These quiet habits were not merely the requirement of old age; they were also a wise and deep-laid precaution on the part of a man of the world to prevent his happiness being troubled by the restless curiosity of his relations, or the petty gossip of a country town. He would concede nothing to the capricious goddess public opinion, whose tyranny—one of the curses of France—was about to be established, and to make

our whole country one single province. So as soon as the
little girl was weaned and could walk, he sent away the cook
whom his niece, Madame Minoret-Levrault, had found for
him, on discovering that she reported to the postmistress
everything that went on in his house.

Little Ursule's nurse, the widow of a poor laborer owning
no name but that he was christened by, and who came from
Bougival, had lost her last baby at the age of six months; and
the doctor, knowing her to be an honest creature, engaged
her as wet nurse, in pity for her destitution. Having no
money, and coming from La Bresse, where her family lived in
poverty, Antoinette Patris, widow of Pierre *dit* de Bougival,
naturally attached herself to Ursule, as foster-mothers do
attach themselves to a sucking child as it grows up. This
blind motherly affection was reinforced by domestic attachment. Warned beforehand of the doctor's intentions, La
Bougival learned to cook on the sly, made herself tidy, and
fell into the old man's ways. She took the greatest care of
the furniture and the rooms; in short, she was indefatigable.
Not only did the doctor insist that his private life should be
screened from the world; he had reasons of his own for keeping all knowledge of his affairs from his heirs. Thus by the
time he had been at Nemours a year there was no one in his
house but La Bougival, on whose discretion he could absolutely rely, and he disguised his real reasons under the all-
powerful plea of economy. To the great joy of his family,
he became miserly. Without underhand wheedling, solely as
a result of her solicitude and devotedness, La Bougival, who
at the time when this drama opens was forty-three years old,
was housekeeper to the doctor and his little protégé, the
pivot on which the whole house turned, in fact, his confidential servant. She had been named La Bougival in consequence of the impossibility of calling her by her Christian
name of Antoinette, for names and faces must follow a law of
harmony.

The doctor's avarice was not an empty word; but it was for a purpose. From 1817 he gave up two of his newspapers, and ceased to subscribe to periodical magazines. His annual outlay, which all Nemours could reckon, was not more than eighteen hundred francs. Like all old men, his requirements in linen, clothing, and shoes were a mere trifle. Every six months he made a journey to Paris, no doubt to draw and invest his dividends. In fifteen years he never said a word that had anything to do with his affairs. His confidence in Bongrand was of later date; he never spoke to him of his plans till after the Revolution of 1830. These were the only things in the doctor's life known at that time to the townsfolk and his heirs. As to his political opinions, as his house was rated at no more than a hundred francs in taxes, he never interfered, and would have nothing to say to subscriptions on either the Royalist or the Liberal side. His well-known horror of priests and his deism so little loved demonstrations, that when his nephew, Minoret-Levrault, sent a traveling bookseller to his house to propose that he should buy the "Curé Meslier" and "General Foy's Addresses," he turned the man out of the house. Tolerance on such terms was quite inexplicable to the Liberals of Nemours.

The doctor's three collateral heirs, Minoret-Levrault and his wife, Monsieur and Madame Massin-Levrault, junior, Monsieur and Madame Crémière-Crémière—who shall be called simply Crémière, Massin, and Minoret, since such elaborate distinctions are only needed in the Gatinais—these three families, too busy to create another centre, met constantly, as people only meet in small towns. The postmaster gave a grand dinner on his son's birthday, a ball at the Carnival, and another on the anniversary of his wedding-day, and to these he asked all the townsfolk of Nemours. The tax-receiver also gathered his relations and friends about him twice a year. The justice's registrar being, as he said, too poor to launch out in such extravagance, lived narrowly in a house half-way down the High Street, of which the ground floor was let to his sister, the mistress of the letter-post—another benefaction of the doctor's. But in the course of the year these three inheritors or their wives met in the town or out walking, at the market in the morning, on their door-steps, or on Sunday, after mass, on the church square, as at this moment, so that they saw each other every day.

Now for the last three years more especially, the doctor's age, his miserliness, and his fortune justified allusions or direct remarks relating to their prospects, which, passing from one to another, at last made the doctor and his heirs equally famous. For these six months not a week had passed without the friends and neighbors of the Minoret˙ family speaking to them with covert envy of the day when the old man's eyes would be closed and his money-boxes opened.

"Doctor Minoret may be a physician, and have come to an understanding with death," said one; "but only God is eternal."

"Bah! he will bury us all; he is in better health than we are," one of the expectant heirs would reply hypocritically.

"Well, if you don't get it, your children will—unless that little Ursule——"

"He will not leave her everything?" another would reply, interrupting the last speaker.

Ursule, as Madame Massin had prognosticated, was the real bugbear of the family, the Damocles' sword; and Madame Crémière's favorite last word, "Those who live will know," showed plainly enough that they wished her ill rather than well.

The tax-receiver and the registrar, who were poor by comparison with the postmaster, had often, by way of conversation, calculated the doctor's property. As they walked along by the canal or on the high-road, if they saw their uncle coming they looked at each other piteously.

"He has provided himself with some elixir of life, no doubt," said the one.

"He is in league with the devil," said the other.

"He ought to leave us the lion's share, for that fat Minoret wants for nothing."

"Oh, Minoret has a son who will get rid of a great deal of his money for him!"

"How much, now, do you suppose the doctor's fortune may run to?" said the registrar.

"Well, at the end of twelve years, twelve thousand francs saved every year come to a hundred and forty-four thousand, and compound interest will have produced at least a hundred thousand francs more; but as, under his Paris lawyer's advice, he must have turned his money to advantage now and again, and as he would have invested up to 1822 at eight or seven and a half per cent. in government securities, the old fellow must at this time have about four hundred thousand francs to turn over, to say nothing of his fourteen thousand francs at five per cent., worth one hundred and sixteen at the present moment. If he were to die to-morrow and leave Ursule an equal share, we should get seven to eight hundred thousand francs, not to mention the house and furniture."

"Well, a hundred thousand to Minoret, a hundred thousand to the little girl, and three hundred thousand to each of us. That would be the fair thing."

"Yes, that would keep us in shoe-leather."

"If he should do that," cried Massin, "I would sell my appointment and buy a fine estate. I would try to be made judge at Fontainebleau, and be elected deputy."

"I would buy a stockbroker's business," said the tax-receiver.

"Unfortunately, that little girl on his arm and the curé have so blockaded him that we cannot get at him."

"At any rate, we are quite certain that he will leave nothing to the church."

It may now be understood that the heirs were in agonies at seeing their uncle going to mass. The most stupid have wit enough to imagine injury to their interests. Interest is the moving spirit of the peasant as of the diplomat, and on that ground the most stupid in appearance may perhaps prove the sharpest. Hence this terrible argument: "If that little Ursule is able to bring her protector within the pale of the church, she will certainly have power to secure her own inheritance," blazed out in letters of fire in the mind of the most obtuse of the inheritors. The postmaster had forgotten the enigma in his son's letter in hurrying to the square; for if the doctor were really in church following the order of prayer, they might lose two hundred and fifty thousand francs. It must be admitted that their fears were based on the strongest and most legitimate of social sentiments, namely, on family interest.

"Well, Monsieur Minoret," said the mayor—a retired miller who had turned Royalist, a Levrault-Crémière—"when the devil was old, the devil a monk would be! Your uncle, I am told, has come over to us."

"Better late than never, cousin," replied the postmaster, trying to conceal his annoyance.

"How that man would laugh if we were disappointed! He is quite capable of making his son marry that cursed little hussy. May the devil get his tail round her!" cried Crémière, shaking his fist at the mayor as he went in under the porch.

"What on earth is the matter with old Crémière?" said the butcher, the eldest son of a Levrault-Levrault. "Is he not pleased to see his uncle take the road to paradise?"

"Who would ever have believed it?" said the registrar.

"It is never safe to say to the well, 'I will never drink of your water!'" replied the notary, who, seeing the group from afar, left his wife to go on to church alone.

"Now, Monsieur Dionis," said Crémière, taking the

lawyer by the arm, "what do you advise us to do in these circumstances?"

"I advise you," said Dionis, addressing the expectant heirs, "to go to bed and get up at the usual hours, to eat your soup before it gets cold, to put your shoes on your feet and your hat on your head; in short, to go on exactly as if nothing had happened."

"You are a poor comforter!" said Massin with a cunning glance.

In spite of his short, fat figure, and his thick, crushed-looking features, Crémière-Dionis was as slippery as silk. To make a fortune he was in secret partnership with Massin, whom he no doubt kept informed when peasants were in difficulties, and which plots of ground he might devour. So the two men could pick and choose, never letting a good chance escape them, and dividing the profits of this usury on mortgage, which delays, though it cannot hinder, the action of the peasantry on the land. Hence Dionis felt a keen interest in the doctor's will, less on account of Minoret the postmaster and Crémière the tax-receiver than for his friend the registrar's sake. Massin's share would, sooner or later, come to swell the capital on which the partners traded in the district.

"We must try to find out, through Monsieur Bongrand, who has fired this shot," replied the lawyer in a low voice, as a warning to Massin to lay low.

"What are you doing here, Minoret?" was suddenly heard from a little woman who bore down on the group, in the midst of which the postmaster was visible as a tower. "You do not know what has become of Désiré, and you seem to have taken root there on your two feet when I fancied you were on horseback! Good-morning, ladies and gentlemen!"

This spare little woman, pale and fair, dressed in a cotton gown—white, with a large flowered pattern in chocolate-color—in an embroidered cap trimmed with lace, and a small green shawl over her flat shoulders, was the postmistress, who made the stoutest postillions quake, the servants, and the carters; who kept the till and the books; and managed the house with her finger and eye, as the neighbors were in the habit of saying. Like a true, thrifty housewife, she had not a single article of jewelry. She did not "favor frippery and trash," as she put it; she liked what was durable, and, in spite of its being Sunday, she had on her black silk apron with pockets, in which a bunch of keys jingled. Her shrill voice was ear-splitting. In spite of the sweet blue of her eyes, her hard gaze was in evident harmony with the thin lips of a tightly set mouth, and a high, projecting, and very despotic brow. Her glance was sharp, sharper still were her gestures and words. "Zélie being obliged to have will enough for two, had always had enough for three," Goupil used to say; and it was he who noted the successive reigns of three young post-boys, very neatly kept, whom Zélie had set up after seven years' service. Indeed, the spiteful clerk always called them Postillion I., Postillion II., and Postillion III. But the small influence exerted in the house by these young men, and their perfect obedience, proved that Zélie had simply and purely taken an interest in really good fellows.

"Ay, Zélie values zeal," the clerk would reply to any one who made such a remark.

This piece of scandal was, however, improbable. Since the birth of her son, whom she nursed herself, though it was impossible to see how, the postmistress had thought only of adding to her fortune, and devoted herself without respite to the management of her immense business. To rob her of a truss of straw or a few bushels of oats, to detect her in error in the most complicated accounts, was a thing impossible, though she wrote a cat's scrawl, and knew nothing of arithmetic beyond addition and subtraction. She walked out solely to inspect her hay, her oats, and her after-crops; then she would send her man to fetch in the crops, and her postillions to pack

the hay, and tell them within a hundredweight how much
they could get off this or that field.   Though she was the soul
of the huge body known as Minoret-Levrault, and led him by
his idiotically snub nose, she was liable to the frights which
more or less constantly agitate those who quell and lead wild
beasts, and she quarreled with him frequently.   The post-
boys knew by the rowings they got from Minoret when his
wife had scolded him, for her rage glanced off on to them.
But, indeed, Madame Minoret was as shrewd as she was
avaricious.

"Where would Minoret be without his wife?" was a by-
word in more than one household in the town.

"When you hear what is happening to us you will be beside
yourself too," replied the Master of Nemours.

"Well, what is it?"

"Ursule has taken Doctor Minoret to mass."

Zélie Levrault's eyes seemed to dilate; for an instant she
was silent, yellow with rage; then crying, "I must see it to
believe it," she rushed into the church.   The Host was just
elevated.   Favored by the general attitude of worship, she
was able to look along each row of chairs and benches as she
went up past the chapels to the place where Ursule knelt, and
by her side she saw the old man bareheaded.

If you can recall the portraits of Barbé-Marbois, Boissy-
d'Anglas, Morellet, Helvétius, and Frederick the Great, you
will have an exact idea of the head of Doctor Minoret, who in
his green old age was a good deal like these famous personages.
These heads, struck as it might seem from the same die, for they
lend themselves to the medalist's art, present a severe and
almost puritanical profile, cold coloring, a mathematical brain,
a certain narrowness of face, as if it had been squeezed, astute
eyes, grave lips, and something aristocratic in sentiment rather
than in habits, in the intellect rather than in the character.
They all have lofty foreheads, receding a little at the top,
which betrays a tendency to materialism.   You will find all

these leading characteristics of the head, and the look of the face, in the portraits of the encyclopedists, of the orators of the Girondins, and of the men of that time whose religious belief was almost a blank, and who, though calling themselves deists, were atheists. A deist is an atheist with an eye to the off-chance of some advantage.

Old Minoret had a forehead of this type, but furrowed with wrinkles, and it derived a sort of childlike ingenuousness from the way in which his silvery hair, combed back like a woman's at her toilet, curled in thin locks on his black coat; for he persisted in dressing, as in the days of his youth, in black silk stockings, shoes with gold buckles, knee-breeches of rich silk, a white waistcoat, across which lay the black ribbon of Saint Michael, and a black coat with the red rosette in the buttonhole. This characteristic head, its cold pallor softened by the ivory-yellow tone of old age, was under the full light from a window. At the moment when the postmistress came in, the doctor's blue eyes, with slightly reddened lids and pathetic lines, were fixed on the altar; new conviction had given them a new expression. His spectacles, laid in his prayer-book, marked the page where he had ceased to read. With his arms folded across his breast, the tall, spare old man, standing in an attitude which proclaimed the full power of all his faculties, and something immovable in his faith, never ceased from gazing at the altar with a humble look, rejuvenescent through hope; not choosing to see his nephew's wife, who stood rooted almost face to face with him, as if to reproach him for this return to God.

On seeing every face turned to look at her, Zélie hastily retired, and came out on to the square again less precipitately than she had gone into the church; she had counted on that inheritance, and the inheritance was becoming problematical. She found the registrar, the tax-receiver, and their wives in even greater consternation than before. Goupil had taken pleasure in tormenting them.

"It is not here, on the square, and under the eyes of the whole town, that we can discuss our private affairs," said the postmistress; "come to my house. You will not be in the way, Monsieur Dionis," she added to the lawyer.

So the probable disinheritance of the Massins, the Crémières, and the postmaster was to become the talk of the country.

Just as the heirs and the notary were about to cross the square on their way to the house, the clatter of the diligence arriving at top-speed made a tremendous noise; it stopped at the coach-office, a few yards from the church, at the top of the High Street.

"Why, like you, Minoret, I had forgotten Désiré," said Zélie. "Let us go to meet him; he is almost a lawyer now, and this business is partly his concern."

The arrival of a diligence is always a diversion, and when it is behind time something interesting may be expected; so the crowd rushed to see the "Ducler."

"There is Désiré," was a general cry.

At once the tyrant and the ringleader of fun in Nemours, Désiré's visits always brought some excitement to the town. A favorite with the young men, to whom he was liberal, his presence was to them a stimulant; but his pleasures were so much dreaded, that more than one family was glad that his studies for the law should be carried on in Paris. Désiré Minoret, slight, thin, and fair like his mother, with her blue eyes and colorless complexion, smiled at the crowd from the coach door, and jumped out to embrace her. A slight sketch of this youth will explain Zélie's flattered pride on beholding him.

The young law student wore neat little boots, white English drill trousers with patent-leather straps, a handsome cravat carefully folded, and a still handsomer pin, a smart fancy waistcoat, and in its pocket a flat watch with a dangling chain; a short blue cloth overcoat, and a gray hat. But

vulgar riches were betrayed in the gold buttons to his waistcoat, and a ring worn outside his gloves of purplish kid.   He
carried a cane with a chased gold knob.

"You will lose your watch," said his mother as she kissed
him.

"It is worn so," said he, submitting to his father's embrace.

"Well, cousin, so you will soon be a full-blown lawyer,"
said Massin.

"I am to be sworn when the courts reopen," said he,
waving an acknowledgment of the friendly greetings of the
crowd.

"Then we shall have some fun?" said Goupil, shaking
hands with him.

"Ah! there you are, old ape!" answered Désiré.

"Having worked for your license, you think you may take
it, I suppose!" retorted the clerk, mortified at being so
familiarly treated before so many people.

"For his lies?   Take what?" asked Madame Crémière of
her husband.

"You know all my things, Cabirolle!" cried Désiré to the
old purple and pimply-faced conductor.   "Have them all
taken down to the house."

"Your horses are in a lather," said Zélie roughly to Cabirolle.   "Have you no sense at all that you drive them like
that?   You are a greater brute than they are."

"But Monsieur Désiré insisted on getting on as fast as
possible, to relieve your anxiety."

"As there has been no accident, why risk killing your
horses?" said she.

Friendly greetings, hand-shaking, and the eagerness of his
young acquaintance surrounding Désiré, all the incidents of
arrival, and details as to the accident which had occasioned
the delay, took up so much time that the party of inheritors,
increased by their friends, got back to the church just as mass

was ended. By a trick of chance, which allows itself strange caprices, Désiré saw Ursule under the church porch as he passed, and was quite startled by her beauty. The young man suddenly paused, and necessarily checked the movements of his parents.

Ursule had taken her godfather's arm, which obliged her to hold her prayer-book in her right hand and her parasol in the left; and, in doing so, she displayed the native grace with which graceful women manage to get over the little difficulties of their dainty womanhood. If the mind betrays itself in everything, it may be said that her demeanor expressed her exquisite ingenuousness.

Ursule wore a white muslin dress, shaped loosely like a dressing-gown, with blue bows at intervals; the cape, trimmed with similar ribbon run into a wide hem, and fastened like the dress with bows, suggested the beauty of her figure; her throat, of ivory whiteness, was thrown into charming relief by all this blue—the true cosmetic for fair complexions.

A blue sash, with floating ends, marked a girlish waist and what seemed a pliant figure, one of the most seductive graces of woman. She wore a rice-straw hat, simply trimmed with ribbons to match those on her dress. It was tied with a bow under her chin; and this, while enhancing the excessive whiteness of the hat, did not detract from that of her lovely complexion.

Her fine, bright hair, which she herself dressed in wide plaits, fastened into loops on each side of her face *à la Berthe*, caught the eye by the shining bosses of the crossing tresses. Her gray eyes, soft, though proud, harmonized with a well-moulded brow. A delicate color flushed her cheeks like a rosy cloud, and gave life to a face that was regular without being insipid, for nature had bestowed on her the rare privilege of a pure outline with an expressive countenance.

The virtue of her life was written in the perfect accordance of her features, her movements, and the general expression

of her individuality, which might serve as a model of trust-
fulness or of modesty.

Her health was excellent, but not coarsely robust, so that she
looked elegant.   Her light gloves left it to be inferred that
she had pretty hands.   Her arched and slender feet were shod
with dainty little bronze kid boots, trimmed with a fringe of
brown silk.   Her blue sash, in which a little flat watch made
a boss, while a blue purse with gold tassels hung through it,
attracted the eye of every woman there, and gave cause for
remark.

"He has given her a new watch," said Madame Crémière,
squeezing her husband's arm.

"Why, it is Ursule!" exclaimed Désiré.   "I did not
recognize her."

"Well, my dear uncle, this is an event!" said the postmaster, pointing to where the whole town had fallen into two
lines along the old man's way.   "Everybody wants to see
you."

"Is it the Abbé Chaperon or Ursule who has converted
you, uncle?" said Massin, bowing with jesuitical obsequious-
ness to the doctor and his companion.

"It is Ursule," said the old man curtly, and without stopping, as a man who is annoyed.

The evening before, as he finished his rubber with Ursule,
the town doctor, and Bongrand, he had said, "I shall go to
mass to-morrow;" and even if the justice had not then replied, "Your heirs will never have another night's sleep!" a
single glance now would have sufficed to enable the sagacious
and clear-sighted old man to read the temper of his heirs in
the look of their faces.   Zélie's irruption into the church, the
flash he had caught in her eye, the meeting of all the interested parties on the square, and the expression of their countenances on seeing Ursule—all revealed freshly revived hatred
and sordid fears.

"This is your doing, mademoiselle," said Madame Crémière, interposing with a low courtesy. " It is no trouble to you to work miracles."

" The miracle is God's, madame," replied Ursule.

" Oh, indeed! God's," exclaimed Minoret-Levrault. " My father-in-law used to say that God was a name for many a dark horse."

" His ideas were those of a horse coper !" said the doctor severely.

" Now, then," said Minoret to his wife and son, "are you not coming to pay your respects to my uncle ?"

" I could not contain myself face to face with that sneaking slut !" exclaimed Zélie, leading away her son.

" You would be wise, uncle," said Madame Massin, " not to go to church without a little black velvet cap ; the parish church is very damp."

" Pah ! niece," said the old man, looking round at his followers. " The sooner I am laid to rest, the sooner you will dance."

He walked on, dragging Ursule with him, and seeming in such haste that they were left to themselves.

" Why do you answer them with such hard words? It is not kind," said Ursule, shaking his arm with a little refractory gesture.

" My hatred for hypocrites has always been the same, before as well as since my conversion. I have done them all kindness, and I do not ask for gratitude ; but not one of all those people sent a flower on your birthday, the only day I keep."

At some little distance from the doctor and Ursule, Madame de Portenduère was dragging herself along, overwhelmed, as it seemed, with suffering. She was one of those old women in whose dress we may still trace the spirit of the last century, who wear pansy-colored gowns with tight sleeves of a cut now only to be seen in portraits by Madame Lebrun ; black lace scarfs, and bonnets of extinct shapes, in harmony with their

4

slow and solemn gait ; as if they still walked in hoops, and felt them about them, as those who have had an arm cut off sometimes move the limb they have lost.   Their long, pale faces, with deeply shadowed eyes and blighted brows, are not devoid of a certain melancholy grace in spite of a front of dejected curls ; they drape their heads in old lace, which now has no light flutter over their cheeks ; but over the whole mass of ruins predominates an indescribable dignity of manner and look.

This old lady's red and puckered eyes plainly showed that she had wept during the service.   She walked like a person in some anxiety, and seemed to be expecting somebody, for she looked back.   Now, that Madame de Portenduère should look back was an event as serious as Doctor Minoret's conversion.

"To whom can Madame Portenduère owe a grudge?" said Madame Massin, as she came up with the heirs, who were dumfounded by the doctor's retorts.

"She is looking for the curé," said Dionis, striking his forehead like a man suddenly struck by a remembrance or some forgotten idea.   "I have it!   I see my way; the inheritance is saved!   Come, we will all breakfast cheerfully with Madame Minoret."

The eagerness with which the whole party followed the notary to the posting-house may easily be imagined.   Goupil clung to his comrade, taking his arm, saying in his ear with a revolting smile: "There are crayfish!"

"What do I care?" replied the son of the house with a shrug.   "I am madly in love with Florine, the most heavenly creature in the world."

"What on earth is Florine without a surname?" asked Goupil.   "I am too much your friend to allow you to be made a fool of by hussies."

"Florine is adored by the famous Nathan, and my folly is of no use, for she positively refuses to marry me."

"Girls who are rash with their bodies are sometimes prudent with their brains," said Goupil.

"If you could but see her, only once, you would not make use of such expressions," said Désiré languishingly.

"If I saw you destroying your prospects for what can be only a fancy," retorted Goupil, with a warmth that might perhaps have taken in Bongrand, "I would go and wreck that doll as Varney wrecked Amy Robsart in Kenilworth! Your wife ought to be a d'Aiglemont, a Mademoiselle du Rouvre, and open your way to being a deputy to the Chamber. My future is mortgaged to yours, and I will not allow you to play the fool."

"I am rich enough to be content with happiness," replied Désiré.

"Well, what are you two plotting?" said Zélie to Goupil, hailing the two young men, who were standing together in the wide stable-yard.

The doctor turned down the Rue des Bourgeois, and walked on, as briskly as a young man, to his house, where, in the course of the past week, the strange event had taken place which was just now the ruling thought of all the town of Nemours, and of which some account must be given to render this story, and the notary's singular remark to the heirs, more perfectly intelligible.

The doctor's father-in-law, the famous harpsichord player and instrument-maker, Valentin Mirouët, one of our most celebrated organists, died in 1785, leaving a natural son, the child of his old age, whom he had recognized and called by his name, but who was a thorough scapegrace. He had not the consolation of seeing this spoilt child when on his death-bed; Joseph Mirouët, a singer and composer, after coming out in Italian opera under an assumed name, had run away to Germany with a young girl. The old instrument-maker recommended this lad, who was full of talent, to his son-in-law, explaining that his object in not marrying the boy's mother was to protect the interests of his daughter, Madame Minoret. The doctor promised to give the unfortunate youth half of the property left by the old man, whose stock and business were bought up by Erard.

He set to work diplomatically to find his natural half-brother, Joseph Mirouët; but one evening Grimm told him that, after enlisting in a Prussian regiment, the artist had deserted, and, taking a false name, had escaped all search.

Joseph Mirouët, gifted by nature with an enchanting voice, a fine figure, and a handsome face, being a composer of taste and spirit into the bargain, led for fifteen years the Bohemian existence which Hofmann of Berlin has so well described. But at the age of forty he was reduced to such misery that in 1806 he seized the opportunity of becoming a Frenchman again. He then settled at Hamburg, where he married the daughter of a respectable citizen, who, being music-mad, fell in love with the singer, whose fame was still in the future, and who devoted herself to its attainment. But after fifteen years of penury, Joseph Mirouët's head could not stand the wine of opulence; his extravagant nature reasserted itself; and, though he made his wife happy, in a few years he had spent all her fortune. Misery again came upon them. The household must indeed have been living wretchedly for Joseph Mirouët to come down to enlisting as one of the band in a French regiment.

In 1813, by the merest chance, the surgeon-major of this regiment, struck by the name of Mirouët, wrote to Doctor Minoret, to whom he owed some obligation. The reply came at once. In 1814, before the capitulation of Paris, Joseph Mirouët had found a home there, and there his wife died in giving birth to a little girl whom the doctor named Ursule, after his wife. The bandmaster did not long survive his wife; he, like her, was worn out by fatigue and privation. On his death-bed the hapless musician bequeathed his little girl to the

doctor, who was her godfather, in spite of his repugnance for
what he called church mummeries.

After losing every child, either by miscarriage, at the time
of its birth, or within the first year of its life, the doctor had
anxiously looked forward to their last hope. But when a
sickly, nervous, delicate woman begins with a miscarriage, it
is common enough to see her successive failures, as in the case
of Ursule Minoret, in spite of her husband's care, watchful-
ness, and learning. The poor man had often blamed himself
for their persistent desire to have children. The last of the
little ones born to them, after an interval of more than two
years, died in 1792, the victim of constitutional nervousness,
inherited from its mother, if we may believe the physiologists,
who say that, in the inscrutable phenomena of generation, a
child takes its blood from the father and its nervous system
from the mother. The doctor, compelled to forego the joys
of his strongest feelings, no doubt found in benevolence some
indemnity for disappointed fatherhood.

All through his married life, so cruelly agitated, he had
wished above everything for a little fair girl, one of those
flowers which are the delight of a household; so he gladly
accepted his half-brother's bequest, and transferred all his
vanished hopes and dreams to the little orphan. For two
years he watched over the minutest details of Ursule's life, as
Cato over Pompey; he would not have her fed, or taken up,
or put to bed without his superintendence. His experience
and his science were all devoted to this child. After enduring all the pangs, the alternations of fear and hope, the
anxieties and joys of a mother, he was so happy as to find
vigorous vitality and a deeply sensitive nature in this child of
the flaxen-haired German mother and the artistic Frenchman.
The happy old man watched the growth of that yellow hair
with the feelings of a mother—first pale down, then silk, then
light, fine hair, so caressing to the touch of caressing fingers.
He would kiss the tiny feet, the toes through whose fine skin

the blood shows pink, making them look like rosebuds.   He
was crazy over the child.

When she tried to speak, or when she fixed her lovely, soft
blue eyes on the objects about her, with the wondering look
which would seem to be the dawning of ideas, and which she
ended with a laugh, he would sit in front of her for whole
hours, and he and Jordy would try to find out the reasons—
which to many have seemed mere caprices—concealed under
the smallest manifestations of that delightful phase of life
when the child is at once flower and fruit, a bewildered intelligence, perpetual motion, and vehement desire.   Little
Ursule's beauty and sweetness made her so precious to the
doctor that for her he would gladly have changed the laws of
nature ; he would sometimes tell his friend Jordy that he
suffered from pain in his teeth when Ursule was cutting hers.

When old men love a child there is no limit to their passion ; they adore it.   For this tiny creature's sake they
silence their pet manias, and recall every detail of their past
life.   Their experience, their forbearance, their patience, all
the acquisitions of life—a treasure so painfully amassed—are
poured out for this young life by which they grow young
again, and they make up for motherliness by intelligence.
Their wisdom, always on the alert, is as good as a mother's
intuition ; they remember the exquisite care which in a
mother is divination, and infuse it into the exercise of a
pitifulness whose strength is great, no doubt, in proportion to
that excessive weakness.   The slowness of their movements
supplies the place of maternal gentleness.   And then, in
them, as in children, life is reduced to the simplest expression ; if a mother is a slave from feeling, the negation of all
passion and the absence of all self-interest allow the old man
to sacrifice himself wholly.   Hence it is not uncommon to see
children and old men make great friends.

The old officer, the old curé, and the old doctor, happy in
Ursule's caresses and caprices, were never tired of answering

her or playing with her. Her childish petulance, far from fretting them, was their delight; and they indulged all her desires, while making everything a subject of instruction. Thus the little girl grew up in the midst of old men, who smiled on her, and were to her like so many mothers, all equally attentive and watchful. Thanks to this learned education, Ursule's soul developed in a congenial sphere. This rare plant found the soil that suited it, inhaled the elements of its true life, and assimilated the flood of its native sunshine.

"In what faith will you bring this child up?" asked the Abbé Chaperon of Minoret, when Ursule was six years old.

"In yours," replied the doctor.

He, an atheist after the pattern of Monsieur de Wolmar in the "Nouvelle Héloïse," did not see that he had any right to deprive Ursule of the benefits offered by the Catholic faith.

The physician, just then sitting on a bench outside the window of the Chinese summer-house, felt his hand warmly pressed by that of the curé.

"Yes, curé, whenever she asks me about God, I shall refer her to her friend 'Sapron,' " said he, mimicking Ursule's baby accent. "I wish to see whether religious feeling is innate. So far, therefore, I have done nothing either for or against the tendencies of this young soul; but I have already, in my heart, appointed you her spiritual director."

"It will be accounted to you by God, I trust!" said the curé, gently patting his hands together, and raising them to heaven, as though he were putting up a short mental prayer.

So, at the age of six, the little orphan came under the religious influence of the curé, as she had already under that of her old friend Jordy.

The captain, formerly a professor in one of the old military schools, and interested in grammar and the divergencies of European tongues, had studied the problem of an universal language. This learned man, patient as all old teachers are, made it his pleasure to teach Ursule to read and write, instructing her in French, and in so much arithmetic as it was needful that she should know. The doctor's extensive library allowed of a choice of books fit to be read by a child, and adapted to amuse as well as to instruct her. The soldier and the priest left her mind to develop naturally and easily, as the doctor left her body. Ursule learned in play. Religion included reflection.

Thus left to the divine culture of a nature guided by these three judicious teachers into a realm of purity, Ursule tended towards feeling rather than duty, and took as her rule of life the voice of conscience rather than social law. In her, beauty of sentiment and action would always be spontaneous; her judgment would come in to confirm the impulse of her heart. She was fated to do right as a pleasure before doing it as an obligation. This tone is the peculiar result of a Christian education. These principles, quite unlike those to be inculcated in a man, are suited to a woman, the soul and conscience of the family, the latent elegance of home life, the queen, or little less, of the household.

They all three acted in the same manner with this child. Far from being startled by the audacity of childish innocence, they explained to Ursule the purpose of things and their known processes, without ever giving her an inaccurate impression. When in her questioning about a plant, a flower, or a star, she went directly to God, the professor and the doctor alike told her that only the curé could answer her. Neither of them intruded on the ground of the other. Her godfather took charge of her physical progress and the matters of daily life; her lessons were Jordy's affair; morality, metaphysics, and all higher matters were left to the curé.

This excellent education was not counteracted by bad servants, as is sometimes the case in wealthier houses. La Bougival, well lectured on the subject — and, indeed, far too simple in mind and nature to interfere—did nothing to mar the work of these great spirits.

Thus Ursule, a privileged creature, had to nurture her three good genii, who found their task easy and pleasant with so sweet a nature as hers. This manly tenderness, this seriousness tempered by smiles, this freedom without risk, this incessant care of mind and body, had made her, at the age of nine, a delightful and lovely child. Then, unfortunately, the fatherly trio was broken up. In the following year the old captain died, leaving it to the doctor and the curé to carry on his work, after he had achieved the most difficult part of it. Flowers would spring up naturally in a soil so well prepared. The good gentleman had, during these nine years, saved a thousand francs a year, and left ten thousand francs to his little Ursule, that she might have something to remember him by all her life through. In his will, full of pathetic feeling, he begged his legatee to spend the four or five hundred francs a year of interest on this little capital exclusively on dress.

When the justice placed seals on his old friend's possessions, he found, in a closet which no one had ever been allowed to enter, a quantity of toys, most of them broken, and all used; toys of the past, piously treasured, which Monsieur Bongrand himself was to burn, by the poor captain's desire.

Not long after this, Ursule was to take her first communion. The Abbé Chaperon devoted a whole year to instructing the young girl, in whom heart and brain, so early developed, but so wisely dependent on each other, required a specific spiritual nourishment. And this initiation into a knowledge of divine things was of such a nature that from this period, when the soul takes its religious mould, Ursule became a pious and mystical young creature, whose character was always superior to events, and whose heart could triumph over adversity. Then it was that a secret struggle began between infidel old age and fully-believing youth; a struggle of which she who had challenged it was long unaware, but of which the issue had set the town by the ears, while it was destined to have

great influence on Ursule's future life, by unchaining against
her the doctor's collateral relations.

During the first six months of the year 1824, Ursule almost
always spent the morning at the curé's house. The old doctor
divined the abbé's intention ; he wanted to make Ursule
herself an invincible argument. The unbeliever, beloved by
his god-daughter as though she were his own child, would
believe in her simplicity, and be attracted by the touching
effects of religion in the soul of a girl whose love, like the
trees of the tropical forest, was always loaded with flowers
and fruit, always fresh, and always fragrant. A beautiful life
is more powerful than the most cogent arguments. It is
impossible to resist the charm of certain images. And
the doctor's eyes filled with tears, he knew not why, when he
saw the child of his heart set out for church dressed in a
frock of white gauze, with white satin shoes, graced with
white ribbons, a fillet of white round her head tied on one
side with a large bow, her hair rippling in a thousand
waves over her pretty white shoulders, her bodice trimmed
with a pleating mixed with narrow bows, her eyes shining
like stars, from new hopes, loving her godfather all the
more since her soul had risen to God. When he perceived
the idea of eternity supplying nourishment to the soul
hitherto wrapped in the darkness of childhood, as the sun
brings life to the world after the night is past, he felt
vexed to remain alone at home, still without knowing why.
Seated on the balcony steps, his eyes remained long fixed on
the bars of the gate through which his godchild had passed,
saying, " Why are you not coming too, godfather? Am I
to be happy without you ? "

Though shaken to the foundations, the encyclopedist's
pride did not once give way. However, he went out to
look at the little procession, and saw his little Ursule
radiant with exaltation under her veil. She flashed an
inspired look at him, which struck to the stoniest corner

of his heart, the spot closed against God. Still the deist was firm. "Mummery!" he said to himself. "To imagine that if a Maker of worlds exists, such an Organizer of infinitude can trouble Himself about this foolish trumpery!"

He laughed, and pursued his walk along the heights which overhang the road through the Gatinais, where the church bells, ringing loud peals, announced the gladness of many a home.

The clatter of backgammon is intolerable to those who do not know the game, one of the most difficult that exist. Not to disturb his little girl—whose extreme delicacy of ear and nerves did not allow of her enduring this rattle and their talk without apparent meaning—the curé, old Jordy during his lifetime, and Dr. Minoret postponed their game till the child was in bed or out walking. It often happened that it was unfinished when she came in again, and she then submitted with the best possible grace, and sat down by the window to sew. She disliked the game, which at the beginning is no doubt dry and dull, to many minds repellent, and so difficult to master, that those who have not become accustomed to it in their youth find it almost impossible to learn in later life.

Now on the evening after her first communion, when Ursule came back to her guardian and found him alone for that day, she set the backgammon board in front of the old man.

"Now whose throw will it be?" said she.

"Ursule," said the doctor, "is it not sinful to make game of your godfather on the very day of your first communion?"

"I am not making game," said she, seating herself. "I must think of your pleasure—you who are always thinking of mine. Whenever Monsieur Chaperon was pleased with me, he gave me a lesson in backgammon, and he has given me so many that I am prepared to beat you. You will not have to put yourself to inconvenience for me. I have conquered every difficulty, not to interfere with your amusement, and I really like the rattle of the dice."

Ursule won the game. The curé came in, taking them by surprise, and enjoyed her triumph.

Next day Minoret, who had hitherto refused to allow the girl to learn music, went to Paris, bought a piano, and made arrangements with a mistress at Fontainebleau, submitting to the annoyance which Ursule's constant practicing could not fail to cause him. One of his lost friend Jordy's phrenological prognostics proved true—the girl became an excellent musician. The doctor, proud of his god-daughter, now got an old German named Schmucke, a learned professor of music, to come from Paris once a week, and paid the cost of an art which he had at first contemned as perfectly useless in home life. Unbelievers do not love music, that heavenly language worked out by Catholicism, which found the names of the seven notes in one of its hymns. Each note is called by the first syllable of the seven first lines of the hymn to St. John.

The impression produced on the old man by Ursule's first communion, though vivid, was transient. The calm contentment which acts of resolution and prayer diffused in her young soul were also examples of which he took no account. Minoret, having no subjects for remorse or repentance, enjoyed perfect serenity of mind. Doing all his acts of benevolence without any hope of an eternal harvest, he thought himself superior to the Catholic, who, as he always said, was merely making a profitable bargain with God.

"And yet," the Abbé Chaperon would say, "if all men went in for this business, you must admit that society might be perfect. There would be no more misery. To be benevolent on your lines, a man must be a great philosopher. You raise yourself to your principles by reason—you are a social exception ; now you need only be a Christian to be benevolent on ours. With you it is an effort ; with us it is natural."

" Which is as much as to say, curé, that I think and you feel. That is all."

Meanwhile, having reached the age of twelve, Ursule, whose womanly tact and shrewdness were brought into play by a superior education, and whose sense, now in its blossom, was enlightened by a religious spirit, fully understood that her godfather believed not in a future life, nor in the immortality of the soul, nor in Providence, nor in God. The doctor, pressed by her innocent questioning, found it impossible any longer to hide the terrible secret. Ursule's naïve consternation at first made him smile ; but then, seeing that she was sometimes sad, he understood how great an affection this dejection revealed. Unqualified love has a horror of every kind of discord, even in things which have no connection with itself. The old man would sometimes lend himself, as to a caress, to the arguments of his adopted child, spoken in a gentle and tender voice, and the outcome of the most pure and ardent feeling. But believers and unbelievers speak two different languages, and cannot understand each other. The young girl in pleading the cause of God was hard upon her godfather, as a spoilt child is sometimes hard upon its mother.

The curé gently reproved her, telling her that God reserved to Himself the power of humbling such proud spirits. The young girl answered the abbé by saying that David slew Goliath. These religious differences, these sorrows of the child who longed to lead her guardian to God, were the only griefs of their home-life, so simple and so full, and hidden from the gaze of the inquisitive little town.

Ursule grew up and developed into the modest, Christianly trained maiden whom Désiré had admired as she came out of church. The culture of the flowers in the garden, music, amusing her guardian and all the attentions she paid him—for Ursule had relieved La Bougival by taking care of the old man—all filled up the hours, days, and months of this tranquil existence. For a year past, indeed, some little ailments of Ursule's had made the doctor anxious; but they did not disturb him beyond making him watchful of her health. Meanwhile, however, the sagacious observer and experienced practitioner fancied he could discern that to her physical disorders there was some corresponding disturbance in her mind. He watched her with a mother's eye, but, seeing no one in their circle worthy to inspire her with love, he made himself easy.

Under these circumstances, just a month before the day when this drama had its beginning, an event occurred in the doctor's intellectual life—one of those incidents which plough into the subsoil, so to speak, of our convictions, and turn up its very depths. But it will first be necessary to give a brief account of some facts of his medical career, which will also lend fresh interest to this narrative.

At the end of the eighteenth century science was as deeply rent by the apparition of Mesmer as art was by that of Gluck. After his rediscovery of magnetism, Mesmer came to France, whither from time immemorial inventors have resorted to find protection for their discoveries. France, thanks to the lucidity of her language, is as it were the trumpeter of the world.

"If homœopathy gets to Paris, it is safe!" said Hahnemann.

"Go to France," said Metternich to Gall, "and if they laugh at your 'bumps,' you are a made man."

Mesmer, then, had his disciples and his antagonists, as ardent as the Piccinists against the Gluckists. Scientific France was stirred, and a serious debate was set on foot. Until judgment should be pronounced, the faculty of medicine, in a body, proscribed what they called Mesmer's quackery, his tub, his conducting wires, and his theories. But it must be said that the German compromised his splendid discovery by preposterous pecuniary demands. Mesmer failed through unproven facts, through his ignorance of the part played in nature by imponderable fluids not as yet investigated, and through his inability to study all sides of a science which has three aspects. Magnetism has more applications; in Mesmer's hands it was in relation to its future development what a principle is to results. But though the discoverer lacked genius, it is sad for human reason and for France to have to own that a science contemporaneous with the earliest civilization, cultivated in Egypt and Chaldea, in Greece and in India, met in Paris at the high-tide of the eighteenth century with the same fate as the truth embodied in Galileo in the sixteenth; and that magnetism was put out of court by the twofold attainder of religious believers and of materialist philosophers, both equally alarmed. Magnetism, the favorite science of Jesus, and one of the powers conferred on the apostles, seems to have been as little recognized by the church as by the followers of Jean-Jacques and Voltaire, of Locke and Condillac. Neither the encyclopedia nor the priesthood could come to terms with this ancient human force which seemed to them so novel. The miracles of the *convulsionnaires* were smothered by the church and by the indifference of the learned, in spite of the valuable works of Carré de Montgeron; still, they were the first summons to make experiments on the fluids in the human body which supply the power of calling up enough spontaneous forces to nullify the pain caused by an external agency. But it would have necessitated the recognition of fluids that are intangible, invisible, and imponderable, the three negations which science at that time regarded as the definition of a vacuum.

To modern science a vacuum is impossible. Given ten feet of vacuum, and the world is in ruins! To materialists especially the world is absolutely full, everything is closely linked and connected, and acts mechanically.

"The world," said Diderot, "as a result of mere change

is more intelligible than God. The multiplicity of causes, and the immeasurable number of throws that chance presupposes, sufficiently account for creation. Given the 'Æneid' and all the letters necessary to set it up, if you grant me time and space, by dint of tossing the letters, I should bring out the combination forming the 'Æneid.'" These wretched men, who would deify everything rather than confess a God, shrank no less from the infinite divisibility of matter which is implied in the nature of an imponderable force. Locke and Condillac at that time delayed by fifty years the immense advance which natural science is now making under the conception of unity which we owe to the great Geoffroy Saint-Hilaire.

Some honest minds, devoid of system, convinced by the facts they had conscientiously studied, persisted in holding the doctrine of Mesmer, who discerned the existence in man of a penetrating influence, giving one individual power over another, and brought into play by the will; an influence which is curative when the fluid is abundant, and which acts as a duel between two wills—the evil to be cured and the will to cure it. The phenomena of somnambulism, hardly suspected by Mesmer, were detected by MM. de Puységur and Deleuze; but the Revolution brought a pause in these discoveries, which left the men of learning and the scoffers in possession of the field.

Among the small number of believers were some physicians; these seceders were persecuted by their brethren till the day of their death. The respectable faculty of doctors in Paris turned against the Mesmerists with all the rigor of a religious warfare, and were as cruel in their hatred as it was possible to be in a period of Voltairean tolerance. The orthodox physicians refused to meet in consultation with those who adhered to the Mesmerian heresy. In 1820, these reputed heresiarchs were still the object of this unformulated proscription. The disasters and storms of the Revolution did

THE HEIRS IN ALARM. 65

not extinguish this scientific hostility. None but priests, lawyers, and physicians can hate in this way. The "gown" is always terrible. But are not ideas certain to be more implacable than things? Doctor Bouvard, a friend of Minoret, accepted the new creed, and to his dying day persisted in the scientific faith to which he sacrificed the peace of his whole life—for he was the pet aversion of the Paris faculty. Minoret, one of the bravest supporters of the encyclopedists, and the most redoubtable adversary of Deslon, Mesmer's chief disciple, since his pen had great weight in this dispute, quarreled beyond remedy with his old comrade; he did worse, he persecuted him. His behavior to Bouvard must have caused him the only repentance that can have clouded the serenity of his declining life.

Since Doctor Minoret's retirement to Nemours, the science of imponderable agents—the only name applicable to magnetism of which the phenomena ally it so closely with electricity and light—had made immense progress, in spite of the unfailing mockery of the Paris world of science. Phrenology and physiognomy, the sciences of Gall and Lavater, twins, of which one is to the other as cause to effect, demonstrated to the eyes of more than one physiologist certain traces of the intangible fluid which is the basis of the phenomena of human will, giving rise to passions and habits, to the forms of the features and of the skull. Magnetic facts too, the miracles of somnambulism, and those of divination and ecstasy, allowing us to enter into the world of spirit, were multiplying. The strange tale of the apparitions seen by Martin, a farmer, which were amply proved, and that peasant's interview with Louis XVIII.; the statements as to Swedenborg's intercourse with the dead, seriously accepted in Germany; Walter Scott's narratives of the results of second-sight; the amazing faculties displayed by some fortune-tellers, who combined into one science chiromancy, card-reading, and horoscopy; the facts of catalepsy, and of the peculiar action of the diaphragm

5

under certain morbid influences ; all these phenomena, curious, to say the least, and all emanating from the same source,
undermined much doubt, and led the most indifferent into the
province of experiment.   Minoret knew nothing of this
movement of mind, vast in Northern Europe, though still
small in France, where, nevertheless, certain facts occurred
which superficial observers called marvelous, but which fell
like stones to the bottom of the sea in the whirlpool of events
in Paris.

At the beginning of this year the anti-mesmerist was greatly
disturbed by receiving the following letter :

" MY OLD COMRADE :—Every friendship, even a lost friendship, has rights which it is not easy to set aside.   I know that
you are still alive, and I remember less of our hostilities than
of our happy days in the little dens of Saint-Julien-le-pauvre.
Now that I am about to quit this world, I cling to a hope of
proving to you that magnetism is destined to be one of the
most important of sciences—unless, indeed all science should
not be regarded as *one*.   I can wreck your incredulity by positive proofs.   Perhaps I may gain from your curiosity the
happiness of once more clasping your hand as we used to
clasp hands before the days of Mesmer.   Always yours,

" BOUVARD."

The anti-mesmerist, stung as a lion by a gadfly, rushed off
to Paris and left his card on old Bouvard, who lived in the
Rue Férou, near Saint Sulpice.   Bouvard sent a card to his
hotel, writing on it, " To-morrow at nine o'clock, Rue St.
Honoré, opposite the Church of the Assumption."

Minoret, grown young again, did not sleep.   He went to
call on the old physicians of his acquaintance, and asked
them if the world were turned upside down, if there were
still a school of medicine, and if the four faculties still existed.
The doctors reassured him by telling him that the old spirit

of resistance still survived; only, instead of persecuting the new science, the academies of medicine and of sciences roared with laughter, and classed magnetic demonstrations with the tricks of Comus, Comte, and Bosco, as jugglery, sleight-of-hand, and what is known as amusing physics.

These speeches did not hinder Minoret from going to the rendezvous appointed by old Bouvard. After forty-four years of alienation the antagonists met again under a courtyard gate in the Rue St. Honoré.

Frenchmen live in too constant a change to hate each other very long. In Paris, especially, events expand space and make life so wide—in politics, in science, and in literature—that men cannot fail to find countries in it to conquer where their demands find room to dwell and rule. Hatred requires so many forces always in arms that those who mean to hate persistently begin with a good supply. And then, only bodies of men can bear it in mind. At the end of forty-four years Robespierre and Danton would fall on each other's neck.

Neither of the two doctors, however, offered to shake hands. Bouvard was the first to say to Minoret (with the familiar *tu* of French good-fellowship)—

" You are looking very well."

" Yes, not so badly; and you?" said Minoret, the ice being broken.

" I—as you see me."

" Has magnetism kept you from dying?" asked Minoret in a bantering tone, but not bitterly.

" No ; but it has almost kept me from living."

" You are not rich then?" said Minoret.

" Rich?" said Bouvard.

" Well, but I am rich!" cried Minoret.

" It is not your fortune, but your conviction, that I aim at. Come," replied Bouvard.

" Obstinate fellow!" exclaimed Minoret.

The believer in Mesmer led his incredulous friend into a

dark stairway, and made him mount cautiously to the fourth floor.

At this time there was in Paris an extraordinary man endowed by faith with stupendous powers, and a master of magnetic forces in every form of their application. Not only did this great unknown, who is still living, cure unaided, and at any distance, the most painful and inveterate diseases—cure them suddenly and radically, as of old did the Redeemer of man—but he also could produce at any moment the most curious phenomena of somnambulism by quelling the most refractory wills. The countenance of the unknown, who, like Swedenborg, declares himself to be commissioned by God and in communion with the angels, is that of a lion; it is radiant with concentrated and irresistible energy. His features, of a singular cast, have a terrible and overwhelming power; his voice, coming from the depths of his being, seems charged with magnetic fluid, and enters the listener by every pore.

Disgusted with the ingratitude of the public after thousands of cures, he had thrown himself into unapproachable solitude, voluntary annihilation. His all-powerful hand, which has restored dying daughters to their mothers, fathers to their weeping children, adored mistresses to lovers crazed with love; which has cured the sick when physicians have given them over, and caused thanksgivings to be sung in the synagogue, in the conventicle, and in the church by priests of different creeds, all brought to the same God by the same miracle; which has mitigated the agony of death to those for whom life was no longer possible—that sovereign hand, the sun of life which dazzled the closed eyes of the sleep-walker, he now would not lift to restore the heir of a kingdom to a queen. Wrapped in the memory of the good he has done as in a luminous shroud he has shut his door on the world, and dwells in the skies.

But, in the early days of his reign, almost startled by his

THE HEIRS IN ALARM. 69

own powers, this man, whose disinterestedness was as great as
his influence, allowed a few inquirers to witness his miracles.
The rumor of his fame, which had been immense, and which
might revive any day, aroused Doctor Bouvard on the brink
of the tomb. The persecuted believer in Mesmer could at last
behold the most brilliant manifestation of the science he
cherished, like a treasure, in his heart. The old man's misfortunes had touched the great unknown, who granted him
certain privileges. So Bouvard, as they climbed the stairs,
took his old adversary's banter with malicious satisfaction.
He made no reply but, "You will see, you will see," with
the little tosses of the head that mark a man sure of his case.

The two doctors entered a suite of rooms of the plainest
simplicity. Bouvard went to speak with the master for a
moment in a bedroom adjoining the drawing-room, where he
left Minoret, whose distrust was now aroused. But Bouvard
immediately came back, and led him into the bedroom, where
he found the famous Swedenborgian with a woman seated in
an armchair. The woman did not rise, and seemed not to
observe the arrival of the two old men.

"What, no tub?" said Minoret, with a smile.

"Nothing but the power of God," gravely replied the
Swedenborgian, whom Minoret supposed to be a man of about
fifty.

The three men sat down, and the stranger made conversation. They spoke of the weather and indifferent matters, to
old Minoret's great surprise; he fancied he was being fooled.
The Swedenborgian questioned his visitor as to his scientific
views, and was evidently taking time to study him.

"You have come here out of pure curiosity, monsieur," he
said at length. "I am not in the habit of prostituting a
power which, it is my full conviction, emanates from God;
if I made a frivolous or evil use of it, it might be taken from
me. However, Monsieur Bouvard tells me our aim is to be
the conversion of an opinion antagonistic to ours, and the

enlightenment of a man of learning and good faith. I shall therefore satisfy you. The woman, you see there," he went on, pointing to the armchair, " is in a magnetic sleep. From the accounts and revelations of all such somnambulists, the state is one of great beatitude, during which the inner being, set free from the fetters by which visible nature hinders the full exercise of its faculties, wanders through the world which we erroneously call invisible. Sight and hearing are then far more perfectly active than in the state which we call being awake, and independent, perhaps, of the medium of those organs which are but as a sheath to the blades of light that we call sight and hearing. To a man in that condition distance and material obstacles have ceased to exist, or are pierced through by an internal vitality of which our body is the container, the necessary fulcrum, a mere wrapper. Terms are lacking for results so recently rediscovered; for the words imponderable, intangible, invisible have no meaning in relation to the fluid whose action is perceptible through magnetism. Light is ponderable by heat, which, when it penetrates a body, increases its volume ; and electricity is only too tangible. We have passed judgment on things instead of blaming the imperfection of our instruments."

" She is asleep ? " asked Minoret, examining the woman, who seemed to him of the lower class.

" Her body is in a certain sense annihilated," replied the Swedenborgian. "Ignorant persons mistake this state for sleep. But she will prove to you that there is a spiritual world, where the spirit does not obey the laws of the physical universe. I will send her to any region whither you may choose that she shall go, twenty leagues away, or as far as China; she will tell you what is happening there."

" Send her only to my house at Nemours," replied Minoret.

"I will not interfere between you," said the mysterious man. " Give me your hand ; you shall be at once actor and spectator, cause and effect."

HE TOOK MINORET'S HAND——AND WITH HIS OTHER HAND
HE TOOK THAT OF THE WOMAN IN THE CHAIR.

He took Minoret's hand, Minoret yielding; he held it for a minute with an apparent concentration of thought, and with his other hand he took that of the woman in the chair; then he placed the doctor's hand in the woman's, signing to the old skeptic to sit down by the side of this Pythoness without a tripod. Minoret observed a slight thrill in the excessively calm face of the woman when the Swedenborgian placed them in contact; but the movement, though marvelous in its results, was in itself extremely simple.

"Obey this gentleman," said the unknown, extending his hand over the head of the woman, who seemed to inhale light and life from him. "And remember that all you do for him will please me. Now, you can speak to her," he said to Minoret.

"Go to Nemours, Rue des Bourgeois, to my house," said the doctor.

"Give her time; hold her hand till she shows by what she says that she is there," said Bouvard to his old friend.

"I see a river," replied the woman in a low voice, and seeming to be looking attentively within herself, in spite of her closed eyes. "I see a pretty garden."

"Why have you begun by the river and the garden?" asked Minoret.

"Because they are in the garden."

"Who?"

"The young lady and her nurse, of whom you are thinking."

"What is the garden like?" asked Minoret.

"As you go into it by the steps that lead to the river there is a long gallery to the right, built of brick, in which I see books, and at the end there is a little gazebo trimmed up with wooden bells and red eggs. The wall on the left is covered with creepers—Virginia creeper and yellow jasmine. There is a little sun-dial in the middle; there are a great many pots of flowers. Your ward is looking at the flowers and showing them to her nurse; she makes holes with a dibble and sows some seeds. The nurse is raking the path. Though the girl is as pure as an angel, there is a dawning of love in her, as faint as the first light of morning."

"For whom?" asked the doctor, who had so far heard nothing that any one might not have told him without being a clairvoyant. He still believed it was a trick.

"You know nothing of it, though you were somewhat anxious not long since as she grew up," said the woman, smiling. "The instincts of her heart followed the development of her nature."

"And it is quite a common woman who speaks thus?" exclaimed the old doctor.

"In this state they all speak with peculiar lucidity," replied Bouvard.

"But who is it that Ursule loves?"

"Ursule does not know that she is in love," answered the woman, with a little shake of her head. "She is too angelically innocent to be conscious of desire, or of love in any kind; but she wonders over him, she thinks of him; she even forbids herself to do so, and returns in spite of her determination to avoid it. Now she is at the piano——"

"But who is he?"

"The son of the lady who lives opposite."

"Madame de Portenduère?"

"Portenduère, did you say?" replied the clairvoyant. "I daresay. But there is no danger; he is not at home?"

"Have they ever spoken to each other?"

"Never. They have looked at each other. She thinks him charming. And he really is very good-looking, and he has a good heart. She has watched him out of her window, and they have seen each other at church; but the young man thinks no more about it."

"What is his name?"

"I cannot tell you unless I should read it or hear it——

His name is Savinien; she has just spoken it; she likes the
sound of it; she had looked in the calendar for his saint's
day, and had marked it with a tiny red spot. Childish! Oh,
she will love very truly, and with a love as pure as it is strong.
She is not the girl to love twice; love will color her whole
soul, and fill it so completely, that she will reject every other
feeling."

"Where do you see that?"

"I see it in her. She will know how to bear suffering;
she has inherited that power, for her father and mother suffered
much."

The last words overset the doctor, who was surprised rather
than shaken. It is desirable to note that ten or fifteen minutes passed between each of the woman's statements; during
these her attention became more and more self-centred. He
could see that she saw! Her brow showed peculiar changes;
internal effort was to be seen there; it cleared or was knit by
a power whose effects Minoret had never seen but in dying
people at the moment when the prophetic spirit is upon them.
She not unfrequently made gestures reminding him of Ursule.

"Oh, question her," said the mysterious master to Minoret.
"She will tell you secrets that none but yourself can know."

"Does Ursule love me?" said Minoret.

"Almost as she loves God," replied the sleeper, with a
smile. "And she is very unhappy about your infidelity. You
do not believe in God, as if you could hinder His being!
His voice fills the world! And so you are the cause of the
poor child's only distress. There! she is playing her scales;
she wishes to be a better musician than she is, and is vexed
with herself. What she thinks is: ' If I only could sing
well, if I had a fine voice, when he was at his mother's it
would be sure to reach his ears! '

Doctor Minoret took out a note-book and wrote down the
exact hour.

"Can you tell me what seeds she has sown?"

" Mignonette, sweet peas, balsams——"

" And lastly ? "

" Larkspur."

" Where is my money ? "

" At your lawyer's; but you invest as it comes in without losing a day's interest."

" Yes ; but where is the money I keep at home for the half-yearly housekeeping ? "

" You keep it in a large book bound in red, called ' The Pandects of Justinian,' vol. ii., between the two last pages; the book is above the sideboard with glass doors, in the division for folios. There is a whole row of them. The money is in the last volume at the end next the drawing-room. By the way, vol. iii. is placed before vol. ii. But it is not money —it is in——"

" Thousand franc notes? " asked the doctor.

"I cannot see clearly ; they are folded up. No, there are two notes for five hundred francs each."

" You can see them ? "

" Yes."

" What are they like ? "

" One is old, and very yellow; the other is white, and almost new."

This last part of the interview left Doctor Minoret thunderstruck. He looked at Bouvard in blank amazement; but Bouvard and the Swedenborgian, who were accustomed to the astonishment of skeptics, were conversing in an undertone, without showing any surprise or amazement.

Minoret begged them to allow him to return after dinner. The anti-mesmerist wanted to think it over, to shake off his extreme terror, so as to test once more this immense power, to submit it to some decisive experiment, and ask some questions which, if answered, could leave no shadow of a doubt.

" Be here by nine o'clock," said the unknown. " I shall be at your service."

Minoret was so violently agitated that he went away without taking leave, followed by Bouvard, who called after him—

"Well? Well?"

"I believe I am mad," replied Minoret, as they reached the outer door. "If that woman has told the truth about Ursule, as there is no one on earth but Ursule who can know what the sorceress has revealed—*you are right.* I only wish I had wings to fly to Nemours and verify her statements. But I will hire a post-chaise and start at ten this evening. Oh! I am going crazy!"

"What would you think, then, if you had known a man incurable for years made perfectly well in five seconds; if you could see that great magnetizer make a leper sweat profusely; or make a crippled woman walk?"

"Let us dine together, Bouvard, and stay with me till nine o'clock. I want to devise some decisive and irrefutable test."

"Certainly, old friend," replied the Mesmerian doctor.

The reconciled enemies went to dine at the Palais Royal. After an eager conversation, which helped Minoret to escape from the turmoil of ideas that racked his brain, Bouvard said to him—

"If you discern in this woman a real power to annihilate space, if you can but convince yourself that she, here, from the Church of the Assumption, can see and hear what is going on at Nemours, you must then admit all other effects of magnetism; they are to a skeptic quite as impossible as these. Ask her, therefore, one single proof that may satisfy you, for you may imagine that we have procured all this information. But we cannot possibly know, for instance, what will happen this evening at nine o'clock in your house, in your ward's bedroom. Remember or write down exactly what the clairvoyant may tell you, and hasten home. Little Ursule, whom I never saw, is not our accomplice; and, if she shall have done or said what you will have written down, bow thy head, proud infidel!"

The two friends returned to the Swedenborgian's rooms, and there found the woman, who did not recognize Doctor Minoret. Her eyes gently closed under the hand which the master stretched out to her from afar, and she sank into the attitude in which Minoret had seen her before dinner. When his hand and hers were placed in connection he desired her to tell him all that was happening in his house at Nemours at that moment.

"What is Ursule doing?" he asked.

"She is in her dressing-gown; she has finished putting in her curl-papers; she is kneeling on her prie-Dieu in front of an ivory crucifix fastened on to a panel of red velvet."

"What is she saying?"

"Her evening prayers; she commends herself to God; she beseeches Him to keep her soul free from evil thoughts; she examines her conscience, going over all she has done during the day to see whether she has failed in obedience to His commandments or those of the church; she is stripping her heart bare, poor dear little thing." There were tears in the clairvoyant's eyes. "She has committed no sin; but she blames herself for having thought too much of Monsieur Savinien," she went on. "She stops to wonder what he is doing in Paris, and prays to God to make him happy. She ends with you, and says a prayer aloud."

"Can you repeat it?"

"Yes."

Minoret took out his pencil and wrote at the woman's dictation the following prayer, evidently composed by the Abbé Chaperon—

"'O God, if Thou art pleased with Thy handmaid, who adores Thee and beseeches Thee with all love and fervor, who strives not to wander from Thy holy commandments, who would gladly die, as Thy Son died, to glorify Thy name, who would fain live under Thy shadow, Thou to whom all hearts are open, grant me the mercy that my godfather's eyes may be unsealed, lead him into the way of life, and give him Thy grace, that he may dwell in Thee during his latter days; preserve him from all ill, and let me suffer in his stead! Holy Saint Ursule, my beloved patron saint, and thou, mother of God, queen of heaven, archangels, and saints in paradise, hear me; join your intercessions to mine, and have pity on us!'''

The clairvoyant so exactly imitated the child's innocent gestures and saintly aspirations that Doctor Minoret's eyes filled with tears.

" Does she say anything more ? " he asked.

" Yes."

" Repeat it."

"' Dear godfather! Whom will he play backgammon with in Paris ? ' She has blown out her light, lays down her head, and goes to sleep. She is gone off! She looks so pretty in her little night-cap ! "

Minoret took leave of the great unknown, shook hands with Bouvard, ran downstairs, and hurried off to a stand of coaches, which at that time existed under the gateway of a mansion since demolished to make way for the Rue d'Alger. He there found a driver, and asked him if he would set out forthwith for Fontainebleau. The price having been agreed on, the old man, made young again, set out that very minute. As agreed, he let the horse rest at Essonne, then drove on till they picked up the Nemours diligence, and dismissed his coachman.

He reached home by about five in the morning, and went to bed amid the wreck of all his former notions of physiology, of nature, and of metaphysics; and he slept till nine, he was so tired by his expedition.

On waking, the doctor, quite sure that no one had crossed the threshold since his return, proceeded to verify the facts, not without an invincible dread. He himself had forgotten the difference between the two bank-notes, and the displace-

ment of the two volumes of "The Pandects." The somnambulist had seen rightly. He rang for La Bougival.

"Tell Ursule to come to speak to me," said he, sitting
down in the middle of the library.

The girl came at once, flew to his side, and kissed him;
the doctor took her on his knee, where, as she sat, her fine fair
tresses mingled with her godfather's white hair.

"You have something to say to me, godfather?"

"Yes. But promise me, on your soul, to reply frankly,
unequivocally, to my questions."

Ursule blushed to the roots of her hair.

"Oh! I will ask you nothing that you cannot answer," he
went on, seeing the bashfulness of first love clouding the
hitherto childlike clearness of her lovely eyes.

"Speak, godfather."

"With what thought did you end your evening prayers last
night; and at what hour did you say them?"

"It was a quarter-past nine, or half-past."

"Well, repeat now your last prayer."

The young girl hoped that her voice might communicate
her faith to the unbeliever; she rose, knelt down, and clasped
her hands fervently; a radiant look beamed in her face, she
glanced at the old man, and said—

"What I asked of God last night I prayed for again this
morning, and shall still ask till He grants it me."

Then she repeated the prayer with fresh and emphatic
expression; but, to her great surprise, her godfather interrupted her, ending it himself.

"Well, Ursule," said the doctor, drawing her on to his
knees again, "and as you went to sleep with your head on the
pillow, did you not say, 'Dear godfather! Whom will he
play backgammon with in Paris?'"

Ursule started to her feet as though the trump of judgment
had sounded in her ears; she gave a cry of terror; her
dilated eyes stared at the old man with fixed horror.

" Who are you, godfather ? Where did you get such a power ? " she asked, fancying that as he did not believe in God, he must have made a compact with the angel of hell.

" What did you sow in the garden yesterday ? "

" Mignonette, sweet peas, balsams———"

" And larkspurs to end with ? "

She fell on her knees.

" Do not terrify me, godfather ! But you were here, were you not ? "

" Am I not always with you ? " replied the doctor in jest, to spare the innocent child's reason.

" Let us go to your room." Then he gave her his arm and went upstairs.

" Your knees are quaking, godfather," said she.

" Yes ; I feel quite overset."

" Do you at last believe in God ? " she exclaimed, with innocent gladness, though the tears rose to her eyes.

The old man looked round the neat and simple room he had arranged for Ursule. On the floor was an inexpensive green drugget, which she kept exquisitely clean ; on the walls a paper with a pale-gray ground and a pattern of roses with their green leaves ; there were white cotton curtains, with a pink border, to the windows looking on the courtyard ; between the windows, below a tall mirror, a console of gilt wood with a marble slab, on which stood a blue Sèvres vase for flowers ; and opposite the fireplace a pretty inlaid chest of drawers with a top of fine marble. The bed, furnished with old chintz, and chintz curtains lined with pink, was one of the old *duchesse* four-post beds which were common in the eighteenth century, ornamented with a capital of carved feathers to each of the fluted columns at the corners. On the chimney-shelf was an old clock, mounted in a sort of catafalque of tortoise-shell inlaid with ivory ; the marble chimney-piece and candelabra, the glass, and the pier, painted in shades of gray, had a remarkably good effect of tone, color, and style. A large wardrobe, the doors inlaid with land-scapes in various kinds of wood, some of them of greenish tint, hardly to be met with in these days, no doubt contained her linen and her dresses.

The atmosphere of this room had a fragrance as of heaven. The careful arrangement of everything indicated a spirit of order, a feeling for the harmony of things, that would have struck any one, even a Minoret-Levrault. It was, above all, easy to see how dear to Ursule were the things about her, and how fond she was of the room which was, so to speak, part of all her life as a child and a young girl.

While looking round at it all as an excuse, the guardian convinced himself that from her window Ursule could see across to Madame de Portenduère's house. During the night he had considered the line of conduct to be taken with regard to the secret he had discovered of her budding passion. To question his ward would compromise him in her eyes ; for either he must approve or disapprove of her love ; in either case he would be awkwardly situated. He had therefore determined that he would study for himself the relations of young Portenduère and Ursule, to decide whether he should try to counteract her inclination before it had become irresistible. Only an old man could show so much prudence. Still gasping under the shock of finding the magnetic revelations true, he turned about, examining the smallest things in the room, for he wished to glance at the almanac which hung by a corner of the chimney-piece.

" These clumsy candlesticks are too heavy for your pretty little hands," he said, taking up the marble candlesticks, ornamented with brass.

He weighed them in his hands, looked at the almanac, unhooked it, and said—

" This, too, seems to me very ugly. Why do you hang this common calendar in such a pretty room ? "

" Oh, leave me that, godfather ! "

" No, no ; you shall have another to-morrow."

He went downstairs again, carrying away the convicting document, shut himself into his room, looked for Saint Savinien, and found, as the clairvoyant had said, a small red dot at the 19th of October ; he found such another at Saint Denis' day, his own patron saint ; and at Saint John's day—that of the curé. And this dot, as large as a pin's head, the sleeping woman had discerned in spite of distance and obstacles. The old man meditated till dusk on all these facts, more stupendous to him than to any other man. He was forced to yield to evidence. A thick wall, within himself, as it were, crumbled down ; for he had lived on the double foundation of his indifference to religion and his denial of magnetism. By proving that the senses—a purely physical structure, mere organs whose effects can all be explained—were conterminous with some of the attributes of infinity, magnetism overthrew, or at any rate seemed to him to overthrow, Spinoza's powerful logic : The finite and the infinite, two elements which, according to that great man, are incompatible, existed one in the other. However great the power he could conceive of the divisibility and mobility of matter, he could not credit it with almost divine characters. And he was too old to connect these phenomena with a system, to compare them with those of sleep, of vision, or of light. All his scientific theory, based on the statements of the school of Locke and Condillac, lay in ruins. On seeing his hollow idols wrecked, his incredulity naturally was shaken. Hence all the advantages in this struggle between Catholic youth and Voltairean old age was certain to be on Ursule's side. A beam of light fell on the dismantled fortress in ruins ; from the depths of the wreckage rose the cry of prayer.

And yet the stiff-necked old man tried to dispute his own doubts. Though stricken to the heart, he could not make up his mind ; he still strove with God. At the same time his mind seemed to vacillate ; he was not the same man. He

6

became unnaturally pensive; he read the "Pensées" of Pascal, Bossuet's sublime "Histoire des Variations;" he studied Bonald; he read Saint Augustine; he also read through the works of Swedenborg and of the deceased Saint-Martin, of whom the mysterious stranger had spoken. The structure raised in this man by materialism was splitting on all sides; a shock alone was needed; and when his heart was ripe for God, it fell into the heavenly vineyard as fruits drop. Several times already in the evening, when playing his game with the priest, his goddaughter sitting by, he had asked questions which, in view of his opinions, struck the Abbé Chaperon as strange; for as yet he knew not of the moral travail by which God was rectifying this noble conscience.

"Do you believe in apparitions?" the infidel suddenly asked his pastor, pausing in his game.

"Cardain, a great philosopher of the sixteenth century, said that he had seen some," replied the curé.

"I know of all those that the philosophers have seen; I have just re-read Plotinus. At this moment I ask you as a Catholic: I want to know whether you think that a dead man can return to visit the living."

"Well, Jesus appeared to His apostles after His death," replied the priest. "The church must believe in the apparition of our Lord. As to miracles, there is no lack of them," added the Abbé Chaperon with a smile. "Would you like to hear of the latest? Some were wrought in the eighteenth century."

"Pooh!"

"Yes; the blessed Maria-Alphonzo de Liguori knew of the pope's death when he was far from Rome, at the moment when the holy father expired, and there were many witnesses to the miracle. The reverend bishop, in a trance, heard the pontiff's last words, and repeated them to several persons. The messenger bringing the news did not arrive till thirty hours later——"

"Jesuit!" said Minoret with a smile; "I do not ask you for proofs; I ask you whether you believe it."

"I believe that the apparition depends greatly on the person seeing it," said the curé, still laughing at the skeptic.

"My dear friend, I am not laying a trap for you. What is your belief on this point?"

"I believe that the power of God is infinite," replied the abbé.

"When I die, if I am at peace with God, I will entreat Him to let me appear to you," said the doctor, laughing.

"That is precisely the agreement made by Cardan with his friend," replied the curé.

"Ursule," said Minoret, "if ever a danger should threaten you, call me—I would come."

"You have just put into simple words the touching elegy called 'Néère,' by André Chénier," replied the curé. "But poets are great only because they know how to embody facts or feelings in perennially living forms."

"Why do you talk of dying, my dear godfather?" said the young girl sadly. "We shall not die, we who are Christians; the grave is but the cradle of the soul."

"Well, well," said the doctor with a smile, "we are bound to quit this world; and when I am no more, you will be very much astonished at your fortune."

"When you are no more, my kind godfather, my only consolation will be to devote my life to you."

"To me—when I am dead?"

"Yes. All the good works I may be able to do shall be done in your name to redeem your errors. I will pray to God day by day to persuade His infinite mercy not to punish eternally the faults of a day, but to give a place near to Himself among the spirits of the blest to a soul so noble and so pure as yours."

This reply, spoken with angelic candor and in a tone of absolute conviction, confounded error and converted Doctor

Minoret like another Saint Paul. A flash of internal light stunned him, and at the same time this tenderness, extending even to the life to come, brought tears to his eyes. This sudden effect of grace was almost electrical, The curé clasped his hands and stood up in his agitation. The child herself, surprised at her success, shed tears. The old man drew himself up as though some one had called him, looked into space as if he saw an aurora; then he knelt on his armchair, folded his hands, and cast down his eyes in deep humiliation.

"Great God!" he said, in a broken voice, and looking up to heaven, "if any one can obtain my forgiveness, and lead me to Thee, is it not this spotless creature? Pardon my repentant old age, presented to Thee by this glorious child!"

He lifted up his soul in silence to God, beseeching Him to enlighten him by knowledge after having overwhelmed him by grace; then, turning to the curé, he held out his hand, saying—

"My dear father in God, I am a little child again. I am yours; I give my soul into your hands."

Ursule kissed her godfather's hands, covering them with tears of joy. The old man took her on his knee, gaily calling her his godmother. The curé, much moved, recited the *Veni Creator* in a sort of religious transport. This hymn was their evening prayer as the three Christians knelt together.

"What has happened?" asked La Bougival in astonishment.

"At last my godfather believes in God!" cried Ursule.

"And a good thing too; that was all that was wanting to make him perfect!" exclaimed the old peasant-woman, crossing herself with simple gravity.

"My dear doctor," said the good priest, "you will soon have mastered the grandeur of religion and the necessity for its exercises; and you will find its philosophy, in so far as it is human, much loftier than that of the most daring minds."

The curé, who displayed an almost childlike joy, then agreed to instruct the old man by meeting him as a catechumen twice a week.

Thus the conversion ascribed to Ursule and to a spirit of sordid self-interest had been spontaneous. The priest, who for fourteen years had restrained himself from touching the wounds in that heart, though he had deeply deplored them, had been appealed to, as we go to a surgeon when we feel an injury. Since that scene every evening Ursule's prayers had become family prayers. Every moment the old man had felt peace growing upon him in the place of agitation. And viewing God as the responsible editor of inexplicable facts— as he put it—his mind was quite easy. His darling child told him that by this it could be seen that he was making progress in the kingdom of God.

To-day, during the service, he had just read the prayers with the exercise of his understanding; for, in his first talk with the curé, he had risen to the divine idea of the communion of the faithful. The venerable neophyte had understood the eternal symbol connected with that nourishment, which faith makes necessary as soon as the whole, deep, glorious meaning of the symbol is thoroughly felt. If he had seemed in a hurry to get home, it was to thank his dear little goddaughter for having brought him to the Lord, to use the fine old-fashioned phrase. And so he had her on his knee in his drawing-room, and was kissing her solemnly on the brow, at the very moment when his heirs, defiling her holy influence by their ignoble alarms, were lavishing on Ursule their coarsest abuse. The good man's haste to be at home, his scorn, as they thought it, for his relations, his sharp replies as he left the church, were all naturally attributed by each of the family to the hatred for them which Ursule had implanted in him.

While the girl was playing to her godfather the variations on *La dernière Pensée musicale* of Weber, a plot was being hatched in Minoret-Levrault's dining-room, which was destined to bring on to the stage one of the most important actors in this drama. The breakfast, which lasted two hours, was as noisy as a provincial breakfast always is, and washed down by capital wine brought to Nemours by canal, either from Burgundy or from Touraine. Zélie had procured some shell-fish too, some sea-fish, and a few rarer dainties to do honor to Désiré's return.

The dining-room, in its midst the round table of tempting aspect, looked like an inn-room. Zélie, satisfied with the extent of her household offices, had built a large room between the vast courtyard and the kitchen-garden, which was full of vegetables and fruit-trees. Here everything was merely neat and substantial. The example set by Levrault-Levrault had been a terror to the countryside, and Zélie had forbidden the master-builder's dragging her into any such folly. The room was hung with satin paper, and furnished with plain walnut-wood chairs and sideboards, with an earthenware stove, a clock on the wall, and a barometer. Though the crockery was ordinary—plain white china—the table shone with linen and abundant plate.

As soon as the coffee had been served by Zélie, who hopped to and fro like a grain of shot in a bottle of champagne, for she kept but one cook; and when Désiré, the budding lawyer, had been fully apprised of the great event of the morning and its results, Zélie shut the door, and the notary Dionis was called upon to speak. The silence that fell, the looks fixed by each expectant heir on that authoritative face, plainly showed how great is the influence exercised by these men over whole families.

"My dear children," he began, "your uncle, having been born in 1746, is at this day eighty-three years old; now old men are liable to fits of folly, and this little——"

"Viper!" exclaimed Madame Massin.

"Wretch!" said Zélie.

"We will only call her by her name," said Dionis.

"Well, then, a thief," said Madame Crémière.

"A very pretty thief," added Désiré Minoret.

"This little Ursule," Dionis went on, "is very dear to him. I have not waited till this morning to make inquiries in the interest of you all as my clients, and this is what I have learned concerning this young——"

"Spoiler!" put in the tax-collector.

"Underhand fortune-hunter," said the lawyer's clerk.

"Hush, my friends, or I shall put on my hat and go, and good-day to you."

"Come, come, old man!" said Minoret, pouring him out a liqueur glassful of rum. "Drink that; it comes from Rome, direct."

"Ursule is no doubt Joseph Mirouët's legitimate offspring. But her father was the natural son of Valentin Mirouët, your uncle's father-in-law. Thus Ursule is the natural niece of Doctor Denis Minoret. As his natural niece, any will the doctor may make in her favor may perhaps be void, and if he should leave her his fortune, you may bring a lawsuit against her; this might be bad enough for you, for it is impossible to say that there is no tie of relationship between the doctor and Ursule; still, a lawsuit would certainly frighten a defenseless girl, and would result in a compromise."

"The law is so rigorous as to the rights of natural children," said the newly-hatched lawyer, eager to display his learning, "that by the terms of a judgment of the Court of Appeals of July 7, 1817, a natural child can claim nothing from its natural grandfather, not even maintenance. So, you see, that the parentage of a natural child carries back. The law is against a natural child, even in his legitimate descendants; for it regards any legacies benefiting the grandchildren as bestowed through the personal intermediary of the natural son, their parent. This is the inference from a comparison of Articles 757, 908, and 911 of the Civil Code. And, in fact, the Royal Court of Paris, on the 26th of December, only last year,

reduced a legacy bequeathed to the legitimate child of a
natural son by its grandfather, who, as its grandfather, was as
much a stranger in blood to his natural grandson as the doctor
is to Ursule as her uncle.''

"All that," said Goupil, "seems to me to relate only to
the question of bequests made by grandparents to their
illegitimate descendants; it has nothing to do with uncles,
who do not appear to me to have any blood relationships to
the legitimate offspring of these natural half-brothers.   Ursule
is a stranger in blood to Doctor Minoret.   I remember a
judgment delivered in the Supreme Court at Colmar in 1825,
when I was finishing my studies, by which it was pronounced
that the illegitimate child being dead, his descendants could
no longer be liable to his interposition.   Now Ursule's father
is dead.''

Goupil's argument produced, what in reports of law cases
journalists are accustomed to designate by this parenthesis:
(*Great sensation*).

"What does that matter?" cried Dionis.   "Even if the
case of a legacy left by the uncle of an illegitimate child has
never yet come before the courts, if it should occur, the rigor
of the French law towards natural children will be all the
more surely applied, because we live in times when religion is
respected.   And I will answer for it that, in such a suit, a
compromise would be offered; especially if it were known
that you were resolved to carry the case against Ursule even
to the court of last resort.''

The delight of heirs who might find piles of gold betrayed
itself in smiles, little jumps, and gestures all round the table.
No one observed Goupil's shake of dissent.   But, then, this
exultation was immediately followed by deep silence and dismay at the notary's next word—

"But——''

Dionis at once saw every eye fixed on him, every face
assuming the same angle, just as if he had pulled the wire of

one of those toy theatres where all the figures move in jerks by the action of wheel-work.

"But there is no law to hinder your uncle from adopting or marrying Ursule," he went on. "As to an adoption, it might be disputed, and you would, I believe, win the case; the high courts are not to be trifled with in the matter of adoption, and you would be examined in the preliminary inquiry. It is all very well for the doctor to display the ribbon of St. Michael, to be an officer of the Legion of Honor, and formerly physician to the ex-Emperor; he would go to the wall. But though you might be warned in case of an adoption, how are you to know if he marries her? The old fellow is quite sharp enough to get married in Paris after residing there for a year, and to secure to his bride a settlement of a million francs under the marriage contract. The only thing, therefore, which really jeopardizes your inheritance is that your uncle should marry the child." Here the notary paused.

"There is another risk," said Goupil, with a knowing air. "He may make a will in favor of a third person, old Bongrand for instance, who would be constituted trustee for Mademoiselle Ursule Mirouët."

"If you worry your uncle," Dionis began again, cutting short his head clerk, "if you are not all as nice as possible to Ursule, you will drive him either into a marriage or into the trusteeship of which Goupil speaks; but I do not think he is likely to have recourse to a trust; it is a dangerous alternative. As to his marrying her, it is easy to prevent it. Désiré has only to show the girl a little attention; she will certainly prefer a charming young fellow, the cock of the walk at Nemours, to an old man."

"Mother," said the postmaster's son in Zélie's ear, tempted both by the money and by Ursule's beauty, "if I were to marry her, we should get it all."

"Are you mad? You who will have fifty thousand francs

a year one of these days and who are sure to be elected deputy ! So long as I live you shall never hang a millstone round your neck by a foolish marriage. Seven hundred thousand francs ? Thank you for nothing ! Why, monsieur, the mayor's only daughter will have fifty thousand a year, and they have already made overtures."

This reply, in which, for the first time in his life, his mother spoke roughly to him, extinguished in Désiré every hope of marrying the fair Ursule, for his father and he could never gain the day against the determination written in Zélie's terrible blue eyes.

"Yes; but, I say, Monsieur Dionis," cried Crémière, whose wife had nudged his elbow, "if the old man took the matter seriously, and let his ward marry Désiré, settling on her the absolute possession of his property, good-by to our chances ! And if he lives another five years, our uncle will have at least a million."

"Never," cried Zélie; "never so long as I live and breathe shall Désiré marry the daughter of a bastard, a girl taken in out of charity, picked up in the streets ! What next, by heaven ? At his uncle's death my son will be the representative of the Minorets ; and the Minorets can show five centuries of good citizenship. It is as good as a noble pedigree. Make your minds easy. Désiré shall marry when we see what he is likely to do in the Chamber of Deputies."

This arrogant pronouncement was seconded by Goupil, who added—

"With eighty thousand francs a year, Désiré may rise to be president of a supreme court, or public prosecutor, which leads to a peerage. A foolish marriage would be the ruin of his prospects."

The heirs all began to talk at once, but they were silenced by the blow of his fist that Minoret struck on the table to enable the notary to speak on.

"Your uncle is an excellent and worthy man," said Dionis.

" He believes himself immortal ; and, like all clever men, he will allow death to overtake him before he has made his will. My opinion, therefore, for the moment, is that he should be induced to invest his capital in such a way as to make it difficult to dispossess you; and the opportunity now offers. Young Portenduère is in Sainte Pélagie, locked up for a hundred and odd thousand francs of debts. His old mother knows he is in prison; she is weeping like a Magdalen, and has asked the Abbé Chaperon to dinner, to talk over the catastrophe, no doubt. Well, I shall go this evening and suggest to your uncle to sell his stock of consolidated five per cents., which are at a hundred and eighteen, and lend the sum necessary to release the prodigal to Madame du Portenduère on the farm at Bordières and her dwelling-house. I am within my rights as a notary in applying to him on behalf of that little idiot of a Portenduère, and it is quite natural that I should wish him to change his investments; I get the commission, the stamps, and the business. If I can get him to take my advice, I shall propose to him to invest the rest of his capital in real estate. I have some splendid lands for sale in my office. When once his fortune is invested in real estate or in mortgages on land in this neighborhood, it will not easily fly away. It is always easy to raise difficulties in the way of realizing the capital if he should wish to do so."

The heirs, struck by the soundness of this logic, much more skillful than that of M. Josse, expressed themselves by approving murmurs.

" So settle it among yourselves," added the notary, in conclusion, " to keep your uncle in this town, where he has his own ways, and where you can keep an eye on him. If you can find a lover for the girl, you will hinder her marrying."

" But if she were to marry him?" said Goupil, urged by an ambitious instinct.

" That would not be so bad after all; your loss would be set down in plain figures, and you would know what the old

man would give her," answered the notary. "Still, if you
set Désiré at her, he might easily play fast and loose with her
till the old man's death. Marriages are arranged and upset
again."

"The shortest way," said Goupil, "if the doctor is likely
to live a long time yet, would be to get her married to some
good fellow, who would take her out of the way by settling
with her at Sens, or Montargis, or Orleans, with a hundred
thousand francs down."

Dionis, Massin, Zélie, and Goupil, the only clear heads of
the party, exchanged glances full of meaning.

"He would be a maggot in the pear," said Zélie in Massin's
ear.

"Why was he allowed to come?" replied the registrar.

"That would just suit you!" exclaimed Désiré to Goupil;
"but how could you ever keep yourself decent enough to
please the old man and his ward?"

"You don't think small beer of yourself!" said Minoret,
understanding Goupil at last.

This coarse jest was greeted with shouts of laughter. But
the lawyer's clerk glared at the laughers with such a sweeping
and terrible gaze that silence was immediately restored.

"In these days," Zélie whispered to Massin, "notaries
think only of their own interests. What if Dionis, to get his
commission, should take Ursule's side?"

"I know he is safe," replied the registrar, with a keen
twinkle in his wicked little eyes; he was about to add, "I
have him in my power," but he abstained, deeming it the
more prudent course.

"I am entirely of Dionis' opinion," he said aloud.

"And so am I," exclaimed Zélie, though she already suspected the notary and Massin to be in collusion for their own
advantage.

"My wife has given our vote," said the postmaster, sipping
a glass of spirits, though his face was already purple with

digesting the meal and from a considerable consumption of wines and liqueurs.

" It is quite right," said the tax-collector.

" Then will I call on him after dinner ?" asked Dionis, good-naturedly.

" If Monsieur Dionis is right," said Madame Crémière to Madame Massin, " we ought to go to see your uncle, as we used to, every Sunday evening, and do all Monsieur Dionis has just told us."

" Yes, indeed ! To be received as we have been," exclaimed Zélie. " After all, we have an income of over forty thousand francs ; and he has refused all our invitations. We are as good as he is. I can steer my own ship, thank you, though I cannot write prescriptions ! "

" As I am far from having forty thousand francs a year," said Madame Massin, nettled, "I am not anxious to lose ten thousand ! "

" We are his nieces ; we will look after him ; we shall see what is going on," said Madame Crémière. " And some day, Cousin Zélie, you will be beholden to us."

" Be civil to Ursule ; old Jordy left her his savings," said the notary, putting his right forefinger to his lip.

" I will mind my P's and Q's," said Désiré.

" You were a match for Desroches, the sharpest attorney in Paris," said Goupil to his master, as they quitted the house.

" And they dispute our bills," remarked the notary, with a bitter smile.

The heirs, seeing out Dionis and his head clerk, found themselves at the gate, all with faces heated from the meal, just as the congregation came out from vespers. As the notary had foretold, the Abbé Chaperon had given his arm to old Madame de Portenduère.

" She has dragged him to vespers ! " cried Madame Massin, pointing out to Madame Crémière Ursule coming out of the church with her uncle.

"Let us go and speak to him," suggested Madame Cré-mière, going forward.

The change which the conclave had produced in all their countenances astonished Doctor Minoret. He wondered what the cause could be of this friendliness to order, and out of curiosity he favored a meeting between Ursule and these two women, who were eager to address her with exaggerated sweet-ness and forced smiles.

"Uncle, will you allow us to call on you this evening?" said Madame Crémière. "We sometimes think we are in the way; but it is long now since our children have paid their respects to you, and our daughters are of an age to make friends with dear Ursule."

"Ursule justifies her name," said the doctor; "she is not at all tame."

"Let us tame her," said Madame Massin. "And besides, my dear uncle," added the prudent housewife, trying to con-ceal her scheming under a semblance of economy, "we have been told that your charming goddaughter has such a talent for the piano, that we should be enchanted to hear her play. Madame Crémière and I are rather inclined to have her master to teach our girls; for if he had seven or eight pupils he might fix a price for his lessons within our means——"

"By all means," said the old man; "all the more, indeed, because I am thinking of getting a singing-master for Ursule."

"Very well; then this evening, uncle; and we will bring your grand-nephew Désiré, who is now a full-fledged attor-ney."

"Till this evening," replied Minoret, who wished to study these mean souls.

His two nieces shook hands with Ursule, saying with affected graciousness, "Till this evening."

"Oh, dear godfather, you can read my heart, I believe!" cried Ursule, with a grateful look at the old man.

"You have a good voice," he said. "And I also mean to

give you drawing and Italian lessons. A woman," he added, looking at Ursule as he opened the gate of his own courtyard, "ought to be educated in such a way as to be equal to any position in which she may be placed by marriage."

Ursule blushed as red as a cherry; her guardian seemed to be thinking of the very person she herself was thinking of. Feeling herself on the point of confessing to the doctor the involuntary impulse which made her think of Savinien, and refer all her strivings after perfection to him, she went to sit under the bower of creepers, against which she looked from a distance like a white and blue flower.

"Now you see, godfather, your nieces were kind to me; they were very nice just now," said she, as he followed her, to mislead him as to the thoughts which had made her pensive.

"Poor little thing!" said the old man. He laid Ursule's hand on his arm, patting it gently, and led her along the terrace by the river, where no one could overhear them.

"Why do you say, ' Poor little thing?'"

"Can you not see that they are afraid of you?"

"But why?"

"My heirs are at this moment very uneasy about my conversion; they ascribe it, no doubt, to your influence, and fancy that I shall deprive them of their inheritance to make you the richer."

"But you will not?" said Ursule with simplicity, and looking in his face.

"Ah, divine comfort of my old age," said the old man, lifting her up, and kissing her on both cheeks. "It was for her sake and not for my own, O God, that I besought Thee just now to suffer me to live till I shall have given her into the keeping of some good man worthy of her! You will see, my angel, the farce that the Minorets and the Crémières and the Massins are going to play here. You want to prolong and beautify my life. They! they think of nothing but my death!"

"God forbids us to hate; but if that is true—oh, I scorn them!" cried Ursule.

"Dinner!" cried La Bougival, from the top of the steps which, on the garden side, were at the end of the gallery.

Ursule and the doctor were eating their dessert in the pretty dining-room, painted to imitate Chinese lacquer, which had ruined Levrault-Levrault, when the justice walked in. The doctor, as his most signal mark of intimacy, offered him a cup of his own coffee, a mixture of Mocha with Bourbon and Martinique berries, roasted, ground, and made by his own hands in a silver coffee-pot of the kind patented by Chaptal.

"Well, well," said Bongrand, putting up his spectacles, and looking at the old man with a sly twinkle, "the town is by the ears! Your appearance at church has revolutionized your relations. You are going to leave everything to the priests and to the poor! You have stirred them up, and they are astir! Oh! I saw their first commotion on the church square; they were as fussy as a nest of ants robbed of their eggs."

"What did I tell you, Ursule?" exclaimed the old man. "Even at the risk of grieving you, my child, am I not bound to teach you to know the world, and to put you on your guard against undeserved enmity."

"I wanted to say a few words to you on that subject," said Bongrand, seizing the opportunity of speaking to his old friend about Ursule's future prospects.

The doctor put a black velvet cap on his white head, and the justice kept on his hat as a protection against the dew, and they walked together up and down the terrace, talking over the means of securing to Ursule the little fortune the doctor proposed to leave her. Bongrand knew the opinion of Dionis as to the invalidity of any will made by the doctor in Ursule's favor, for Nemours was too inquisitive as to the Minoret inheritance for this question not to have been discussed by the wise heads of the town. He himself had decided that Ursule was an alien in blood as regarded Doctor Minoret ; but he was fully aware that the spirit of the law was adverse to the recognition of illegitimate offspring as members of the family. The framers of the Code had only anticipated the weakness of fathers and mothers for their natural children ; it had not been supposed that uncles or aunts might have such tender feelings for an illegitimate relation as to favor his descendants. There was evidently an omission in the law.

"In any other country," said he to the doctor, after setting forth the state of the law which Goupil, Dionis, and Désiré had just explained to the heirs, "Ursule would have nothing to fear. She is a legitimate child, and her father's disabilities ought only to affect the money left by Valentin Mirouët, your father-in-law. But in France the bench is unluckily very clever and very logical ; it insists on the spirit of the law. Pleaders will talk of morality, and prove that the omission in the Code arises from the single-mindedness of the framers, who never foresaw such a case, but who nevertheless established a principle. A lawsuit would be lengthy and costly. With Zélie on the other side it would be carried to the court of appeal ; and I cannot be sure that I should be still living when the case was tried."

"The strongest case is not certain to stand," cried the doctor. "I can see the documents on the subject already : 'To what degree of relationship ought the disabilities of natural children in the matter of inheritance to extend?' and the glory of a clever lawyer is to gain a rotten suit."

"On my honor," said Bongrand, "I would not take it upon myself to assert that the judges would not widen the interpretation of the law so as to extend its protection of marriage, which is the everlasting foundation of society."

Without explaining his intentions, the doctor rejected the idea of a trust. But as to the notion of marrying her, which

7

Bongrand suggested as a means of securing her his fortune—

"Poor little thing!" cried the doctor. "I may live fifteen years yet. What would become of her?"

"Well, then, what do you propose?" said Bongrand.

"We must think about it. I shall see," replied the old doctor, evidently at a loss for an answer.

At this instant Ursule came to tell the friends that Dionis wished to see the doctor.

"Dionis already!" exclaimed Minoret, looking at the justice. "Yes," he said to Ursule; "let him be shown in."

"I will bet my spectacles to a brimstone match that he is your heirs' stalking-horse. They breakfasted together at the posting-house, and something has been plotted there."

The notary, following Ursule, came out into the garden. After the usual civilities and a few commonplace remarks, Dionis begged for a moment's private conversation. Ursule and Bongrand went into the drawing-room.

"We must think about it! I shall see!" said Bongrand to himself, echoing the doctor's last words. "That is what clever people think; then death overtakes them, and they leave those who are dearest to them in the greatest difficulties."

The distrust a man of business feels of a man of talent is extraordinary. He cannot admit that the greater includes the less. But this very distrust, perhaps, implies praise. Seeing these superior minds inhabiting the high peaks of human thought, men of business do not believe them capable of descending to the infinitely small details which, like interest in the world of finance, or microscopic creatures in natural history, at last accumulate till they equal the capital, or constitute a world. It is a mistake. The man of feeling and the man of genius see everything.

Bongrand, nettled by the doctor's persistent silence, but urged, no doubt, by Ursule's interests, which he feared were compromised, determined to protect her against her rivals.

He was in despair at not knowing what was going on between the old man and Dionis.

"However pure-minded Ursule may be," thought he, as he looked at her, "there is one point on which young girls are wont to have their own ideas of jurisprudence and morality. Let us try!" "The Minoret-Levraults," said he to Ursule, as he settled his spectacles, "are quite capable of proposing that you should marry their son."

The poor child turned pale. She had been too well brought up, and had too much perfect delicacy, to go and listen to what her uncle and Dionis were saying; but after a short deliberation she thought she might go into the room, thinking that if she were in the way her godfather would make her understand it. The Chinese summer-house, which was the doctor's private study, had the shutters of the glass door left open. Ursule's idea was that she would go herself to close them. She apologized for leaving the lawyer alone in the drawing-room; but he smiled and said—

"Do so, do so."

Ursule went to the steps leading from the Chinese summer-house down to the garden, and there she stood for some minutes slowly closing the Venetian shutters and looking at the sunset. Then she heard this answer spoken by the doctor as he came towards the summer-house—

"My heirs would be delighted to see me possessed of real estate and mortgages. They fancy that my fortune would be much more safely invested. I can guess all they could say; and you, perhaps, are their representative. But, my dear sir, my arrangements are unalterable. My heirs will have the capital of the fortune I brought here with me; they may accept that as a certainty, and leave me in peace. If either of them should make any change in what I believe it to be my duty to do for that child" (and he pointed to his god-daughter), "I will come back from the other world to torment him! So Monsieur Savinien de Portenduère may remain in prison if his release depends on me," added the doctor. "I shall not sell any of my securities."

As she heard the last words of this speech, Ursule felt the first, the only grief she had ever known. She rested her forehead against the shutter, and clung to it for support.

"Good heavens! what ails her?" cried the old doctor; "she is colorless. Such emotion just after dinner might kill her!"

He put out his arm to hold Ursule, who fell almost fainting.

"Good-evening, monsieur; leave me," he said to the notary.

He carried his goddaughter to a huge easy-chair, dating from Louis XV., which stood in his study, seized a phial of ether from his medicine store, and made her inhale it.

"Go and take my place, my friend," said he to Bongrand, who was alarmed; "I must stay with her."

The justice walked to the gate with the notary, asking him, but without any show of eagerness, "What has come over Ursule?"

"I do not know," said Monsieur Dionis. "She was standing on the steps listening to us; and when her uncle refused to lend the necessary sum to release young Portenduère, who is in prison for debt—for he had not a Monsieur Bongrand to defend him as Monsieur du Rouvre had—she turned pale and tottered. Does she love him? Can there be——?"

"At fifteen!" said Bongrand, interrupting Dionis.

"She was born in February, 1814. In four months she will be sixteen."

"But she has never seen her neighbor," replied the justice. "No, it is just an attack."

"An attack of the heart," said the notary.

Dionis was much delighted by his discovery; it would avert the dreaded marriage by which the doctor might have frustrated the hopes of his heirs, while Bongrand saw his

"WHAT AILS YOU, CRUEL CHILD?" HE SAID.

castles in the air in ruins; he had long dreamed of a marriage between his own son and Ursule.

"If the poor child should be in love with that youth, it would be unfortunate for her. Madame de Portenduère is a Bretonne, and crazy about noble birth," replied the justice, after a pause.

"Happily—for the honor of the Portendueres," said the notary, who had nearly betrayed himself.

To do the worthy and honorable lawyer full justice, it must be said that, on his way from the gate to the drawing-room, he gave up, not without regret for his son's loss, the hope he had cherished of one day calling Ursule his daughter. He intended to give his son six thousand francs a year as soon as he was appointed deputy recorder; and if the doctor would have settled a hundred thousand francs on Ursule, the young couple should have been patterns of a happy household. His Eugène was a loyal and accomplished young fellow. Perhaps he had a little over-praised Eugène, and perhaps old Minoret's suspicions had been aroused by that.

"I will fall back on the mayor's daughter," thought Bongrand. "But Ursule without a penny would be better than Mademoiselle Levrault-Crémière with her million. Now we must see what can be done to get Ursule married to this young Portenduère, if, in fact, she loves him."

After closing the doors on the side next the library and the garden, the doctor led the girl to the window that looked over the river.

"What ails you, cruel child?" he said. "Your life is my life. Without your smile what would become of me?"

"Savinien—in prison!" answered she, and with these words a torrent of tears burst from her eyes, and she began to sob.

"Now all will be well," said the old man to himself, as he stood feeling her pulse with a father's anxiety. "Alas! she has all my poor wife's nervous sensibility!" he thought; and he brought a stethoscope, which he placed over Ursule's heart and listened. "Well, there is nothing wrong there," he said to himself. "I did not know, my sweetheart, that you loved him so much already," he went on, as he looked at her. "But think to me as if to yourself, and tell me all that has occurred between you."

"I do not love him, godfather; we have never spoken to each other," she sobbed out; "but to know that the poor young man is in prison, and to hear that you, who are so kind, refuse sternly to help him out——"

"Ursule, my sweet little angel, if you do not love him, why have you put a red dot to the day of Saint Savinien as you have to that of Saint Denis? Come, tell me all the smallest incidents of this love affair."

Ursule colored, and swallowed down a few tears; for a minute there was silence between them.

"Are you afraid of your father, of your friend, your mother, your physician, your godfather, whose heart has within these few days become even more soft and loving than it was?"

"Well, then, dear godfather," said she, "I will open my soul to you. In the month of May, Monsieur Savinien came to see his mother. Till that visit I had never paid the least attention to him. When he went away to live in Paris I was a little child, and I saw no difference, I swear to you, between a young man—and others like you, excepting that I loved you, and never imagined I could love any one better, whoever he might be. Monsieur Savinien arrived by the mail-coach the night before his mother's birthday without our knowing of it. At seven next morning, after saying my prayers, as I opened the window to air my room, I saw the open windows of Monsieur Savinien's room, and Monsieur Savinien himself in his dressing-gown engaged in shaving himself, and doing everything with such grace in his movements—in short, I thought him very nice. He combed his black mustache, and the little tuft on his chin, and I saw his throat white and round. Oh! must I say it all? I noticed that his fresh neck, and his face, and his beautiful black hair were quite unlike yours when I see you shaving yourself; and something rose up in me from I know not where—like a mist rushing in waves to my heart, to my throat, to my head, and so violently that I had to sit down. I could not stand; I was trembling. But I longed so much to see him that I pulled myself up on tiptoe; then he saw me, and for fun he blew me a kiss from the ends of his fingers, and——"

" And——"

" And I hid myself," she went on, " equally ashamed and happy, without understanding why I was ashamed of my happiness. This feeling, which bewildered my soul while giving it an unexplained sense of power, came over me each time that I saw his young face again in fancy. Indeed, I liked to have that feeling, though it was so painfully agitating. As I went to mass an irresistible force made me look at Monsieur Savinien giving his arm to his mother, and his way of walking, and his clothes—everything about him, to the sound of his boots on the pavement, seemed so pretty. The least thing about him, his hand in its fine kid glove, had a sort of charm for me. And yet I was strong enough not to think of him during the service. As we came out I waited in the church to let Madame de Portenduère go first, so as to walk behind him. I cannot tell you how much I was interested in all these little things. On coming in, as I turned round to shut the gate——"

" And La Bougival?" asked the doctor.

" Oh, I had let her go to the kitchen," said Ursule innocently. " So I could, of course, see Monsieur Savinien standing squarely to look at me. Oh, dear godfather, I felt so proud as I fancied I saw in his eyes a sort of surprise and admiration, and I do not know what I would not have done to give him cause to look at me. I felt as though henceforth I ought to think of nothing but of how to please him. His

look is now the sweetest reward of all I can do right. From
that moment I have thought of him incessantly and in spite
of myself. Monsieur Savinien went away that evening, and
I have not seen him since ; the Rue des Bourgeois has seemed
quite empty, and he has taken my heart away with him, as it
were, without knowing it."

"And that is all?" asked the doctor.

"Yes, all, godfather," she said with a sigh, in which
regret at having no more to tell was lost in the grief of the
moment.

"My dear child," said the old man, drawing Ursule on to
his knee, "you will soon be sixteen years old, and your life
as a woman will begin. You are now between your blissful
childhood, which is coming to an end, and the agitations of
love, which will make life stormy for you, for you have the
highly strung nerves of an excessively sensitive nature. It is
love, my child, that has come upon you," said the old man,
with a look of deep pathos, "love in its holy simplicity, love
as it ought to be, involuntary and swift, coming like a thief
that takes all—yes, all! And I was prepared for it. I have
studied women carefully, and I know that, though with most
of them love does not wholly possess them till after many
proofs, many miracles of affection, if such as these do not
speak nor yield till they are conquered, there are others who,
under the sway of a sympathy which can now be accounted
for by magnetic fluids, are vanquished in a moment. I can
tell you now: as soon as I saw the lovely woman who bore
your name, I felt that I should love her alone and faithfully
without knowing whether in our characters or our persons we
should prove suitable. Is there a second-sight in love? How
can the question be answered, when we see so many unions,
which have been sanctioned by such a sacred contract, destroyed afterwards, and giving rise to almost eternal hatred
and intense aversion? The senses may be in affinity while
minds are discordant, and some persons perhaps live more by

the mind than by the senses. On the other hand, characters are often suited in persons who cannot please each other.

" These two opposite phenomena, which would account for many catastrophes, demonstrate the wisdom of the law which leaves to parents supreme control over the marriage of their children ; for a young girl is often the dupe of one of these two hallucinations. And, indeed, I do not blame you. The feelings you experience, the emotional impulse which rushes from its hitherto unknown focus to your heart and to your brain, the joy with which you think of Savinien, are all quite natural. But, my adored child, as our good Abbé Chaperon will have told you, society demands the sacrifice of many natural impulses. The destiny of men is one thing, the destiny of women another. It was in my power to choose Ursule Mirouët for my wife, to go to her and tell her how much I loved her, whereas a young girl is false to her virtue when she solicits the love of the man she loves; a woman is not, as we are, at liberty to follow up in broad daylight the fulfillment of her hopes. Thus, modesty is in women, and especially in you, the insurmountable barrier which guards the secrets of your heart. Your hesitation to confide even to me what your first emotions had been shows me plainly that you would suffer the worst torments rather than confess to Savinien——"

" Oh, yes ! " she exclaimed.

" But, my child, you must do more. You must repress these impulses of your heart, you must forget them."

" Why ? "

" Because, my little darling, you must love no man but him who will be your husband ; and even if Monsieur Savinien de Portenduère should love you——"

" I had not thought of such a thing."

" Listen to me. Even if he should love you, even if his mother were to ask me to give him your hand, I would not consent to the marriage till I had subjected Savinien to a long and mature course of proof. His recent conduct has placed

him under a cloud in every good family, and raised such
barriers between him and any young girl of fortune as it will
be hard to break down."

A heavenly smile checked Ursule's tears, as she said,
" Misfortune has its good uses ! "

The doctor found nothing to say to her artlessness.

" What has he done, godfather ? " she inquired.

" In two years, my darling, he has run into debt in Paris to
the sum of a hundred and twenty thousand francs ! He has
been so clumsy as to let himself be taken and imprisoned at
Sainte-Pélagie, a blunder which disgraces a young man for
ever in these days. A spendthrift who can bring his mother
to grief and penury would kill his wife with despair, as your
poor father did."

" Do you think he might amend his ways ? " she asked.

" If his mother pays his debts, he will be left without a
penny, and I know no harder punishment for a nobleman than
to be penniless."

This reply made Ursule thoughtful ; she wiped away her
tears, and said to her godfather—

" If you can save him, do so, godfather. Such a service
will give you the right to admonish him ; you will remon-
strate with him——"

" And then," said the doctor, mimicking her tone, " he
may perhaps come here, and the old lady too, and we shall
see them, and——"

" At this moment I am thinking only of him," replied
Ursule, coloring.

" Think of him no more, my poor child. It is madness,"
said the doctor gravely. " Never would Madame de Portenduère—a Kergarouët—if she had but three hundred francs a
year to live on, consent to see the Vicomte Savinien de
Portenduère, grand-nephew of the late Comte de Portenduère,
lieutenant-general of the King's naval forces, and son of the
Vicomte de Portenduère, ship's captain, married to—whom ?

Ursule Mirouët, the daughter of a regimental bandmaster, without a fortune; and whose father—now is the time to tell you—was the bastard son of an organist, my father-in-law.''

" Yes, godfather, you are right. We are equals only in the eyes of God. I will think of him no more—except in my prayers!'' she exclaimed through the sobs with which she received this information. ''Give him all you intended to leave me. What can a poor girl like me want of money!— and he, in prison!''

''Lay all your distresses before God, and He perhaps will intervene to help us.''

For some minutes silence reigned. When Ursule, who dared not look at her godfather, presently raised her eyes to his face, she was deeply moved by seeing tears flowing down his withered cheeks. The tears of an old man are as terrible as those of a child are natural.

''What, oh, what is the matter with you?'' she cried, falling at his feet and kissing his hands. ''Do you not trust me?''

'' I, who only wish to satisfy your every wish, am compelled to cause the first great sorrow of your life! I am as much grieved as you are! I never shed a tear but when my children died and my Ursule. There, I will do anything you like!'' he exclaimed.

Ursule, through her tears, gave her godfather a look that was like a flash of light. She smiled.

'' Now, come into the drawing-room and contrive to keep your own counsel about all this, my child,'' said the doctor, and he went out, leaving her alone in the study.

The fatherly soul was so weak before this smile that he was about to speak a word of hope which might have deluded his goddaughter.

At this moment Madame de Portenduère, alone with the curé in her chilly little ground-floor drawing-room, had just

finished confiding her woes to the good priest, her only
friend. She held in her hand some letters which the abbé
had returned to her after reading them, and which had been
the crown of her misery. Seated in an armchair, on one side
of the square table covered with the remains of the dessert,
the old lady looked at the curé, who, on the other, huddled
into a deep chair, was stroking his chin with that strange
gesture peculiar to the stage valet, to mathematicians, and
priests, as betraying meditation on a problem difficult of
solution.

The little room, lighted by two windows looking on the
street, and lined with wainscoting painted gray, was so damp
that the lower panels displayed the geometrical crackle of de-
caying wood when it is no longer held together by paint.
The floor, of red tiles rubbed smooth by the lady's only servant, made little round hempen mats a necessity in front of
each chair, and on one of these mats were the abbé's feet.
The curtains, of light-green flowered damask, were drawn,
and the shutters closed. Two wax-candles lighted the table ;
the rest of the room was half-dark. Need it be said that
between the windows a fine pastel by Latour showed the portrait of the famous Admiral de Portenduère, the rival of Suf-
fren, of Kergarouët, of Guichen, of Simeuse ? On the wainscot opposite the chimney might be seen the Vicomte de Portenduère and the old lady's mother, a Kergarouët-Ploëgat.

Savinien, then, was great-nephew to Vice-Admiral Kergarouët and cousin to the Comte de Portenduère, the admiral's grandson, both of them very rich. The vice-admiral
lived in Paris, and the Comte de Portenduère at his château
of the same name in Dauphiné. The Count, his cousin, represented the elder branch, and Savinien was the only scion
of the younger branch of the Portenduères.

The Count, a man of past forty, married to a rich wife, had
three children. His fortune, augmented several times by inheritance, brought him in, it was said, sixty thousand francs a

year. He represented the department of the Isère as deputy, spending the winter in Paris, where he had repurchased the mansion of the Portenduères with the indemnity paid him under Villèle's act. The vice-admiral had lately married his niece,* Mademoiselle de Fontaine, solely to settle his fortune on her. Thus the young Vicomte's errors had perhaps deprived him of the interest of two powerful friends.

Savinien, young and handsome, if he had entered the navy, with his name and the interest of an admiral and of a deputy to back him, might perhaps at three-and-twenty have been already first-lieutenant; but his mother, averse to seeing her only son engage in a military career, had had him educated at Nemours by one of the Abbé Chaperon's curates, and had flattered herself that she might keep her son at her side till her death. She had hoped to marry him very prudently to a demoiselle d'Aiglemont, with twelve thousand francs a year; the name of Portenduère, and the farm-lands of Bordières, justifying his pretensions to her hand. This moderate but judicious scheme, which might have re-established the family in another generation, had been frustrated by events. The d'Aiglemonts were now ruined, and one of their daughters, Hélène, the eldest, had vanished without any explanation being offered by the family.

The tedium of a life devoid of outdoor interests, of purpose, and of action, with nothing to support it but the love of a son for his mother, so wearied Savinien that he burst his bonds, light as they were, and vowed he would never live in a country town; discovering, somewhat late, that his future did not lie in the Rue des Bourgeois. So at one-and-twenty he left his mother to introduce himself to his relations, and try his fortune in Paris.

The contrast between life at Nemours and life in the capital could not fail to be fatal to a youth of one-and-twenty, perfectly free, with no one to contradict him, of course greedy

* See " Le Bal de Sceaux."

for pleasure, and to whom the name of Portenduère and the wealth of his connections opened every drawing-room. Convinced that his mother had somewhere stored the savings of twenty years, Savinien had soon squandered the six thousand francs she had given him to spend in Paris. This sum did not defray the expenses of the first six months, and by that time he owed twice as much to his lodging-keeper, his tailor, his bootmaker, to a man from whom he hired carriages and horses, to a jeweler, in short, to all the tradespeople who supply the luxury of youth. He had hardly achieved making himself known, had hardly learned to speak, to enter a room, to wear and choose a waistcoat, to order his clothes and tie his cravat, when he found himself possessed of thirty thousand francs of debts, and had not yet gotten farther than trying to find an insinuating phrase in which to declare his passion to Madame de Sérizy, the sister of the Marquis de Ronquerolles, an elegant woman still, whose youth had shone through the empire.

"And how did you fellows get out of the scrape?" said Savinien one day after breakfast to some young men of fashion with whom he was intimate, as even at this day young men become intimate when their pretensions in all respects tend to the same ends, and when they proclaim an impossible equality. "You were no richer than I; you live on without a care, you support yourselves, and I am already in debt."

"We all began in the same way," they replied, with a laugh—Rastignac, Lucien de Rubempré, Maxime de Trailles, Emile Blondet, the dandies of that day.

"If de Marsay was rich at beginning life, it was a mere chance!" said their host, a parvenu named Finot, who tried to rub elbows with these young men. "And if he had been any one else," he added, bowing to Marsay, "his fortune might have been his ruin."

"You have hit the word," said Maxime de Trailles.

"And the idea too," replied Rastignac.

"My dear boy," said de Marsay gravely to Savinien, "debts are the sleeping partners of experience. A good college education, with masters for the ornamental and the useful, from which you learn nothing, costs sixty thousand francs. If the education the world gives you costs double, it teaches you life, business, and politics; to know men and sometimes women."

Blondet capped the lecture by a parody on a line of La Fontaine's—

"The world sells us dear what we fancy it gives!"

But instead of reflecting on the good sense in what the most skilled pilots of the Paris shoals had said, Savinien took it all as a jest.

"Take care, my dear fellow," said de Marsay, "you have a fine name, and if you cannot acquire the fortune your name demands you may end your days as quartermaster to a cavalry regiment,

"'For nobler heads than thine have had a fall,'"

he added, quoting Corneille, and taking Savinien's arm. "It is about six years," he went on, "since a certain young Comte d'Esgrignon came among us, who did not live more than two years in the paradise of fashion! Alas, his career was as that of the sky-rocket. He rose as high as the Duchesse de Maufrigneuse, and he fell into his native town, where he is now expiating his sins between a snuffling old father and rubbers of whist at two sous a point. Go, then, and frankly explain your position to Madame de Sérizy; do not be ashamed; she will be of great use to you; whereas, if you play a charade of first love, she will pose as a Raphael Madonna, play innocent games, and send you a most expensive excursion round the 'Pays du Tendre'" (Country of Sentiment).

Savinien, still too young and too sensitive to a gentleman's

honor, dared not confess the state of his fortunes to Madame de
Sérizy. Madame de Portenduère, at a moment when her son
knew not which way to turn, sent him twenty thousand francs,
all she had, in answer to a letter in which Savinien, taught by
his companions the tactics of assault by sons on their parents'
strong-boxes, hinted at bills to meet, and the disgrace of dishonoring his endorsements. With this help, he got on to
the end of the first year. During the second year, as a captive at the wheels of Madame de Sérizy's car—for she had
taken a serious fancy to him, and was teaching him his paces
—he availed himself of the perilous aid of money-lenders. A
deputy, named des Lupeaulx, who was his friend, and a friend
of his cousin de Portenduère, introduced him one miserable
day to Gobseck, to Gigonnet, and to Palma, who, being duly
and fully informed as to the value of his mother's property,
made things easy for him. The money-lenders, by the delu-
sive aid of renewals, gave him a happy life for about eighteen
months more. Without daring to neglect Madame de Sérizy,
the hapless boy fell desperately in love with the young Comtesse de Kergarouët, a prude, as all young women are who are
waiting for the death of an old husband, and who are clever
enough to save up their virtue for a second marriage. Savinien, unable to understand that virtue based on reasons is
invincible, paid his court to Emilie de Kergarouët with all
the display of a rich man ; he was never missing from a ball
or a theatre if she was to be there.

" My boy, you have not enough powder to blow up that
rock ! " de Marsay said to him one evening, with a laugh.

This young prince of Paris fashion vainly attempted, out of
commiseration, to make the lad understand Emilie de Fontaine's character, only the gloomy light of disaster and the
darkness of a prison could enlighten Savinien. A bill of
exchange, rashly assigned to a jeweler in collusion with the
money-lenders, who did not choose to take the odium of
arresting him, led to Savinien de Portenduère being con-

signed to Sainte-Pélagie, unknown to his friends. As soon as the news was known to Rastignac, de Marsay, and Lucien de Rubempré, they all three went to see Savinien, and, finding him absolutely destitute, each offered him a note for a thousand francs. His own servant, bribed by two creditors, led them to the apartment where Savinien lodged in secret, and everything had been seized but the clothes and a few trinkets he had on him.

The three young men, fortified by a capital dinner, while they drank some sherry that de Marsay had brought with him, catechised Savinien as to the state of his affairs, ostensibly to make arrangements for the future, but in reality, no doubt, to pass sentence on him.

"When your name is Savinien de Portenduère," cried Rastignac, "when you have a future peer of France for your cousin and the Admiral de Kergarouët for your grand-uncle, if you are such a blunderer as to let yourself be sent to Sainte-Pélagie, at any rate you must get out of it, my dear fellow!"

"Why did you say nothing about it to me?" cried de Marsay. "My traveling carriage was at your orders, ten thousand francs, and letters for Germany. We know Gobseck and Gigonnet, and the other beasts of prey; we would have brought them to terms. To begin with, what has brought you to drink of these poisoned waters?" asked de Marsay.

"Des Lupeaulx."

The three young men looked at each other, communicating the same thought, a suspicion, but without speaking it.

"Explain your resources; show us your hand," said de Marsay.

When Savinien had described his mother and her cap and bows, her little house with its three windows fronting on the Rue des Bourgeois, with no garden but a yard with a well, and an outhouse to hold fire-logs; when he had estimated the value of this dwelling, built of rough stone set in reddish cement, and that of the farm of Bordières, the three dandies

8

exchanged glances, and, with a look of deep meaning, quoted the word spoken by the abbé in Alfred de Musset's play "Les Marrons du feu"—for his "Contes d'Espagne" had just come out—

"Dismal!"

"Your mother would pay in response to a skillful letter?" said Rastignac.

"Yes; but after——?" cried de Marsay.

"If you had only been put into the hackney coach," said Lucien, "the King's government would give you a berth in a foreign mission; but Sainte-Pélagie is not the anteroom to an embassy."

"You are not up to the mark for life in Paris," said Rastignac.

"Let's see," de Marsay began, looking at Savinien from head to foot as a horse-dealer examines a horse. "You have good blue eyes well set, you have a well-shaped white forehead, splendid black hair, a neat little mustache which looks well on your pale skin, and a slight figure; your foot bespeaks a good breed, shoulders and chest strong, and not too like a coal-heaver's. I should call you a good specimen of a dark man. Your face is in the style of that of Louis XIII.; not much color, and a well-shaped nose; and you have besides the thing that appeals to woman, the indescribable something of which men themselves are never conscious, which is in the air, the walk, the tone of voice, the flash of the eyes, the gesture, a hundred little things which women see, and to which they attach a meaning which eludes us. You do not know yourself, my dear fellow. With a little style, in six months you could fascinate an Englishwoman with a hundred thousand francs, especially if you use the title of Vicomte de Portenduère to which you have a right. My charming mother-in-law, Lady Dudley, who has not her equal for skewering two hearts together, will discover the damsel for you in some alluvial district of Great Britain. But then you must be able to stave off your debts for ninety days, and know how to do it by some skillful stroke of high finance. Oh! why did you say nothing of it to me? At Baden these money-lenders would have respected you, have served you perhaps; but after clapping you in prison they despise you. The money-lender is like society, like the mob—on his knees to a man who is clever enough to take advantage of him, and pitiless to a lamb. In the eyes of a certain set, Sainte-Pélagie is a demon which takes the shine off a young man's soul to a terrible extent. Will you have my opinion, my dear boy? I say to you as I did to little d'Esgrignon: Pay your debts cautiously, keeping enough to live on for three years, and get married in the country to the first girl who has thirty thousand francs a year. In three years you will be sure to have found some suitable heiress who will gladly hear herself called Madame de Portenduère. These are the words of wisdom. Let us have a drink. I propose a toast: 'To the girl with money!'"

The young men did not leave their ex-friend till the official hour of parting, and on the threshold of the gate they said to each other, "He is not game! He is very much crushed! Will he pick himself up again!"

The next day Savinien wrote to his mother, a general confession covering twenty-two pages. Madame de Portenduère, after crying for a whole day, wrote first to her son, promising to get him out of prison, and then to the Comtes de Portenduère and de Kergarouët.

The letters the curé had just read, and which the poor mother now held in her hand, moist with her tears, had reached her that morning, and had almost broken her heart.

"PARIS, *September*, 1829.

"To Madame de Portenduère.

"MADAME:—You cannot doubt the great interest which the admiral takes in your troubles. The news you write to M. de Kergarouët distresses me all the more because my house

was open to your son ; we were proud of him. If Savinien
had had more confidence in the admiral, we would have taken
him in charge, and he would now have a suitable appointment ; but the unhappy boy told us nothing ! The admiral
could not possibly pay a hundred thousand francs ; he is himself in debt, and has involved himself for me, for I knew
nothing of his pecuniary position. He regrets it all the more
because Savinien, by allowing himself to be arrested, has for
the moment tied our hands. If my handsome nephew had
not felt for me some foolish passion which smothered the
voice of relationship in the arrogance of a lover, we might
have sent him to travel in Germany while his affairs here were
being arranged. M. de Kergarouët might have asked for a
place for his grand-nephew in the naval department ; but
imprisonment for debt cannot fail to paralyze the admiral's
efforts. Pay off Savinien's debts, let him go into the navy ;
he will then make his way like a true Portenduère ; he has
their fire in his fine black eyes, and we will all help him.

"So do not despair, madame ; you still have friends,
among whom I beg to be accounted one of the sincerest, and
I send you my best wishes with every respect. From your
very devoted servant,

"EMILIE DE KERGAROUËT."

"PORTENDUÈRE, *August,* 1829.
"To Madame de Portenduère.

"MY DEAR AUNT :—I am as much vexed as pained by
Savinien's scapegrace doings. Married, as I am, the father
of two sons and a daughter, my fortune, moderate indeed in
comparison with my position and expectations, does not allow
of my reducing it by such a sum as a hundred thousand francs
to ransom a Portenduère captive to the Lombards. Sell your
farm, pay his debts, and come to Portenduère ; you will here
find the welcome due to you from us, even if our hearts were
not wholly yours. You will live happy, and we will find a

wife for Savinien, whom my wife thinks charming. This disaster is nothing; do not let it distress you; it will never be heard of in our remote district, where we know several girls with money—nay, very rich—who will be enchanted to belong to us.

"My wife joins me in assuring you how happy you would make us, and begs you to accept her hopes that this plan may be carried out, with the assurance of our affectionate respect.

"LUC-SAVINIEN, COMTE DE PORTENDUÈRE."

"What letters to write to a Kergarouët!" cried the old Bretonne, wiping her eyes.

"The admiral does not know that his nephew is in prison," said the Abbé Chaperon presently. "Only the Countess has read your letter, and she alone has answered it. But something must be done," he added after a pause, "and this is the advice I have the honor to offer you. Do not sell your farm. The present lease is nearly out; it has been running four-and-twenty years; in a few months you can raise the rent to six thousand francs, and demand a premium equal to two years' rent. Borrow from some honest man—not from the townspeople, who make a traffic of mortgages. Your neighbor, now, is a worthy man, a man of the world, who knew the upper classes before the Revolution, and who from being an atheist has become a Catholic. Do not feel any repugnance for coming to call on him this evening; he will be deeply sensible of your taking such a step; forget for one moment that you are a Kergarouët."

"Never!" said the old mother in a strident tone.

"At any rate, be an amiable Kergarouët. Come when he is alone; he will only take three-and-a-half per cent., perhaps not more than three, and he will do you the service in the most delicate manner. You will be quite satisfied with him. He will go himself to release Savinien, for he will be obliged to sell some securities, and he will bring him home to you."

"Do you mean that little Minoret?"

"Little Minoret is eighty-three years of age," replied the abbé with a smile. "My dear lady, have a little Christian charity; do not hurt his feelings, as he may be useful to you in more ways than one."

"How, may I ask?"

"Well, he has living with him an angel, the heavenliest young girl——"

"Yes, that little Ursule. Well, and what then?"

The poor curé dared say no more as he heard this inflected interrogation.

"Well, what then?" Its harsh severity cut short beforehand the proposal he had been about to make.

"Doctor Minoret is, I believe, exceedingly rich——"

"So much the better for him."

"You have already been the indirect cause of your son's present misfortunes by giving him no opening in life. Beware for the future," said the abbé sternly. "Shall I announce your proposed visit to your neighbor?"

"But why, if he were told that I want him, should he not come to me?"

"Well, madame, if you go to him, you will pay three per cent., and if he comes to you, you will pay five," said the abbé, hitting on this argument to persuade the old lady. "And if you should be forced to sell your farm through Dionis the notary, or Massin the clerk, who would refuse to advance money in the hope of profiting by your disaster, you would lose half the value of Les Bordières. I have not the smallest influence over the Dionis, the Massins, the Levraults, rich country folks who covet your farm, and know that your son is in prison."

"They know it! They know it!" she cried, throwing up her hands. "Oh, my poor friend, you have let your coffee get cold. Tiennette! Tiennette!"

Tiennette, an old Brittany peasant of sixty, in the jacket

and cap of her province, hastened in and took the curé's coffee to heat it again.

"Wait a minute, Monsieur le Recteur," said she, seeing that the curé was about to drink it. "I will heat it in a bain-marie, and it will be none the worse."

"Very well, then," the priest began again, in his persuasive voice, "I will give the doctor notice of your intended visit, and you will come."

The old lady still would not give in till at the end of an hour's discussion, during which the curé was forced to repeat his arguments ten times over. And even then the haughty daughter of the Kergarouëts only yielded to these last words—

"Savinien would go!"

"Then it had better be I," said she.

Nine o'clock was striking when the little door in the great gate was closed behind the curé, who forthwith rang eagerly at the doctor's entrance. The Abbé Chaperon escaped Tiennette to fall on La Bougival, for the old nurse said to him—

"You are very late, Monsieur le Curé." Just as Tiennette had said, "Why have you left madame so early when she is in trouble?"

The curé found a large party in the doctor's green and brown drawing-room; for Dionis had been to reassure his heirs on his way to see Massin, and repeat to him his uncle's words.

"Ursule," said he, "has I suspect a love in her heart which will bring her nothing but sorrow and care. She seems to be romantic"—the word applied by notaries to a sensitive nature—"and she will long remain unmarried. So do not be suspicious; pay her all sorts of little attentions, and be the humble servants of your uncle, for he is sharper than a hundred Goupils," added the notary, not knowing that Goupil is a corrupt form of the Latin *vulpes*, a fox.

So Mesdames Massin and Crémière, their husbands, the postmaster and Désiré, with the town doctor and Bongrand, formed an unwonted and turbulent crowd at the old doctor's. As the abbé went in he heard the sound of a piano. Poor Ursule was ending Beethoven's sonata in A. With the artfulness permissible to the innocent, the girl, enlightened by her godfather, and averse to the family, had selected this solemn music, which must be studied to be appreciated, to disgust these women with their wish to hear her. The finer the music, the less the ignorant enjoy it. So, when the door opened, and the Abbé Chaperon put in his venerable head, "Ah! here is Monsieur le Curé!" they all exclaimed, delighted to have to rise and put an end to their torment.

The exclamation found an echo at the card-table, where Bongrand, the town doctor, and the old man himself were victims to the audacity with which the tax-collector, to court his great-uncle, had proposed to take the fourth hand at whist. Ursule came away from the piano. The doctor also rose as if to greet the priest, but in fact to put a stop to the game. After many compliments to their uncle on his goddaughter's proficiency, the heirs took their leave.

"Good-night, friends," cried the doctor, as the gate shut.

"So that is what costs so dear!" said Madame Crémière to Madame Massin, when they had gone a little way.

"God forbid that I should pay any money to hear my little Aline make such a noise as that in the house!" replied Madame Massin.

"She said it was by Beethoven, who is supposed to be a great composer," said the tax-collector. "He has a great name."

"My word! not at Nemours," cried Madame Crémière.

"I believe my uncle arranged it on purpose that we should never go there again," said Massin. "For he certainly winked as he pointed out the green volume to that little minx."

"If that is the only tune they care to dance to, they are wise to keep themselves to themselves," said the postmaster.

"The justice must be very fond of his game to listen to those rigmarole pieces," said Madame Crémière.

"I shall never be able to play to people who do not understand music," said Ursule, taking her seat near the card-table.

"In persons of a rich organization feeling can only express itself among congenial surroundings," said the curé. "Just as a priest can give no blessing in the presence of the evil one, and as a chestnut tree dies in a heavy soil, so a musician of genius feels himself morally routed when he is among ignorant listeners. In the arts we need to receive from the souls in which our souls find their medium as much power as we can impart. The axiom, which is a law of human affections, has given rise to the proverbs: 'We must howl with the wolves;' 'Like to like.' But the discomfort you must have felt is known only to tender and sensitive natures."

"Ay, my friends," said the doctor, "and a thing which might only annoy another woman could kill my little Ursule. Ah! when I am no more, raise up between this tender flower and the world such a sheltering hedge as Catullus speaks of— *Ut flos*, etc."

"And yet the ladies were flattering in their remarks to you, Ursule," said the lawyer, smiling.

"Coarsely flattering," observed the town doctor.

"I have always felt such coarseness in insincere praise," replied Monsieur Minoret. "And why?"

"A true thought has its own refinement," said the abbé.

"Did you dine with Madame de Portenduère?" said Ursule, questioning the Abbé Chaperon, with a glance of anxious curiosity.

"Yes; the poor lady is in much distress, and it is not impossible that she may call on you this evening, Monsieur Minoret."

"If she is in trouble and needs me, I will go to her," said the doctor. "Let us finish the first rubber."

Ursule pressed her uncle's hand under the table.

"Her son," said the justice, "was rather too simple to live in Paris without a mentor. When it came to my knowledge that inquiries were being made of the notary here about the old lady's farm, I guessed that he was borrowing on his reversion."

"Do you think him capable of that?" said Ursule, with a terrible flash at Monsieur Bongrand, who said to himself, "Yes, alas! she is in love with him."

"Yes and No," said the town doctor. "There is good in Savinien, and the proof of it is that he is in prison. A thorough rogue never gets caught."

"My friends," said old Minoret, "enough of this for this evening. We must not leave a poor mother to weep for a minute longer when we can dry her tears."

The four friends rose and went out. Ursule accompanied them as far as the gate, watched her godfather and the curé while they knocked at the door opposite; and when Tiennette had admitted them, she sat down on one of the stone piers in the courtyard, La Bougival standing near her.

"Madame la Vicomtesse," said the curé, going first into the little room, "Doctor Minoret could not allow you to have the trouble of going to his house——"

"I am too much of the old school, madame," the doctor put in, "not to know what is due from a man to a person of your rank, and I am only too happy to think, from what Monsieur le Curé tells me, that I may be of some service to you."

Madame de Portenduère, on whom the arrangement she had agreed to weighed so heavily, that, since the abbé had quitted her, she had thought of applying rather to the notary, was so surprised by Minoret's delicate feeling, that she rose to return his bow, and pointed to an arm-chair.

"Be seated, monsieur," said she, with a royal air. "Our dear curé will have told you that the Vicomte is in prison for debt—a young man's debts—a hundred thousand francs. If you could lend him the sum, I would give you as security my farm at Bordières."

"We can talk of that, madame, when I shall have brought you back your son, if you will allow me to represent you in these circumstances."

"Very good, monsieur," replied the old lady, with a bow, and a glance at the curé, which was meant to convey: "You are right; he is a man of good breeding."

"My friend, the doctor, as you see, madame, is full of devotion to your family."

"We shall be grateful to you, monsieur," said Madame de Portenduère, with a visible effort, "for at your age to venture through Paris on the tracks of a scapegrace's misdeeds——"

"Madame, in '65, I had the honor of seeing the illustrious Admiral de Portenduère at the house of the worthy Monsieur de Malesherbes, and at that of the Comte de Buffon, who was anxious to question him as to various curious facts in his voyages. It is not impossible that Monsieur de Portenduère, your late husband, may have been there too. The French navy was then in its glory; it held its own against England, and the captain contributed his quota of courage to the game. How impatiently, in '83 and '84, did we await news from the camp of Saint-Roch! I was very nearly joining as surgeon to the King's forces. Your grand-uncle, Admiral de Kergarouët, who is still living, fought his great battle at that time, for he was on board the 'Belle Poule.'"

"Ah! if he knew that his grand-nephew was in prison?" replied Madame de Portenduère.

"The Vicomte will no longer be there two days hence," said old Minoret, rising.

He put out his hand to take the old lady's, who allowed him to do so; he kissed it respectfully, bowed low, and went out; but he came in again to say to the curé—

"Will you, my dear abbé, secure a place for me in the diligence for to-morrow morning?"

The curé remained another half-hour to sing the praises of the doctor, who had intended to conquer the old lady, and had succeeded.

"He is wonderful for his age," said she. "He talks of going to Paris and settling my son's affairs as if he were no more than five-and-twenty. He has moved in good society."

"In the best, madame; and at this day, more than one son of an impoverished peer of France would be very happy to marry his ward with a million of francs. Ah, if such a notion should enter Savinien's brain, times are so altered that the chief difficulties would not be raised on your side after your son's conduct!"

It was the intense amazement with which the old lady heard this speech that allowed the priest to finish it.

"You have lost your wits, my dear Abbé Chaperon."

"Think it over, madame; and God grant that henceforth your son may behave in such a way as to acquire that old man's esteem!"

"If it were not you, Monsieur le Curé," said Madame de Portenduère; "if it were any one else who spoke to me in these terms——"

"You would never see him again," said the abbé, smiling. "We must hope that your dear son may enlighten you as to what is doing in Paris in the matter of marriages. You will consider Savinien's happiness, and, after compromising his future, you will surely not interfere with his making himself a position?"

"And it is you who say this to me!" responded Madame de Portenduère in amazement.

"If I did not, who would?" cried the priest, rising and beating a prompt retreat.

The curé saw Ursule and her godfather walking up and

down the little courtyard. The submissive doctor had been so teased by his ward that he had at last yielded; she wanted to go to Paris, and had found a thousand pretexts. He called the curé, who joined them, and the doctor begged him to engage the coupé of the diligence for that very night if the coach-office were still open.

At six o'clock on the following afternoon the old man and the young girl reached Paris, and the doctor went, the same evening, to consult his lawyer. Political events looked threatening. The justice at Nemours had been telling the doctor the day before, several times in the course of their conversation, that he would be nothing less than mad to keep a penny in the funds so long as the quarrel between the Court and the Press should remain unsettled. Minoret's notary approved of the advice indirectly given by Bongrand. So the doctor took advantage of his visit to Paris to sell out his commercial investments and state securities, which were all at a premium, and to deposit his capital in the bank. The lawyer also advised his old client to sell the shares left to Ursule by Monsieur Jordy, which, as a good trustee, he had invested. He promised to set to work, with the help of a very knowing agent, to come to terms with Savinien's creditors; but, to achieve every success, it was necessary that the young man should spend yet a few days in prison.

"Hurrying on these matters costs at least fifteen per cent.," said the lawyer to the doctor. "And at any rate you cannot get at your money for seven or eight days."

When Ursule learned that Savinien would be in prison at least a week longer, she entreated her guardian to let her go there with him, if only for once. Old Minoret refused. The uncle and niece were lodging at an hotel in the Rue Croix-des-Petits-Champs, where the doctor had taken a suitable set of rooms; and knowing his ward's religious honor, he made her promise never to go out while he was absent on business. The kind old man took her for walks about Paris, showing her the arcades, the shops, the Boulevards—but nothing interested or amused her.

"What do you want?" asked he.

"To see Sainte-Pélagie," she persistently replied.

Then Minoret hired a hackney coach, and took her to the Rue de la Clef, where the vehicle drew up in front of the squalid building—an ancient convent turned into a prison. The sight of the high gray walls, where every window was closely barred, of the low door, not to be entered without stooping—dreadful lesson!—the gloomy mass standing in a neighborhood full of poverty, where it rises in the midst of deserted streets, itself the supreme misery; the whole combination of dismal ideas choked Ursule, and made her shed tears.

"How is it," said she, "that young men can be imprisoned for money? How is it that a debt gives to a money-lender such power as the King himself does not possess? And *he* is there!" she exclaimed. "Where, godfather?" she added, looking from one window to another.

"Ursule," said her godfather, "you make me commit follies. This is not forgetting him!"

"But," said she, "even if I must give him up, must I feel no interest in him? I may love him, and marry no one."

"Oh!" cried the old man, "there is so much method in your madness, that I repent of having brought you."

Three days later the old man had the receipts in due form, the title-deeds, and all the documents which were necessary to liberate Savinien. The liquidation, including the agent's commission, had been effected for the sum of eighty thousand francs. The doctor had in hand eight hundred thousand francs, which, by his lawyer's advice, he placed in treasury notes, so as not to lose too much interest. He kept twenty thousand in bank-notes for Savinien.

The doctor himself went to release him on Saturday at two o'clock, and the young Vicomte, already informed by a letter from his mother, thanked his deliverer with sincere effusiveness of feeling.

"You must not delay in coming home to see your mother," said old Minoret.

Savinien replied, in some confusion, that even in prison he had contracted a debt of honor; and he told the doctor of the visit of his three friends.

"I suspected you might have some personal debts," said the doctor with a smile. "Your mother has borrowed a hundred thousand francs, but I have paid no more than eighty thousand; here is the remainder, use it with thrift, monsieur, and regard what is left as your stake on the green cloth of fortune."

During the past week Savinien had reflected on the times he lived in. Competition on all sides demands severe labor from those who hope to make a fortune. Illegal methods require more talent and underhand manœuvres than enterprise under the light of day. Success in the gay world, far from securing a position, absorbs time and a great deal of money. The name of Portenduère, omnipotent according to his mother, was nothing in Paris. His cousin the deputy, the Comte de Portenduère, cut but a small figure in the midst of the elective Chamber in comparison with the peerage and the court, and had no more influence than enough for himself. Admiral Kergarouët existed only in the person of his wife. He had seen orators, men who had risen from a social rank beneath the nobility or the simple gentry, become personages of importance. In short, money was the pivot, the only means, the only motor of a society which Louis XVIII. had tried to form in imitation of that of England.

On his way from the Rue de la Clef to the Rue Croix-des-Petits-Champs, the young gentleman summed up his meditations, and laid them before the old doctor, in accordance with de Marsay's advice.

"I must let myself be forgotten," said he, "for three or

four years, and try to find a career. Perhaps I may make a name in political diplomacy or in moral statistics, by some treatise on one of the great questions of the day. At any rate, while finding some young person whom I may marry, and whose position may qualify me for election, I shall work in silence and obscurity."

The doctor studied the young man's countenance, and saw in it the fixed purpose of a man who, having been wounded, hopes for revenge. He greatly approved this scheme.

"My young neighbor," said he, "if you have cast the skin of the old nobility—which is not found to be good wear nowadays—after three or four years of a steady industrious life, I will undertake to find you a superior girl, pretty, amiable, pious, and with a fortune of seven or eight hundred thousand francs, who will make you happy, and of whom you may be proud, though she has no nobility but that of the heart."

"Eh, doctor!" cried the young man, "there is no nobility left—only an aristocracy."

"Go and pay your debts of honor, and return here. I will go to engage the coupé of the diligence, for my ward is with me," said the old man.

That evening, at six o'clock, the three travelers set out from the Rue Dauphine by the "Ducler." Ursule, who wore a veil, spoke not a word. After blowing her the kiss in an impulse of trivial flirtation, which had upset Ursule as much as a whole book of love, Savinien had totally forgotten the doctor's ward in the torments of his debts; and, indeed, his hopeless adoration of Emilie de Kergarouët did not suffer him to bestow a remembrance on the glances he had interchanged with a mere little girl at Nemours. So he did not recognize her when the old man made her get first into the coach and sat next her, dividing her from the young Vicomte.

"I have accounts to settle with you," said the doctor to the youth; "I have all your papers here."

"I was within an ace of not getting away," said Savinien. "I had to order clothes and linen; the Philistines have robbed me of everything, and I am in the state of the prodigal son."

However interesting the subjects of conversation between the old man and the young one, however pertinent some of Savinien's remarks, the young girl sat in silence till it was dark, her green veil hiding her face, and her hands folded over her shawl.

"You do not seem to have found Paris very delightful, mademoiselle," said Savinien at last, somewhat piqued.

"I am glad to return to Nemours," she replied, in an agitated voice, putting up her veil.

In spite of the gloom, Savinien now recognized her by her thick plaits of hair and brilliant blue eyes.

"And, for my part, I can leave Paris without regret to bury myself at Nemours, since I there shall find so fair a neighbor," said he. "I hope, Monsieur le Docteur, that you will allow me to visit you; I am fond of music, and I remember hearing Mademoiselle Ursule's piano."

"I hardly know, monsieur," said the doctor gravely, "whether your mother will be pleased that you should come to see an old man who is obliged to have a mother's care of this dear child."

This measured reply gave Savinien much to think about; he now recollected that kiss, so lightly wafted.

It was now night; the heat was oppressive; the doctor and Savinien were the first to fall asleep. Ursule, who remained a long time awake, her head full of plans, succumbed about midnight. She had taken off her little hat of coarse straw plait. Her head, in a little cap of embroidered muslin, presently dropped on to her godfather's shoulder. At daybreak, near Bouron, Savinien woke the first. He saw Ursule in the untidy state produced by the jolting of the coach; her cap was tumbled and askew; her hair had come unpinned,

9

and the plaits fell about her face, which was rosy with the heat; but in this disorder, which is horrible in a woman to whom dress is indispensable, youth and beauty are triumphant. The sleep of innocence is always lovely. Her parted lips showed pretty teeth; her shawl, thrown back, allowed him to observe, without offense to Ursule, the grace of her figure under the folds of a full bodice of flowered muslin. And through the countenance shone the purity of the maiden's soul, all the more visible because no other expression mingled with it. Old Minoret, who presently woke, arranged her head against the corner of the coach to make her more comfortable; and she did not even feel what he did, so soundly was she sleeping, after spending so many nights in thinking of Savinien's misfortunes.

"Poor little thing!" said he to his companion, "she sleeps like a child—as she is."

"You should be proud of her," said Savinien, "for she seems to be as good as she is pretty."

"Ah! she is the light of the house! If she were my daughter, I could not love her better. She will be sixteen on the 5th of February next. God grant I may live to see her married to a man who will make her happy! I wanted to take her to the play in Paris, where she had never been before; she would not go; the curé at Nemours had forbidden it. 'But,' said I, 'when you are married, if your husband wishes to take you?' 'I shall do whatever my husband desires,' said she. 'If he should ask me to do anything wrong, and I should be so weak as to obey him, he will be held responsible before God; but I should find strength to resist—in his interest, of course.'"

As they reached Nemours, at five in the morning, Ursule woke up, quite ashamed of her untidiness, and of meeting Savinien's gaze of frank admiration. During the hour which the diligence took to drive from Bouron, where it had stopped a few minutes, the young man had fallen in love with Ursule.

He had studied the innocence of her soul, the beauty of her person, the whiteness of her complexion, the delicacy of her features, and the sweet voice which had spoken the brief expressive phrase in which the poor child had told everything while intending to tell nothing. In short, I know not what presentiment led him to think of Ursule as the wife the doctor had suggested to him, set in a gold frame by the magical words—"Seven or eight hundred thousand francs."

"In three or four years she will be twenty; I shall be twenty-seven. The good man spoke of struggles, of work, of good behavior. However cunning he may be, he will end by telling me his secret."

The neighbors parted before their respective houses, and Savinien put much meaning into his leave-taking, with a glance at Ursule full of imploring invitation.

Madame de Portenduère left her son to sleep till noon. The doctor and Ursule, in spite of their fatiguing journey, went to high mass.

Savinien's release, and his return in the doctor's company, had explained the object of his journey to the parochial politicians and to his heirs, who had met in council in the church square, as they had done a fortnight since. To the great surprise of all parties, on coming out of church, Madame de Portenduère stopped old Minoret, who offered her his arm, and conducted her home. The old lady wished to invite him and his ward to dinner that same day, telling him that the curé would be her other guest.

"He wanted to let Ursule see Paris," said Minoret-Levrault.

"Damnation! The old man cannot stir a step without his little housekeeper," cried Crémière.

"There must have been some very private transactions between them, for Mother Portenduère to take his arm," observed Massin.

"It has not occurred to you that your uncle has sold his investments and taken the young 'un out of quod!" cried

Goupil. "He refused my master, but he did not refuse his madame—— Ah! your goose is cooked! The Vicomte will propose a marriage-contract instead of a promise to pay, and the doctor will make the husband settle on his god-daughter all the money he will have to give her to secure such a match."

"It would not be such a bad stroke of business to marry Ursule to Monsieur Savinien," said the butcher. "The old lady is having them to dine with her to-day; Tiennette came over to me at five in the morning to secure a fillet of beef."

"Well, Dionis, this is a pretty piece of work!" said Massin, hurrying to meet the notary, who came out on to the square.

"Why, what's wrong?" said the notary. "All is well; your uncle has sold his securities, and Madame de Portenduère has asked me to go to her house to witness a deed acknowledging a loan of a hundred thousand francs from your uncle on a mortgage of her estates."

"Yes; but if the young folks were to marry each other?"

"You might as well say if Goupil were to be my successor," said the notary.

"Neither case is impossible," said Goupil.

On returning from mass, the old lady sent Tiennette to desire her son to come to her room.

The little house had three rooms on the ground floor. Those of Madame de Portenduère and of her deceased husband were on the same side of the house, divided by a dressing-room with a borrowed light, and a small anteroom opening on to the stairs. The window of the third room, which had always been Savinien's, looked out on the street, as did that of his father's. The staircase lay behind it in such a way as to leave space for a little dressing-room adjoining, with a small round window to the courtyard.

Madame de Portenduère's room, the gloomiest in the house,

also looked on the yard; but the widow spent her life in the sitting-room on the ground floor, which communicated by a passage with the kitchen built on the farther side of the court-yard; so that this room did duty both as drawing-room and dining-room.

The room that had been Monsieur de Portenduère's remained in the state in which it had been left on the day of his death; the dead man alone was missing. Madame de Portenduère herself had made the bed, and laid upon it the captain's uniform, with her husband's sword, red ribbon, orders and hat. The gold snuff-box out of which the Vicomte had taken his last pinch of snuff was on the table by the bed, with his prayer-book, his watch, and the cup he used to drink out of. His white hair, arranged in a frame in a single thick curl, hung above the crucifix and holy-water cup over the bed. Finally, the trifling objects of his daily use were all in their place—his papers, furniture, Dutch spittoon, and field-glass hanging over the fireplace. The widow had stopped the antique clock at the hour of his death, which it thus recorded in perpetuity. The scent of his powder and snuff still hung in the air. The hearth was as he had left it. To go into the room was like seeing him again, on finding all the things that thus spoke of his habits. His tall cane with its gold knob still lay where he had left it, and his large doeskin gloves close beside it. On the console stood a vase of solid gold, coarsely executed, but worth a thousand crowns, a present from the port of Havana, which he had protected during the war of American Independence from an attack of the English, holding his own against a superior force, after getting the vessels under his convoy safe into harbor. As a reward the King of Spain had made him Knight of the Spanish Orders. For this achievement he was promoted on the first opportunity to the command of a squadron, and received the order of the Legion of Honor.

Then, on his next leave, he married his wife, with a fortune of two hundred thousand francs. But the Revolution stopped all further promotion, and Monsieur de Portenduère emigrated.

"Where is my mother?" asked Savinien of Tiennette, on making his appearance.

"She is waiting for you in your father's room," said the old Bretonne.

Savinien could not repress a little shudder. He knew how rigid were his mother's principles, her worship of honor, her loyalty, her faith in noble blood, and he foresaw a scene. So he went as if to lead a forlorn hope, his heart beating and his face almost pallid. In the twilight that filtered through the Venetian shutters he saw his mother dressed in black, and wearing a solemn mien in harmony with this chamber of the dead.

"Monsieur le Vicomte," she said, rising as he entered and taking his hand to lead him to the bedside, "there your father died—a man of honor ; died without having anything to reproach himself with. His spirit is above. He must indeed have groaned there to see his son disgraced by imprisonment for debt. Under the old monarchy you would have been spared this mud-stain, by craving a *lettre de cachet*, by which you would have been shut up for a few days in a state prison. However, you now stand before your father, who can hear you. You, knowing all you had done before being taken to that squalid prison, can you swear to me, before that shade, and before God who sees all things, that you have done no dishonorable action, that your debts were the consequence of a young man's follies—in short, that your honor is unspotted? If your blameless father were there, alive, in that armchair, if he could call you to account for your conduct, would he, after hearing you, embrace you still?"

"Yes, mother," said the young man, with the most respectful gravity.

She opened her arms and clasped her son to her heart, shedding a few tears.

"Then let all be forgotten," said she; "we have lost nothing but the money. I will pray to God that it may be restored to us; and since you still are worthy of your name, kiss me, for I have suffered greatly."

"I swear to you, my dear mother," said he, holding out his hand over the bed, "never again to give you the least trouble of the same kind, and to do all in my power to repair my past errors."

"Come to breakfast, my child," she said, and she left the room.

If the laws of the stage are to be applied to narrative, Savinien's arrival, by introducing at Nemours the only actor as yet missing from the personages of this little drama, here completes the prologue.

THE MINORET PROPERTY.

The action began with a scene so hackneyed in literature, whether old or new, that no one would believe in its effect in 1829 if the principal figure were not an old lady of Brittany, a Kergarouët, and an *émigrée*. But it must at once be made clear that in 1829 the nobility had reconquered in society some of the ground it had lost in political influence. Moreover, the feeling which governs grandparents when matrimonial suitability is in question, is imperishable; it is closely implicated with the existence of civilized society, and founded in family spirit. It is supreme at Geneva as at Vienna, and as at Nemours, where Zélie Levrault had refused her consent to her son's marrying the daughter of a bastard.

Still, every social law has its exceptions. Savinien proposed trying to bend his mother's pride before Ursule's innate nobility. The battle began forthwith. As soon as he was seated at table his mother began to tell him of the dreadful letters, as she called them, written to her by the Kergarouëts and the Portenduères.

"The family has ceased to exist, my dear mother," replied Savinien. "Nothing is left but the individual. The nobility no longer forms a compact body. Nowadays no one asks if you are a Portenduère, or if you are brave, or a statesman; all that any one inquires is, 'How much do you pay in rates and taxes?'"

"And the King?" asked the old lady.

"The King stands between the two Chambers, like a man between his lawful wife and his mistress. So I must contrive to marry some rich girl whatever her family may be—a peasant's daughter if she has a million of francs, and if she is

(136)

fairly well brought up; that is to say, if she comes from a convent-school."

"This is quite another matter!" said the old lady.

Savinien knit his brows over this reply. He knew that granite will, called Breton obstinacy, which characterized his mother; and was anxious to know, as soon as possible, what her views were on this delicate subject.

"And so," said he, "if I should fall in love with a girl— say, for instance, our neighbor's ward, little Ursule—you would oppose my marrying her?"

"To my dying day," said she. "After my death you alone will be responsible for the honor and the blood of the Portenduères and the Kergarouëts."

"Then you would leave me to die of hunger and despair for the sake of a chimera which, in these days, can only become real by acquiring the splendor of wealth."

"You can serve France and trust in God."

"You will postpone my happiness till the day after your death."

"It will be horrible on your part, that is all," calmly replied his mother.

"Louis XIV. was very near marrying Mazarin's niece—a parvenu."

"Mazarin himself opposed it."

"And the widow Scarron?"

"She was a d'Aubigné! Besides, the marriage was secret. But I am a very old woman, my son," she added, shaking her head. "When I am gone, you can marry to please your own fancy."

Savinien loved and respected his mother; but at once, though in silence, he set against the obstinacy of the daughter of the Kergarouëts, an obstinacy equal to her own, and determined never to have any wife but Ursule, to whom this opposition gave all the charm of a forbidden joy—as always happens in such cases.

When, after vespers, Doctor Minoret, with Ursule, dressed
in pink and white, entered the chilly sitting-room, the poor
child was seized with nervous trembling, just as if she had
found herself in the presence of the Queen of France, and
had some favor to ask of her. Since her talk with the doctor, the little house had assumed, to her, the proportions of
a palace, and the old lady all the social importance that a
duchess must have had in the eyes of a villein's daughter in
the middle ages. Never had Ursule measured more hope-
lessly the distance which divided a Vicomte de Portenduère
from the daughter of a bandmaster, a singer in the opera, the
natural son of an organist, herself living on the bounty of a
physician.

"What ails you, child?" said the lady, making her sit
down by her side.

"Madame, I am overcome by the honor you condescend
to pay me."

"Why, child," replied Madame de Portenduère in her
most vinegary accent, "I know how much your guardian loves
you, and I wish to do what is agreeable to him, for he has
brought home the prodigal son."

"But, my dear mother," said Savinien, for it went to his
heart to see Ursule's deep blushes, and the terrible effort by
which she repressed her tears, "even if you were under no
obligation to Monsieur Minoret, it seems to me we might
be gratified by the pleasure mademoiselle is good enough to
do us by accepting your invitation." And the young man
pressed the doctor's hand with meaning as he added—

"You, monsieur, wear the order of Saint Michael, the oldest
French order, which in itself confers nobility."

Ursule's great beauty, to which her almost hopeless love
had, within the last few days, given the depth of expression
which the greatest painters have always stamped on those
portraits in which the soul is made strongly visible, had suddenly struck Madame de Portenduère, and led her to suspect

some ambitious interest under the doctor's generosity. And
the speech to which Savinien had replied was uttered with a
pointedness that wounded the old man in what was dearest
to him. Still, he could not forbear from smiling as he heard
himself addressed as " Chevalier " by Savinien, and discerned
in this audacious exaggeration a lover's fearlessness of the
ridiculous.

"The order of Saint Michael, to obtain which so many
follies were committed of old, is fallen, Monsieur le Vicomte,"
replied the old court physician. "Fallen, like so many other
privileges ! It is no longer bestowed on any but doctors and
poor artists. And so kings have done well to unite it to that
of Saint Lazarus, a saint who was, I believe, an unhappy
wretch brought back to life by a miracle ! Viewed in this
light, the order of Saint Michael and Saint Lazarus to us may
be symbolical."

After this reply, full of irony and dignity, silence reigned,
no one caring to break it ; and it was becoming uncomfortable, when a knock was heard.

"Here is our good curé," said the old lady, rising, and
leaving Ursule to herself, while she went forward to receive
the priest—an honor she had not paid to Ursule or the doctor.

Minoret smiled as he looked from his ward to Savinien.
To complain or to take offense at Madame de Portenduère's
bad manners was a rock on which a small mind might have
run aground ; but the old man had too much breeding not
to avoid it. He began talking to the Vicomte of the danger
Charles X. was in at that time, after intrusting the direction
of his policy to the Prince de Polignac. When a long enough
time had elapsed to obviate any appearance of retaliation on
the old lady by speaking of business matters, he handed to
her, almost jestingly, the documents of the prosecution and
the receipted bills which proved the accounts drawn up by
the lawyer.

"My son acknowledges them?" she asked with a glance

at Savinien, who bowed in reply. "Well, then, they can be handed to Dionis," and she pushed away the papers, treating the affair with the contempt due in her eyes to money matters.

To look down on wealth was, in Madame de Portenduère's opinion, to enhance nobility, and leave the middle class without a foot to stand on.

A few minutes later Goupil called on behalf of his master, to ask for the accounts as between Savinien and Monsieur Minoret.

"And what for?" asked the old lady.

"To serve as a basis for the mortgage deed; there is no direct payment of money," replied the clerk, looking insolently about him.

Ursule and Savinien, who looked in this odious person's face for the first time, felt such a sensation as is produced by a toad, aggravated by a sense of ill omen. They both had that indefinable and vague anticipation of the future which has no name in speech, but which might be accounted for by an impulse of that inner self of which the Swedenborgian had spoken to Doctor Minoret. A conviction that this venomous Goupil would be fatal to them made Ursule quake; but she got over her agitation as she perceived with unspeakable joy that Savinien shared her feelings.

"Monsieur Dionis' clerk is not a handsome man," said Savinien, when Goupil shut the door.

"What can it matter whether people of that class are ugly or handsome?" said Madame de Portenduère, with an elevation of her eyebrows.

"I have no objection to his ugliness," said the curé, "but only to his malignity, which is unbounded, and he adds to it by villainy."

In spite of his wish to be amiable, the doctor grew cold and dignified, the lovers were uncomfortable. But for the simple good-humor of the Abbé Chaperon, whose gentle

cheerfulness made the dinner lively, the position of the doctor
and his ward would have been almost intolerable.

At dessert, seeing Ursule turn pale, he said to her, "If you
do not feel well, my child, there is only the street to cross."

"What ails you, my dear?" said the old lady to the girl.

"Unfortunately, madame," said the doctor severely, "her
soul feels chilled, accustomed as she is to see nothing but
smiles."

"A bad education, monsieur," said Madame de Portenduère. "Do you not think so, Monsieur le Curé?"

"Yes, madame," Minoret put in, with a glance at the curé,
who could not say a word. "I have, I see, made life impossible to this seraphic nature if she were to be cast on the world;
but before I die, I will find means to protect her from cold-
ness, indifference, and hatred——"

"Godfather! I beg of you—that is enough. I feel nothing
unpleasant here," she said, ready to meet Madame de Portenduère's eye rather than lend too much meaning to her words
by looking at Savinien.

"Whether Mademoiselle Ursule is uncomfortable I know
not, madame," said Savinien to his mother, "but I know that
you are torturing me."

On hearing this speech, wrung from the generous young
man by his mother's behavior, Ursule turned pale; she begged
Madame de Portenduère to excuse her, rose, took her guardian's
arm, courtesied, and went out.   Then, as soon as she was at
home, she rushed into the drawing-room, and, sitting down by
the piano, hid her face in her hands and burst into tears.

"Why will you not leave it to my long experience to guide
your feelings, cruel child?" cried the doctor in despair.
"The nobility never think themselves under any obligation
towards us of the middle class.   In serving them, we do no
more than our duty, that is all.   Besides, the old lady perceived that Savinien looked at you with pleasure; she is afraid
lest he should fall in love with you."

"At any rate, he is safe!" she said. "But to try to set down such a man as you are——!"

"Wait till I come back, my child."

When the doctor returned to Madame de Portenduère's he found Dionis there, and with him Monsieur Bongrand, and Levrault the mayor, the witnesses required by law to give validity to acts drawn up in communes where there is no official above a notary. Minoret led Dionis aside and spoke a word in his ear, after which the notary read the deed of mortgage; Madame de Portenduère pledged all her property until the hundred thousand francs loaned by the doctor to the Vicomte should be repaid, with the interest, calculated at five per cent. When reading this clause, the curé looked at Minoret, who answered the abbé by an approving nod. The good priest went to speak a few words to the lady in a low voice, and she replied quite audibly—

"I do not choose to owe anything to people of that kind."

"My mother leaves the pleasantest part to me," said Savinien to the doctor. "She will pay you all the money, and leave it to me to be grateful."

"But you will have to find eleven thousand francs the first year," observed the curé, "to pay the law costs."

"Monsieur," said Minoret to Dionis, "as Monsieur and Madame de Portenduère are not in a position to pay for the registration, add the costs to the capital sum, and I will pay them."

Dionis made some calculations, and the whole sum was fixed at a hundred and seven thousand francs. When all the documents were signed, Minoret pleaded fatigue, and withdrew at the same time as the notary and the witnesses.

"Madame," said the abbé, who remained with the Vicomte, "why affront that excellent Minoret, who has saved you at least twenty-five thousand francs in Paris, and who had the good feeling to leave twenty thousand in your son's hands for his debts of honor?"

"Your Minoret is a sly fox," said she, taking a pinch of snuff. "He knows very well what he is about."

"My mother fancies that he wants to force me to marry his ward by swallowing up our farm, as if a Portenduère and the son of a Kergarouët could be made to marry against his will."

An hour later Savinien made his appearance at the doctor's, where the heirs had come together, moved by curiosity. The arrival of the young Vicomte produced a great sensation, all the more because in each person it proceeded from a different emotion. Mesdemoiselles Crémière and Massin whispered together, and stared at Ursule, who blushed. The mothers murmured to Désiré that Goupil was very likely in the right as regarded the marriage. The eyes of all were then centred on the doctor, who did not rise to greet the young nobleman, but merely gave him a curt bow, without setting down his dice-box, for he was playing backgammon with Monsieur Bongrand. The doctor's cold manner surprised them all.

"Ursule, my dear," he said, "give us a little music.

The young girl was only too happy to have some occupation; and on seeing her hurry to the piano and turn over the green-bound volumes, the expectant heirs resigned themselves with expressions of pleasure to the torment and silence about to be inflicted on them, so eager were they to detect what was going on between their uncle and the Portenduères.

It happens not unfrequently that a piece, poor enough in itself, but played by a young girl under the stress of deep feeling, may produce more impression than a grand overture pompously given by a fine orchestra. In all music there lies, besides the idea of the composer, the soul of the performer, who, by a privilege peculiar to this art alone, can lend purpose and poetry to phrases of no great intrinsic value. Chopin, in our day, proves the truth of this fact on the piano, a thankless instrument, as Paganini had already done on the violin. This great genius is not so much a musician as a soul, which becomes incarnate, and which could express itself in any form of music, even in simple chords.

Ursule, by her exquisite and perilous organization, belonged to this school of rare genius ; but old Schmucke, the master who came to her every Saturday, and who, during her stay in Paris, had gone to her every day, had developed his pupil's gifts to the utmost perfection. "Rousseau's Dream," the piece Ursule now selected, one of Hérold's youthful compositions, is not lacking in a certain fullness which the player can bring out; Ursule gave it a variety of agitated feeling which justified the title of *Caprice*, which the fragment bears. By her playing, at once mellifluous and dreamy, her soul spoke to the soul of the young man, and wrapped him, as it were, in a cloud of almost visible thoughts. He, seated at the end of the piano, his elbow resting on the top, and his head supported by his left hand, gazed in admiration at Ursule, whose eyes, fixed on the wainscot beyond, seemed to be questioning some mystic world. A man might have fallen desperately in love for less.

True feelings have a magnetic power, and Ursule intended to reveal her soul to some extent, as a coquette dresses herself. to attract. Savinien was admitted to that beautiful realm, carried away by her heart, which, in order to express itself, borrowed the power of the only art which speaks to the mind through the mind, without the aid of words, of color, or of form. Candor has the same power over men as childhood has, the same charms and irresistible attractions; and Ursule had never been more candid than at this moment, when she was waking to a new life.

The curé came to snatch the young man from his dreams by asking him to take the fourth hand at whist. Ursule went on playing ; the heirs left, with the exception of Désiré, who remained to investigate the intentions of his uncle, of the Vicomte, and of Ursule.

"You have as much talent as feeling, mademoiselle," said

"

Savinien, when the young girl closed the piano, and came to sit down by her godfather. "Who is your master?"

"A German who lives quite close to the Rue Dauphine, on the Quai-Conti," said the doctor. "If he had not been giving Ursule a lesson every day during our stay in Paris, he would have been here this morning."

"He is not only a great musician," said Ursule, "but a man of the most adorable simplicity."

"Such lessons must cost very dear!" cried Désiré.

The players exchanged ironical glances. When the game was ended, the doctor, who had been thoughtful all the evening, turned to Savinien with the expression of a man grieved to fulfill a painful duty.

"Monsieur," he said, "I am much gratified by the feeling which has prompted you to call on me so immediately; but your mother ascribes to me a double purpose of an ignoble kind, and I should give her the right to do so if I did not beg of you to come here no more, in spite of the honor your visits do me, and the pleasure I should take in cultivating your society. My honor and my peace of mind require that we should give up all neighborly intercourse. Pray tell your mother that if I do not request her to honor us—my ward and myself—by dining with us next Sunday, it is because I am perfectly certain that on that day she would be indisposed."

The old man offered his hand to the Vicomte, who pressed it respectfully, and merely said, "You are right, monsieur."

He went away, not without bowing to Ursule with an expression of regret rather than of disappointment. Désiré left the room at the same moment, but he could not speak a word with him, for Savinien rushed home.

For two days the coolness between the Portenduères and he doctor was the sole subject of conversation among the heirs, who did justice to the acumen of Dionis, and believed that the inheritance was safe. And thus, in an age when ranks are leveled, when the mania for equality puts all

10

individuals on the same footing, and threatens every institution, even military discipline—the last entrenchment of power
in France ; when, consequently, passion finds no obstacles to
be overcome but personal antipathies or inequality of fortune,
the obstinacy of an old woman and the dignity of Doctor
Minoret had raised between these two lovers barriers which,
as usual, were fated to strengthen rather than to destroy their
love.   To an impassioned man a woman is worth just what
she costs him ; now Savinien, foreseeing a struggle, efforts,
and suspense, which already made the young girl precious to
him, was determined to win her.   Perhaps our feelings obey
the law of nature as to the duration of all her creations—a
long life has a long childhood.

Next morning, on waking, Ursule and Savinien had the
same idea.   This community of feeling would give birth to
love if it were not the most delightful proof of its existence.
When the young girl opened her curtains a little way, so as to
give her eyes exactly space enough to look across to Savinien's
room, she saw her lover's face above the window-fastening
opposite.   When we remember the immense service done to
lovers by windows, it seems quite natural that they should be
taxed.   After thus protesting against her godfather's hard-
heartedness, Ursule let the curtains fall to again, and opened
the window to close the venetians, through which she could
see without being seen.   She went up to her room at least
seven or eight times in the course of the day, and always saw
the young Vicomte writing, tearing up papers, and writing
again—to her, no doubt !

Next morning, when La Bougival woke Ursule, she handed
her the following letter :

" To Mademoiselle Ursule.
" MADEMOISELLE :—I am under no misapprehension as to
the suspicion of which a young man must be the object when
he has placed himself in the position from which your guar-

dian rescued me. I henceforth must offer better guarantees
than another man; hence, mademoiselle, it is with the greatest humility that I throw myself at your feet to avow my
love. This declaration is not prompted by passion; it is
based on a certainty which will last my life through. A mad
passion for my young aunt, Madame de Kergarouët, brought
me to imprisonment; will you not regard as a mark of the
sincerest love the complete effacement of every memory, the
substitution for that image in my heart of your own? From
the moment when I saw you asleep, and so lovely in your
childlike slumbers, at Bouron, you have filled my soul as a
queen holds possession of her realm. I will have no wife but
you. You have every perfection I can look for in the woman
who is to bear my name. The education you have received
and the dignity of your soul qualify you for the highest position. But I am too diffident of myself to attempt to paint
you to yourself; I can only love you. After hearing you
play last night, I remembered these lines, which seem to have
been written on you :

"'Made to attract the heart and charm the eye, at once
gentle and intellectual, witty and reasonable, as polished as
though she had spent her life at courts, as simple as the re-
cluse who has never seen the world, the fire of her soul is
tempered in her eyes by divine modesty.'

"I have felt the value of the beautiful soul which reveals
itself in you by the smallest things. This is what gives me
the courage to ask you—if as yet you love no one—to allow
me to prove to you, by my care and my conduct, that I am
worthy of you. My life depends on it ; you cannot doubt
that all my powers shall be employed not merely to please
you, but yet more to merit your esteem, which will to me
outweigh that of all the rest of the world. In this hope,
Ursule, if you will permit me so to name you in my heart
as one I worship, Nemours will be my paradise, and the most
difficult undertakings will only bring me joys which I shall

lay at your feet, as we lay all at the throne of God. Tell me, then, that I may call myself   YOUR SAVINIEN.''

Ursule kissed this letter; then, after reading it again, and clasping it with rapturous gestures, she dressed to go and show it to her godfather.

"Gracious heaven! I was on the point of going without saying my prayers!" she exclaimed, turning back and kneeling down on her *prie-Dieu*.

A few minutes later she went down to the garden, where she found her guardian, to whom she gave Savinien's letter to read. They sat down together on a bench under the clump of creepers facing the Chinese pavilion. Ursule waited for the old man to speak, and he sat meditating much too long a time for an impatient girl. Finally, the outcome of their secret conference was the following letter, which the doctor had no doubt dictated in part:

"MONSIEUR:—I cannot fail to be much honored by the letter in which you offer me your hand; but at my age, and in accordance with the rules I have been brought up in, I had to lay it before my guardian, who constitutes my whole family, and whom I love as both a father and a friend. These, then, are the painful objections he has raised, and which must serve as my reply.

"I, Monsieur le Vicomte, am but a poor girl, whose future fortune depends entirely not only on my godfather's good-will, but also on the doubtful issue of the measures he can take to evade the ill-will towards me of his next-of-kin. Though I am the legitimate child of Joseph Mirouët, bandmaster to the 45th Infantry Regiment, as he was my guardian's illegitimate half-brother, a suit, however unreasonable, may be brought against a young girl, who will then be defenseless. You see, monsieur, that my slender prospects are not the worst of my misfortunes. I have many reasons for humility. It is for your sake, and not for my own, that I lay before you these considerations, which often weigh but lightly on loving and devoted hearts. But you must take into consideration the fact that if I did not represent them to you, I might be suspected of wishing to induce your affection to overlook obstacles which the world, and, above all, your mother, would think insurmountable. In four months I shall be sixteen. You will perhaps acknowledge that we are, both of us, too young and too inexperienced to struggle with the penury of a life begun on no fortune but what I possess through the kindness of the late Monsieur de Jordy. Besides, my guardian wishes that I should not marry before the age of twenty. Who can tell what fate may have in store for you during these four years, the best of your life? Do not spoil it for the sake of a poor girl.

"Having thus explained to you, monsieur, the reasons given by my dear guardian, who, far from opposing my happiness, desires to contribute to it with all his power, and who hopes to see his protection—which will soon be but feeble— replaced by an affection equal to his own, it only remains for me to say how deeply I am touched by your offer and the warm compliments you have added to it. The prudence which dictates this answer is that of an old man who knows life well; but the gratitude I must express is that of a young girl whose soul no other emotion has as yet entered.

"I can therefore in all truth sign myself your faithful servant,   URSULE MIROUËT.''

Savinien did not reply. Was he trying to influence his mother? Had her letter extinguished his love? A thousand such questions, all unanswerable, tortured Ursule, and by reflex action the doctor, too, for he suffered under the slightest agitation that disturbed his dear child. Ursule often went up to her room and looked across at Savinien, whom she could see seated at his table, deep in thought, and often turning to

glance at her windows.   It was not till the end of the week
that she received this letter from Savinien, whose delay was
explained by an increase of his love :

"To Mademoiselle Ursule Mirouët.

"DEAR URSULE :—There is something of the Breton in
me, and when once I have made up my mind, nothing can make
me alter it.   Your guardian—whom may God long preserve!
—is perfectly right.   But am I to blame, then, for loving
you ?   And all I ask is to know whether you love me.   Tell
me, if only by a sign, and then these four years will indeed
be the best of my life!

"A friend of mine has conveyed to my uncle, Admiral de
Kergarouët, a letter, in which I asked his influence to get me
into the navy.   The kind old man, touched by my mishaps,
has answered that the King's nomination would be contrary
to rule if I wished to take rank.   However, after three months
of study at Toulon, the minister can place me in a ship as
foreman of the steerage ; then, after a cruise against Algiers,
with whom we are at war, I can pass an examination and
become a naval cadet.   If I should distinguish myself in the
expedition to be sent against Algiers, I should certainly be
made sub-lieutenant ; but how soon ?   No one can tell.   But,
at any rate, the regulations will be made as elastic as possible
to reinstate the name of Portenduère on the navy-list.

"I can win you only through your guardian, I see, and
your respect for him makes you the dearer to my heart.   So,
before replying, I will seek an interview with him ; on his
answer my whole future must depend.   Come what may,
believe me that, rich or poor, the daughter of a bandmaster
or of a king, you are to me her whom the voice of my heart
has chosen.

"Dear Ursule, we live at a time when prejudice, which of
old would have parted us, has no longer power enough to
hinder our marriage.   All the feelings of my heart are yours,

and to your uncle I will give such guarantees as may assure
him of your happiness. He does not know that I have loved
you more in a few minutes than he has loved you in fifteen
years! Till this evening."

"See here, godfather!" said Ursule, holding out the letter
with an impulse of pride.

"Ah! my child," cried the doctor, after reading the letter,
"I am more glad than you are. By this determination the
Vicomte has made up for all his misdeeds."

After dinner, Savinien called upon the doctor, who was
just then walking with Ursule by the balustrade of the river-
terrace. The Vicomte had received his clothes from Paris,
and the lover had not omitted to enhance his personal advantages by dressing as carefully, as elegantly, as though it were
to charm the handsome and haughty Comtesse de Kergarouët.
On seeing him advance from the outside steps, the poor
child clung to her uncle's arm exactly as if she were trying to
save herself from falling into an abyss, and the doctor heard
the deep, hollow throbbing of her heart; it made him
shudder.

"Leave us, my child," he said to his ward, who went to
sit down on the steps of the pavilion after suffering Savinien
to take her hand and kiss it respectfully.

"Monsieur, will you give that dear creature to a ship's
captain?" said the young Vicomte to the doctor in a low
voice.

"No," said Minoret with a smile, "we might have too long
to wait; but—to a ship's lieutenant."

Tears of joy stood in the young man's eyes, and he grasped
the old man's hand very warmly.

"Then I shall go," he said, "to study, and try to learn in
six months what the pupils of the naval college learn in six
years."

"Go?" cried Ursule, flying towards them from the steps.

"Yes, mademoiselle, to deserve you. So, the more haste I put into it, the more affection I shall show for you."

"To-day is the 3d of October," said she, looking at him with infinite tenderness. "Start after the 19th."

"Yes," said the old man; "we will keep the feast of Saint-Savinien."

"Then, good-by," exclaimed the youth. "I must spend this week in Paris to take the preliminary steps, make my preparations, and buy the books and the mathematical instruments I need; to make my way, too, in the minister's good graces, and win the most favorable conditions possible."

Ursule and her godfather went with Savinien to the gate. After seeing him go into his mother's house, they saw him come out again, followed by Tiennette, carrying a little portmanteau.

"Why, if you are rich, do you compel him to serve in the navy?" said Ursule to the doctor.

"I believe you will soon think it was I who contracted his debts!" said her uncle, smiling. "I do not compel him. But, my darling, a uniform and the cross of the Legion of Honor won in battle will wipe out many a smirch. In four years he may rise to command a ship, and that is all I ask of him."

"But he may be killed," she said, showing the doctor a white face.

"Lovers, like drunkards, have a Providence of their own," replied the doctor lightly.

The poor child, unknown to her godfather, cut off at night enough of her beautiful long fair hair to make a chain; then, two days later, she persuaded her music-master, old Schmucke, to promise that he would see that the hair was not changed, and that the chain should be finished for the following Sunday.

On Savinien's return, he informed the doctor and his ward that he had signed his papers; he was to be at Brest by the

25th. As the doctor invited him to dinner on the 18th, he spent almost the whole of two days at his house ; and, in spite of the most prudent warnings, the lovers could not hinder themselves from betraying their mutual understanding to the curé, the justice, the town doctor, and La Bougival.

"Children," said the old man, "you are risking your happiness by not keeping your secret to yourselves."

At last, on the fête day, after mass, during which they had exchanged glances, Savinien, watched for by Ursule, crossed the street and came into the little garden, where they found themselves almost alone. To indulge them, the good man sat reading his paper in the Chinese pavilion.

"Dear Ursule," said Savinien, "will you give me a greater boon than my mother could if she were to give me life a second time ? "

"I know what you would ask me," said Ursule, interrupting him. "Here, this is my answer," she added, as she took out of the pocket of her apron the chain made of her hair, and gave it him with a nervous trembling that betrayed her excessive joy. "Wear this for my sake," she said. "May my gift avert from you every peril by reminding you that my life is one with yours ! "

"Ah, the little rogue! she is giving him a chain of her hair," said the doctor to himself. "How could she do it ? Cut her beautiful fair hair ! Why, she would give him my blood ! "

"And will you think it very odious of me if I ask you, before we part, to give me your formal promise that you will never have any husband but me ? " said Savinien, kissing the chain, and looking at Ursule, while he could not restrain one tear.

"If I have not told you so too plainly already—I who went to gaze at the walls of a prison when you were inside," she answered with a deep blush, "I repeat it now, Savinien. I shall never love any one but you, and will never marry any one else,"

Seeing that Ursule was half-hidden among the creepers, the young man could not resist the pleasure of clasping her to his heart and kissing her forehead; but she gave a low scream and dropped on to the bench; and when Savinien sat down by her, imploring her pardon, he saw the doctor standing in front of them.

"My good fellow," said he, "Ursule is a sensitive plant; a hard word might kill her. For her sake you should moderate the expression of your love. Ah! if you had loved her for fifteen years, you would have taken her word," he added, in revenge for the last words of Savinien's letter.

Two days later Savinien left. In spite of the letters he wrote regularly to Ursule, she was a victim to a malady that had no evident cause. Like a fine fruit attacked by a maggot, one thought was eating her heart out. She lost her appetite and her bright color. When her godfather first asked her how she was feeling—

"I want to see the sea," she said.

"It is difficult to take you to a seaport in the month of December?" said the old man.

"Then shall I go?" said she.

If the wind was high, Ursule was in agonies, believing, in spite of the learned observations of her godfather, the curé, and the justice, that Savinien was warring with a hurricane. The justice made her happy for a few days with a print representing a naval cadet in his uniform. She read the newspapers, believing that they would give her news of the cruise in which Savinien was engaged. She devoured the seafaring novels of Cooper, and learned the meaning of sea words. These proofs of a fixed idea, so often affected by other women, were so perfectly natural in Ursule that she foresaw in a dream every letter from Savinien, and never failed to predict their arrival by relating the premonitory dream.

"Now," said she to the doctor, on the fourth occasion

when this had happened without the doctor and the curé
being at all surprised; " now, I am easy; however far away
Savinien may be, if he were wounded, I should feel it at the
same moment."

The old physician sat plunged in deep meditation, which,
to judge from the expression of his face, the justice and the
curé thought must be sorrowful.

"What is wrong?" they asked him, when Ursule had left
them together.

"Will she live?" replied the old doctor. "Can so frail
and tender a flower withstand the anguish of her heart?"

Meanwhile the "little dreamer," as the curé called her,
worked indefatigably; she understood the importance to a
woman of the world of extensive information; and when she
was not studying singing, harmony, or composition, she spent
her time in reading the books chosen for her in her godfather's
extensive library.

While leading this busy life she suffered much, but she did
not complain. Sometimes she would sit for hours gazing at
Savinien's window opposite. On Sunday, as she came from
church, she followed Madame de Portenduère, watching her
tenderly, for in spite of her sternness she loved her as being
Savinien's mother. Her piety was doubled; she went to mass
every morning, for she firmly believed that her dreams were a
special grace from God.

Alarmed by the ravages of this nostalgia of love, on
Ursule's birthday her godfather promised to take her to
Toulon to see the departure of the fleet for Algiers without
announcing their purpose to Savinien, who was sailing with it.
The justice and the curé kept the secret of the doctor's intentions with regard to this journey, which seemed to be undertaken for the benefit of Ursule's health, and which puzzled
the heirs very greatly.

After having seen Savinien once more in his uniform, and
after going on board the fine flagship of the admiral, to whom

the minister had especially recommended young Portenduère, Ursule, at her friend's desire, went to inhale the soft air of Nice, and traveled along the Mediterranean coast as far as Genoa, where she had news of the arrival of the fleet before Algiers and a good report of the landing.   The doctor would gladly have continued the journey across Italy, as much to divert Ursule's mind as to complete her education and enlarge her ideas by comparing manners and scenery, and by the delights of a land where the greatest works of art are to be seen, and where so many civilizations have left glorious traces ; but the news of the opposition to the throne shown by the electors of the famous Chamber of 1830 called him back to France, whither he brought his ward home in a blooming state of health, and happy in the possession of a small model of the ship on which Savinien was serving.

The elections of 1830 gave cohesion to the Minoret heirs; for, by the advice of Goupil and of Désiré Minoret, they formed a committee at Nemours, by whose efforts the Liberal candidate was returned for Fontainebleau.   Massin exerted immense influence over the country voters.   Five of the post-master's farmers also had votes.   Dionis represented more than eleven votes.   By meeting at the notary's, Crémière, Massin, the postmaster, and their adherents got into a habit of assembling there.   On the doctor's return, Dionis' room had thus become their camping ground.

The justice and the mayor, who then combined to resist the Liberals of Nemours, were beaten by the Opposition in spite of the·efforts of the gentry in the neighborhood, and their defeat bound them very closely together.   When Bongrand and the Abbé Chaperon told the doctor of the result of this antagonism, which had divided Nemours, for the first time, into two parties, and had given importance to his next-of-kin, Charles X. was actually leaving Rambouillet for Cherbourg. Désiré Minoret, whose opinions were those of the Paris bar, had invited fifteen of his friends, with Goupil at their head,

to come from Nemours ; the postmaster gave them horses to
hurry to Paris, where they joined Désiré on the night of the
28th of July. Désiré and Goupil led this little troop to
assist in the seizure of the Hôtel de Ville (Town Hall).

Désiré Minoret received the ribbon of the Legion of Honor,
and was appointed deputy to the public prosecutor at Fontainebleau. Goupil won the cross of July. Dionis was
elected mayor of Nemours, in the place of the Sieur Levrault,
and the town council was then composed of Minoret-Levrault,
deputy-mayor, of Massin, Crémière, and all the followers of
Dionis.

Bongrand only kept his appointment as justice by the influence of his son, who was made public prosecutor at Melun,
his marriage with Mademoiselle Levrault seeming at that time
probable.

When three per cents. were down to forty-five, the doctor
set out by post to Paris, and invested five hundred and forty
thousand francs in certificates to the bearer. The rest of his
fortune, amounting to about two hundred and seventy thousand
francs, placed likewise in the funds, yielded nominally fifteen
thousand francs a year. He invested in the same way the
money left to Ursule by the old professor, as well as the
eight thousand francs of nine years' accumulated interest,
which, with the help of a small addition on his part to
make it up to a round sum, brought in fourteen hundred
francs a year to his ward. In obedience to her master's
advice, La Bougival also would get three hundred and fifty
francs a year by investing in the same way her five thousand
and odd francs of savings. These prudent steps, as planned
by the doctor and his friend Bongrand, were taken in perfect
secrecy under favor of the political excitement. When calm
was more or less restored, the doctor purchased a little house
adjoining his own, and pulled it down, as well as the wall of
his courtyard, to construct on the ground a coach-house and
stables. That he should spend capital bearing a thousand

francs interest seemed to all the Minoret heirs pure insanity. This supposed craziness was the beginning of a new era in the doctor's life; at a moment when horses and carriages were being almost given away, he brought from Paris three fine horses and a chariot.

The first time the old man came to mass in a carriage, on a rainy day at the beginning of November, 1830, and got out to give his hand to Ursule, all the townsfolk rushed to the square, as much to see the doctor's carriage and cross-question the coachman, as to comment on his ward, to whose excessive ambition Massin, Crémière, and the postmaster ascribed their uncle's follies.

"A chariot ! heh, Massin ? " cried Goupil. " Your inheritance promises well, hein ! "

" You asked good wages, I suppose, Cabirolle ? " said the postmaster to the son of one of his guards, who took charge of the horses, " for it is to be hoped that you will not see many horseshoes worn through in the service of a man of eighty. How much did those horses cost ? "

" Four thousand francs. The chariot, though second-hand, cost him two thousand ; but it is a good one. The wheels have the patent axle-box."

" What do you call it, Cabirolle ? " asked Madame Crémière.

" He says they have latent axle-hocks," replied Goupil. " It is an English notion ; they invented those wheels. Look how neat it is; all covered up, nothing to be seen, nothing to catch, no ugly square iron peg projecting beyond the axle."

" What does axer-hock mean, then ? " asked Madame Crémière very innocently.

" Surely," said Goupil, " you need hardly axe that."

" Ah ! I understand," said she.

" No, no ; you are a good soul," said Goupil. " It is a shame to take you in. The real word is patent axe-locks, because you must axe how it is fastened."

"That's it, madame," said Cabirolle, who was himself taken in by Goupil's explanation, the clerk spoke with such gravity.

"It is a handsome carriage, at any rate," said Crémière, "and he must be rich to set up in such style."

"She is going ahead, that little girl!" remarked Goupil. "But she is right; she is showing you how to enjoy life. Why have you not fine horses and chariots—you, Father Minoret? Will you submit to be humiliated? In your place I would have a coach like a prince's."

"I say, Cabirolle," said Massin, "is it the little girl who puts my uncle up to all this luxury?"

"I don't know," replied Cabirolle, "but she is, so to speak, mistress of the whole place. And now master after master comes from Paris. She is to learn to paint, they say."

"I will take the opportunity of having my likeness done," said Madame Crémière. Country folks still speak of having a likeness done instead of a portrait taken.

"But the old German is not dismissed," said Madame Massin.

"No, he is here to-day," replied Cabirolle.

"There is safety in numbers," observed Madame Crémière, making everybody laugh.

"You need no longer count on the inheritance," cried Goupil. "Ursule is nearly seventeen; she is prettier than ever; traveling forms the youthful mind, and she knows the length of your uncle's foot. The coach brings her five or six parcels a week, and dressmakers and milliners are always coming to try her gowns and things. My mistress is furious, I can tell you. Just wait till Ursule comes out, and look at her little neckerchief—a real India square, that must have cost six hundred francs."

If a thunderbolt had fallen in their midst, it could not have produced a greater effect on the group of inheritors than this speech from Goupil, who rubbed his hands.

The doctor's old green drawing-room was redecorated by an upholsterer from Paris. Judged by the prodigality of his outlay, the doctor was accused first of having concealed the amount of his fortune and of having sixty thousand francs a year, and then of spending his capital to humor Ursule. He was regarded alternately as a millionaire and a spendthrift. " He is an old fool ! " summed up the opinion of the neighbors. The misguided verdict of the little town had this advantage : it deceived the next-of-kin, who never suspected Savinien's love for Ursule, which was the real cause of the doctor's expenditure, for he was enchanted to accustom his goddaughter to play her part as a vicomtesse ; and having an income now of fifty thousand francs, he indulged himself in the pleasure of beautifying his idol.

In the month of February, 1832, on the day when Ursule was seventeen, as she rose in the morning she saw Savinien at his window in his sub-lieutenant's uniform.

" How is it that I knew nothing about it ? " she asked herself.

After the taking of Algiers, where Savinien had distinguished himself by a deed of valor that had won him the cross, the corvette on which he sailed having remained at sea for many months, he had been quite unable to send a letter to the doctor, and he did not choose to retire from the service without consulting him. The new government, wishing to keep so illustrious a name on the navy-list, had taken advantage of the general scramble of July to promote Savinien. Having obtained a fortnight's leave, the young lieutenant had come by mail from Toulon in time for Ursule's birthday, and to ask the doctor's advice at the same time.

" He is come ! " cried the girl, rushing into her godfather's room.

" That is well," he replied. " I can guess his reason for quitting the service ; he can now remain at Nemours."

"This is my birthday treat! It is all in those words!" she exclaimed, throwing her arms arouud the doctor's neck and kissing him.

In reply to a signal she made him, Savinien came across at once. She wanted to admire him; he seemed to her changed for the better. In fact, military discipline gives to a man's gestures, gait, and demeanor a mixture of gravity and decision, a certain rectitude, which enables the most superficial observer to recognize a soldier under a civilian's coat; nothing can more clearly prove that man is made to command. Ursule loved Savinien all the more for it, and felt a child's delight in walking arm in arm with him in the little garden, while she made him tell her the part he had played "in his capacity of naval cadet" in the siege of Algiers. Evidently it was Savinien who had taken Algiers. She saw everything red, she declared, when she looked at Savinien's decoration. The doctor, who, while dressing in his room, watched the pair, presently joined them. Then, without telling the Vicomte everything, he explained to him that in the event of Madame de Portenduère's consenting to his marriage with Ursule, his goddaughter's fortune was such as to make his pay superfluous in any rank he might be promoted to.

"Alas!" said Savinien, "it will take a long time to overcome my mother's opposition. Before I left, when she had the alternative of keeping me near her if she would agree to my marrying Ursule, or of seeing me only at long intervals, and knowing that I was exposed to the risk of my profession, she let me go——"

"But, Savinien, we shall be together," said Ursule, taking his hand and shaking it with a kind of irritation.

That they should see each other and never part was to her the sum-total of love; she saw nothing beyond; and her pretty impatience and the petulance of her tone expressed such perfect innocence that the doctor and Savinien were touched.

11

Savinien, after his consultation with the doctor, sent in his letter of resignation, and Ursule's birthday was crowned with joy by her lover's presence.

A few months later, by the beginning of May, Doctor Minoret's home life had settled into calm regularity again, but with another constant visitor. The young Vicomte's assiduity was at once interpreted as that of a future bridegroom; all the more so since, whether at mass or out walking, his manner and Ursule's plainly betrayed the mutual understanding of their hearts.   Dionis remarked to the heirs that the old man never claimed interest from Madame de Portenduère, who already owed it for three years.

"She will be forced to give in, to consent to her son's marrying beneath him," said the notary.   "If such a misfortune should happen, it is probable that the larger part of your uncle's fortune will prove, as Basile says, an irresistible argument."

When the expectant heirs understood that the old man's preference for Ursule was too great for him not to secure her happiness at their expense, their wrath became as cunning as it was deep.   Every evening since the revolution of July had seen them meet at Dionis' house, and there they cursed the lovers; and the evening hardly ever ended without their having tried in vain to hit on some way of thwarting the old man.   Zélie, who had, no doubt, like the doctor, taken advantage of the fall in the funds to invest her enormous savings, was the most furious against the orphan and the Portenduères.   One evening, when Goupil—who, however, as a rule, took care not to spend his evenings too dully—had come in to pick up some information as to the affairs of the town, which were under discussion, Zélie had a recrudescence of hatred.   She had that morning seen the doctor, with Ursule and Savinien, returning from a drive in the neighborhood, with an appearance of intimacy that told all.

"I would give thirty thousand francs, gladly, if only God

would take our uncle to Himself before that Portenduère and that little minx could be married," said she.

Goupil walked home with Monsieur and Madame Minoret; and when they were in the middle of their vast courtyard, he said, looking suspiciously about him to make sure that they were alone:

" Will you give me money enough to buy Dionis out of his business, if I will see that the marriage of Monsieur de Portenduère is broken off ? "

" How ? " asked the colossus.

" Do you think I am fool enough to tell you my plan ? " replied the clerk.

" Well, my boy, make them quarrel, and we will see," said Zélie.

" I am not going to plunge into such a job on the strength of ' we will see.' The young gentleman is hot-headed, and might kill me; and I must be well rough-shod, and his match with the rapier and pistol. Set me up in life, and I will keep my word."

"Stop the marriage, and I will set you up," retorted the postmaster.

" For nine months now you have been debating whether you will lend me a wretched fifteen thousand francs to buy Lecœur's business—the usher's—and you expect me to take your word ? Get along ! You will lose your uncle's fortune; and serve you right ! "

" If it were only a matter of fifteen thousand francs and Lecœur's business, I should not say no," replied Zélie; "but to be security for fifty thousand crowns——! "

" But I will repay you," said Goupil, with a fascinating leer at Zélie, which the postmistress met with an imperious stare.

It was like vitriol on steel.

" We will wait," said Zélie.

" Possessed by the genius of evil ! " thought Goupil. " If

ever I get hold of these two," said he to himself as he went away, "I will squeeze them like lemons!"

Savinien, while cultivating the society of the doctor, the justice, and the curé, showed them the excellence of his character. The young man's love for Ursule, so absolutely disinterested, so constant, appealed so strongly to the three friends that they no longer separated the two young people in their thoughts. Before long the monotony of this patriarchal life, and the confidence the lovers felt in their future, had given their affection a fraternal aspect. The doctor often left Savinien and Ursule together. He had rightly estimated the admirable young man who kissed Ursule's hand when he entered, and would never have asked such a privilege when alone with her, so deep was his respect for the innocence and candor of the child ; and the extreme sensitiveness which she had often betrayed had taught him that a harsh word, a cold look, or alternations of gentleness and roughness might kill her. The utmost boldness of the lovers always showed itself in the presence of the old men in the evening.

Two years, full of secret delight, thus slipped away, unbroken by any event but the useless efforts of the young man to obtain his mother's consent to his marriage with Ursule. He would sometimes talk for the whole morning, his mother listening to his entreaties and arguments, but making no reply but by the obstinate silence of a Bretonne or by curt refusals.

At nineteen, Ursule, elegant, well educated, and an excellent musician, had nothing more to learn ; she was perfection. And she had a reputation for beauty, grace, and information which reached far and wide. One day the doctor had to refuse the proposals of the Marquise d'Aiglemont, who would have married her to her eldest son. Six months later, in spite of the absolute silence preserved by Ursule, by her guardian, and by Madame d'Aiglemont, Savinien heard by chance of this affair. Touched by such delicate conduct, he spoke of it

as an argument to overcome his mother's aversion, but she
would only say—

"If the d'Aiglemonts choose to marry beneath them, is
that any reason why we should?"

In the month of December, 1834, the worthy and pious
old man was visibly breaking. As they saw him come out of
church, his face pinched and yellow, his eyes dim, all the
town began to speak of his approaching end, for the good
man was now eighty-eight years of age.

"Now you will know where you stand," they said to the
heirs.

The doctor's death had, in fact, the fascination of a problem. But the old man did not think that he was ill; he had
illusions on the subject, and neither poor Ursule, nor Savinien,
nor Monsieur Bongrand, nor the curé, could, in decency,
explain his danger to him; the town doctor of Nemours, who
came to see him every evening, dared prescribe nothing more.
Old Minoret felt no pain; he was gently burning out. In
him the intellect remained clear, strong, and exact. In old
men of this stamp the soul is potent over the body, and gives
it strength to die standing. To postpone the fatal hour, the
curé granted his parishioner a dispensation from attending
mass at church, and allowed him to read prayers at home, for
the doctor carefully fulfilled all his religious duties; the nearer
he was to the grave, the more he loved God.

At the New Year, Ursule persuaded him to sell his carriage
and horses, and dismiss Cabirolle. The justice, whose uneasiness as to Ursule's prospects was far from being lulled by
the old man's half-confidences, touched on the delicate
question of his fortune, explaining to him one evening the
necessity for making Ursule independent by law, by declaring
her to be of age. She would then be competent to receive
an account of his guardianship and possess property; this
would enable him to leave her money. In spite of this

opening, the old man, though he had formerly consulted the
justice, did not confide to him what his purpose was with
regard to Ursule ; however, he formally declared her of age.
The more eager the lawyer showed himself to know what
steps his old friend had taken to provide for Ursule, the
more suspicious the doctor became. In short, Minoret was
actually afraid to confide to the justice the secret of the
thirty-six thousand francs in bonds payable to the bearer
on demand.

"Why," said Bongrand, "set chance against you?"

"Of two chances," replied the doctor, "one must avoid
the most risky."

Bongrand carried through the matter of the "emancipa-
tion" so briskly that Mademoiselle Mirouët was legally
independent on the day when she was twenty. This anniversary was destined to be the last festival kept by the old
doctor, who, feeling no doubt some presentiment of his
approaching end, celebrated the occasion magnificently by
giving a little ball, to which he invited the young people
of the four families of Dionis, Crémière, Minoret, and Massin. Savinien, Bongrand, the curé and his two assistant
priests, the town doctor, Mesdames Zélie Minoret, Massin,
and Crémière, with old Schmucke, were his guests at a grand
dinner before the dance.

"I feel that I have not long to stay," said the old man to the
notary towards the end of the evening. "I beg you to come
to-morrow to draw up the report and accounts I have to hand
over to Ursule as her guardian, so as to avoid all complica-
tions after my death. Thank God, I have not robbed my
heirs of a sou, and have spent nothing but my income.
Messieurs Crémière, Massin, and my nephew Minoret are
the family trustees appointed for Ursule, and they must be
present at the auditing of the account."

These words, overheard by Massin, and repeated in the
ballroom, filled the three families with joy, after they .had

spent three years in constant alternations of feeling, believing themselves sometimes rich and sometimes disinherited.

"It is a lamp flying out," said Madame Crémière. (She meant dying out.)

When, at about two in the morning, no one remained in the room but Savinien, Bongrand, and the Abbé Chaperon, the old doctor said, as he pointed to Ursule, lovely in her ball-dress, having just said good-night to the young Crémière and Massin girls—

"I place her in your hands, my friends. In a few days I shall no longer be here to protect her; stand between her and the world until she is married—I am afraid for her——"

These words made a painful impression. The account drawn up and read a few days later in the presence of a family council proved that Doctor Minoret was indebted to Ursule in the sum of ten thousand six hundred francs, partly as arrears of the shares bearing interest to the amount of fourteen thousand francs, which was accounted for by the investment of Captain de Jordy's legacy, and partly as a small capital of five thousand francs derived from certain gifts made to his ward during the last fifteen years, on their respective birthdays or namedays.

This authenticated schedule of the account had been advised by the justice, who feared what might be the result of the old man's death; and, unhappily, not without reason. The day after the account was passed which made Ursule the mistress of ten thousand six hundred francs in shares and of fourteen hundred francs a year, the doctor had an attack of weakness which compelled him to keep his bed.

It spite of the caution which shrouded the house, a rumor spread in the town that he was dead, and the heirs flew about the streets like the beads of a rosary of which the thread is snapped. Massin, who came to inquire, heard from Ursule herself that the old man was in bed. Unfortunately, the town doctor had prognosticated that when Minoret took to his bed he would die at once.   From that moment the whole family stood posted in the street, in the square, or on their front doorsteps, in spite of the cold, absorbed in discussing the long-expected event, and waiting for the moment when the curé should carry to the old man the last sacraments with all the ceremony usual in provincial towns.   Hence, when two days later the Abbé Chaperon crossed the High Street, accompanied by his curate and the choir boys, the inheritors followed him to take possession of the house and prevent anything being removed, and to clutch with greedy hands all the imaginary treasure.   When the doctor saw, beyond the clerics, all his heirs on their knees, and, far from praying, watching him with gleaming eyes as bright as the twinkling tapers, he could not repress a mischievous smile.   The curé looked round, saw them, and read the prayers very slowly.   The postmaster was the first to rise from his uncomfortable attitude, his wife followed his example ; Massin, fearful lest Zélie and her husband should lay a hand on some little possession, went after them to the drawing-room, and there, a few minutes later, all the party had assembled.

"He is too honest a man to steal extreme unction," said Crémière ; "so we may be easy."

"Yes ; we shall each have about twenty thousand francs a year," replied Madame Massin.

"I have gotten it into my head," said Zélie, "that for the last three years he has not been investing ; he liked to hoard the money——"

"The treasure is in his cellar no doubt ? " said Massin to Crémière.

"If we are so lucky as to find anything at all ! " observed Minoret-Levrault.

"But after what he said at the ball," cried Madame Massin, "there can be no doubt."

"Whatever there may be," said Crémière, "how shall we proceed?   Shall we divide?   Or put it into the lawyer's hands? Or distribute it in lots? For, after all, we are all of age.''

A discussion, which soon became acrid, arose as to the method of procedure. At the end of half an hour a noise of loud voices, above them all Zélie's shrill tones, rang across the courtyard out into the street.

"He must be dead," said the curious crowd that had collected there.

The uproar reached the doctor's ears, who could hear these words—

"But there is the house; the house is worth thirty thousand francs!" shouted, or rather bellowed, by Crémière.

"Very well, we will pay for it as much as it is worth," retorted Zélie sharply.

"Monsieur le Curé," said the old man to the abbé, who had remained with his friend after the sacrament, "let me die in peace. My heirs, like those of Cardinal Ximenes, are capable of pillaging my house before I am dead, and I have no monkey to make restitution. Go and explain that I will have no one in the house."

The curé and the physician went downstairs and repeated the dying man's orders, adding, in their indignation, some severe words of reproof.

"Madame Bougival," said the town-doctor, "shut the gate, and let no one in; a man cannot even die quietly, it would seem. Make a cup of mustard, to apply plasters to Monsieur Minoret's feet."

"Your uncle is not dead; he may live some time yet," said the abbé to the family who had brought all their children. "He desires perfect silence, and will have no one near him but his ward. What a difference between that young creature's conduct and yours!"

"Old hypocrite!" cried Crémière. "I will keep guard. It is quite possible that he may plot something against our interests."

The postmaster had already disappeared into the garden, intending to watch over his uncle with Ursule, and to gain admission into the house as her assistant. He came back on tiptoe without his boots making a sound, for there were carpets in the passages and on the stairs. He thus came close to his uncle's door without being heard. The curé and the physician had left; La Bougival was preparing the mustard plasters.

"Are we quite alone?" said the old man to his ward.

Ursule stood on tiptoe to look out on the courtyard.

"Yes," said she, "Monsieur le Curé shut the gate as he went out."

"My darling child," said the dying man, "my hours, my minutes are numbered. I have not been a doctor for nothing; the mustard plasters recommended by the apothecary will not carry me through till to-night. Do not cry, Ursule," he said, finding himself interrupted by his ward's sobs, "but listen to me: the point is that you should marry Savinien. As soon as La Bougival comes up with the sinapism, go down to the Chinese pavilion; here is the key; lift up the marble top of the Boule cabinet, and under it you will find a letter addressed to you; take it, and come up and show it to me, for I shall not die easy unless I know that it is in your hands. When I am dead, do not at once announce the fact; first send for Monsieur de Portenduère, read the letter together, and swear to me in his name and in your own that you will obey my last injunctions. When he has done what I desire, you can announce my death, and then the comedy of the inheritance will begin. God grant that those monsters may not ill-use you."

"Yes, godfather."

The postmaster did not wait for the end of the scene; he took himself off on tiptoe, remembering that the locked door of the pavilion opened from the book-gallery. He himself had been present at the time of a discussion between the architect and the locksmith, who had insisted that if there were to be a way into the house through the window looking out on the river there must be a lock to the door leading into the book gallery, the pavilion being a sort of summer-house.

Minoret, his eyes dim with greed and his blood singing in his ears, unscrewed the lock with a pocket-knife as dexterously as a thief. He went into the pavilion, took the packet of papers without stopping to open it, replaced the lock and restored order, and then went to sit in the dining-room, waiting till La Bougival should be gone upstairs with the mustard plaster, to steal out of the house. This he achieved with all the greater ease because Ursule thought it more necessary to see that the mustard was applied than to obey her godfather's injunctions.

"The letter, the letter," said the old man in a dying voice. "Do as I bid you—there is the key. I must see the letter in your hands."

He spoke with such a wild look that La Bougival said to Ursule: "Do as your godfather tells you, at once, or you'll be the death of him."

She kissed his forehead, took the key, and went down, but was immediately recalled by a piercing cry from La Bougival, and ran back. The old man glanced at her, saw that her hands were empty, sat up in bed, and tried to speak—and then died with a last fearful gasp, his eyes staring with terror.

The poor child, seeing death for the first time, fell on her knees, and melted into tears. La Bougival closed the old man's eyes and laid him straight. Then, when she had "dressed the corpse," as she said, she went to call Monsieur Savinien; but the heirs, who were prowling at the top of the street, surrounded by an inquisitive crowd, exactly like a flock of crows waiting till a horse is buried to come and scratch up the earth, and ferret with beak and claws, came running in with the swiftness of birds of prey.

The postmaster, meanwhile, had gone home to master the contents of the mysterious packet.   This was what he read:

"To my dear Ursule Mirouët, daughter of my illegitimate brother-in-law, Joseph Mirouët, and of his wife, Dinah Grollman.

"NEMOURS, *January* 15, 1830.

"MY LITTLE ANGEL:—My fatherly affection, which you have so fully justified, is based not merely on the promise I swore to your poor father to fill his place, but also on your likeness to Ursule Mirouët, my late wife, of whom you constantly remind me by your grace and nature, your artlessness and charm.

"Your being the child of my father-in-law's natural son might lead to any will in your favor being disputed——"

"The old rascal!" exclaimed the postmaster.

"My adopting you would have given rise to a lawsuit. Again, I have always been averse to the notion of marrying you myself to leave you my fortune, for I might have lived to a great age and spoilt your future happiness, which is delayed only by the life of Madame de Portenduère.   Having regard to the difficulties, and wishing to leave you a fortune adequate to a handsome position——"

"The old wretch, he thought of everything!"

"Without doing any injury to my heirs——"

"Miserable Jesuit!   As if we had not a right to his whole fortune!"

"I have put aside for you the sum-total of my savings for the last eighteen years, which I have regularly invested by my lawyer's assistance, in the hope of leaving you as happy as money can make you.   Without wealth your education and superior ideas would be a misfortune; besides, you ought to bring a good dowry to the excellent young man who loves you.   So look in the middle of the third volume of the

'Pandects,' in folio, bound in red morocco, the last volume on the lower shelf above the library cupboard, in the third division on the drawing-room side, and you will find three certificates to bearer of three per cent. consols, each for 12,000 francs.''

''What a depth of villainy!'' cried the postmaster. ''Ah, God will not permit me to be thus thwarted!''

''Take them at once, with the small savings left at the moment of my death, which are in the next volume. Remember, my darling child, that you are bound to obey blindly the wish that has been the joy of my whole life, and which will compel me to appeal for help to God if you should disobey me. But to guard against any scruple of your dear conscience, which is, I know, ingenious in tormenting you, you will find with this a will in due form, bequeathing these certificates to Monsieur Savinien de Portenduère; so, whether you own them, or they are the gift of your lover, they will be legitimately yours. Your godfather

''DENIS MINORET.''

Subjoined to this letter, on a sheet of stamped paper, was the following document:

''THIS IS MY WILL.

''I, DENIS MINORET, Doctor of Medicine, resident at Nemours, sound in mind and body, as the date of this will proves, dedicate my soul to God, beseeching Him to forgive my long errors in favor of my sincere repentance. Then, having discerned in the Vicomte Savinien de Portenduère a sincere affection for me, I bequeath to him thirty-six thousand francs in perpetual consols at three per cent., to be paid out of my estate as a first charge.

''Made and written all by my own hand at Nemours, January 11, 1831.

''DENIS MINORET.''

Without a moment's hesitation the postmaster, who, to make sure of being alone, had locked himself into his wife's room, looked about for the tinder-box; he had two warnings from heaven by the extinction of two matches which would not light. The third blazed up. He burnt the letter and the will on the hearth, and took the needless precaution of burying the ashes of the paper and wax in the cinders. Then, licking his lips at the idea of having thirty-six thousand francs unknown to his wife, he flew back to his uncle's house, spurred by one idea—the single fixed idea that his dull brain could master. On seeing his uncle's dwelling invaded by the three families, at last in possession of the stronghold, he quaked lest he should be unable to carry out a project which he gave himself no time to think over, considering only the obstacles in the way.

"What are you doing here?" he said to Massin and Crémière. "Do you suppose that we are going to leave the house and papers to be pillaged? There are three of us; we cannot encamp on the spot. You, Crémière, go at once to Dionis and tell him to come and certify the death. Though I am an official, I am not competent to draw up the death certificate of my own uncle. You, Massin, had better ask old Bongrand to seal up everything. You," he added to his wife, Madame Massin, and Madame Crémière, "you should sit with Ursule, ladies, and so nothing can be taken. Above all, lock the gate, so that no one can get out."

The women, who felt the weight of this advice, went at once to Ursule's room, where they found the noble girl, already the object of such cruel suspicions, on her knees in prayer, her face bathed in tears.

Minoret, guessing that they would not remain long with Ursule, and suspicious of his co-heirs' want of trust in him, hastened to the library, saw the volume, which he opened, took out the three certificates, and found in the other thirty bank-notes. Notwithstanding his base nature, the big man fancied a whole chime was ringing in each ear, the blood hissed in his brain, as he achieved the theft. In spite of the cold weather, his shirt was wet with perspiration down his back; and his legs shook to such a degree that he dropped into an armchair in the drawing-room as if he had been struck on the head with a sledge-hammer.

"Dear me, how glib the idea of a fortune has made old Minoret!" Massin had said, as they hurried through the town. "Did you notice it?" he observed to Crémière. 'Come here, and go there!' How well he knows the game, and how to play it!"

"Yes, for a fat-head he had a style——"

"I say," said Massin in alarm, "his wife is with him. They are two too many. Do you run the errands; I will go back again."

So just as the postmaster had seated himself, he saw the registrar's hot face at the gate, for he had run back with the nimbleness of a ferret.

"Well, what is it?" asked the postmaster, as he let in his co-heir.

"Nothing; I came back to witness the sealing," replied Massin, glaring at him like a wildcat.

"I wish it were done, and that we could all go quietly home," said Minoret.

"And we will put some one in charge," said the registrar. "La Bougival is capable of anything in the interest of that little minx. We will put in Goupil."

"Goupil!" cried Minoret; "he would find the hoard, and we should see nothing but smoke."

"Let us see," replied Massin; "this evening they will watch by the dead. We shall have everything sealed up in an hour, so our wives will be on guard themselves. The funeral must be to-morrow at noon. The inventory cannot be made till after a week."

"But," said the colossus smiling, "we can turn out that

minx, and we will engage the mayor's drummer to stop in the house and guard the property."

" Very good," said the registrar, "see to that yourself; you are the head of the Minorets."

" Now, ladies, ladies, be so good as to wait in the drawing-room. You cannot be off to dinner yet; we must witness the affixing of the seals for our common interest."

He then took Zélie aside to impart to her Massin's idea about Ursule. The women, whose hearts were full of vengeance, and who longed to turn the tables on "the little hussy," hailed the idea of turning her out of the house with glee.

When Bongrand arrived he was indignant at the request made to him, as a friend of the deceased, by Zélie and Madame Massin, to desire Ursule to leave the house.

" Go yourselves and turn her out of the home of her father, her godfather, her uncle, her benefactor, her guardian ! Go —you who owe your fortunes to her nobility of character— take her by the shoulders—thrust her into the street in the face of the whole town ! You think her capable of robbing you? Well, then, engage a guardian of the property; you have a perfect right to do so. But understand clearly that I will put seals on nothing in her room; it is her own, all that is in it is her property; I shall inform her what her rights are, and advise her to place everything there that belongs to her. —Oh ! in your presence ! " he added, hearing a murmur of disapproval.

" What ? " cried the tax-receiver to the postmaster and the women, who were struck speechless at Bongrand's angry address.

" A pretty magistrate ! " said Minoret.

Ursule, on a low chair, half-fainting, her head thrown back, her hair undone, was sobbing from time to time. Her eyes were heavy, their lids swollen ; in short, she was in a state of moral and physical prostration, which might have touched the heart of the fiercest creatures excepting heirs.

"Ah, Monsieur Bongrand, after my happy fête, here are death and despair," she said, with the unconscious poetry of a sweet nature. "You know what he was. In twenty years he never spoke an impatient word to me! I thought he would live to a hundred! He was a mother to me," she cried, "and a kind mother!"

The utterance of her broken ideas brought on a torrent of tears, broken by sobs, and she fell back half-senseless.

"My child," said the justice, hearing the inheritors on the stairs, "you have the rest of your life to weep in, and only a moment for business. Bring into your own room everything in the house that belongs to you. The heirs insist on my affixing seals——"

"Oh, his heirs may take everything!" cried Ursule, starting up in a spasm of fierce indignation. "I have here all that is precious to me!" and she struck her bosom.

"What? what?" asked the postmaster, who, with Massin, now showed his horrible face.

"The memory of his virtues, of his life, of all his words, the image of his heavenly mind," she replied, her eyes and cheeks flaming as she raised her hand with a proud gesture.

"Ay, and you have a key there too," cried Massin, going on all fours like a cat to seize a key which slipped out of the folds of her bodice as she lifted her arm.

"It is the key of his study," she said, coloring. "He was sending me there just when he died."

The two men exchanged a hideous smile, and turned to the justice with a look that expressed a blighting suspicion. Ursule saw and interpreted the look, malignant on Minoret's part, involuntary on Massin's, and drew herself up, as pale as if all her blood had ebbed; her eyes glistened with the lightnings that can only flash at the cost of vitality, and in a choking voice she said—

"Ah, Monsieur Bongrand, all that is in this room is mine only by my godfather's kindness; they may take it all; I have

12

nothing about me but my clothes; I will go out of it and never come in again."

She went into her guardian's room, and no entreaties could bring her forth—for the heirs were a little ashamed of their conduct. She desired La Bougival to engage two rooms at the Old Posting Inn till she should find some lodging in the town, where they might stay together. She went into her room only to fetch her prayer-book, and remained all night with the curé and another priest and Savinien, weeping and praying. Savinien came in after his mother had gone to bed, and knelt down without speaking by Ursule, who gave him the saddest smile, while thanking him for coming so faithfully to share in her sorrows.

"My child," said Monsieur Bongrand, bringing in a large bundle, "one of your uncle's relations has taken out of your wardrobe all that you need, for the seals will not be removed for some days, and you will then have everything that belongs to you. In your own interest I have placed seals on your things too."

"Thank you," she said, pressing his hand. "Come and look at him once more. You would think he was sleeping."

The old man's face had at this moment the transient bloom of beauty which is seen on the face of those who have died without pain ; it seemed radiant.

"Did he not give you anything privately before he died?" asked the justice of Ursule in a whisper.

"Nothing," she replied. "He only said something about a letter——"

"Good! that will be found," said Bongrand. "Then it is lucky for you that they insisted on the seals."

At daybreak Ursule bade adieu to the house where her happy childhood had been spent, and above all to the room where her love had had its birth, and which was so dear to her that in the midst of her deep grief she had a tear of regret for this peaceful and happy nook. After gazing for the last time

on her windows and on Savinien in turn, she went off to the
inn, accompanied by La Bougival, who carried her bundle;
by the justice, who gave her his arm; and by Savinien, her
kind protector.

And so, in spite of every precaution, the suspicious lawyer
was in the right; Ursule would be bereft of fortune, and at
war with the heirs-at-law.

Next day the whole town followed Doctor Minoret's funeral.
When they heard of the conduct of the next-of-kin to Ursule,
most people thought it natural and necessary; there was an
inheritance at stake; the old man was miserly; Ursule might
fancy she had rights; the heirs were only protecting their
property; and, after all, she had humiliated them enough in
their uncle's time—he had made them as welcome as a dog
among ninepins. Désiré Minoret, who was doing no great
things in his office, said the neighbors who were envious of
the postmaster, came for the funeral. Ursule, unable to
attend, was in bed, ill of a nervous fever, brought on as much
by the insults offered her as by her deep grief.

"Just look at that hypocrite in tears," said some of the
faction, pointing to Savinien, who was in great sorrow for
the doctor's death.

"The question is whether he has any good cause for tears,"
remarked Goupil. "Do not laugh too soon; the seals have
not yet been removed."

"Pooh!" said Minoret, who knew more than he did,
"you have always frightened us for nothing."

Just as the procession was starting for the church, Goupil
had a bitter mortification; he was about to take Désiré's arm,
but the young man turned away, thus denying his comrade in
the eyes of all Nemours.

"It is of no use to be angry," said the clerk to himself;
"I should lose all chance of revenge," and his dry heart
swelled in his bosom like a sponge.

Before breaking the seals and making the inventory, they

had to wait for the public prosecutor's commission, as public guardian of all orphans, to be issued to Bongrand as his representative.   Then the Minoret property, of which every one had talked for ten days, was released, and the inventory was made and witnessed with every formality of the law. Dionis made a job of it ; Goupil was glad to have a finger in any mischief ; and as the business was a paying one, they took their time over it.   They generally breakfasted on the spot.   The notary, the clerks, heirs, and witnesses drank the finest wines in the cellar.

In a country town, where every one has his own house, it is rather difficult to find lodgings ; and when any business is for sale, the house commonly goes with it.   The justice, who was charged by the court with the guardianship of the orphan girl, saw no way of housing her out of the inn but by buying for her, in the High Street, at the corner of the bridge over the Loing, a small house, with a door opening into a passage ; on the ground floor was a sitting-room with two windows on the street, and a kitchen behind it, with a glass door looking into a yard of about a hundred square feet.   A narrow stair, with a borrowed light from the river-side, led to the first floor, containing three rooms, and to two attics above.

Monsieur Bongrand borrowed two thousand francs of La Bougival's savings to pay the first installment of the price of this house, which was six thousand francs, and he obtained a delay for the remainder.   To make room for the books which Ursule wished to buy back, Bongrand had a partition pulled down between two of the first-floor rooms, having ascertained that the depth of the house was sufficient to hold the bookshelves.   He and Savinien hurried on the workmen, who cleaned, painted, and restored this little dwelling with such effect, that, by the end of March, Ursule could move from the inn and find in the plain little house a bedroom just like that from which the heirs had ejected her, for it was full of the furniture brought away by the justice at the removal of the seals. La Bougival, sleeping overhead, could be brought down at the call of a bell which hung by her young mistress' bed.

The room intended for the library, the ground-floor sitting-room, and the kitchen, as yet unfurnished, were colored, repapered, and painted, awaiting the purchases the young girl might make at the sale of her godfather's household goods.

Though they well knew Ursule's strength of character, the justice and the curé both dreaded for her the sudden transition to a life so devoid of the elegance and luxury to which the doctor had always accustomed her. As to Savinien, he fairly wept over it; and he had secretly given the workmen and the upholsterer more than one gratuity in order that Ursule should find no difference, in her own room at least, between the old and the new. But the young girl, who found all her happiness in Savinien's eyes, showed the sweetest resignation. In these circumstances she charmed her two old friends, and proved to them, for the hundredth time, that only grief of heart could give her real suffering. Her sorrow at her godfather's death was too deep for her to feel the bitterness of her changed fortunes, which, nevertheless, raised a fresh obstacle in the way of her marriage. Savinien's dejection at seeing her brought so low was such that she felt obliged to say in his ear, as they came out of church the morning of her moving into her new abode :

"Love cannot live without patience; we must wait."

As soon as the preamble to the inventory was drawn up, Massin, advised by Goupil, who turned to him in his covert hatred of Minoret, hoping for more from the usurer's self-interest than from Zélie's thriftiness, foreclosed on Madame and Monsieur de Portenduère, whose term for payment had lapsed. The old lady was stunned by a summons to pay up 129,517 francs 55 centimes to the heirs-at-law within twenty-four hours, and interest from the day of the demand, under

penalty of the seizure of her landed estate.   To borrow money
to pay with was impossible.   Savinien went to consult a lawyer
at Fontainebleau.

"You have had a bad set to deal with who will make no compromise; their point is to drive you to extremities and take
possession of the farm at Bordières," said the lawyer.   "The
best thing will be to effect a voluntary sale so as to avoid costs."

This melancholy news was a blow to the old Bretonne, to
whom her son mildly remarked that if she had but consented
to his marriage during Minoret's lifetime, the doctor would
have placed all his possessions in the hands of Ursule's husband.   At this moment they would have been enjoying wealth
instead of suffering misery.   Though spoken in no tone of
reproach, this argument crushed the old lady quite as much as
the notion of an immediate and violent eviction.

Ursule, hardly recovered from her fever and the blow dealt
her by the doctor's next-of-kin, was bewildered with dismay
when she heard of this fresh disaster.   To love, and be unable
to help the person beloved, is one of the most terrible pangs
that the soul of a high-minded and delicately constituted
woman can suffer.

"I meant to buy my uncle's house," she said.   "I will
buy your mother's instead."

"Is it possible?" said Savinien.   "You are under age,
and cannot sell your securities without elaborate formalities,
to which the public prosecutor would not give his consent.
And, indeed, we shall attempt no resistance.   All the town
will look on with satisfaction at the discomfiture of a noble
house.   These townsfolk are like hounds at the death.   Happily, I still have ten thousand francs, on which my mother can
live till this deplorable business is wound up.   And, after all,
the inventory of your godfather's property is not yet complete.   Monsieur Bongrand still hopes to find something for
you.   He is as much surprised as I am to find you left penniless.   The doctor so often spoke to him and to me of the

handsome future he had prepared for you, that we cannot at all understand this state of things.''

"Oh," said she, "if I can but buy the books and my god-father's furniture, that they may not be dispersed or pass into strange hands, I am content with my lot."

"But who knows what price those rascally people may not set on the things you wish to have!"

From Montargis to Fontainebleau the Minoret heirs, and the million they hoped to find, were the talk of the country; but the most careful search made throughout the house since the removal of the seals had led to no discovery. The hundred and twenty-nine thousand francs of the Portenduère mortgage, the fifteen thousand francs a year in three per cents., then quoted at sixty-five, and yielding a capital of three hundred and eighty thousand, the house, valued at forty thousand francs, and the handsome furniture, amounted to a total of about six hundred thousand francs, which the outer world thought a very consoling figure.

Minoret had at this time some moments of acute uneasiness. La Bougival and Savinien, who, like the justice, persisted in believing in the existence of a will, came in after every day's cataloguing to ask Bongrand the result of the investigations. The doctor's old friend would exclaim, as the clerks and the heirs-at-law quitted the premises: "I cannot understand it?"

As, in the eyes of many superficial observers, two hundred thousand francs apiece to each inheritor seemed a very fair fortune for the provinces, it never occurred to any one to inquire how the doctor could have kept house as he had done on an income of no more than fifteen thousand francs, since he had never drawn the interest on the Portenduère mortgage. Bongrand, Savinien, and the curé alone asked this question in Ursule's interest, and, on hearing them give it utterance, the postmaster more than once turned pale.

"And yet we have certainly hunted everywhere—they to find a hoard, and I to find a will, in favor probably of Monsieur de Portenduère," said the justice the day the inventory was finished and signed. "They have sifted the ash-heap, raised the marble tops, felt in his slippers, pulled the bed-steads to pieces, emptied the mattresses, run pins into the counterpanes and coverlets, turned out his eiderdown quilt, examined every scrap of paper, every drawer, dug over the ground in the cellar ; and I was ready to bid them pull the house down."

"What do you think about it ?" asked the curé. "The will has been made away with by one of them."

"And the securities ?"

"Try to find them! Try to guess what such creatures would be at—as cunning, as wily, and as greedy as these Massins and Crémières. Make what you can of such a fortune as this Minoret's ; he gets two hundred thousand francs for his share, and he is going to sell his license, his house, and his interest in the Messageries for three hundred and fifty thousand! What sums of money! To say nothing of the savings on his thirty-odd thousand francs derived from real estate. Poor doctor!"

"The will might have been hidden in the library!" said Savinien.

"And, therefore, I did not dissuade the child from buying the books. But for that, would it not have been folly to let her spend all her ready money in books she will never look into ?"

The whole town had believed that the doctor's godchild was in possession of the undiscoverable securities ; but when it was known beyond a doubt that her fourteen thousand francs in consols and her little personalty constituted her whole fortune, the doctor's house and furniture excited the greatest curiosity. Some thought that bank-notes would be found in the stuffing of the chairs ; others that the old man must have hidden them in his books. The sale accordingly afforded the spectacle of the strange precautions taken by the heirs. Dionis, as auctioneer, explained with regard to each article put up for sale that the heirs-at-law were selling the piece of furniture only, and not anything that might be found in it ; then, before parting with it, they all submitted it to the closest scrutiny, pinched it, tapped it, shook it ; and then gazed after it with the fond looks of a father parting with his only son for a voyage to the Indies.

"Oh, mademoiselle," said La Bougival, on her return from the first morning's sale. "I will not go again. Monsieur Bongrand is right ; you could not bear to see it. Everything is upside down. They come and go as if it were the street ; the handsomest furniture is used for anything that is wanted ; they stand upon it ; there is such a mess that a hen could not find her chicks ! You might think there had been a fire. Everything is turned out into the courtyard, the wardrobes all open and empty ! Oh, poor, dear man, it is lucky for him he is dead ! This sale would have been the death of him !"

Bongrand, who was buying for Ursule the things of which the old man had been fond, and which were suitable for her small house, did not appear when the library was sold. Sharper than the heirs-at-law, whose greed would have made him pay too dear for the books, he gave a commission to a second-hand book-dealer at Melun, who came to Nemours on purpose, and who managed to secure several lots. As a consequence of the suspicions of the heirs, the books were sold one by one. Three thousand volumes were turned over, shaken one by one, held by the boards and fluttered, to make any paper fly out that might be hidden between the leaves ; finally, the bindings and backs were closely examined. The lots secured for Ursule mounted up to about six thousand five hundred francs, half of her claims on the estate.

The bookcase was not delivered over until it had been carefully examined by a cabinetmaker, noted for his experience of secret drawers and panels, who was sent for expressly, from Paris. When the justice gave orders that the bookcase and books should be conveyed to Mademoiselle Mirouët's house, the heirs-at-law felt some vague alarms, which were subsequently dissipated by seeing that she was no richer than before.

Minoret bought his uncle's house, which the co-heirs ran up to about fifty thousand francs, imagining that the postmaster hoped to find a treasure in the walls. And the deed of sale contained stipulations on this point. A fortnight after the conclusion of the whole business, Minoret, having sold his post-horses and his business to the son of a wealthy farmer, moved into his uncle's house, on which he spent considerable sums in improvements and repairs. So Minoret condemned himself to live within a few yards of Ursule.

"I only hope," said he to Dionis the day when Savinien and his mother had notice of the foreclosure, "that now we shall be rid of this precious nobility. We will turn them out, one by one."

"The old lady, with her fourteen quarterings, will not stay to witness the disaster," said Goupil. "She will go to die in Brittany, where, no doubt, she will find a wife for her son."

"I don't think so," replied the notary, who, that morning, had drawn up the agreement of purchase for Bongrand. "Ursule has just bought the widow Richard's little house."

"That cursed little fool does not know what to do next to annoy us!" cried Minoret, very rashly.

"Why, what can it matter to you if she lives at Nemours?" asked Goupil, astonished at the vehement disgust shown by the great simpleton.

"Do you not know," said Minoret, turning as red as a poppy, "that my son is fool enough to be in love with her? I would give a hundred crowns to see Ursule well out of Nemours."

From this it is easy to understand how much Ursule, poor and resigned as she was, would be in Minoret's way, with all

his money. The worry of securities to be realized, of selling
his business, the expeditions consequent on such unwonted
affairs, his disputes with his wife over every little detail, and
the purchase of the doctor's house, where Zélie wished to live
quite plainly for her son's sake—all this turmoil, so unlike
the quiet course of his usual life, prevented the great Minoret
from thinking of his victim. But a few days after he had
settled in the Rue des Bourgeois, about the middle of May,
on returning from a walk, he heard the sounds of a piano,
and saw La Bougival sitting in the window, like a dragon
guarding a treasure; and at the same moment he heard an
importunate voice within himself.

An explanation of the reason why, in a man of his temper,
the sight of Ursule, who did not even suspect the theft he
had committed to her injury, became at once unendurable,
why the sight of her dignity in misfortune filled him with the
desire to get her out of the town, and why this desire assumed
the character of hatred and passion, would lead perhaps to a
complete moral treatise. Perhaps he felt that he was not the
legitimate possessor of the thirty-six thousand francs while
she to whom they belonged was so close to him. Perhaps he
thought that by some chance his theft would be discovered, so
long as those he had robbed were within reach. Perhaps,
even, in a nature so primitive, so rough-hewn as his was, and
hitherto always law-abiding, Ursule's presence awoke some
kind of remorse. Perhaps this remorse was the more poig-
nant because he had so much more wealth than had been
legitimately acquired.

He no doubt ascribed these stirrings of his conscience
wholly to Ursule's presence, fancying that if she were out of
sight these uncomfortable pangs would vanish too. Or perhaps, again, crime has its own counsel of perfection. An ill
deed begun may demand its climax, a first blow may require
a second—a death-blow. Robbery, perhaps, inevitably leads
to murder. Minoret had committed the theft without a mo-

ment's pause for reflection, events had crowded on so swiftly; reflection came afterwards. Now, if the reader has fully pictured the appearance and build of this man, he will understand the prodigious results on him of an idea. Remorse is more than an idea; it is the outcome of a feeling which can no more be smothered than love can, and which is tyrannous too. But just as Minoret had not hesitated for an instant to possess himself of the fortune intended for Ursule, so he mechanically felt the need of getting her away from Nemours when the sight of her cheated innocence stung him. Being an imbecile, he never considered consequences; he went on from danger to danger, urged by his instinctive cupidity, like a wild animal which cannot foresee the wiles of the hunter; and trusts to its swiftness and strength.

Before long the richer townspeople, who were wont to meet at the notary's office, observed a change in the manners and demeanor of the man who had always been so light-hearted.

"I cannot think what has come over Minoret," said his wife, to whom he had never revealed his bold stroke. "He is ill anyhow."

The world at large accounted for Minoret's being sick of himself—for in his face the expression of thought was one of boredom—by the fact that he had absolutely nothing to do, and by the transition from an active to an indolent life. While Minoret was scheming to crush Ursule's life, La Bougival never let a day pass without making to her foster-child some allusion to the fortune she ought to have had, or comparing her humble lot with that which the late "Monsieur" had intended her to enjoy, and of which he had spoken to her—La Bougival.

"And besides," said she, "it is not out of greediness; but would not monsieur, so kind as he was, have left me some little money?"

"Am I not here?" Ursule would reply, and forbid any further words on the subject.

She could not bear the taint of any self-interested thought to touch the loving, melancholy and sweet memories which clung round the image of the old doctor, of whom a sketch in black and white chalk, done by her drawing-master, hung in her little sitting-room. To her fresh and strong imagination the sight of this sketch was sufficient to bring her godfather before her; she thought of him constantly, and was surrounded by the objects he had loved—his deep armchair, the furniture of his study, his backgammon-board, and the piano he had given her. The two old friends who remained to her, the Abbé Chaperon and Monsieur Bongrand, the only persons whose visits she would receive, were like two living memories of the past in the midst of the objects to which her regrets almost gave life—of that past which was linked to the present by the love which her godfather had approved and blessed.

Ere long the sadness of her thoughts, insensibly softened by time, cast its hue on all her life, bringing everything into indefinable harmony; exquisite neatness, perfect order in the arrangement of the furniture, a few flowers brought every morning by Savinien, pretty nothings, a stamp of peace set on everything by the young girl's habits, and which made her home attractive. After breakfast and after church she regularly practiced and sang; then she took her embroidery, sitting in the window towards the street. At four o'clock Savinien, on his return from the walk he took in all weathers, would find the window half-open, and sit on the outer sill to chat with her for half an hour. In the evening the curé or the justice would call, but she would never allow Savinien to accompany them. Nor would she accept a proposal from Madame de Portenduère, whom her son persuaded to invite Ursule to live with her.

The young girl and La Bougival lived with the strictest economy; they did not spend, on all included, more than sixty francs a month. The old nurse was indefatigable; she

washed and ironed, she cooked only twice a week, and kept
the remains of the cooked food, which the mistress and maid
ate cold ; for Ursule hoped to save seven hundred francs a
year to pay the remainder of the price of her house.   This
austere conduct, with her modesty and resignation to a penuri-
ous life, after having enjoyed a luxurious existence, when her
lightest whims were worshiped, gained her the regard of certain persons.   She was respected, and never talked about.
The heirs, once satisfied, did her full justice.   Savinien admired such strength of character in so young a girl.   Now
and again, on coming out of church, Madame de Portenduère would say a few kind words to Ursule ; she invited her
to dinner twice, and came herself to fetch her.   If it were
not indeed happiness, at any rate it was peace.

   But a successful transaction, in which the justice displayed
his old skill as a lawyer, brought to a head Minoret's persecution of Ursule, which had hitherto smoldered, and not gone
beyond covert ill-will.   As soon as the old doctor's estate was
fairly settled, the justice, at Ursule's entreaty, took up the
cause of the Portenduères, and undertook to get them out of
their difficulties ; but, in calling on the old lady, whose opposition to Ursule's happiness made him furious, he did not
conceal from her that he was devoting himself to her interests
solely to please Mademoiselle Mirouët.   He selected one of
his former clerks to plead for the Portenduères at Fontainebleau, and himself conducted the appeal for a decree against
foreclosure.   He intended to take advantage of the interval
of time which must elapse between the granting of this decree
and Massin's renewed appeal to re-let the farm at a rent of
six thousand francs, and to extract from the lessee a good
premium and the payment of a year's rent in advance.
Thenceforth the whist parties met again at Madame de Portenduère's, consisting of himself and the curé, Savinien and
Ursule, for whom the justice and the abbé called every evening, and they saw her home again.

In June, Bongrand got his decree annulling the proceedings
taken by Massin against the Portenduères.   He at once signed
a new lease ; got thirty-two thousand francs from the farmer,
and a rent of six thousand francs a year for eight years ; then,
in the evening, before the transactions could get abroad, he
went to Zélie, who, as he knew, was puzzled for an investment
for her savings, and suggested to her that she should buy
Bordières for two hundred and twenty thousand francs.

"I would clinch the bargain on the spot," said Minoret,
"if only I were sure that the Portenduères were going to live
anywhere than at Nemours."

"Why?" asked the justice.

"We want to be quit of nobles at Nemours," frankly answered Minoret.

"I fancy I have heard the old lady say that if she could
settle matters, she could live nowhere but in Brittany on what
would be left.   She talks of selling her house."

"Well, sell it to me then," said Minoret.

"But you talk as if the money were yours !" said Zélie.
"What are you going to do with two houses?"

"If I do not settle the matter of the farm with you this
evening," said the justice, "our lease will become known ;
we shall have fresh proceedings against us in three days, and
I shall fail to pull the thing through.   My heart is set on it ;
I shall go on, this very hour, to Melun, where some farmers I
know will take Bordières off my hands with their eyes shut.
Then you will have lost the opportunity of an investment at
three per cent. in the district of Le Rouvre."

"And why then did you come to us?" said Zélie.

"Because I know you to be rich, while my older clients
will want a few days to enable them to hand over a hundred
and twenty-nine thousand francs.   I want no delays."

"Get *her* away from Nemours, and they are yours !" said
Minoret.

"You must see that I cannot pledge the Portenduères in

any way," replied Bongrand, "but I feel sure that they will not remain at Nemours."

On this assurance Minoret, to whom Zélie gave a nudge, undertook to pay off the Portenduères' debt to the doctor's estate. The contract for the sale was made out by Dionis, and the justice, very content, made Minoret agree to the terms of the renewed lease, though he perceived rather late, as well as Zélie, that the rent was payable a year in advance, leaving the last year, in point of fact, rent free.

By the end of June, Bongrand could take Madame de Portenduère a receipt in full and the remnant of her fortune, a hundred and twenty-nine thousand francs, which he advised her to invest in state securities at five per cent., as well as Savinien's ten thousand; this yielded an income of about six thousand francs a year. Thus, instead of having lost, the old lady had gained two thousand francs a year by the sale of her estate. She and her son therefore remained at Nemours.

Minoret thought he had been tricked, as if the justice could possibly have known that it was Ursule's presence that was intolerable to him, and felt a deep resentment, which added to his hatred of his victim. Then began the covert drama, terrible in its effects, the struggle between two persons' feelings: Minoret's, which prompted him to drive Ursule to leave Nemours; and Ursule's, which gave her the fortitude to endure a persecution of which the cause for long remained inexplicable, a singular state of things to which previous events had all led up and conduced, and to which they had been the prologue.

Madame Minoret, to whom her husband presented plate and a dinner service worth altogether twenty thousand francs, gave a handsome dinner every Sunday, the day on which her son brought friends over from Fontainebleau. For these banquets Zélie would send for some rare dainties from Paris, thus inciting Dionis the notary to imitate her display. Goupil, whom the Minorets did their utmost to banish as a man of ill-repute and a blot on their magnificence, was not invited to the house till the end of July, a month after the retirement into private ease of the old postmaster and mistress. The clerk, quite alive to this deliberate neglect, was obliged to treat even Désiré with formality, and drop the familiar *tu;* and Désiré, since his appointment to official life, had assumed a grave and haughty air even among his family.

"You have forgotten Esther, then, since you are in love with Mademoiselle Mirouët?" said Goupil to the young lawyer.

"In the first place, Esther is dead, monsieur. And, in the second, I never thought of Ursule," was the reply.

"Hey day—what did you tell me, Daddy Minoret?" cried Goupil audaciously.

Minoret, caught in the very act by so formidable a foe, would have been put out of countenance but for the scheme for which he had invited Goupil to dinner, remembering the proposal formerly made by the clerk to hinder Ursule's marriage to young Portenduère. His only answer was to lead the clerk abruptly away and out into the garden.

"You are nearly eight-and-twenty, my good fellow," said he, "and I do not see that you are on the high-road to fortune. I wish you well; for, after all, you were my son's companion. Listen to me: If you can persuade that little Mirouët to become your wife—she has forty thousand francs at any rate—as sure as my name is Minoret, I will give you the money to buy a business at Orleans."

"No," said Goupil, "I should never become known. At Montargis——"

"No," interrupted Minoret, "but at Sens——"

"Very good, say Sens," replied the hideous clerk. "It is an archbishop's see, and I have no objection to a religious centre. A little hypocrisy helps one to get on. Besides, the girl is very pious; she will be a success there."

13

" It must be quite understood that I only give the hundred thousand francs in consideration of my young relative's marriage. I wish to provide for her out of regard for my deceased uncle."

"And why not out of regard for me ? " said Goupil mischievously, for he suspected some secret motive for Minoret's conduct. " Was it not information given by me that enabled you to get twenty-four thousand francs in rent from a single holding in a ring fence round the Château du Rouvre? With your meadows and mill on the other side of the Loing you can add sixteen thousand to that. Come, old Burly, will you play your game with me above board ? "

" Yes."

"Well, just to make you feel my claws, I was brewing a plan with Massin to get possession of Le Rouvre—park, gardens, preserves, timber, and all."

" You had better ! " exclaimed Zélie, interrupting them.

" Well," said Goupil, with a viperine glance at her, "if I choose, Massin will have it all to-morrow for two hundred thousand francs."

" Leave us, wife," said the colossus, taking Zélie by the arm, and turning her about. " We understand each other. We have had so much business on our hands," he went on, coming back to Goupil, " that we have not been able to think of you; but I rely on your friendship to let us get Le Rouvre."

" An old marquisate," said Goupil slyly, " which in your hands will soon be worth fifty thousand francs a year—more than two millions at the present price of money."

" And then our boy can marry the daughter of a Marshal of France, or the heiress of some ancient house, which will help him on to be a judge in Paris," said the postmaster, opening his huge snuff-box, and offering it to Goupil.

" Well, then, all is square and above board ? " asked Goupil, shaking his fingers.

Minoret wrung his hand and said—

"My word of honor."

Like all cunning men, the clerk fancied, happily for Minoret, that this marriage with Ursule was a mere excuse for making up to him, now he had been playing off Massin against them.

"It is not his doing," said he to himself. "I know my Zélie's hand ; she has taught him his part. Bah ! Let Massin slide ! Within three years I shall be returned as député for Sens," he thought.

Then, catching sight of Bongrand on his way to his game of whist over the way, he rushed into the street.

"You take a great interest in Ursule Mirouët, my dear Monsieur Bongrand," said he ; "you cannot be indifferent to her future prospects. This is our programme. She may marry a notary whose business is to be in a large district town. This notary, who will certainly be député in three years, will settle a hundred thousand francs on her."

"She can do better," said Bongrand stiffly. "Since Madame de Portenduère's misfortunes her health is failing. Yesterday she looked dreadfully ill ; she is dying of grief. Savinien will have six thousand francs a year ; Ursule has forty thousand francs ; I will invest their capital on Massin's principle—but honestly—and in ten years they will have a little fortune."

"Savinien would be a fool. He can marry Mademoiselle du Rouvre any day he likes, an only daughter, to whom her uncle and aunt will also leave splendid fortunes."

" 'When love has gotten hold of us, farewell prudence,' says La Fontaine. But who is this worthy notary, for, after all——? " said Bongrand, out of curiosity.

"I," said Goupil, in a tone that made the justice start.

"You ? " said he, not attempting to conceal his disgust.

"Very good, sir ; your servant," retorted Goupil, with a glare of venom, hatred, and defiance.

"Would you like to be the wife of a notary who will settle a hundred thousand francs on you?" cried Bongrand, entering the little sitting-room, and speaking to Ursule, who was sitting by Madame de Portenduère. Ursule and Savinien started as if by one impulse, and looked at each other; she with a smile, he not daring to show his uneasiness.

"I am not my own mistress," replied Ursule, holding out her hand to Savinien in such a way that his old mother could not see it.

"I refused the offer without consulting you even."

"But why?" said Madame de Portenduère. "It seems to me, my dear, that a notary's profession is a very respectable one."

"I prefer my peaceful poverty," she replied, "for it is opulence in comparison with what I had a right to expect of life. My old nurse spares me many anxieties, and I would not exchange my present lot, which suits me, for an unknown future."

Next morning the post brought a poisoned dart to two hearts in the shape of two anonymous letters—one to Madame de Portenduère, and one to Ursule. This is the letter received by the old lady:

"You love your son, you would wish to see him married as beseems the name he bears, and you are fostering his fancy for an ambitious little thing without any fortune, by receiving at your house one Ursule, the daughter of a regimental bandmaster; while you might marry him to Mademoiselle du Rouvre, whose two uncles, the Marquis de Ronquerolles and the Chevalier du Rouvre, each having thirty thousand francs a year, intend to settle a large sum on their niece on her marriage, so as not to leave their fortune to her foolish old father, M. du Rouvre, who wastes his substance. Madame de Sérizy—Aunt Clémentine du Rouvre—who has just lost her only son in Algiers, will no doubt also adopt her niece. Some one who wishes you well believes that Savinien would be accepted."

This is the letter written to Ursule:

"DEAR URSULE:—There is in Nemours a young man who idolizes you; he cannot see you at work at your window without such emotions as prove to him that his love is for life. This young man is gifted with a will of iron and a perseverance which nothing can daunt. Accept his love with favor, for his intentions are of the purest, and he humbly asks your hand in the hope of making you happy. His fortune, though suitable even now, is nothing to what he will make it when you are his wife. You will some day be received at court as the wife of a minister, and one of the first ladies in the land. As he sees you every day, though you cannot see him, place one of La Bougival's pots of pinks in your window, and that will tell him that he may appear before you."

Ursule burnt this letter without mentioning it to Savinien. Two days later she received another, in these terms:

"You were wrong, dear Ursule, not to reply to him who loves you better than his life. You fancy you will marry Savinien, but you are strangely mistaken. That marriage will never take place. Madame de Portenduère, who will see you no more at her house, is going this morning to La Rouvre, on foot, in spite of the weak state she is in, to ask Mademoiselle du Rouvre in marriage for Savinien. He will finally yield. What objection can he make? The young lady's uncles will settle their fortune on their niece at her marriage. That fortune amounts to sixty thousand francs a year."

This letter tortured Ursule's heart by making her acquainted with the torments of jealousy, pangs hitherto unknown, which, to her finely organized nature, so alive to suffering, swamped the present, the future, and even the past in grief. From the

moment when she received this fatal missive, she sat motionless in the doctor's armchair, her eyes fixed on vacancy, and
lost in a sorrowful reverie. In an instant the chill of death had
come on her instead of the glow of exquisite life. Alas! It
was worse; it was, in fact, the dreadful awakening of the
dead to find that there is no God—the masterpiece of that
strange genius Jean Paul. Four times did La Bougival try to
persuade Ursule to eat her breakfast; she saw the girl take up
her bread and lay it down again, unable to carry it to her
lips. When she ventured to offer a remonstrance, Ursule
stopped her with a wave of the hand, saying Hush! in a
terrible tone, as despotic as it had hitherto always been sweet.
La Bougival, watching her mistress through a glass door between the rooms, saw her turn alternately as red as if fever
were consuming her, and then blue, as though an ague fit had
followed the fever. By about four o'clock, when Ursule rose
every few minutes to look whether Savinien was coming, and
Savinien came not, she became evidently worse. Jealousy
and doubt destroy all the bashfulness of love. Ursule, who
till now had never allowed her passion to be detected in the
least gesture, put on her hat and her little shawl, and ran into
the passage to go out and meet Savinien; but a remnant of
reserve brought her back into the little sitting-room. There
she wept.

When the curé came in the evening, the poor old nurse
stopped him on the threshold.

" Oh, Monsieur le Curé, I do not know what ails mademoiselle; she——"

" I know," said the priest sadly, silencing the frightened
attendant.

The abbé then told Ursule what she had not dared to ask :
" Madame de Portenduère had gone to dine at Le Rouvre."

" And Savinien ? "

" He too."

Ursule shuddered nervously—a shudder which thrilled the

Abbé Chaperon as though he had received a shock from a Leyden jar, and he felt a painful turmoil at his heart.

"So we shall not go to her house this evening," said he. "But, indeed, my child, you will be wise never to go there again. The old lady might receive you in a way that would wound your pride. We, having brought her to listen to the idea of your marriage to Savinien, cannot imagine what ill-wind has blown to change her views in an instant."

"I am prepared for anything; nothing can astonish me now," said Ursule in a tone of conviction. "In such extremities it is a great comfort to feel that I have done nothing to offend God."

"Submit, my dear daughter, and never try to inquire into the ways of Providence," said the curé.

"I do not wish to show any unjust suspicion of M. de Portenduère's character——"

"Why do you no longer call him Savinien?" asked the abbé, observing a certain bitterness in Ursule's tone.

"My dear Savinien!" she went on, with a burst of tears. "Yes, my good friend," she said, sobbing, "a voice assures me that his heart is as noble as his birth. He has not merely told me that he loves me; he has proved it in a thousand delicate ways, and by heroically controlling the ardor of his passion. Lately, when he took my hand that I held out to him, when Monsieur Bongrand proposed to me for a notary, I declare to you that it was the first time I had ever offered it to him. Though he began, by a jest, blowing me a kiss across the street, since then our affection has never once, as you know, overstepped the strictest limits; but I may tell you—you who read my whole soul excepting the one spot which is open only to the angels—well, this affection is in me the foundation of many virtues. It has enabled me to accept my poverty; it has, perhaps, softened the bitterness of the irreparable loss for which I mourn now more in my garments than in my heart! Yes, I have done wrong—for my love has been greater than my gratitude to my godfather; and God has avenged him! How could I help it? What I valued myself for was as Savinien's wife. I have been too proud; and it is that pride, perhaps, that God is punishing. God alone, as you have often told me, ought to be the spring and end of all we do."

The curé was touched as he saw the tears rolling down her cheeks, already paler. The greater the poor girl's confidence had been, the lower she had fallen.

"However," she went on, "reduced once more to my orphaned state, I shall be able to accustom myself to the proper frame of mind. After all, could I bear to be a stone round the neck of the man I love! What should he do here? Who am I that I should aspire to him? Do I not love him with such perfect love that it is equal to a complete sacrifice of my happiness, of my hopes? And you know I have often blamed myself for setting my love on a tomb, and looking forward to the morrow of that old lady's death. If Savinien can be rich and happy through another woman, I have just money enough to purchase my admission to a convent, to which I shall at once retire. There ought not to be two loves in a woman's heart, any more than there are two Lords in heaven. The religious life will have its charms for me."

"He could not allow his mother to go alone to Le Rouvre," said the kind priest gently.

"We will talk no more of it, my dear Monsieur Chaperon. I will write to him this evening to give him his liberty. I am glad to be obliged to close the windows of my sitting-room."

She then told him about the anonymous letters, saying that she would offer no encouragement to this unknown suitor.

"Ah! then it is an anonymous letter that has prompted Madame de Portenduère's expedition to Le Rouvre!" exclaimed the curé. "You are, no doubt, the object of some malignant persecution."

"But why? Neither Savinien nor I have injured any one, and we are doing no harm to any one here."

"Well, well, my child. We will take advantage of this tornado which has broken up our little party to arrange our poor old friend's books; they are still piled in disorder. Bongrand and I will set them straight, for we had thought of hunting through them. Put your trust in God; but remember, too, that in the justice and myself you have two devoted friends."

"And that is much," she said, walking to the end of the little alley with the priest, and craning her neck like a bird looking out of its nest, still hoping to see Savinien.

At this instant Minoret and Goupil, coming home from a walk in the country, stopped as they were passing, and the heir-at-law said to Ursule—

"What is the matter, cousin?—for we are still cousins, are we not? You look altered."

Goupil cast such ardent eyes on Ursule that she was frightened. She ran in without replying.

"She is a wild bird," said Minoret to the curé.

"Mademoiselle Mirouët is quite right not to talk to men on her doorstep; she is too young——"

"Oh!" said Goupil; "you must be well aware that she does not lack lovers!"

The curé bowed hastily, and hurried off to the Rue des Bourgeois.

"Well," said the lawyer's clerk to Minoret, "the fat is burning. She is as pale as death already; within a fortnight she will have left the town. You will see."

"It is better to have you for a friend than for an enemy," said Minoret, struck by the horrible smile which gave to Goupil's face the diabolical expression which Joseph Bridau gave to Goethe's Mephistopheles.

"I believe you!" replied Goupil. "If she will not marry me, I will make her die of grief."

"Do so, boy, and I will give you money enough to start in business in Paris. Then you can marry a rich wife——"

"Poor girl!—why, what harm has she done to you?" asked the clerk in surprise.

"I am sick of her," said Minoret roughly.

"Only wait till Monday, and you shall see how I will make her squirm," replied Goupil, studying the postmaster's countenance.

Next morning La Bougival went to see Savinien, and as she gave him a note, she said, "I don't know what the dear child has written to you about, but she looks like a corpse this morning."

Who, on reading this letter to Savinien, can fail to picture the sufferings Ursule must have endured during the past night?

"My dear Savinien:—Your mother wishes you to marry Mademoiselle du Rouvre, I am told; perhaps she is right. You see yourself between a life almost of poverty and a position of wealth, between the wife of your heart and a woman of fashion, between obedience to your mother and obedience to your own choice—for I still believe that I am your choice. Savinien, since you must decide, I wish that you should do so in perfect freedom. I give you back your word—given not to me, but to yourself, at a moment which I can never forget, and which, like all the days that have passed since then, was angelically pure and sweet. That memory will be enough for me to live on. If you should persist in adhering to your vows, a dark and dreadful thought would always trouble my happiness. In the midst of our privations, which you now take so lightly, you might afterwards reflect that, if you had but followed the rules of the world, things might have been very different with you. If you were the man to utter such a thought, it would be my death-warrant in bitter anguish; and if you did not say it, I should be suspicious of the slightest cloud on your brow. Dear Savinien, I have always cared for you more than for anything on earth. I might do so; for my godfather, though jealous of you, said to me, 'Love him, my child! you will certainly be his, and he yours some day.' When I went to Paris I loved you without hope, and that love was enough for me. I do not know whether I can revert to that state of mind, but I will try. What are we to each other at this moment? A brother and sister. Let us remain so. Marry the happy girl, whose joy it will be to restore to your name the lustre due to it, which I, according to your mother, must tarnish. You shall never hear me mentioned. The world will applaud you; I, believe me, shall never blame you, and shall always love you. So, farewell."

"Wait!" cried the young man. He made La Bougival sit down, and, going to his desk, he hastily wrote these few lines:

"MY DEAR URSULE :—Your letter breaks my heart, for you are inflicting on yourself much useless pain, and for the first time our hearts have failed to understand each other. That you are not already my wife is because I cannot yet marry without my mother's consent. After all, are not eight thousand francs a year, in a pretty cottage on the banks of the Loing, quite a fortune? We calculated that, with La Bougival, we could save five thousand francs a year. You allowed me one evening in your uncle's garden to regard you as my promised wife, and you cannot by yourself alone break the ties which bind us both. Need I tell you that I plainly declared, yesterday, to Monsieur du Rouvre that, even if I were free, I would not accept a fortune from a young lady whom I did not know? My mother refuses to see you any more; I lose the happiness of my evenings, but do not abridge the brief moments when I may speak with you at your window. Till this evening, then—— Nothing can part us."

"Go now, my good woman. She must not have a moment's needless anxiety."

That afternoon, on his return from the walk he took every day on purpose to pass by Ursule's dwelling, Savinien found her somewhat the paler for all these sudden agitations.

"I feel as though I had never till this moment known what a happiness it is to see you," said she.

"You yourself said to me," replied Savinien, with a smile, "that 'Love cannot exist without patience; I will wait'— for I remember all your words. But have you, my dear child, divided love from faith? Ah! this is the end of all our differences. You have always said that you loved me more than I could love you. But have I ever doubted you?" he asked, giving her a bunch of wildflowers chosen so as to symbolize his feelings.

"You have no reason to doubt me," she replied. "Besides, you do not know all," she added, in a tone of uneasiness.

She had given orders that no letters to her by post should be taken in. But without her being able to guess by what conjuring trick the thing had been done, a few minutes after Savinien had left her, and she had watched him round the turning of the Rue des Bourgeois out of the High Street, she found on her armchair a piece of paper on which was written—

"Tremble! the lover scorned will be worse than a tiger."

Notwithstanding Savinien's entreaties, she would not, out of prudence, trust him with the dreadful secret of her fears. The ineffable joy of seeing him again, after believing him lost to her, could alone enable her to forget the mortal chill which came over her. Every one knows the intolerable torment of awaiting an indefinite misfortune. Suffering then assumes the proportions of the unknown, which is certainly infinitude, to the mind. To Ursule it was the greatest anguish. She found herself starting violently at the slightest sound; she distrusted the silence; she suspected the walls of conspiracies. Her peaceful sleep was broken. Goupil, without knowing anything of her constitution—as fragile as that of a flower—had, by the instinct of wickedness, hit on the poison that would blight it—kill it.

The next day, however, passed without any shock. Ursule played the piano till very late, and went to bed almost reassured, and overpowered by sleep. At about midnight she was roused by a band, consisting of a clarionet, a hautboy, a flute, a cornet-à-pistons, a trombone, a bassoon, a fife, and a triangle. All the neighbors were at their windows. The poor child, upset by seeing a crowd in the street, was struck to the heart on hearing a hoarse, vulgar man's voice crying out—

"For the fair Ursule Mirouët, a serenade from her lover!"

At church next morning all the town was in a hubbub; and as Ursule entered and quitted the church, she saw the square filled with groups staring at her, and displaying the most odious curiosity. The serenade had set every tongue wagging, for every one was lost in conjecture. Ursule got home more dead than alive, and went out no more, the curé having advised her to say vespers at home. On going in she saw, lying in the passage paved with red brick that ran from the street to the courtyard behind, a letter that had been slipped under the door; she picked it up and read it, prompted by the desire for some explanation. The least sensitive reader can imagine her feelings as she saw these terrible words:

"Make up your mind to be my wife, rich and adored. I will have you. If you are not mine alive, you shall be, dead. You may ascribe to your refusal misfortunes which will not fall on you alone. HE WHO LOVES YOU AND WILL SOME DAY POSSESS YOU."

Strange irony! at the moment when the gentle victim

of this conspiracy was drooping like a plucked flower, Mesdemoiselles Massin, Dionis, and Crémière were envying her lot.

"She is a happy girl," they were saying. "Men are devoted to her, flatter her taste, are ready to quarrel for her. The serenade was delightful, it would seem! There was a cornet-à-pistons!"

"What is a cornet-à-pistons?"

"A new sort of musical instrument—there—as long as that!" said Angélique Crémière to Paméla Massin.

Early the next day Savinien went off to Fontainebleau to inquire who had ordered the musicians of the regiment stationed there; but, as there were two men to each instrument, it was impossible to ascertain which one had gone to Nemours, since the colonel prohibited them from playing for private persons without his leave. Monsieur de Portenduère had an interview with the public prosecutor, Ursule's legal guardian, and explained to him the serious effect such scenes must have on a young girl so delicate and fragile as she was, begging him to find out the instigator of this serenade by means that the law could set in motion.

Three days later, in the middle of the night, a second serenade was given by three violins, a flute, a guitar, and a hautboy. On this occasion the musicians made off by the road to Montargis, where there was just then a troupe of actors. Between two pieces a strident and drunken voice had proclaimed:

"To the daughter of Bandmaster Mirouët."

Thus all Nemours was apprised of the profession of Ursule's father, the secret the old doctor had so carefully kept.

But this time Savinien did not go to Montargis; he received in the course of the day an anonymous letter from Paris containing this terrible prophecy:

"You shall not marry Ursule. If you wish her to live, make haste and surrender her to him who loves her more than

you do ; for he has become a musician and an artist to please
her, and would rather see her dead than as your wife.''

By this time the town doctor of Nemours was seeing Ursule
three times a day, for this covert persecution had brought her
to the point of death. Plunged, as she felt herself, by a
diabolical hand into a slough of mud, the gentle girl behaved
like a martyr; she lay perfectly silent, raising her eyes to
heaven, without tears, awaiting further blows with fervent
prayer, and hoping for the stroke that might be her death.

"I am glad to be unable to go downstairs," said she to
Monsieur Bongrand and the abbé, who stayed with her as
much as possible. *"He* would come, and I feel unworthy
to meet the looks with which he is in the habit of making me
blest. Do you think he doubts me ?"

"Why, if Savinien cannot discover the moving spirit of all
this shameful business, he means to ask for the intervention of
the Paris police," said Bongrand.

"The unknown persons must know that they have killed
me," she replied. " They will be quiet now."

The curé, Bongrand, and Savinien puzzled themselves with
conjectures and suppositions. Savinien, Tiennette, La Bougival, and two devoted adherents of the curé's constituted
themselves ˋspies, and were constantly on the watch for a
whole week ; but Goupil could never be betrayed by a sign,
he pulled all the wires with his own hand. The justice was
the first to suspect that the author of the evil was frightened
at his own success. Ursule was as pale and weak as a consumptive English girl. The spies relaxed their efforts. There
were no more serenades nor letters. Savinien ascribed the
cessation of these odious means to the secret energy of the
law officers, to whom he had sent the letters written to Ursule,
to himself, and to his mother.

The armistice was of no long duration. When the doctor
had checked the course of Ursule's nervous fever, just as she

was recovering her spirit, one morning, about the middle of
July, a ladder of ropes was found attached to her window.
The postillion who had ridden with the night mail deposed
that a little man was in the act of coming down it just as he
was passing; but in spite of his wishing to stop, his horses,
having set off down hill from the bridge, at the corner of
which stood Ursule's little house, had carried him some way
out of Nemours.

An opinion, suggested in Dionis' drawing-room, attributed
these manœuvres to the Marquis du Rouvre, at that time in
great need of money, who, it was supposed, by hastening
Savinien's marriage with his daughter, would be able to save
the Château of Le Rouvre from his creditors. Madame de
Portenduère also, it was said, looked with favor on anything
that could discredit, dishonor, and blight Ursule; but when
the young girl seemed likely to die, the old lady was almost
conquered.

This last stroke of malice so much distressed the Curé
Chaperon that it made him ill enough to compel him to
remain at home for some days. Poor Ursule, in whom this
cruel attack had brought on a relapse, received by post a
note from the curé, which was not refused, as his writing
was familiar.

" My child, leave Nemours, and so discomfort the malice
of your unknown enemies. Perhaps what they aim at is to
imperil Savinien's life. I will tell you more when I can go
to see you." This note was signed, " Your devoted friend
Chaperon."

When Savinien, almost driven mad, went to call on the
priest, the poor man read and re-read the letter, so much was
he horrified at the perfection with which his writing and
signature had been imitated, for he had written nothing, and,
if he had written, he would not have employed the post to
carry a letter to Ursule. The mortal anguish to which this
last villainy reduced Ursule compelled Savinien once more to

apply to the public prosecutor, showing him the forged letter
from the abbé.

"It is murder," said the young man to the lawyer. "Murder is being committed by means not provided against by law,
on the person of an orphan placed under your protection by
the Civil Code."

"If you can discover any means of interfering," replied
the public prosecutor, "I am ready to adopt them; but I
know of none. This rascally anonymous letter gives the best
advice. Mademoiselle Mirouët must be sent to the care of
the Ladies of the Adoration. Meanwhile, by my order, the
commissary of police at Fontainebleau will authorize you to
carry weapons in your own defense. I myself have been to
Le Rouvre, and Monsieur du Rouvre is justifiably indignant
at the suspicions that have attached to him. Minoret, my
deputy's father, is in treaty for the purchase of his château.
Mademoiselle du Rouvre is to marry a rich Polish count.
Monsieur du Rouvre himself was about to leave the neighborhood on the day of my visit, to escape being seized for debt."

Désiré, questioned by his chief, dared not say what he
thought; he recognized Goupil in all this. Goupil alone
was capable of conducting a plot which should thus shave
close to the Penal Code without being amenable to any of its
provisions. The impunity, the secrecy, the success of it, increased Goupil's audacity. The terrible man had set Massin,
who had become his dupe, on the tracks of the Marquis du
Rouvre, to compel that gentleman to sell the rest of his land
to Minoret. After opening negotiations with a notary at
Sens, he determined to try a last stroke to gain possession of
Ursule. He thought he could imitate some young men of
Paris, who owed their wife and fortune to an elopement. His
services done to Minoret, Massin, and Crémière, and the protection of Dionis, mayor of Nemours, would allow of his
hushing the matter up. He at once determined to cast off his
mask, believing that Ursule was incapable of resistance in the

14

state of weakness to which he had brought her. However, before risking the last card of his base game, he thought it well to havé an explanation at Le Rouvre, whither he went with Minoret, who was going there for the first time since the agreement was signed.

Minoret had just received a confidential letter from his son, asking him for information as to what was going on with regard to Ursule, before going himself with the public prosecutor to place her in a convent safe from any further atrocity. The young lawyer besought his fathor to give him his best advice, if this persecution were the work of one of their friends. Though justice could not always punish, she would at last find everything out and make good note of it. Minoret had achieved his great end ; he was now the immovable owner of the Château du Rouvre, one of the finest in all the Gâtinais, and he could derive forty-odd thousand francs a year from the rich and beautiful land surrounding the park. The colossus could laugh at Goupil now. Moreover, he meant to live in the country, where the memory of Ursule would haunt him no more.

"My boy," said he to Goupil, as they paced the terrace, "leave my little cousin in peace ! "

"Pooh ! " said the clerk, who could make nothing of his capricious behavior, for even stupidity has its depths.

"Oh, I am not ungrateful : you have helped me to get, for two hundred and eighty thousand francs, this fine mansion of brick and hewn stone, which certainly could not now be built for nearly five times the price, with the home farm, the park, the gardens, and timber—Well, yes, I will, on my word—I will give you ten per cent.—twenty thousand francs, with which you can buy a bailiff's practice at Nemours. And I guarantee your marriage with one of the Crémière girls—the elder."

"The one who talked of the cornet-à-pistons ? " cried Goupil.

"But her mother will give her thirty thousand francs,"
said Minoret. "You see, my boy, you were born to be a
bailiff, just as I was made to be a postmaster, and we must all
obey our vocation."

"Very well," said Goupil, fallen from his high hopes,
"here are the stamps; sign me bills for twenty thousand
francs, that I may make my bargain cash in hand."

Eighteen thousand francs were due to Minoret, the half-
yearly interest on securities of which his wife knew nothing;
he thought he should thus be rid of Goupil, and he signed
the bills. Goupil, seeing this huge and stupid Machiavelli
of the Rue des Bourgeois in a fit of seignorial fever, took
leave of him with an "Au revoir," and a look that would
have made any one but a parvenu simpleton tremble as he
looked down from a high terrace on the gardens, and the
handsome roof of a château built in the style fashionable
under Louis XIII.

"You will not wait for me?" he cried to Goupil, seeing
the clerk set out on foot.

"You can pick me up on the road, old man," replied the
prospective bailiff, thirsting for vengeance, and curious to
know the answer to the riddle presented to his mind by the
strangely tortuous conduct of this old man.

Ever since the day when the most infamous calumny had
darkened her life, Ursule, a prey to one of those unaccount-
able maladies whose seat is in the soul, was hastening to the
grave. Excessively pale, speaking rarely a few weak, slow
words, looking about her with a gentle, indifferent gaze,
everything in her appearance, even her brow, showed that she
was possessed by a consuming thought. She believed that
the ideal crown of pure flowers, with which in every age and
nation the brow of a maiden has been supposed to be crowned,
had fallen from hers. In the void and silence she seemed to
hear the slanderous remarks, the malignant comments, the
mean laughter of the little town. The burden was too heavy

for her; her innocence was too sensitive to endure such a stoning. She did not complain, a melancholy smile lay on her lips, and her eyes were constantly raised to heaven as though to appeal to the Lord of Angels against the injustice of men.

When Goupil got back to Nemours, Ursule had been brought down from her room to the ground floor, leaning on the arm of La Bougival and of the doctor. This was in honor of a great event. Madame de Portenduère, having heard that the young girl was dying as the ermine dies, though her honor was less cruelly attacked than that of Clarissa Harlowe, had come to see her and to comfort her. The sight of her son, who had been talking all night of killing himself, had been too much for the old lady. Madame de Portenduère, indeed, found it quite becoming to her dignity to carry encouragement to so pure a creature, and regarded her own visit as an antidote to all the ill done by the gossips of the place. Her opinion, so much more influential, no doubt, than that of the vulgar, would consecrate the power of the nobility.

This step, announced by the Abbé Chaperon, had produced a revulsion in Ursule which revived the hopes of the physician, who had been in despair, and had talked of holding a consultation with the most eminent Paris doctors. Ursule had been placed in her old guardian's armchair, and the character of her beauty was such that in mourning and in suffering she looked more lovely than at any time in her happy days. When Savinien came in, with his mother on his arm, the young invalid's color mounted to her cheeks once more.

"Do not rise, my dear," said the old lady, in a tone of command. "However ill and feeble I may be myself, I was determined to come and tell you what I think of all that is going on. I esteem you as the purest, saintliest, and sweetest girl in the Gâtinais, and regard you as worthy to make a gentleman of family happy."

At first Ursule could make no reply; she held the withered hands of Savinien's mother and kissed them, dropping tears upon them.

"Ah, madame!" she answered, in a weak voice, "I should never have been so bold as to think of raising myself so far above my position if I had not been encouraged by promises, and my only claim was a love without limits; but means have been found to separate me for ever from him whom I love. I have been made unworthy of him. Never!" she exclaimed, with a vehemence of tone that startled the listeners painfully—"never will I consent to give to any man a hand so vilified, a reputation so tarnished! I loved too well—— I may say it now, wreck that I am; I love a creature almost as much as God. And so God——"

"Come, come, child, do not calumniate God. Come, my daughter," said the old lady, making a great effort, "do not exaggerate the importance of an infamous jest which no one believes in. You shall live—I promise it—live and be happy."

"You shall be happy!" cried Savinien, kneeling by Ursule, and kissing her hand. "My mother calls you her daughter!"

"That will do," said the doctor, who was feeling his patient's pulse. "Do not kill her with joy."

At this instant Goupil, who had found the gate into the alley ajar, pushed open the drawing-room door and showed his hideous face, beaming with the thoughts of revenge that had blossomed in his heart in the course of his walk.

"Monsieur de Portenduère," said he, in a voice like the hiss of a viper at bay in its hole.

"What do you want?" said Savinien, rising.

"I want to say two words to you."

Savinien went out into the passage, and Goupil led him into the yard.

"Swear to me by the life of Ursule whom you love, and by your honor as a gentleman which you prize, so to behave as though there were nothing known between us of what I am going to tell you, and I will explain to you the sole cause of the persecutions turned against Mademoiselle Mirouët."

"Can I put an end to them?"

"Yes."

"Can I be revenged?"

"Yes, on the prime mover—not on the instrument."

"Why?"

"The instrument is—— I am the instrument."

Savinien turned white.

"I just caught sight of Ursule——" the clerk began again.

"Ursule?" said Savinien, with a look at the clerk.

"Mademoiselle Mirouët," said Goupil, made respectful by Savinien's tone; "and I would shed all my blood to undo what has been done. I repent. If you were to kill me in a duel or in any other way, of what use would my blood be to you? Could you drink it? At this moment it would poison you."

The man's cool reasonableness and his own curiosity quelled Savinien's boiling blood; he glared at this hunchback spoiled, with an eye that made Goupil look down.

"And who set you on the job?" asked the young man.

"You swear?"

"You wish to escape unharmed?"

"I wish that you and Mademoiselle Mirouët should forgive me."

"She will forgive you. I never will!"

"Well, you will forget?"

How terrible is the force of logic seconded by interest! Two men, each longing to rend the other, were standing there, close together, in a little yard, forced to speak to each other, united by one feeling in common.

"I will forgive you, but I shall not forget."

"Of no use whatever," said Goupil, coldly.

Savinien lost patience. He dealt the clerk a slap on the cheek that rang through the yard; it almost upset Goupil, and he himself staggered back.

"I have gotten no more than I deserve," said Goupil. "I have been a fool. I thought you a finer fellow than you are. You have taken a mean advantage of the opportunity I offered you. You are in my power now!" he added, with a flash of hatred at Savinien.

"You are a murderer!" exclaimed Savinien.

"No more than the knife in the assassin's hand," replied Goupil.

"I ask your forgiveness," said Savinien.

"Are you sufficiently revenged?" said the clerk with savage irony. "Will you now rest satisfied?"

"Forgive and forget on both sides," replied Savinien.

"Your hand on it?" said Goupil, holding out his.

"Here it is," said Savinien, swallowing the indignity out of love for Ursule. "But speak: who was behind you?"

Goupil paused, considering the two dishes of the scale, so to speak, with Savinien's slap on one side, and on the other his hatred of Minoret. For two seconds he doubted; then a voice said to him: "You can be a notary!" and he replied, "Forgive and forget? Yes, on both sides, monsieur," and he clasped Savinien's hand.

"Who is it, then, that is persecuting Ursule?" said Savinien.

"Minoret. He would like to see her dead and buried. Why, I do not know; but we will find out the reason. Do not mix me up in the matter. I can do nothing more for you if once I am suspected. Instead of attacking Ursule, I will defend her; instead of serving Minoret, I will try to spoil his game. I live only to ruin him, to crush him. And I will see him under my feet, I will dance on his dead body, I will make dominoes of his bones! To-morrow, on all the walls of Nemours, of Fontainebleau, of Le Rouvre, the words shall be seen in red chalk—*Minoret is a thief!* Oh, I will do it, by all that is holy! I will blow him to the four winds! Now, we are allies by my having peached. Well, if you like, I will go on my knees to Mademoiselle Mirouët, and tell her that I curse the insane passion which drove me to kill her. I will entreat her to forgive me. That will do her good. The justice and the curé are there ; those two witnesses are enough ; but Monsieur Bongrand must pledge his word that he will not damage me in my career. For I have a career now," concluded Goupil.

" Wait a moment," replied Savinien, quite bewildered by this revelation.

" Ursule, my child," said he, going back to the drawing-room, " the cause of all your misery has lived to feel the horror of his work ; he repents, and would be glad to ask your pardon in the presence of these gentlemen, on condition that all shall be forgotten."

" What ! Goupil ? " exclaimed the curé, the justice, and the doctor in a breath.

" Keep his secret," said Ursule, putting a finger on her lips.

Goupil heard her words, and saw the gesture, and it touched him.

" Mademoiselle," he said, with feeling, " I wish that all Nemours might hear me confess to you that a fatal passion turned my head, and suggested to me a series of crimes deserving the blame of all honest folks. What I have said I will repeat everywhere, deploring the evil result of my practical jokes, though they may, in fact, have hurried on your happiness," he added, a little maliciously, as he rose, " since I see Madame de Portenduère here."

" That is right, Goupil," said the curé; "Mademoiselle forgives you. But do not forget that you have been very near committing murder."

" Monsieur Bongrand," Goupil went on, turning to the justice, " I am going this evening to try to bargain with Lecœur for his place as summonsing officer. I hope this confession will have done me no injury in your mind, and that you will support my candidature among the superior lawyers, and to the ministry."

The justice gravely bowed, and Goupil went off to treat for the better of the two appointments in Nemours. The others remained with Ursule, and endeavored that evening to restore calmness and peace in her mind, which was already relieved by the satisfaction given her by the clerk.

"All Nemours shall know it," said Bongrand.

" You see, my child, God was not against you," said the curé.

Minoret returned late from Le Rouvre, and dined late. At about nine in the evening he was sitting in his Chinese pavilion digesting his dinner, his wife by his side, and laying plans with her for Désiré's future prospects. Désiré had quite settled down since he had held an appointment; he worked steadily, and had a good chance, it was said, of succeeding the public prosecutor of the district of Fontainebleau, who was to be promoted to Melun. They must find him a wife now, a girl wanting money, but belonging to some old and noble family; then he might rise to a judgeship in Paris. Possibly they might be able to get him elected député for Fontainebleau, where Zélie thought it would be well to settle for the winter, after spending the summer at Le Rouvre. Minoret, very much pleased with himself for having arranged everything for the best, had ceased to think of Ursule at the very moment when the drama he had so clumsily begun had become so fatally complicated.

"Monsieur de Portenduère would like to speak to you," said Cabirolle, coming in.

"Bring him here," said Zélie.

The shades of dusk prevented Madame Minoret's seeing her husband suddenly turn pale; he shuddered as he heard Savinien's boots creak on the inlaid flooring of the passage, where the doctor's books had formerly lined the wall. A vague presentiment ran like a congestive chill through the spoiler's veins.

Savinien came in. He stood still, keeping his hat on, his stick in his hand, his arms folded—motionless, face to face with the couple.

"I have come to know, Monsieur and Madame Minoret, the reasons which have led you to torture in the most infamous manner the young girl who is, to the knowledge of all Nemours, my future wife; why you have tried to brand her honor; why you wish her dead; and why you have abandoned her to the insults of such a creature as Goupil? Answer."

"What a queer notion, Monsieur Savinien," said Zélie, "to come and ask us our reasons for a thing which is to us inexplicable! I do not care for Ursule one snap. Since Uncle Minoret's death I have no more given her a thought than to an old smock! I have never breathed her name to Goupil—and a queer rascal he is, whom I would not trust with the interests of my dog. Well, Minoret, why don't you answer? Are you going to let monsieur attack you and accuse you of rascality that is beneath you? As if a man who has forty-eight thousand francs a year in landed estate round a château fit for a prince would demean himself to such folly! Wake up, man—sitting there like a dummy!"

"I don't know what monsieur would be at," said Minoret at last, in his thin voice, of which the clear accents betrayed its trembling. "What reason could I have for persecuting the girl? I may have said to Goupil that it vexed me to know that she was in Nemours; my son Désiré had taken a

fancy to her, and I would not have him marry her, that
was all.''

"Goupil has confessed everything, Monsieur Minoret.''

There was a moment's silence—a terrible moment, while
these three persons watched each other. Zélie had detected
a nervous movement in the broad face of her colossus.

"Though you are but vermin, I intend to be publicly revenged on you,'' the young nobleman went on. "I shall not
ask satisfaction from you, a man of sixty-seven, for the insults
heaped on Mademoiselle Mirouët; but from your son. The
first time Monsieur Minoret, junior, sets foot in Nemours, we
meet. He will have to fight me, and he shall fight! Or he
shall be so utterly disgraced that he will not dare to show his
face anywhere; if he does not come to Nemours, I will go to
Fontainebleau! I will have satisfaction. It shall never be
said that you have basely tried to bring shame on a defenseless girl.''

"But the calumnies of such a fellow as Goupil—really—
are not——'' said Minoret.

"Would you like me to confront you with him?'' cried
Savinien, interrupting him. "Believe me, you had better
not noise the matter; it is between you and Goupil and me;
leave it so, and God will decide the issue in the duel to which
I shall do your son the honor of challenging him.''

"But things cannot go on like that!'' cried Zélie. "What?
Do you suppose that I shall allow Désiré to fight with you, a
naval officer, whose business it is to use the sword and pistol?
If you have a score against Minoret, here is Minoret; take
Minoret, fight with Minoret! But why should my boy, who,
by your own confession, is innocent of it all, suffer the penalty?
I will set a dog of mine to hinder that, my fine gentleman!
Come, Minoret, there you sit gaping like a great idiot! You
are in your own house, and you allow this young fellow to
keep his hat on in your wife's presence! Now, young man,
to begin with, take yourself off. Every man's house is his

castle. I do not know what you are at with all your rhodo-
montade, but just turn on your heel; and if you lay a finger
on Désiré, you will have me to settle with—you and your
precious slut, Ursule."

She rang violently, and called the servants.

" Remember what I have said," repeated Savinien, who,
heedless of Zélie's diatribe, went away, leaving this sword of
Damocles suspended over their heads.

" Now, Minoret, will you tell me the meaning of all this?"
said Zélie to her husband. " A young man does not come
into a decent house and kick up all this tremendous dust for
nothing, and insist on the blood of an only son and heir."

" It is some trick of that nasty ape, Goupil; I had promised to help him to be made notary if he would get Le Rouvre
on reasonable terms. I gave him ten per cent., twenty thousand francs, in bills of exchange, and I suppose he is not satisfied."

" Yes; but what previous reason can he have had to get up
serenades and rascalities to trouble Ursule?"

" He wanted to marry her."

" A girl without a sou? He? Fiddlesticks! Look here,
Minoret, you are cramming me with nonsense, and you are
by nature too stupid to make it take, my man. There is something behind it all, and you must tell it me."

" There is nothing."

" There is nothing? Well, I tell you that is a lie, and we
shall see."

" Will you leave me in peace?"

" I will turn on the tap of that barrel of poison, Goupil,
whom you know, I think; and you will not get the best of
the bargain then."

" As you please."

" Certainly, it will be as I please! And what I please, first
and foremost, is that no one shall lay a finger on Désiré;
if anything happens to him—there, I tell you, I should do

something that would take me to the block. Désiré! Why! And there you sit without stirring!"

A quarrel thus begun between Minoret and his wife was not likely to end without long domestic broils. The thieving fool now found his struggle with himself and Ursule made harder by his blundering, and complicated by a fresh and terrible adversary. Next day, when he went out to go to Goupil, hoping to silence him with money, he read on all the walls: *Minoret is a thief!* Every one he met pitied him, and asked him who was at the bottom of this anonymous placarding, and every one overlooked the evasiveness of his replies by ascribing it to his stupidity. Simpletons gain more advantages from their weakness than clever men get from their strength. We look on at a great man struggling against fate, but we raise a fund for a bankrupt grocer. Do you know why? We feel superior when we protect an idiot, and are aggrieved at being no more than equal to the man of genius. A clever man would have been ruined if, like Minoret, he had stammered out preposterous replies with a scared look. Zélie and the servants effaced the libelous inscription wherever they saw it; but it weighed on Minoret's conscience.

Though Goupil had, only the day before, given the summonsing officer his word, he most audaciously refused now to sign the agreement.

"My dear Lecœur, you see I am in a position to buy Dionis' practice, and I can help you to sell yours to some one else. Put your agreement in your pocket again. It is the loss only of a couple of stamps. Here are seventy centimes."

Lecœur was too much afraid of Goupil to make any complaints. All Nemours was forthwith informed that Minoret had offered his guarantee to Dionis to enable Goupil to purchase his place. The budding notary wrote to Savinien retracting all his confession regarding Minoret, and explaining to the young nobleman that his new position, the decisions of the supreme court, and his respect for justice forbade his fighting a duel. At the same time, he warned him to take care henceforth how he behaved, as he—Goupil—was practiced in kicking, and at the first provocation would have the pleasure of breaking his leg.

The walls of Nemours spoke no more. But the quarrel between Minoret and his wife continued, and Savinien kept angry silence. Within ten days of these events the marriage of the elder Mademoiselle Massin to the future notary was publicly rumored. Mademoiselle Massin had eighty thousand francs and her ugly face ; Goupil, his misshapen body and his appointment ; so the union seemed suitable and probable.

At midnight, as Goupil was quitting the Massins' house, he was seized in the street by two strangers, who thrashed him soundly and disappeared. Goupil never breathed a word about this nocturnal scene, and gave the lie to an old woman who, looking out of her window, fancied she had recognized him.

All these great little events were watched by the justice, who clearly saw that Goupil had some mysterious power over Minoret, and promised himself that he would find out the reason of it.

Though public opinion in the little town acknowledged Ursule's perfect innocence, she recovered but slowly. In this state of physical prostration, which left her soul and mind free, she became the passive medium of certain phenomena of which the effects indeed were terrible, and of a nature to attract the attention of science, if science had only been taken into the secret. Ten days after Madame de Portenduère's visit, Ursule had a dream which presented the characteristics of a supernatural vision, as much in its moral facts as in its physical conditions, so to speak.

Her godfather, old Doctor Minoret, appeared to her, and signed to her to follow him ; she dressed and went with him, through the darkness, as far as the house in the Rue des Bourgeois, where she found everything, to the most trivial details, just as they had been at the time of her godfather's death. The old man wore the clothes he had had on the day before he died; his face was pale, not a sound was heard as he moved ; nevertheless, Ursule distinctly heard his voice, though it was faint, as if repeated by a distant echo. The doctor led his ward into the Chinese pavilion, where he made her raise the marble top of the little Boule chiffonier, as she had done the day of his death; but instead of finding nothing there, she saw the letter her godfather had desired her to fetch. She unsealed it and read it, as well as the will in Savinien's favor.

"The letters of the writing," she said to the curé, "shone as though they had been traced with sunbeams; they scorched my eyes."

When she looked up at her uncle to thank him, she saw a kindly smile on his pale lips. Then, in his weak but quite clear voice, the spectre showed her Minoret in the passage listening to his secret, unscrewing the lock, and taking the packet of papers. Then, with his right hand, he took hold of the girl and obliged her to walk with the tread of the dead to follow Minoret home to his house. Ursule crossed the town, went into the posting-house, and up to Zélie's room, where the spectre made her see the spoiler unsealing the letters, reading and burning them.

"He could only make the third match burn," said Ursule, "to set light to the papers, and he buried the ashes among the cinders. After that, my godfather took me back to our house, and I saw Monsieur Minoret-Levrault steal into the library, where he took out of the third volume of the 'Pandects' the three bonds bearing twelve thousand francs a year, as well as the money saved in the house, all in bank-notes. Then my guardian said to me: 'All the torments that have brought you to the brink of the grave are his work, but God wills that you shall be happy. You will not die yet; you will marry Savinien. If you love me, if you love Savinien, you will ask for the restoration of your fortune by my nephew. Swear that you will.' "

Shining like the Lord at His Transfiguration, the spectre had had such a violent effect on Ursule's mind, in the oppressed state in which she was at the time, that she promised all her uncle asked her to be rid of the nightmare. She woke to find herself standing in the middle of her room, in front of the portrait of her godfather, which she had had brought there when she was ill. She went to bed again, and to sleep after great excitement, remembering this strange vision when she woke; but she dared not speak of it. Her refined good sense, and her delicacy of feeling, took offense at the thought of revealing a dream of which the cause and object were her own pecuniary interests; she naturally attributed it to La Bougival's chat, as she was going to sleep, of the doctor's liberality, and the convictions her old nurse still cherished on the subject.

But the dream returned with aggravated details, which made her dread it greatly. The second time her godfather laid his ice-cold hand on her shoulder, causing her the acutest pain, an indescribable sensation. "The dead must be obeyed!" he said in sepulchral tones.

"And tears," she added, "fell from his hollow blank eyes."

The third time the dead man took her by her long plaits of hair, and showed her Minoret talking with Goupil, and promising him money if he would take Ursule to Sens. Then she made up her mind to tell her three dreams to the Abbé Chaperon.

"Monsieur le Curé," she said to him one evening, "do you believe that the dead can walk?"

"My child, sacred history, profane history, modern history bear witness in many passages to their appearing. Still, the church has never made it an article of faith; and as to science, in France it laughs it to scorn."

"What do you believe?"

"The power of God, my child, is infinite."

"Did my godfather ever speak to you of these things?"

"Yes; often. He had completely changed his views of such matters. His conversion dated from the day, as he told me twenty times, when a woman at Paris heard you, at Nemours, praying for him, and saw the red dot you had made on the calendar at the name of Saint Savinien."

Ursule gave a scream that made the priest shudder; she remembered the scene when, on his return from Paris, her guardian had read her heart, and had taken away her calendar.

"If that is the case," said she, "my visions are possible. My godfather has appeared to me as Jesus appeared to His disciples. He stands in a golden light, and he speaks to me. I wanted to beg you to say a mass for the repose of his soul, and to beseech the interposition of God to stop these apparitions which overwhelm me."

She then related her three dreams in every detail, insisting on the absolute truthfulness of the facts, the freedom of her own movements, and the clear vision of an inner self which, as she described it, followed the guidance of her uncle's spectre with perfect ease. What most surprised the priest, to whom Ursule's perfect veracity was well known, was her exact description of the room formerly occupied by Zélie Minoret at the posting-house, into which Ursule had never been, and which, indeed, she had never even heard mentioned.

"By what means can these strange apparitions be produced?" said Ursule. "What did my godfather think?" .

"Your godfather, my child, argued from hypotheses. He acknowledged the possible existence of a spiritual world, a world of ideas. If ideas are a creation proper to man, if they subsist and live a life peculiar to themselves, they must have forms imperceptible to our external senses, but perceptible to

15

our interior senses under certain conditions.   Thus your godfather's ideas may enwrap you, and you perhaps have lent
them his aspect.   Then, if Minoret has committed these ac-
tions, they are dissolved into ideas; for every action is the
outcome of several ideas.   Now, if ideas have their being in
the spiritual world, your spirit may have been enabled to see
them when transported thither.   These phenomena are not
more strange than those of memory; and those of memory
are as surprising and as inexplicable as those of the perfume
of plants, which are perhaps the plants' ideas."

"Dear me! how you expand the world!   But is it really
possible to hear a dead man speak, to see him walk and act?"

"Swedenborg, in Sweden," replied the abbé, "has proved
to demonstration that he held intercourse with the dead.
But, at any rate, come into the library, and in the life of the
famous Duc de Montmorency, who was beheaded at Toulouse,
and who certainly was not the man to invent a cock-and-bull
story, you will read of an adventure almost like your own,
which also occurred, above a hundred years before, to
Cardan."

Ursule and the curé went up to the second floor, and the good
man found for her a little duodecimo edition, printed in Paris
in 1666, of the "History of Henri de Montmorency," written
by a contemporary priest who had known that prince.

"Read," said the curé, giving her the volume open at
pages 175 and 176.   "Your godfather often read this passage;
see, here are some grains of his snuff."

"And he is no more!" said Ursule, taking the book to
read this passage:

"The siege of Privas was remarkable for the loss of some
of the persons in command.   Two colonels were killed, to
wit: the Marquis d'Uxelles, who died of a wound received in
the trenches, and the Marquis de Portes, by a gunshot in the
head.   He was to have been made a marshal of France the
very day he was killed.   Just about the moment when the

Marquis died, the Duc de Montmorency, who was sleeping in his tent, was roused by a voice like that of the Marquis, bidding him farewell. The love he had for one who was so dear to him caused him to attribute the illusion of this dream to the power of his imagination; and the toil of the night, which he had spent as usual in the trenches, made him go to sleep again without any fear. But the same voice suddenly broke it again; and the phantom, which he had only seen in his sleep, compelled him to wake once more, and to hear distinctly the same words that it had spoken before disappearing. The Duc then recollected that one day when they had heard Pitrat the philosopher discoursing of the separation of the soul from the body, they had promised to bid each other farewell, whichever died first, if he were permitted. Whereupon, unable to hinder his dread of the truth of this warning, he at once sent one of his servants to the Marquis' lodgings, which were distant from his own. But before his man could return he was sent for by the King, who caused him to be told, by persons who could comfort him, of the misfortune he had already apprehended.

"I leave it to the learned to discuss the cause of this event, which I have often heard the Duc de Montmorency relate, and which I have thought worthy to be set down for its marvelousness and its truth."

"But, then," asked Ursule, "what ought I to do?"

"My child," said the curé, "the case is so serious, and so much to your own advantage, that you must keep complete silence. Now that you have trusted me with the secret of this apparition, perhaps it will come no more. Besides, you are strong enough now to go to church; well, then, to-morrow you can come to thank God, and to pray for the peace of your godfather's soul. Be quite sure, at any rate, that your secret is in safe hands."

"If you could know in what terror I go to sleep! What awful looks my godfather gives me! The last time he held on to my dress to see me longer. I woke with my face streaming with tears."

" Rest in peace ; he will come no more," said the curé.

Without losing any time the Abbé Chaperon went to Minoret's house and begged him to grant him a minute's conversation in the Chinese pavilion, insisting that they must be alone.

" No one can hear us ?" asked the priest.

" No one," said Minoret.

" Monsieur, my character is known to you," said the worthy priest, looking Minoret mildly but steadfastly in the face.   " I must speak to you of some serious, extraordinary matters, which concern you alone, and which you may rely on me to keep a profound secret ; but it is impossible that I should not reveal them to you.   When your uncle was alive, there stood just there——" said the abbé, pointing to the spot, "a little chiffonier of Boule with a marble top" (Minoret turned pale), " and under the marble slab your uncle placed a letter for his ward——"

The curé went on to tell Minoret the whole story of Minoret's conduct, without omitting the smallest detail.   The retired postmaster, when he heard of the circumstance of the two matches that went out before burning up, felt his hair creep on his thick-set scalp.

" Who has invented such a cock-and-bull story ?" he said in a husky voice, when the tale was finished.

" The dead man himself ! "

This reply made Minoret shiver slightly, for he too saw the doctor in his dreams.

" God is most good to work miracles for me, Monsieur le Curé," said Minoret, inspired by his peril to utter the only jest he ever perpetrated in his life.

" All that God does is natural," replied the priest.

" Your phantasmagoria does not frighten me," said the colossus, recovering his presence of mind a little.

"I have not come to frighten you, my dear sir, for I shall never speak of this to any living creature," said the curé. "You alone know the truth. It is a matter between you and God."

"Come, now, Monsieur le Curé, do you believe me capable of such a breach of faith?"

"I believe in no crimes but those which are confessed to me, and of which the sinner repents," said the priest in apostolic tones.

"A crime?" exclaimed Minoret.

"A crime, terrible in its results."

"In what way?"

"In the fact that it evades human justice. The crimes which are not expiated here will be expiated in the other world. God Himself avenges the innocent."

"You think that God troubles Himself about such mere trifles?"

"If He could not see all the worlds and every detail at a glance, as you hold a landscape in your eye, He would not be God."

"Monsieur le Curé, do you give me your word of honor that you have heard all this story from no one but my uncle?"

"Your uncle has now appeared three times to Ursule, to reiterate it. Worn out by these dreams, she confided these revelations to me, under the seal of secrecy; she herself regards them as so entirely irrational that she will never allude to them. So on that point you may be quite easy."

"But I am quite easy on all points, Monsieur Chaperon."

"I can but hope so," said the old priest. "Even if I should regard such warnings given in dreams as utterly absurd, I should still think it necessary to communicate them to you on account of the singularity of the details. You are a respectable man; and you have earned your fine fortune too legitimately to wish to add to it by robbery. You are, too, a

very simple man; remorse would torture you too cruelly.
We have in ourselves an instinct of justice, in the civilized
man as in the savage, which does not allow of our enjoying
in peace anything we have acquired dishonestly according to
the laws of the society we live in; for well-organizad communities are modeled on the plan given to the universe by
God Himself.   In so far, society has a divine origin.   Man
does not evolve ideas, does not invent forms; he imitates the
eternal relations he finds in all that surrounds him.   Consequently, this is what happens: no criminal going to the
scaffold with the full power of carrying out of the world the
secret of his crimes, allows himself to be executed without
making the confession to which he is urged by a mysterious
impulse.   So, my dear Monsieur Minoret, if you are easy I
may go away happy.''

Minoret was so dazed that he left the curé to let himself
out.   As soon as he was alone he flew into the rage of a full-
blooded nature; he broke out in the wildest blasphemies, and
called Ursule by every odious name.

"Why, what has that little wench done to you?" asked
Madame Minoret, who had come in on tiptoe after seeing the
curé depart.

For the first and only time in his life, Minoret, drunk with
fury and driven to extremities by his wife's persistent questioning, beat her so soundly that when she fell helpless he
was obliged to lift her in his arms, and, very much ashamed
of himself, to put her to bed.

He himself had a short fit of illness; the doctor was
obliged to bleed him twice.   When he was about again,
every one, within a short time, noticed that he was altered.
Minoret would take walks alone, and often wander about the
streets like a man uneasy in his mind.   He seemed absent-
minded when spoken to—he, who had never had two ideas
in his head.   At last, one day, he addressed the justice, in
the High Street, as he was going, no doubt, to fetch Ursule

to take her to Madame de Portenduère's, where the whist
parties had begun again.

"Monsieur Bongrand, I have something rather important
to say to my cousin Ursule," said he, taking the justice by
the arm, "and I am glad that you should be present; you
may give her some advice."

They found Ursule at the piano; she rose with an air of
cold dignity when she saw Minoret.

"Monsieur Minoret wishes to speak with you on business,
my dear," said the justice. "By the way, do not forget to
give me your dividend warrants. I am going to Paris, and I
will get your six months' interest, and La Bougival's."

"Cousin," said Minoret, "our uncle had accustomed you
to an easier life than you now enjoy."

"It is possible to be very happy without much money,"
said she.

"I have been thinking that money would help to make you
happy," replied Minoret, "and I came to offer you some, out
of respect for my uncle's memory."

"You had a very natural course open to show your respect for
him," said Ursule severely. "You might have left his house
just as it was, and have sold it to me, for you ran the price
up so high only in the hope of finding treasure hoarded
there——"

"At any rate," said Minoret, evidently ill at ease, "if you
had twelve thousand francs a year, you would be in a position
to marry the better."

"I have not such an income."

"But if I were to give it to you, on condition of your pur-
chasing an estate in Brittany, in Madame de Portenduère's
part of the country, she would then consent to your marrying
her son?——"

"Monsieur Minoret, I have no right to so large a sum, and
could not possibly accept it from you. We are scarcely
related, and still less are we friends. I have suffered too

much already from slander to wish to give any cause for evil speaking. What have I done to deserve such a gift? On what pretext could you make me such a present? These questions, which I have a right to ask you, every one will answer in his own way. It will be interpreted as compensation for some injury, and I decline to recognize any. Your uncle did not bring me up in ignoble sentiments. We can accept gifts only from a friend. I could not feel any affection for you, and should necessarily prove ungrateful, so I do not choose to run the risk of such ingratitude."

"You refuse!" exclaimed the colossus; the idea of anybody refusing a fortune would never have entered his head.

"I refuse," repeated Ursule.

"But on what grounds have you any claim to offer such a fortune to mademoiselle?" asked the old lawyer. "You have an idea; have you an idea?"

"Well, yes; the idea of getting her away from Nemours, that my son may leave me in peace; he is in love with her, and insists on marrying her."

"Well, we will see about that," replied the justice, settling his spectacles. "Give us time to reflect."

He escorted Minoret home, quite approving his anxiety as to the future on Désiré's account, gently blaming Ursule's hasty decisiveness, and promising to make her listen to reason. As soon as Minoret was within doors, Bongrand went to the posting stables, borrowed a horse and gig, and hurried off to Fontainebleau, where he inquired for Désiré, and was informed that he was at an evening party at the sous-préfet's. The justice, quite delighted, went on thither. Désiré was playing a rubber with the public prosecutor's wife, the wife of the sous-préfet, and the colonel of the regiment stationed there.

"I have come the bearer of good news," said Monsieur Bongrand to Désiré. "You are in love with Ursule Mirouët, and your father no longer objects to the marriage."

" Ursule Mirouët ! I am in love with her ? " cried Désiré, laughing. " What put Ursule Mirouët into your head ? I remember seeing her occasionally at old Doctor Minoret's, my great grand-uncle, a little girl who is certainly lovely ; but she is outrageously pious; and if I, like everybody else, did justice to her charms, I never troubled my head with caring for her washed-out complexion," and he smiled at the lady of the house—a "sprightly brunette," to use a last-century phrase. " Where were you dug up, my dear Monsieur Bongrand ? All the world knows that my father is sovereign lord over lands worth forty-eight thousand francs a year, lying round his Château du Rouvre, so all the world knows that I have forty-eight thousand perpetual and funded reasons for not caring for the ward of the law. If I were to marry a mere nobody, these ladies would think me a great fool."

" You have never teased your father about Ursule ? "

" Never."

" You hear him, monsieur," said the justice to the lawyer, who had been listening, and whom he now buttonholed in a corner, where they stood talking for about a quarter of an hour.

An hour later the justice, having returned to Nemours and to Ursule's house, sent La Bougival to fetch Minoret, who came at once.

" Mademoiselle——" said Bongrand, as Minoret came in.

" Accepts? " Minoret put in, interrupting him.

" No, not yet," replied the justice, settling his spectacles. " She had some scruples regarding your son's condition, for she had been very much ill-used on the score of a similar passion, and knows the value of peace and quiet. Can you swear to her that your son is crazed with love, and that you have no object in view but that of preserving our dear Ursule from some fresh Goupilleries? "

" Oh yes, I swear it ! " said Minoret.

" Stop a minute, Master Minoret ! " said the justice, taking one of his hands out of his trousers-pocket to slap Minoret on the back, making him start. "Do not so lightly commit perjury."

" Perjury ! "

" It lies between you and your son, who, at Fontainebleau, at the sub-prefect's house, and in the presence of four persons and the public prosecutor of the district, has just sworn that he never once thought of his cousin Ursule Mirouët. You must therefore have had other reasons for offering her such an immense sum? I perceived that you were making very rash statements, and I have been to Fontainebleau myself."

Minoret stood aghast at his own blunder.

" Still, there is no harm, Monsieur Bongrand, in offering to a young relative what will facilitate a marriage, which, as it would seem, will make her happy, and in seeking some excuse to overcome her modesty."

Minoret, who in his extremity had hit on an almost admissible plea, wiped his brow, wet with large drops of sweat.

" You know my motives for refusing," replied Ursule. " I can but beg you to come here no more. Monsieur de Portenduère has not told me his reasons, but he has a feeling of contempt, even of hatred, of you, which forbids me to receive you. My happiness is my whole fortune ; I do not blush to own it ; and I will do nothing to compromise it, for Monsieur de Portenduère is waiting only till I am of age to marry me."

" The proverb, ' Money is all-powerful,' is very false ! " said the huge, burly Minoret, looking at the justice, whose observant eyes disturbed him greatly.

He rose and went away; but he found the air outside as oppressive as that in the little sitting-room.

" I must somehow put an end to this ! " said he to himself as he got home.

" Now, your dividend warrant, my child," said the justice, a good deal surprised at Ursule's calmness after so strange a scene.

When she returned with her own warrant and La Bougival's, Ursule found the justice walking up and down the room.

"You have no idea what could have led to that huge lout's offer?" he asked her.

"None that I can tell you," she replied.

Monsieur Bongrand looked at her in surprise—

"Then we both have the same notion," he said. "Here, make a note of the numbers of the two warrants, in case I should lose them; that is always a necessary precaution." Bongrand himself noted on a card the numbers of the warrants.

"Good-by, my child; I shall be away two days, but I shall be back on the third for my sitting."

That night Ursule had a vision of a very strange character. It seemed to her that her bed was in the graveyard of Nemours, and that her uncle's grave was at the foot of the bed. The white stone on which she read the epitaph dazzled her eyes, and opened endways like the front cover of an album. She shrieked loudly, but the figure of the doctor slowly sat up. She first saw his yellow head and white hair, that shone as if surrounded by a halo. Under his bald forehead his eyes glittered like beams of light, and he rose as if drawn up by some superior force. Ursule trembled horribly in her bodily frame; her flesh felt like a burning garment; and, as she subsequently described it, there seemed to be another self moving within it.

"Mercy, godfather!" she cried.

"Mercy? It is too late," he answered in the voice of the dead, to use the poor girl's inexplicable expression when she related this fresh dream to the Abbé Chaperon. "He has been warned. He has paid no heed to the warning. His son's days are numbered. If he does not ere long confess all and make full restitution, he will mourn his son, who is to perish by a horrible and violent death. Tell him this!" The

spectre pointed to a row of figures, which flashed on the wall
as if they had been written with fire, and said: "That is his
sentence!"

When her uncle had lain down in the grave again, Ursule
heard the noise of the stone falling into place, and then, far
away, a strange noise as of tramping horses, and men loudly
shouting.

Next day Ursule was prostrate. She could not get up, this
dream had so overwrought her. She begged her old nurse to
go at once to the Abbé Chaperon and bring him back with
her. The good man came as soon as he had performed mass;
but he was not at all astonished by Ursule's dream. He was
convinced of the fact of the robbery, and no longer sought any
explanation of the abnormal state of his "little dreamer."
He left Ursule, and went straight to Minoret.

"Dear me, Monsieur le Curé," said Zélie, "my husband's
temper is so spoilt, I don't know what is the matter with him.
Until lately, he was a perfect child; but these two months
past I hardly know him. That he should have gotten into such
a rage as to strike me—me, when I am so gentle! The man
must be completely and utterly altered. You will find him
among the rocks; he spends his life there. What does he do
there?"

. In spite of the heat—it was September, 1836—the priest
crossed the canal, and turned up a pathway, where he saw
Minoret sitting under a boulder.

"You are in some great trouble, Monsieur Minoret," said
the priest, appearing before the guilty man. "You belong to
me, you know, for you are unhappy. Unfortunately, I have
come to add, perhaps, to your apprehensions. Ursule has
just had a terrible dream. Your uncle lifted up his grave-
stone to prophesy misfortune to your family. I have not
come to frighten you, believe me, but you ought to be told
what he said——"

"Really, Monsieur le Curé, I cannot be left in peace any-

"YOU STOLE THE THREE CERTIFICATES."

where, not even in this wilderness. I want to know nothing of what goes on in the next world," dejectedly replied the miserable old man.

"I will leave you, monsieur. I have not taken this walk in the heat for my own pleasure," said the priest, wiping his brow.

"Well, then, what was it the old fellow said?" asked Minoret.

"You are threatened with the loss of your son. If your uncle could tell things which you alone knew, you must tremble at the things which we none of us know. Restitution, my dear sir, restitution! Do not lose your soul for a little gold."

"Restitution of what?"

"Of the fortune the doctor intended for Ursule. You stole the three certificates; I now know it. You began by persecuting the poor girl, and you now end by offering her a dowry; you have fallen so low as lying; you are entangled in its mazes, and make a false step at every turn. You are yourself clumsy, and you have been badly served by your accomplice, Goupil, who only laughs at you. Make haste, for you are being watched by clever and clear-sighted persons, Ursule's friends. Restitution! And even if you do not save your son, who may not be in any danger, you will save your own soul, and your honor. In a society constituted as ours is, in a little town where you all have your eyes on each other, and where what is not known is surely guessed, can you hope to hide an ill-gotten fortune? Come, my son, an innocent man would not have allowed me to say so much?"

"Go to the devil!" cried Minoret. ' "I do not know what you are all at, setting on me. I like these stones better, for they leave me in peace."

"Good-by. You have been warned by me, my dear sir, without a soul in the world having heard a single word about the matter, either from me or from that poor girl. But beware! There is a man who has his eye on you. God have mercy on you!"

The curé turned and left him. When he had gone a few steps, he looked back once more at Minoret. He was sitting with his head between his hands, for his head ached. Minoret was a little mad.

In the first place, he had kept the three certificates; he did not know what to do with them; he dared not present them himself; he was afraid lest he should be recognized; he did not wish to sell them, and was trying to hit on some way of transferring them. His day dreams were romances of business, of which the climax always was the transfer of those cursed certificates. In this dreadful predicament he thought, however, of confessing to his wife, so as to have some advice. Zélie, who had steered her own ship so well, would know how to get him out of this scrape.

Three per cents. were now quoted at eighty; thus, with arrears, the restitution in question would amount to nearly a million francs. Give up a million, without any proof against him that he had taken them! This was no joke. And during the whole of September and part of October Minoret remained a prey to remorse and irresolution. To the amazement of the whole town, he grew thinner.

A fearful circumstance hastened the imparting of his secret to Zélie; the sword of Damocles swayed over their heads. Towards the middle of October Monsieur and Madame Minoret received the following letter from their son Désiré:

"MY DEAR MOTHER:—If I have not been to see you since the vacation, it is because, in the first place, I have been on duty in the absence of my chief, and also because I knew that Monsieur de Portenduère only awaited my going to Nemours to pick a quarrel with me. Tired, perhaps, of the long postponement of the revenge he is anxious to take on our family, the Vicomte has been to Fontainebleau, where he appointed

to meet one of his friends from Paris, after making sure of
the assistance of the Vicomte de Soulanges, brigadier of the
hussars quartered here.

" He called on me very politely, accompanied by these two
gentlemen, and told me that my father was undoubtedly the
originator of the infamous persecution directed against Ursule
Mirouët, his future wife ; he gave me proof by telling me that
Goupil had confessed before witnesses, and by giving me an
account of my father's conduct ; he, it seems, after refusing
at first to carry out his promises to Goupil as the price of his
villainous devices, found the necessary funds for acquiring
the place of summonsing officer at Nemours, and, finally, out
of fear, stood surety to Monsieur Dionis for the purchase of
his practice, and so disposed of Goupil. The Vicomte, who
cannot fight a man of sixty-seven, and who insists on aveng-
ing the insults heaped on Ursule, formally asked satisfaction
of me. His purpose, thought out and determined on in
silence, was not to be altered. If I should refuse to fight, he
meant to meet me in a drawing-room in the presence of those
persons whose opinion I most value, and there to insult me so
grossly that either I must fight or my hopes in life be at an
end. In France a coward is universally contemned. Moreover, his motives for demanding such reparation would be
laid before me by gentlemen of honor.

" He was sorry, he said, to be driven to such extremities.
In the opinion of his seconds, the wisest thing I could do
would be to arrange a meeting, as men of honor are in the
habit of doing, in such a way that Ursule's name should not
appear in the matter. Finally, to avoid all scandal in France,
we could, with our seconds, cross the frontier at the nearest
point. Thus everything would be arranged for the best.
His name, he said, was worth ten times my fortune, and his
prospects of happiness were a greater stake for him to risk
than anything I could risk in this duel, which is to be fatal.
He desired me to choose seconds and settle the matter. My

seconds met his yesterday, and they unanimously decided that I owe him this reparation.

"In a week I set out for Geneva with two of my friends. Monsieur de Portenduère, Monsieur de Soulanges, and Monsieur de Trailles will go their own way. We fight with pistols; all the details are arranged. Each is to fire three shots, and then, whatever may have come of it, the matter is at an end. To avoid all talk of such a dirty business—for I cannot possibly justify my father's conduct—I am writing to you only at the last minute. I will not go to see you on account of the violence you might display, which would be quite out of place. To make my way in the world I must obey its laws; and where a Vicomte finds ten reasons for a duel, the son of a postmaster must have a hundred. I shall pass through Nemours at night, and will there bid you good-by."

When they had read this letter, there was a scene between Zélie and Minoret, which ended in his confessing the theft, with all the circumstances connected with it, and the strange scenes to which it had everywhere given rise, even in the realm of dreams. The million had the same fascination for Zélie as it had for Minoret, and she did not propose to let it give her any uneasiness.

"Do you stay quietly here," said Zélie, without the smallest reproach to her husband for his blundering; "I will take the matter in hand. We will keep the money, and Désiré shall not fight."

Madame Minoret put on her shawl and bonnet and hurried off to Ursule with her son's letter; she found her alone, for it was about twelve o'clock.

In spite of her audacity, Zélie Minoret was abashed by the girl's cold looks, but she scolded herself for her cowardice, and took an airy tone.

"Here, Mademoiselle Mirouët, have the kindness to read

this letter, and tell me what you think of it," she exclaimed, holding out her son's letter.

Ursule felt a thousand conflicting emotions on reading this letter, which proved to her how deeply she was loved, and what care Savinien would take of the honor of the woman he was about to marry ; but she was at once too pious and too charitable to desire to be the cause of death or suffering to her worst enemy.

"I promise you, madame, that I will hinder this duel, and your mind may be easy ; but I beg you to leave me the letter."

"Let us see, my beauty, if we cannot do better than that. Listen to me. We have estates to the tune of forty-eight thousand a year round Le Rouvre, which is a real royal château ; besides that we can give Désiré twenty-four thousand francs a year in consols ; seventy-two thousand francs a year in all. You will allow that there are not many matches to compare with him. You are an ambitious little puss—and you are very right," added Zélie, noting Ursule's eager gesture of denial. "I have come to ask your hand for Désiré ; you will take your godfather's name—that will do it honor. Désiré, as you may have seen, is a good-looking young fellow ; he is very much liked at Fontainebleau, and will soon be public prosecutor. You, who are such a coaxing charmer, will get him to Paris. At Paris we will give you a fine house ; you will shine and play a part in society ; for with seventy-two thousand francs a year and the salary of a good appointment, you and Désiré will be in the highest circles. Consult your friends ; you will see what they say."

"I need only consult my heart, madame."

"Pooh, pooh ! Now you will be talking of that little lady-killer, Savinien ! Hang it all ! you will pay very dear for his name, his little mustache twirled into two curly spikes, and his black hair. A pretty boy he is ! A nice business you will make of housekeeping on seven thousand francs a year, and a husband who ran into debt for a hundred thousand in two

16

years in Paris. You don't know it yet, my child, but all men are alike ; and though I say it that shouldn't, my Désiré is every bit as good as a king's son.''

"You are forgetting, madame, the danger that your son is in at this moment, which can only be averted by Monsieur de Portenduère's wish to oblige me. The danger would be quite inevitable if he should learn that you are making such a dishonoring proposal. I may assure you, madame, that I shall be happier with the small income to which you allude than with the wealth you describe to dazzle me. For reasons unknown as yet—for everything will be known, madame— Monsieur Minoret, by his odious persecution, has brought to light the affection which binds me to Monsieur de Portenduère, and which I may openly avow since his mother will give us her blessing ; I may tell you that this affection, now sanctioned and legitimate, is all I live for. No lot, however splendid, however elevated, would induce me to change. I love beyond all possibility of repentance or change. Hence it would be a crime, undoubtedly punished, if I were to marry a man to whom I could only bring a heart that is wholly Savinien's. And, indeed, madame, since you drive me to it, I will say more : even if I did not love Monsieur de Portenduère, I could never make up my mind to go through the sorrows and joys of life as your son's companion. If Monsieur Savinien has been in debt, you have often paid Monsieur Désiré's. Our natures have neither the points of resemblance nor of difference which would allow of our living together without covert bitterness. I, perhaps, should not show him the tolerance that a woman owes to her husband ; I should therefore soon become a burden to him. Think no more of a marriage of which I am unworthy, and which I may decline without causing you the smallest regret, since, with such advantages, you will not fail to find plenty of girls handsomer than I am, of higher rank, and much richer.''

"Swear to me, child,'' said Zélie, "that you will prevent these two young men from taking their journey and fighting."

"It will, I know, be the greatest sacrifice Monsieur de Portenduère can make for my sake. But my bridal wreath must not be claimed by blood-stained hands."

"Very well, little cousin; I am much obliged to you, and I hope you may be happy."

"And I, madame, hope you may realize the promise of your son's future."

This reply struck to the mother's heart; she remembered the predictions of Ursule's last dream; she stood up, her little eyes fixed on Ursule's face—so pale, pure, and fair in her half-mourning dress—for Ursule had risen, as a hint to her self-called cousin to leave.

"Then you believe in dreams?" asked Zélie.

"I suffer from them too much not to believe in them."

"But then——" Zélie began.

"Good-morning, madame," said Ursule, with a bow to Madame Minoret, as she heard the curé's step.

The Abbé Chaperon was surprised to find Madame Minoret with Ursule. The anxiety depicted on the retired postmistress' pinched and wrinkled face naturally led the priest to study the two women by turns.

"Do you believe in ghosts?" Zélie asked the curé.

"Do you believe in dividends?" replied the curé, smiling.

"Sharpers—all of them!" thought Zélie; "they want to get round us. The old priest, the old justice, and that rascally little Savinien have arranged it all. There are no more dreams in it than there are hairs in the palm of my hand." She then courtesied twice with curt abruptness, and went away.

"I know why Savinien went to Fontainebleau," said Ursule to the Abbé Chaperon, and she informed him of the duel, begging him to use his influence to prevent it.

"And Madame Minoret proposed to you to marry her son?" asked the old man.

"Yes."

"Minoret has probably confessed his crime to his wife," added the curé.

The justice, who came in at this moment, heard of the proceedings and the offer made by Zélie, whose hatred of Ursule was known to him, and he glanced at the curé as much as to say—"Come out ; I want to speak to you about Ursule out of her hearing."

"Savinien will hear that you have refused eighty thousand francs a year and the cock of the walk of Nemours!" he said.

"Is that any sacrifice?" answered she. "Is anything a sacrifice to those who truly love? And is there any merit in my refusing the son of a man we despise? If others can make a virtue of their aversions, that should not be the moral code of a girl brought up by a Jordy, an Abbé Chaperon, and our dear doctor!" and she looked up at the portrait.

Bongrand took Ursule's hand and kissed it.

"Do you know," said the justice to the curé when they were in the street, "what Madame Minoret came for?"

"What?" said the priest, looking at his friend with a keen eye that only revealed curiosity.

"She wanted to make a kind of restitution."

"Then, do you think——?" began the Abbé Chaperon.

"I do not think, I am sure—here, only look." The justice pointed to Minoret, who was coming towards them on his way home, for on leaving Ursule's house the two friends had turned up the High Street.

"Having to plead in court, I have naturally studied many cases of remorse, but I never saw one to compare with this. What can have produced that flaccid pallor in cheeks of which the skin was tight as a drum, bursting with the coarse, rude health of a man without a care? What has set dark rings

round those eyes, and deadened their rustic twinkle? Could
you have believed that there would ever be a wrinkle on that
brow, or that that colossus could ever have felt his brain
reel! At last he is conscious of a heart! I know the phases
of remorse, my dear curé, as you know those of repentance.
Those that have hitherto come under my observation were
awaiting punishment, or condemned to endure it, to settle
their score with the world; they were resigned, or breathed
vengeance. But here we have remorse without expiation;
remorse pure and simple, greedy of its prey, and rending it.
You are not yet aware," said the justice, stopping Minoret,
"that Mademoiselle Mirouët has just refused your son's
hand?"

"But," added the curé, "you may be easy; she will prevent his duel with Monsieur de Portenduère."

"Ah! my wife has been successful," said Minoret; "I am
very glad. I was more dead than alive."

"You are indeed so altered that you are not like yourself,"
said the justice.

Minoret looked from one to the other to see if the curé
had betrayed him, but the abbé preserved a fixity of countenance, a calm melancholy, that at once greatly reassured the
guilty man.

"And the change is all the more surprising," the lawyer
went on, "because you ought to be perfectly happy. Why,
here you are, lord of Le Rouvre, to which you have added
Les Bordières, all your farms, your mills, your meadows. You
have a hundred thousand francs a year in consols——"

"I hold no consols," said Minoret, hastily.

"Bah!" said the justice. "Why, it is just the same with
that as with your son's love for Ursule. One day he will have
nothing to say to her, and the next asks her to marry him.
After having tried to kill Ursule with misery, you want to
have her for a daughter-in-law! My dear sir, there is something at the bottom of all this!"

Minoret wanted to answer; he tried to find words; he could only bring out—

"You are funny, Mr. Justice of the Peace. Good-day, gentlemen."

And with this reply he slowly turned down the Rue des Bourgeois.

"He has stolen our poor Ursule's fortune. But how can we prove it?"

"God grant——" said the curé.

"God has endowed us with a feeling which is now speaking in that man," replied the justice. "But we call that presumptive evidence, and human justice requires something more."

The Abbé Chaperon kept silent, as a priest. As happens in such cases, he thought much more often than he wished of the robbery Minoret had almost confessed, and of Savinien's happiness, so evidently delayed by Ursule's lack of fortune; for the old lady owned in secret to her spiritual director how wrong she had been not to consent to her son's marriage during the doctor's lifetime.

Next day, as he came down the altar steps after mass, he was struck by an idea, which came upon him with the force of a voice calling to him. He signed to Ursule to wait for him, and went home with her without breakfasting.

"My dear child," said he, "I want to see the two volumes in which your godfather, as you dream of him, says that he placed the certificates and notes."

Ursule and the curé went upstairs to the library and took down the third volume of the "Pandects." On opening it, the curé observed, not without surprise, the mark left by some papers on the pages, which, offering less resistance than the boards of the binding, still showed the impression made by the certificates; and in the other volume it was easy to see the readiness to open caused by the long pressure of a packet of papers between two pages of the folio.

"Come in, come up!" cried the abbé to the justice, who was just passing the house.

Bongrand entered the room at the very moment when the priest was putting on his spectacles to read three numbers written by the dead doctor's hand on the colored vellum-paper guard placed inside the boards by the binder, and which Ursule had just detected.

"What is the meaning of that? Our worthy friend was too great a book-lover to spoil the guard of a binding," said the Abbé Chaperon; "here are three numbers written between a first number, preceded by an M, and another preceded by an U."

"What do you say?" cried Bongrand. "Let me look at that. Good God!" he exclaimed, "is not this enough to open the eyes of an atheist, by proving to him the existence of Providence? Human justice is, I believe, the development of a divine idea brooding over the universe."

He seized Ursule and kissed her on the forehead.

"Oh! my child, you shall be happy—rich—and through me!"

"What is it?" said the curé.

"My dear monsieur!" cried La Bougival, taking the tail of the justice's blue coat, "let me embrace you for what you say."

"But explain yourself," said the curé, "that we may not rejoice vainly."

"If, in order to be rich, I must give anybody pain," said Ursule, who had an inkling of a criminal trial, "I——"

"But think," said the lawyer, interrupting Ursule, "of the happiness you will give our dear Savinien."

"But you are mad!" said the curé.

"No, my dear curé," said Bongrand. "Listen. Certificates of consols are numbered in as many series as there are letters of the alphabet, and each number bears the letter of its series; but certificates to bearer cannot have any letter, since they are inscribed in no name. Hence, what you here see proves that, on the day when the good man placed his money in state securities, he made a note of the number of his certificate for fifteen thousand francs a year under the letter M—for Minoret ; of the numbers of three certificates to bearer ; and of that of Ursule Mirouët under the letter U, number 23,534, which, as you see, immediately follows that of the certificate for fifteen thousand francs. This coincidence proves that these numbers are those of five certificates acquired on the same day, and noted by the old man in case of loss. I had advised him to put Ursule's money into certificates to bearer, and he must have invested his own money, the money he intended for Ursule, and her little property all on the same day. I am now going to Dionis to look at the inventory. If the number of the certificate he left in his own name is 23,533, letter M, we may be certain that he invested through the same stockbroker, and on the same day : Firstly, his own money in one lump sum ; secondly, his savings in three sums, in certificates to bearer ; and, thirdly, his ward's money ; the register of transfer will afford irrefutable proof. Ah, Minoret the wisehead, I have gotten you! Mum's the word, my friends ! ''

The justice left the curé, Ursule, and La Bougival lost in admiration of the ways by which God brings innocence to happy issues.

" The finger of God is here ! '' cried the Abbé Chaperon.

" Will they do him any hurt ? '' asked Ursule.

" Oh, mademoiselle,'' cried La Bougival, '' I would give the rope to hang him with ! ''

The justice was by this time at the house where Goupil was already the successor designate of Dionis, and went into the office with a careless air.

" I want a little information,'' said he to Goupil, '' as to the estate of Doctor Minoret.''

" What is it ? '' asked Goupil.

"Did the old man leave one or more certificates of investment in three per cents.?"

"He left fifteen thousand francs of income in three per cents.," said Goupil, "in one certificate. I entered it myself."

"Then just look in the inventory," said the justice.

Goupil took down a box, turned over the contents, took out the document in question, looked through it, and read, "Item, one certificate—there, read for yourself—number 23,533, letter M."

"Be so kind as to hand over to me an extract of the particulars from the inventory before one o'clock. I will wait for it."

"What can you want it for?" asked Goupil.

"Do you wish to become notary?" retorted the justice, looking sternly at the expectant successor to Dionis.

"I should think so!" cried Goupil. "I am sure I have eaten dirt enough to earn my title of 'Master.' I beg you to understand, monsieur, that the wretched office clerk known as Goupil has no connection with 'Master' Jean-Sebastien-Marie Goupil, notary at Nemours, and husband to Mademoiselle Massin. The two men do not know each other; they are not even alike in any particular. Do you not see me?"

Monsieur Bongrand then remarked Goupil's dress. He wore a white stock, a shirt of dazzling whiteness with ruby studs, a red velvet waistcoat, a coat and trousers of fine black cloth and Paris make. He had neat boots, and his hair, carefully combed and smoothed, was elegantly scented. In short, he seemed to have been metamorphosed!

"You are, in fact, another man," said Bongrand.

"Morally as well as physically, monsieur. Wisdom comes with work; and money is the fountain of cleansing——"

"Morally as well as physically?" said the justice, settling his spectacles.

"Dear me, monsieur, is a man with a hundred thousand crowns a year ever a democrat?· Regard me as a respectable man, who has a taste for refinement, and for loving his wife," he added, as Madame Goupil came in. "I am so much altered," said he, "that I think my cousin Madame Crémière quite witty. I have taken her in hand; and even her daughter no longer talks about pistons. Why, only yesterday, in speaking of Monsieur Savinien's dog, she said he was making a point. Well, I did not repeat her blunder, though it is a funny one. I at once explained to her the difference between pointing, making a point, and standing at point. So, you see, I am quite another man, and would not allow a client to get into a mess."

"Well, make haste then," said Bongrand. "Give me that copy within an hour, and Goupil, the notary, will have done something towards repairing the misdeeds of the clerk."

After borrowing from the town doctor his cab and horse, the justice went to fetch the two accusing folios, Ursule's certificate, and the extract from the inventory; armed with these, he drove to Fontainebleau to the public prosecutor there. Bongrand easily proved the abstraction of the three certificates to be the act of one or another of the heirs-at-law, and then demonstrated Minoret's guilt.

"It accounts for his conduct," said the lawyer.

Then, as a measure of precaution, he stopped the transfer of the three certificates by a minute to the treasury, he desired Bongrand to ask what was the amount of interest due on the three certificates, and ascertain if they had been sold.

While the justice went to do all this at Paris, the public prosecutor wrote a polite note to Madame Minoret to beg her to come to the assize town. Zélie, anxious about her son's duel, dressed, had her own carriage out, and drove post-haste to Fontainebleau. The public prosecutor's scheme was simple but formidable. By separating the husband and wife, he felt sure of learning the truth as a result of the terrors of the law.

Zélie found the magistrate in his private room, and was absolutely thunderstruck by this unceremonious speech :

"Madame, I do not imagine that you are an accomplice in a robbery made at the time of Doctor Minoret's death ; justice is now on the traces, and you will save your husband from appearing at the bar by making a full confession of all you know about it. The punishment that threatens your husband is not, indeed, all you have to fear ; you must try to save your son from degradation, and not cut his throat. In a few minutes it will be too late ; the gendarmes are already on horseback, and the warrant for Minoret's apprehension will be sent to Nemours."

Zélie fainted. When she came to herself, she confessed everything. After proving easily to this woman that she was an accomplice, the magistrate told her that, to avoid ruining her husband and son, he would proceed cautiously.

"You have had to deal with a man and not with a judge," said he. "There is no charge on the part of the victim, nor has the theft been made public ; but your husband has committed dreadful crimes, madame, which are usually tried before a tribunal less accommodating than I am. In the present circumstances of the case you will be obliged to remain a prisoner. Oh, in my house, and on parole," he added, seeing Zélie ready to faint again. "Remember that my strict duty would be to demand a warrant for your imprisonment, and institute an inquiry ; however, I am acting at present as the legal guardian of Mademoiselle Ursule Mirouët, and in her interests, wisely understood, a compromise will be advisable."

"Ah !" said Zélie.

"Write as follows to your husband." And he dictated this letter to Zélie, who wrote it at his desk, with preposterously bad spelling :

"MY DEAR :—I am arrested, and I have told all. Give

up the certificates left by our uncle to Monsieur de Portenduère by virtue of the will you burned, for monsieur the public prosecutor has stopped them at the treasury."

" By this means you will prevent his making denials, which would be his ruin," said the lawyer, smiling at the spelling. " We will see about having the restitution carried out in a proper manner. My wife will make your stay at my house as little unpleasant as possible ; I advise you to say nothing to any one, and not to show your distress."

As soon as his deputy's mother had confessed and been placed in safety, the magistrate sent for Désiré, told him point by point the story of the robbery committed by his father, secretly to Ursule's detriment, evidently to that of the co-heirs, and showed him the letter his mother had written. Désiré immediately begged to be sent to Nemours, to see that his father made restitution.

" The whole case is very serious," said his chief. " The will having been destroyed, if the thing becomes known, the co-heirs, Massin and Crémière, your relations, may intervene. I have now sufficient evidence against your father. I give your mother back to you ; this little ceremony has sufficiently enlightened her as to her duty. In her eyes I shall seem to have yielded to your entreaties in releasing her. Go to Nemours with her, and guide all these difficulties to a happy issue. Fear nobody. Monsieur Bongrand loves Mademoiselle Mirouët too well to commit any indiscretion."

Zélie and Désiré set out at once for Nemours. Three hours after his deputy's departure, the public prosecutor received by express messenger the following letter, of which the spelling is corrected, not to make an unhappy man ridiculous :

" To the Public Prosecutor of the Court of Assizes at Fontainebleau.

" MONSIEUR :—God has not been so merciful to us as you

have been, and an irreparable misfortune has fallen on us.
On arriving at the bridge of Nemours, a strap came unfast-
ened. My wife was at the back of the chaise without a servant ; the horses smelt the stable. My son, afraid of their
restiveness, would not let the coachman get down, and got
out himself to buckle it up. At the moment when he turned
to get up again by his mother, the horses started off; Désiré
did not make way quickly enough by squeezing back against
the parapet, the iron step cut his legs ; he fell, and the hind
wheel went over his body. The messenger riding express to
Paris to fetch the first surgeons will carry you this letter,
which my son, in the midst of his suffering, desires me to
write, to express to you our entire submission to your decisions in the business which was bringing him home.

"I shall be grateful to you till my latest breath for the
way in which you have proceeded, and will justify your
confidence.

"FRANÇOIS MINORET."

This terrible event upset the whole town of Nemours. The
excited crowd that gathered round Minoret's gate showed
Savinien that his revenge had been taken in hand by one
more powerful than he. The young man went at once to
Ursule, and the young girl and the curé alike felt more horror
than surprise. The next day, after the first treatment, when
the Paris doctors and surgeons had given their advice, which
was unanimous as to the necessity for amputating both legs,
Minoret, pale, dejected, and heart-broken, came, accompanied
by the curé, to Ursule's house, where he found Bongrand and
Savinien.

" Mademoiselle," said he, " I am guilty towards you ; but
though all the ill I have done cannot be entirely repaired,
some I can expiate. My wife and I have made up our minds
to give you, as an absolute possession, our estate of Le Rouvre
if we preserve our son—as well as if we have the terrible grief

of losing him." As he ceased speaking, the man melted into tears.

"I may assure you, my dear Ursule," said the curé, "that you may and ought to accept a part of this gift."

"Do you forgive us?" said the colossus humbly, and kneeling at the feet of the astonished girl. "In a few hours the operation is to be performed by the first surgeon of the Hôtel-Dieu ; but I put no trust in human science ; I believe in the omnipotence of God ! If you forgive me, if you will go and ask God to preserve us our son, he will have strength to endure this torment, and we shall have the happiness of keeping him, I am sure of it."

"Let us all go to the church !" said Ursule, rising. She was no sooner on her feet than she gave a piercing shriek, fell back in her chair, and fainted away. When she recovered her senses, she saw her friends, with the exception of Minoret, who had rushed off to find a doctor, all with their eyes fixed on her, anxiously expecting her to speak a word. That word filled every heart with horror.

"I saw my godfather at the door," she said. "He signed to me that there was no hope."

And, in fact, the day after the operation, Désiré died, carried off by fever and the revulsion of the humors which follows on such operations. Madame Minoret, whose heart held no sentiment but that of motherhood, went mad after her son's funeral, and was taken by her husband to the care of Doctor Blanche for medical treatment, where she died in January, 1841.

Three months after these events, in January, 1837, Ursule married Savinien, with Madame de Portenduère's consent. Minoret intervened at the signing of the contract to settle on Mademoiselle Mirouët, by deed of gift, his estate of Le Rouvre, and twenty-eight thousand francs a year in consols, reserving of all his fortune only his uncle's house and six thousand francs a year. He has become the most charitable and pious man in Nemours, churchwarden of the parish, and the providence of the unfortunate.

"The poor have taken the place of my child," he says.

If you have ever observed by the roadside, in districts where the oak is lopped low, some old tree, bleached, and, as it would seem, blasted, but still throwing out shoots, its sides riven, crying out for the axe, you will have an idea of the old postmaster, white-haired, bent, and lean, in whom the old folks of the district can trace nothing of the happy lout whom we saw watching for his son at the beginning of this tale; he no longer takes snuff in the same way even; he bears some burden besides his body. In short, it is perceptible in everything that the hand of God has been heavily laid on that form to make it a terrible example. After hating his uncle's ward so bitterly, this old man, like Doctor Minoret himself, has so set his affections on Ursule, that he is the self-constituted steward of her property at Nemours.

Monsieur and Madame de Portenduère spend five months of the year in Paris, where they have purchased a splendid house in the Faubourg St.-Germain. After bestowing her house at Nemours on the Sisters of Charity to be used as a free school, Madame de Portenduère the elder went to live at Le Rouvre, where La Bougival is the head gatekeeper. Cabirolle's father, formerly the guard of the "Ducler," a man of sixty, has married La Bougival, who owns twelve hundred francs a year in consols, besides the comfortable profits of her place. Cabirolle's son is Monsieur de Portenduère's coachman.

When, in the Champs-Élysées, you see one of those neat little low carriages, known as *escargots* (or snail-shells), drive past, and admire a pretty, fair woman leaning lightly against a young man, her face surrounded by a myriad of curls, like light foliage, and eyes like luminous periwinkle flowers, full of love—if you should feel the sting of envious wishes, remember that this handsome couple, the favorites of God, have paid in advance their tribute to the woes of life. These married lovers will probably be the Vicomte de Portenduére and his wife. There are not two such couples in Paris.

"It is the prettiest happiness I ever saw," said the Comtesse d'Estorade, not long since.

So give those happy children your blessing instead of envying them, and try to find an Ursule Mirouët—a young girl brought up by three old men, and that best of mothers—adversity.

Goupil, who is helpful to everybody, and justly regarded as the wittiest man in Nemours, is esteemed by the little town; but he is punished in his children, who are hideous, rickety, and hydrocephalous. His predecessor, Dionis, flourishes in the Chamber of Deputies, of which he is one of the greatest ornaments, to the great satisfaction of the King of the French, who sees Madame Dionis at every state ball. Madame Dionis relates to all the town of Nemours the particulars of her reception at the Tuileries, and the grandeurs of the King's court. She is queen at Nemours, by virtue of a king who is certainly popular in that sense.

Bongrand is president of the court of justice at Melun, and his son is on the high road to becoming a very respectable public prosecutor.

Madame Crémière still says the funniest things in the world. She writes tambour *tambourg*, and says it is because her pen splutters. On the eve of her daughter's marriage, she told her, in concluding her advice to her, that a wife ought to be the toiling caterpillar of her home, and keep a sphinx's eye on everything. Indeed, Goupil is making a collection of his cousin's absurd blunders, a *Crémièriana*.

"We have had the grief of losing our good Abbé Chaperon this winter," says the Vicomtesse de Portenduère, who nursed him during his illness. All the district attended his funeral. Nemours is fortunate, for this saintly man's successor is the venerable Curé de Saint-Lange.

PARIS, *June–July*, 1841.

MADAME FIRMIANI.

*(To my dear Alexandre de Berny, from his old
friend De Balzac.)*

MANY tales, rich in situations, or made dramatic by the
endless sport of chance, carry their plot in themselves, and
can be related artistically or simply by any lips without the
smallest loss of the beauty of the subject ; but there are some
incidents of human life to which only the accents of the heart
can give life; there are certain anatomical details, so to
speak, of which the delicacy appears only under the most
skillful infusions of mind. Again, there are portraits which
demand a soul, and are nothing without the more ethereal
features of the responsive countenance. Finally, there are
certain things which we know not how to say, or to depict,
without I know not what unconceived harmonies that are
under the influence of a day or an hour, of a happy conjunc-
tion of celestial signs, or of some occult moral predisposition.

Such revelations as these are absolutely required for the
telling of this simple story, in which I would fain interest
some of those naturally melancholy and pensive souls which
are fed on bland emotions. If the writer, like a surgeon by
the side of a dying friend, has become imbued with a sort of
respect for the subject he is handling, why should not the
reader share this inexplicable feeling? Is it so difficult to
throw one's self into that vague, nervous melancholy which
sheds gray hues on all our surroundings, which is half an illness, though its languid suffering is sometimes a pleasure?

If you are thinking by chance of the dear friends you have
lost; if you are alone, and it is night, or the day is dying,
read this narrative; otherwise, throw the book aside, here.
If you have never buried some kind aunt, an invalid or poor,

you will not understand these pages. To some, they will be odorous as of musk; to others, they will be as colorless, as strictly virtuous as those of Florian. In short, the reader must have known the luxury of tears; must have felt the wordless grief of a memory that drifts lightly by, bearing a shade that is dear but remote; he must possess some of those remembrances that make us at the same time regret those whom the earth has swallowed, and smile over vanished joys.

And now the author would have you believe that for all the wealth of England he would not extort from poetry even one of her fictions to add grace to this narrative. This is a true story, on which you may pour out the treasure of your sensibilities, if you have any.

In these days our language has as many dialects as there are men in the great human family. And it is a really curious and interesting thing to listen to the different views or versions of one and the same thing, or event, as given by the various species which make up the monograph of the Parisian —the Parisian being taken as a generic term. Thus you might ask a man of the matter-of-fact type, " Do you know Madame Firmiani?" and this man would interpret Madame Firmiani by such an inventory as this: "A large house in the Rue du Bac, rooms handsomely furnished, fine pictures, a hundred thousand francs a year in good securities, and a husband who was formerly receiver-general in the department of Montenotte." Having thus spoken, your matter-of-fact man—stout and roundabout, almost always dressed in black— draws up his lower lip, so as to cover the upper lip, and nods his head, as much as to say, "Very respectable people, there is nothing to be said against them." Ask him no more. Your matter-of-fact people state everything in figures, dividends, or real estate—a great word in their dictionary.

Turn to your right, go and question that young man, who belongs to the lounger species, and repeat your inquiry.

"Madame Firmiani?" says he. "Yes, yes, I know her very well. I go to her evenings. She receives on Wednesdays; a very good house to know." Madame Firmiani is already metamorphosed into a house. The house is not a mere mass of stones architecturally put together; no, this word, in the language of the lounger, has no equivalent. And here your lounger, a dry-looking man, with a pleasant smile, saying clever nothings, but always with more acquired wit than natural wit, bends to your ear, and says with a knowing air: "I never saw Monsieur Firmiani. His social position consists in managing estates in Italy. But Madame Firmiani is French, and spends her income as a Parisian should. She gives excellent tea! It is one of the few houses where you really can amuse yourself, and where everything they give you is exquisite. It is very difficult to get introduced, and the best society is to be seen in her drawing-rooms." Then the lounger emphasizes his last words by gravely taking a pinch of snuff; he applies it to his nose in little dabs, and seems to be saying: "I go to the house, but do not count on my introducing you."

To folks of this type Madame Firmiani keeps a sort of inn without a sign.

"Why on earth can you want to go to Madame Firmiani's? It is as dull there as it is at court. Of what use are brains if they do not keep you out of such drawing-rooms, where, with poetry such as is now current, you hear the most trivial little ballad just hatched out."

You have asked one of your friends who comes under the class of petty autocrats—men who would like to have the universe under lock and key, and have nothing done without their leave. They are miserable at other people's enjoyment, can forgive nothing but vice, wrong-doing, and infirmities, and want nothing but protégés. Aristocrats by taste, they are republicans out of spite, simply to discover many inferiors among their equals.

"Oh, Madame Firmiani, my dear fellow, is one of those adorable women whom nature feels to be a sufficient excuse for all the ugly ones she has created by mistake; she is be-witching, she is kind! I should like to be in power to be king, to have millions of money, solely" (and three words are whispered in your ear). "Shall I introduce you to her?"

This young man is a schoolboy, known for his audacious bearing among men and his extreme shyness in private.

"Madame Firmiani!" cries another, twirling his cane in the air. "I will tell you what I think of her. She is a woman of between thirty and thirty-five, face a little *passée*, fine eyes, a flat figure, a worn contralto voice, dresses a great deal, rouges a little, manners charming; in short, my dear fellow, the remains of a pretty woman which are still worthy of a passion."

This verdict is pronounced by a specimen of the genus cox-comb, who, having just breakfasted, does not weigh his words, and is going out riding. At such moments a coxcomb is piti-less.

"She has a collection of magnificent pictures in her house. Go and see her," says another; "nothing can be finer."

You have come upon the species amateur. This individual quits you to go to Pérignon's, or to Tripet's. To him Madame Firmiani is a number of painted canvases.

A WIFE.—"Madame Firmiani? I will not have you go there." This phrase is the most suggestive view of all. Madame Firmiani. A dangerous woman! A siren! She dresses well, has good taste; she spoils the night's rest of every wife. The speaker is of the species shrew.

AN ATTACHÉ TO AN EMBASSY.—"Madame Firmiani? From Antwerp, is she not? I saw that woman, very handsome, about ten years ago. She was then at Rome."

Men of the order of attachés have a mania for utterances *à la* Talleyrand, their wit is often so subtle that their perception is imperceptible. They are like those billiard players who

miss the balls with infinite skill.   These men are not generally
great talkers; but when they talk it is of nothing less than
Spain, Vienna, Italy, or Saint Petersburg.   The names of
countries act on them like springs; you press them and the
machinery plays all its tunes.

"Does not that Madame Firmiani see a great deal of the
Faubourg Saint-Germain?"   This is asked by a person who
desires claims to distinction.   She adds a *de* to everybody's
name—to Monsieur Dupin, senior, to Monsieur Lafayette;
she flings it right and left and spatters people with it.   She
spends her life in anxieties as to what is *correct;* but, for her
sins, she lives in the unfashionable Marais, and her husband
was an attorney—but an attorney in the King's court.

"Madame Firmiani, monsieur? I do not know her."   This
man is of the class of dukes.   He recognizes no woman who
has not been presented.   Excuse him; he was created duke
by Napoleon.

"Madame Firmiani?   Was she not a singer at the Italian
opera house?"   A man of the genus simpleton.   The individuals of this genus must have an answer to everything.
They would rather speak calumnies than be silent.

TWO OLD LADIES (*the wives of retired lawyers*).   THE FIRST
(she has a cap with bows of ribbon, her face is wrinkled, her
nose sharp; she holds a prayer-book, and her voice is harsh).—
"What was her maiden name—this Madame Firmiani?"

THE SECOND (she has a little red face like a lady-apple,
and a gentle voice).—"She was a Cadignan, my dear, niece
of the old Prince de Cadignan, and cousin, consequently, to
the Duc de Maufrigneuse."

Madame Firmiani then is a Cadignan.   Bereft of virtues,
fortune, and youth, she would still be a Cadignan; that, like
a prejudice, is always rich and living.

AN ECCENTRIC.—"My dear fellow, I never saw any clogs
in her anteroom; you may go to her house without compromising yourself, and play there without hesitation; for if

there should be any rogues, they will be people of quality, consequently there is no quarreling."

AN OLD MAN OF THE SPECIES OBSERVER.—"You go to Madame Firmiani's, my dear fellow, and you find a handsome woman lounging indolently by the fire. She will scarcely move from her chair; she rises only to greet women, or ambassadors, or dukes—people of importance. She is very gracious, she charms you, she talks well, and likes to talk of everything. She bears every indication of a passionate soul, but she is credited with too many adorers to have a lover. If suspicion rested on only two or three intimate visitors, we might know which was her gallant slave. But she is all mystery; she is married, and we have never seen her husband; Monsieur Firmiani is purely a creature of fancy, like the third horse we are made to pay for when traveling post, and which we never see; madame, if you believe the professionals, has the finest contralto voice in Europe, and has not sung three times since she came to Paris; she receives numbers of people, and goes nowhere."

The observer speaks as an oracle. His words, his anecdotes, his quotations must all be accepted as truth, or you risk being taken for a man without knowledge of the world, without capabilities. He will slander you lightly in twenty drawing-rooms, where he is as essential as the first piece in the bill—pieces so often played to the benches, but which once upon a time were successful. The observer is a man of forty, never dines at home, and professes not to be dangerous to women; he wears powder and a maroon-colored coat; he can always have a seat in various boxes at the Théâtre des Bouffons. He is sometimes mistaken for a parasite, but he has held too high positions to be suspected of sponging, and, indeed, possesses an estate, in a department of which the name has never leaked out.

"Madame Firmiani? Why, my dear boy, she was a mistress of Murat's." This gentleman is a contradictory. They supply the errata to every memory, rectify every fact, bet you a hundred to one, are cock-sure of everything. You catch them out in a single evening in flagrant delictions of ubiquity. They assert that they were in Paris at the time of Mallet's conspiracy, forgetting that half an hour before they had crossed the Beresina. The contradictories are almost all members of the Legion of Honor; they talk very loud, have receding foreheads, and play high.

"Madame Firmiani, a hundred thousand francs a year? Are you mad? Really some people scatter thousands a year with the liberality of authors, to whom it costs nothing to give their heroines handsome fortunes. But Madame Firmiani is a flirt who ruined a young fellow the other day, and hindered him from making a very good marriage. If she were not handsome, she would be penniless."

This speaker you recognize; he is one of the envious, and we will not sketch his least feature. The species is as well known as that of the domestic cat. How is the perpetuity of envy to be explained! A vice which is wholly unprofitable!

People of fashion, literary people, very good people, and people of every kind were, in the month of January, 1824, giving out so many different opinions on Madame Firmiani that it would be tiresome to report them all. We have only aimed at showing that a man wishing to know her, without choosing, or being able, to go to her house, would have been equally justified in the belief that she was a widow or a wife— silly or witty, virtuous or immoral, rich or poor, gentle or devoid of soul, handsome or ugly; in fact, there were as many Mesdames Firmiani as there are varieties in social life, or sects in the Catholic Church. Frightful thought! We are all like lithographed plates, of which an endless number of copies are taken off by slander. These copies resemble or differ from the original by touches so imperceptibly slight that, but for the calumnies of our friends and the witticisms of newspapers, reputation would depend on the balance struck by each hearer between the limping truth and the lies to which Parisian wit lends wings.

Madame Firmiani, like many other women of dignity and noble pride, who close their hearts as a sanctuary and scorn the world, might have been very hardly judged by Monsieur de Bourbonne, an old gentleman of fortune, who had thought a good deal about her during the past winter. As it happened, this gentleman belonged to the Provincial land-owner class, folks who are accustomed to inquire into everything, and to make bargains with peasants. In this business a man grows keen-witted in spite of himself, as a soldier, in the long run, acquires the courage of routine. This inquirer, a native of Touraine, and not easily satisfied by the Paris dialects, was a very honorable gentleman who rejoiced in a nephew, his sole heir, for whom he planted his poplars. Their more than natural affection gave rise to much evil-speaking, which individuals of the various species of Tourangeau formulated with much mother wit; but it would be useless to record it; it would pale before that of Parisian tongues. When a man can think of his heir without displeasure, as he sees fine rows of poplars improving every day, his affection increases with each spadeful of earth he turns at the foot of his trees. Though such phenomena of sensibility may be uncommon, they still are to be met with in Touraine.

This much-loved nephew, whose name was Octave de Camps, was descended from the famous Abbé de Camps, so well known to the learned, or to the bibliomaniacs, which is not the same thing.

Provincial folks have a disagreeable habit of regarding young men who sell their reversions with a sort of respectable horror. This Gothic prejudice is bad for speculation, which the government has hitherto found it necessary to encourage. Now, without consulting his uncle, Octave had on a sudden disposed of an estate in favor of the speculative builders. The

château of Villaines would have been demolished but for the
offers made by his old uncle to the representatives of the de-
molishing fraternity.   To add to the testator's wrath, a friend
of Octave's, a distant relation, one of those cousins with small
wealth and great cunning, who lead their prudent neighbors
to say, "I should not like to go to law with him!" had
called, by chance, on Monsieur de Bourbonne and informed
him that his nephew was ruined.   Monsieur Octave de Camps,
after dissipating his fortune for a certain Madame Firmiani,
and not daring to confess his sins, had been reduced to giving
lessons in mathematics, pending his coming into his uncle's
leavings.   This distant cousin—a sort of Charles Moor—had
not been ashamed of giving this disastrous news to the old
country gentleman at the hour when, sitting before his spacious
hearth, he was digesting a copious provincial dinner.   But
would-be legatees do not get rid of an uncle so easily as they
could wish.   This uncle, thanks to his obstinacy, refusing to
believe the distant cousin, came out victorious over the in-
digestion brought on by the biography of his nephew.   Some
blows fall on the heart, others on the brain; the blow struck
by the distant cousin fell on the stomach, and produced little
effect, as the good man had a strong one.

Monsieur de Bourbonne, as a worthy disciple of Saint
Thomas, came to Paris without telling Octave, and tried to
get information as to his heir's insolvency.   The old gentleman, who had friends in the Faubourg Saint-Germain—the
Listomères, the Lenoncourts, and the Vandenesses—heard so
much slander, so much that was true, and so much that was
false concerning Madame Firmiani, that he determined to call
on her, under the name of Monsieur de Rouxellay, the name
of his place.   The prudent old man took care, in going to
study Octave's mistress—as she was said to be—to choose an
evening when he knew that the young man was engaged on
work to be well paid for; for Madame Firmiani was always at
home to her young friend, a circumstance that no one could

account for.   As to Octave's ruin, that, unfortunately, was
no fiction.

Monsieur de Rouxellay was not at all like a stage uncle.
As an old musketeer, a man of the best society, who had his
successes in his day, he knew how to introduce himself with a
courtly air, remembered the polished manners of the past, had
a pretty wit, and understood almost all the rôle of nobility.
Though he loved the Bourbons with noble frankness, believed
in God as gentlemen believe, and read only the *Quotidienne*,
he was by no means so ridiculous as the Liberals of his department would have wished.   He could hold his own with men
about the court, so long as he was not expected to talk of
" Moses," or the play, or romanticism, or local color, or rail-
ways.   He had not gotten beyond Monsieur de Voltaire, Monsieur le Comte de Buffon, Peyronnet, and the Chevalier
Gluck, the Queen's private musician.

" Madame," said he to the Marquise de Listomère, to
whom he had given his arm to go into Madame Firmiani's
room, " if this woman is my nephew's mistress, I pity her.
How can she bear to live in the midst of luxury and know
that he is in a garret ?   Has she no soul ?   Octave is a fool to
have invested the price of the estate of Villaines in the heart
of a——"

Monsieur de Bourbonne was of a fossil species, and spoke
only the language of a past day.

" But suppose he had lost it at play ? "

" Well, madame, he would have had the pleasure of
playing."

" You think he has had no pleasure for his money ?   Look,
here is Madame Firmiani."

The old uncle's brightest memories paled at the sight of
his nephew's supposed mistress.   His anger died in a polite
speech wrung from him by the presence of Madame Firmiani.
By one of those chances which come only to pretty women,
it was a moment when all her beauties shone with particular

brilliancy, the result, perhaps, of the glitter of wax-lights, of an exquisitely simple dress, of an indefinable reflection from the elegance in which she lived and moved. Only long study of the petty revolutions of an evening party in a Paris salon can enable one to appreciate the imperceptible shades that can tinge and change a woman's face. There are moments when, pleased with her dress, feeling herself brilliant, happy at being admired and seeing herself the queen of a room full of remarkable men, all smiling at her, a Parisian is conscious of her beauty and grace; she grows the lovelier by all the looks she meets; they give her animation, but their mute homage is transmitted by subtle glances to the man she loves. In such a moment a woman is invested, as it were, with supernatural power, and becomes a witch, an unconscious coquette; she involuntarily inspires the passion which is a secret intoxication to herself, she has smiles and looks that are fascinating. If this excitement which comes from the soul lends attractiveness even to ugly women, with what splendor does it not clothe a naturally elegant creature, finely made, fair, fresh, bright-eyed, and, above all, dressed with such taste as artists and even her most spiteful rivals must admit.

Have you ever met, for your happiness, some woman whose harmonious tones give to her speech the charm that is no less conspicuous in her manners, who knows how to talk and to be silent, who cares for you with delicate feeling, whose words are happily chosen and her language pure? Her banter flatters you, her criticism does not sting; she neither preaches nor disputes, but is interested in leading a discussion, and stops it at the right moment. Her manner is friendly and gay, her politeness is unforced, her eagerness to please is not servile; she reduces respect to a mere gentle shade; she never tires you, and leaves you satisfied with her and yourself. You will see her gracious presence stamped on the things she collects about her. In her home everything charms the eye, and you breathe, as it seems, your native air. This woman is quite natural. You never feel an effort, she flaunts nothing, her feelings are expressed with simplicity because they are genuine. Though candid, she never wounds the most sensitive pride ; she accepts men as God made them, pitying the vicious, forgiving defects and absurdities, sympathizing with every age, and vexed with nothing because she has the tact to forefend everything. At once tender and lively, she first constrains and then consoles you. You love her so truly that, if this angel does wrong, you are ready to justify her. Then you know Madame Firmiani.

By the time old Bourbonne had talked with this woman, for a quarter of an hour, sitting by her side, his nephew was absolved. He understood that, true or false, Octave's connection with Madame Firmiani no doubt covered some mystery. Returning to the illusions of his youth, and judging of Madame Firmiani's heart by her beauty, the old gentleman thought that a woman so sure of her dignity as she seemed, was incapable of a base action. Her black eyes spoke of so much peace of mind, the lines of her face were so noble, the forms so pure, and the passion of which she was accused seemed to weigh so little on her heart, that, as he admired all the pledges given to love and to virtue by that adorable countenance, the old man said to himself, " My nephew has committed some folly."

Madame Firmiani owned to twenty-five. But the matter-of-facts could prove that, having been married in 1813 at the age of sixteen, she must be at least eight-and-twenty in 1825. Nevertheless the same persons declared that she had never at any period of her life been so desirable, so perfectly a woman. She had no children, and had never had any ; the hypothetical Firmiani, a respectable man of forty in 1813, had, it was said, only his name and fortune to offer her. So Madame Firmiani had come to the age when a Parisian best understands what passion is, and perhaps longs for it innocently in her unemployed hours: she had everything that the world can

sell, or lend, or give. The attachés declared she knew everything; the contradictories said she had yet many things to
learn; the observers noticed that her hands were very white,
her foot very small, her movements a little too undulating;
but men of every species envied or disputed Octave's good
fortune, agreeing that she was the most aristocratic beauty in
Paris.

Still young, rich, a perfect musician, witty, exquisite;
welcomed, for the sake of the Cadignans, to whom she was
related through her mother, by the Princess de Blamont-
Chauvry, the oracle of the aristocratic quarter; beloved by
her rivals the Duchesse de Maufrigneuse her cousin, the
Marquise d'Espard, and Madame de Macumer, she flattered
every vanity which feeds or excites love. And, indeed, she
was the object of too many desires not to be the victim of
fashionable detraction and those delightful calumnies which
are wittily hinted behind a fan or in a whispered *aside*.
Hence the remarks with which this story opened were necessary to mark the contrast between the real Firmiani and the
Firmiani known to the world. Though some women forgave
her for being happy, others could not overlook her respecta-
bility; now there is nothing so terrible, especially in Paris,
as suspicion without foundation; it is impossible to kill it.

This sketch of a personality so admirable by nature can
only give a feeble idea of it; it would need the brush of an
Ingres to represent the dignity of the brow, the mass of fine
hair, the majesty of the eyes, all the thoughts betrayed by the
varying hues of the complexion. There was something of
everything in this woman; poets could see in her both Joan
of Arc and Agnes Sorel; but there was also the unknown
woman—the soul hidden behind this deceptive mask—the
soul of Eve, the wealth of evil and treasures of goodness,
wrong and resignation, crime and self-sacrifice—the Doña
Julia and Haidee of Byron's " Don Juan."

The old soldier very boldly remained till the last in Madame

Firmiani's drawing-room; she found him quietly seated in an armchair, and staying with the pertinacity of a fly that must be killed to be gotten rid of. The clock marked two in the morning.

"Madame," said the old gentleman, just as Madame Firmiani rose in the hope of making her guest understand that it was her pleasure that he should go. "Madame, I am Monsieur Octave de Camps' uncle."

Madame Firmiani at once sat down again, and her agitation was evident. In spite of his perspicacity, the planter of poplars could not make up his mind whether shame or pleasure made her turn pale. There are pleasures which do not exist without a little coy bashfulness—delightful emotions which the chastest soul would fain keep behind a veil. The more sensitive a woman is, the more she lives to conceal her soul's greatest joys. Many women, incomprehensible in their exquisite caprices, at times long to hear a name spoken by all the world, while they sometimes would sooner bury it in their hearts. Old Bourbonne did not read Madame Firmiani's agitation quite in this light; but forgive him; the country gentleman was suspicious.

"Indeed, monsieur?" said Madame Firmiani, with one of those clear and piercing looks in which we men can never see anything, because they question us too keenly.

"Indeed, madame; and do you know what I have been told—I, in the depths of the country? That my nephew has ruined himself for you; and the unhappy boy is in a garret, while you live here in gold and silks. You will, I hope, forgive my rustic frankness, for it may be useful to you to be informed of the slander."

"Stop, monsieur," said Madame Firmiani, interrupting the gentleman with an imperious gesture, "I know all that. You are too polite to keep the conversation to this subject when I beg you to change it. You are too gallant, in the old-fashioned sense of the word," she added, with a slightly ironical emphasis, "not to acknowledge that you have no right to cross-question me. However, it is ridiculous in me to justify myself. I hope you have a good enough opinion of my character to believe in the utter contempt I feel for money, though I was married without any fortune whatever to a man who had an immense fortune. I do not know whether your nephew is rich or poor; if I have received him, if I still receive him, it is because I regard him as worthy to move in the midst of my friends. All my friends, monsieur, respect each other; they know that I am not so philosophical as to entertain people whom I do not esteem. That, perhaps, shows a lack of charity; but my guardian angel has preserved in me, to this day, an intense aversion for gossip and dishonor."

Though her voice was not quite firm at the beginning of this reply, the last words were spoken by Madame Firmiani with the cool decision of *Célimène* rallying the *Misanthrope*.

"Madame," the Count resumed in a broken voice, "I am an old man—I am almost a father to Octave—I therefore must humbly crave your pardon beforehand for the only question I shall be so bold as to ask you; and I give you my word of honor as a gentleman that your reply will die here," and he laid his hand on his heart with a really religious gesture. "Does gossip speak the truth; do you love Octave?"

"Monsieur," said she, "I should answer any one else with a look. But you, since you are almost a father to Monsieur de Camps, you I will ask what you would think of a woman who, in reply to your question, should say, Yes. To confess one's love to the man we love—when he loves us—well, well; when we are sure of being loved for ever, believe me, monsieur, it is an effort to us and a reward to him; but to any one else!——"

Madame Firmiani did not finish her sentence; she rose, bowed to the good gentleman, and vanished into her private rooms, where the sound of doors opened and shut in succession had language to the ears of the poplar planter.

"Damn it !" said he to himself, "what a woman ! She is either a very cunning hussy or an angel;" and he went down to his hired fly in the courtyard, where the horses were pawing the pavement in the silence. The coachman was asleep, after having cursed his customer a hundred times.

Next morning, by about eight o'clock, the old gentleman was mounting the stairs of a house in the Rue de l'Observance, where dwelt Octave de Camps. If there was in this world a man amazed, it was the young professor on seeing his uncle. The key was in the door, Octave's lamp was still burning; he had sat up all night.

"Now, you rascal," said Monsieur de Bourbonne, seating himself in an armchair. "How long has it been the fashion to make fools (speaking mildly) of uncles who have twenty-six thousand francs a year in good land in Touraine ? and that when you are sole heir ? Do you know that formerly such relations were treated with respect ? Pray, have you any fault to find with me ? Have I bungled my business as an uncle ? Have I demanded your respect ? Have I ever refused you money ? Have I shut my door in your face, saying you had only come to see how I was ? Have you not the most accommodating, the least exacting uncle in France ?—I will not say in Europe, it would be claiming too much. You write to me, or you don't write. I live on your professions of affection. I am laying out the prettiest estate in the neighborhood, a place that is the object of envy in all the department ; but I do not mean to leave it you till the latest date possible—a weakness that is very pardonable. And my gentleman sells his property, is lodged like a groom, has no servants, keeps no style——"

"My dear uncle——"

"It is not a case of uncle, but of nephew. I have a right to your confidence ; so have it out all at once ; it is the easiest way, I know by experience. Have you been gambling ? Have you been speculating on the Bourse ? Come, say,

' Uncle, I am a wretch,' and we kiss and are friends. But if
you tell me any lie bigger than those I told at your age, I will
sell my property, buy an annuity, and go back to the bad ways
of my youth, if it is not too late."

"Uncle——"

"I went last night to see your Madame Firmiani," said the
uncle, kissing the tips of all his fingers together. "She is
charming," he went on. "You have the King's warrant and
approval,.and your uncle's consent, if that is any satisfaction
to you. As to the sanction of the church, that I suppose is
unnecessary—the sacraments, no doubt, are too costly. Come;
speak out. Is it for her that you have ruined yourself?"

"Yes, uncle."

"Ah! the hussy! I would have bet upon it. In my day a
woman of fashion could ruin a man more cleverly than any
of your courtesans of to-day. I saw in her a resuscitation of
the last century."

"Uncle," said Octave, in a voice that was at once sad and
gentle, "you are under a mistake. Madame Firmiani de-
serves your esteem, and all the adoration of her admirers."

"So hapless youth is always the same!" said Monsieur de
Bourbonne. "Well, well! go on in your own way; tell me
all the old stories once more. At the same time, you know,
I dare say, that I am no chicken in such matters."

"My dear uncle, here is a letter which will explain everything," replied Octave, taking out an elegant letter-case—*her*
gift, no doubt. "When you have read it I will tell you the
rest, and you will know Madame Firmiani as the world knows
her not."

"I have not my spectacles with me," said his uncle.
"Read it to me."

Octave began: "'My dear love——'"

"Then you are very intimate with this woman?"

"Why, yes, uncle."

"And you have not quarreled?"

18

"Quarreled!" echoed Octave in surprise. "We are married—at Gretna Green."

"Well, then, why do you dine for forty sous?"

"Let me proceed."

"Very true. I am listening."

Octave took up the letter again, and could not read certain passages without strong emotion.

"'My beloved husband, you ask me the reason of my melancholy. Has it passed from my soul into my face, or have you only guessed it? And why should you not? Our hearts are so closely united. Besides, I cannot lie, though that perhaps is a misfortune. One of the conditions of being loved is, in a woman, to be always caressing and gay. Perhaps I ought to deceive you; but I would not do so, not even if it were to increase or to preserve the happiness you give me—you lavish on me—under which you overwhelm me. Oh, my dear, my love carries with it so much gratitude! And I must love for ever, without measure. Yes, I must always be proud of you. Our glory—a woman's glory—is all in the man she loves. Esteem, consideration, honor, are they not all his who has conquered everything? Well, and my angel has fallen. Yes, my dear, your last confession has dimmed my past happiness. From that moment I have felt myself humbled through you—you, whom I believed to be the purest of men, as you are the tenderest and most loving. I must have supreme confidence in your still childlike heart to make an avowal which costs me so dear. What, poor darling, your father stole his fortune, and you know it, and you keep it! And you could tell me of this attorney's triumph in a room full of the dumb witnesses of our love, and you are a gentleman, and you think yourself noble, and I am yours, and you are two-and-twenty! How monstrous all through!

"'I have sought excuses for you; I have ascribed your indifference to your giddy youth; I know there is still much of the child in you. Perhaps you have never yet thought seriously of what is meant by wealth, and by honesty. Oh, your laughter hurt me so much! Only think, there is a family, ruined, always in grief, girls perhaps, who curse you day by day, an old man who says to himself every night, "I should not lack bread if Monsieur de Camps' father had only been an honest man." ' "

" What ! " exclaimed Monsieur de Bourbonne, interrupting him, " were you such an idiot as to tell that woman the story of your father's affair with the Bourgneufs? Women better understood spending a fortune than making one——"

" They understand honesty. Let me go on, uncle !

" ' Octave, no power on earth is authorized to garble the language of honor. Look into your conscience, and ask it by what name to call the action to which you owe your riches.' "

And the nephew looked at his uncle, who bent his head.

" ' I will not tell you all the thoughts that beset me ; they can all be reduced to one, which is this: I cannot esteem a man who knowingly soils himself for a sum of money whether large or small. Five francs stolen at play, or six times a hundred thousand francs obtained by legal trickery, disgrace a man equally. I must tell you all : I feel myself sullied by a love which till now was all my joy. From the bottom of my soul there comes a voice I cannot stifle. I have wept to find that my conscience is stronger than my love. You might commit a crime, and I would hide you in my bosom from human justice if I could ; but my devotion would go no farther. Love, my dearest, is, in a woman, the most un-limited confidence, joined to I know not what craving to reverence and adore the being to whom she belongs. I have never conceived of love but as a fire in which the noblest feelings were yet further purified—a fire which develops them to the utmost.

" ' I have but one thing more to say: Come to me poor, and I shall love you twice as much if possible; if not, give me up. If I see you no more, I know what is left to me to do.

" ' But, now, understand me clearly, I will not have you make restitution because I desire it. Consult your conscience. This is an act of justice, and must not be done as a sacrifice to love. I am your wife, and not your mistress; the point is not to please me, but to inspire me with the highest esteem. If I have misunderstood, if you have not clearly explained your father's action, in short, if you can regard your fortune as legitimately acquired—and how gladly would I persuade myself that you deserve no blame—decide as the voice of conscience dictates; act wholly for yourself. A man who truly loves, as you love me, has too high a respect for all the holy inspiration he may get from his wife to be dishonorable.

" ' I blame myself now for all I have written. A word would perhaps have been enough, and my preaching instinct has carried me away. So I should like to be scolded—not much, but a little. My dear, between you and me, are not you the power? You only should detect your own faults. Well, master mine, can you say I understand nothing about political discussion ? '

"Well, uncle?" said Octave, whose eyes were full of tears.

"I see more writing, finish it."

"Oh, there is nothing further but such things as only a lover may read."

"Very good," said the old man. "Very good, my dear boy. I was popular with the women in my day; but I would have you to believe that I too have loved; *et ego in Arcadiâ.* Still, I cannot imagine why you give lessons in mathematics."

"My dear uncle, I am your nephew. Is not that as much as to say that I have made some inroads on the fortune left to me by my father? After reading that letter a complete revolution took place in me, in one instant I paid up the arrears of remorse. I could never describe to you the state in which I was. As I drove my cab to the Bois a voice cried to me, ' Is that horse yours?' As I ate my dinner, I said to myself, ' Have you not stolen the food?' I was ashamed of myself. My honesty was ardent in proportion to its youth. First I flew off to Madame Firmiani. Ah, my dear uncle, that day I had such joys of heart, such raptures of soul as were worth millions. With her I calculated how much I owed the Bourgneuf family; and I sentenced myself, against Madame Firmiani's advice, to pay them interest at the rate of three per cent. But my whole fortune was not enough to refund the sum. We were both of us lovers enough—husband and wife enough—for her to offer and for me to accept her savings——"

"What, besides all her virtues, that adorable woman can save money!" cried the uncle.

"Do not laugh at her. Her position compels her to some thrift. Her husband went to Greece in 1820, and died about three years ago; but to this day it has been impossible to get legal proof of his death, or to lay hands on the will he no doubt made in favor of his wife; this important document was stolen, lost, or mislaid in a country where a man's papers are not kept as they are in France, nor is there a consul. So, not knowing whether she may not some day have to reckon with other and malignant heirs, she is obliged to be extremely careful, for she does not wish to have to give up her wealth as Chateaubriand has just given up the ministry. Now I mean to earn a fortune that shall be mine, so as to restore my wife to opulence if she should be ruined."

"And you never told me—you never came to me. My dear nephew, believe me I love you well enough to pay your honest debts, your debts as a gentleman. I am the uncle of the fifth act—I will be revenged."

"I know your revenges, uncle; but let me grow rich by my own toil. If you wish to befriend me, allow me a thousand crowns a year until I need capital for some business. I declare at this moment I am so happy that all I care about is to live. I give lessons that I may be no burden on any one.

"Ah, if you could but know with what delight I made restitution. After making some inquiries I found the Bourg-

neufs in misery and destitution. They were living at Saint-
Germain in a wretched house. The old father was manager
in a lottery office; the two girls did the work of the house
and kept the accounts. The mother was almost always ill.
The two girls are charming, but they have learned by bitter
experience how little the world cares for beauty without fortune. What a picture did I find there! If I went to the
house as the accomplice in a crime, I came out of it an honest
man, and I have purged my father's memory. I do not judge
him, uncle; there is in a lawsuit an eagerness, a passion which
may sometimes blind the most honest man alive. Lawyers
know how to legitimize the most preposterous claims; there
are syllogisms in law to humor the errors of conscience, and
judges have a right to mistakes. My adventure was a
perfect drama. To have played the part of Providence, to
have fulfilled one of these hopeless wishes: 'If only twenty
thousand francs a year could drop from heaven!'—a wish we
all have uttered in jest; to see a sublime look of gratitude,
amazement and admiration take the place of a glance fraught
with curses; to bring opulence into the midst of a family
sitting round a turf-fire in the evening, by the light of a
wretched lamp. No words can paint such a scene. My
excessive justice to them seemed unjust. Well, if there be a
paradise, my father must now be happy. As for myself, I am
loved as man was never loved before. Madame Firmiani has
given me more than happiness; she has taught me a delicacy
of feeling which perhaps I lacked. Indeed, I call her Dear
Conscience, one of those loving names that are the outcome
of certain secret harmonies of spirit. Honesty is said to pay;
I hope ere long to be rich myself; at this moment I am bent
on solving a great industrial problem, and if I succeed I shall
make millions.''

"My boy, you have your mother's soul," said the old man,
hardly able to restrain the tears that rose at the remembrance
of his sister.

At this instant, in spite of the height above the ground of Octave's room, the young man and his uncle heard the noise of a carriage driving up.

"It is she! I know her horses by the way they pull up."

And it was not long before Madame Firmiani made her appearance.

"Oh!" she cried, with an impulse of annoyance on seeing Monsieur de Bourbonne. "But our uncle is not in the way," she went on with a sudden smile. "I have come to kneel at my husband's feet and humbly beseech him to accept my fortune. I have just received from the Austrian embassy a document proving Firmiani's death. The paper, drawn up by the kind offices of the Austrian envoy at Constantinople, is quite formal, and the will which Firmiani's valet had in keeping for me is subjoined. There, you are richer than I am, for you have there," and she tapped her husband's breast, "treasures which only God can add to." Then, unable to disguise her happiness, she hid her face in Octave's bosom.

"My sweet niece, we made love when I was young," said the uncle, "but now you love. You women are all that is good and lovely in humanity, for you are never guilty of your faults; they always originate with us."

PARIS, *February*, 1831.

A FORSAKEN WOMAN.

(La Femme Abandonnée.)

Translated by ELLEN MARRIAGE.

To Her Grace the Duchesse d'Abrantes,
from her devoted servant,

HONORÉ DE BALZAC.

PARIS, *August,* 1835.

IN the early spring of 1822, the Paris doctors sent to
Lower Normandy a young man just recovering from an
inflammatory complaint, brought on by overstudy, or perhaps
by excess of some other kind. His convalescence demanded
complete rest, a light diet, bracing air, and freedom from
excitement of every kind, and the fat lands of Bessin seemed
to offer all these conditions of recovery. To Bayeux, a
picturesque place about six miles from the sea, the patient
therefore betook himself, and was received with the cordiality
characteristic of relatives who lead very retired lives, and
regard a new arrival as a godsend.

All little towns are alike, save for a few local customs.
When M. le Baron Gaston de Nueil, the young Parisian in
question, had spent two or three evenings in his cousin's
house, or with the friends who made up Mme. de Sainte-
Sevère's circle, he very soon had made the acquaintance of the
persons whom this exclusive society considered to be "the
whole town." Gaston de Nueil recognized in them the invar-
iable stock characters which every observer finds in every one
of the many capitals of the little states which made up the
France of an older day.

First of all comes the family whose claims to nobility are

(280)

regarded as incontestable, and of the highest antiquity in the department, though no one has so much as heard of them a bare fifty leagues away. This species of royal family on a small scale is distantly, but unmistakably, connected with the Navarreins and the Grandlieu family, and related to the Cadignans, and the Blamont-Chauvrys. The head of the illustrious house is invariably a determined sportsman. He has no manners, crushes everybody else with his nominal superiority, tolerates the sub-prefect much as he submits to the taxes, and declines to acknowledge any of the novel powers created by the nineteenth century, pointing out to you as a political monstrosity the fact that the prime minister is a man of no birth. His wife takes a decided tone, and talks in a loud voice. She has had adorers in her time, but takes the sacrament regularly at Easter. She brings up her daughters badly, and is of the opinion that they will always be rich enough with their name.

Neither husband nor wife has the remotest idea of modern luxury. They retain a livery only seen elsewhere on the stage, and cling to old fashions in plate, furniture, and equipages, as in language and manner of life. This is a kind of ancient state, moreover, that suits passably well with provincial thrift. The good folk are, in fact, the lords of the manor of a bygone age, *minus* the quit-rents and heriots, the pack of hounds and the laced coats ; full of honor among themselves, and one and all loyally devoted to princes whom they only see at a distance. The historical house *incognito* is as quaint a survival as a piece of ancient tapestry. Vegetating somewhere among them there is sure to be an uncle or a brother, a lieutenant-general, an old courtier of the King, who wears the red ribbon of the order of Saint-Louis, and went to Hanover with the Maréchal de Richelieu, and here you find him like a stray leaf out of some old pamphlet of the time of Louis Quinze.

This fossil greatness finds a rival in another house, wealthier,

though of less ancient lineage.   Husband and wife spend a
couple of months of every winter in Paris, bringing back
with them its frivolous tone and short-lived contemporary
crazes.   Madame is a woman of fashion, though she looks
rather conscious of her clothes, and is always behind the
mode.   She scoffs, however, at the ignorance affected by
her neighbors.   *Her* plate is of modern fashion; she has
"grooms," negroes, a valet-de-chambre, and what not.   Her
oldest son drives a tilbury, and does nothing (the estate is
entailed upon him); his younger brother is auditor to a council of state.   The father is well posted up in official scandals,
and tells you anecdotes of Louis XVIII. and Mme. du Cayla.
He invests his money in the five per cents., and is careful to
avoid the topic of cider, but has been known occasionally to
fall a victim to the craze for rectifying the conjectural sums-
total of the various fortunes of the department.   He is a
member of the departmental council, has his clothes from
Paris, and wears the cross of the Legion of Honor.   In short,
he is a country gentleman who has fully grasped the signifi-
cance of the Restoration, and is coining money at the Chamber, but his Royalism is less pure than that of the rival house ;
he takes the *Gazette* and the *Débats*, the other family only
reads the *Quotidienne.*

His lordship the bishop, a sometime vicar-general, fluctuates
between the two powers, who pay him the respect due to
religion, but at times they bring home to him the moral
appended by the worthy La Fontaine to the fable of the "Ass
laden with Relics."   The good man's origin is distinctly
plebeian.

Then come stars of the second magnitude, men of family
with ten or twelve hundred livres a year, captains in the navy
or cavalry regiments, or nothing at all.   Out on the roads,
on horseback, they rank half-way between the curé bearing
the sacraments and the tax-collector on his rounds.   Pretty
nearly all of them have been in the Pages or in the Horse

Guards, and now are peaceably ending their days in worthy manorial duties; more interested in felling timber and the cider prospects than in the monarchy.

Still they talk of the Charter and the Liberals while the cards are making, or over a game at backgammon, when they have exhausted the usual stock topic of *dots*, and have married everybody off according to the genealogies which they all know by heart. Their womenkind are haughty dames, who assume the airs of court ladies in their basket-chaises. They huddle themselves up in shawls and caps by way of full-dress; and twice a year, after ripe deliberation, have a new bonnet from Paris, brought as opportunity offers. Exemplary wives are they for the most part, and garrulous.

These are the principal elements of aristocratic gentility, with a few outlying old maids of good family, spinsters who have solved the problem: given a human being, to remain absolutely stationary. They might be sealed up in the houses where you see them; their faces and their dresses are literally part of the fixtures of the town, and the province in which they dwell. They are its tradition, its memory, its quintessence, the local genus incarnate. There is something frigid and monumental about these ladies; they know exactly when to laugh and when to shake their heads, and every now and then give out some utterance which passes current as a witticism.

A few rich townspeople have crept into the miniature Faubourg Saint-Germain, thanks to their money or their aristocratic leanings. But despite their forty years, the circle still says of them, "Young So-and-so has sound opinions," and of such do they make deputies. As a general rule, the elderly spinsters are their principal patronesses, and not without comment.

Finally, in this exclusive little set include two or three ecclesiastics, admitted for the sake of their cloth, or for their wit; for these great nobles find their own society rather dull, and introduce the bourgeois element into their drawing-rooms, as a baker puts leaven into his dough.

The sum-total contained by all heads put together consists of a certain quantity of antiquated notions; a few new reflections brewed in company of an evening being added from time to time to the common stock. Like sea-water in a little creek, the phrases which represent these ideas surge up daily, punctually obeying the tidal laws of conversation in their flow and ebb; you hear the hollow echo of yesterday, to-day, to-morrow, a year hence, and for evermore. On all things here below they pass immutable judgments, which go to make up a body of tradition into which no power of mortal man can infuse one drop of wit or sense. The lives of these persons revolve with the regularity of clockwork in an orbit of use and wont which admits of no more deviation or change than their opinions on matters religious, political, moral, or literary.

If a stranger is admitted to the *cénacle*,* every member of it in turn will say (not without a trace of irony), "You will not find the brilliancy of your Parisian society here," and proceed forthwith to criticise the life led by his neighbors, as if he himself were an exception who had striven, and vainly striven, to enlighten the rest. But any stranger, so ill-advised as to concur in any of their freely expressed criticism of each other, is pronounced at once to be an ill-natured person, a heathen, an outlaw, a reprobate Parisian "as Parisians mostly are."

Before Gaston de Nueil made his appearance in this little world of strictly observed etiquette, where every detail of life is an integrant part of a whole, and everything is known; where the values of personalty and real estate are quoted like stocks on the last sheet of the newspaper—before his arrival he had been weighed in the unerring scales of Bayeusaine judgment.

* Guest-chamber.

His cousin, Mme. de Sainte-Sevère, had already given out the amount of his fortune, and the sum of his expectations, had produced the family tree, and expatiated on the talents, breeding, and modesty of this particular branch. So he received the precise amount of attention to which he was entitled; he was accepted as a worthy scion of a good stock; and, for he was but twenty-three, was made welcome without ceremony, though certain young ladies and mothers of daughters looked not unkindly upon him.

He had an income of eighteen thousand livres from land in the valley of the Auge; and sooner or later his father, as in duty bound, would leave him the château of Manerville, with the lands thereunto belonging. As for his education, political career, personal qualities, and qualifications—no one so much as thought of raising the questions. His land was undeniable, his rentals steady; excellent plantations had been made; the tenants paid for repairs, rates, and taxes; the apple-trees were thirty-eight years old; and, to crown all, his father was in treaty for two hundred acres of woodland just outside the paternal park, which he intended to enclose with walls. No hopes of a political career, no fame on earth, can compare with such advantages as these.

Whether out of malice or design, Mme. de Sainte-Sevère omitted to mention that Gaston had an elder brother; nor did Gaston himself say a word about him. But, at the same time, it is true that the brother was consumptive, and to all appearance would shortly be laid in earth, lamented and forgotten.

At first Gaston de Nueil amused himself at the expense of the circle. He drew, as it were, for his mental album, a series of portraits of these folk, with their angular, wrinkled faces and hooked noses, their crotchets and ludicrous eccentricities of dress, portraits which possessed all the racy flavor of truth. He delighted in their "Normanisms," in the primitive quaintness of their ideas and characters. For a short time

he flung himself into their squirrel's life of busy gyrations in a
cage. Then he began to feel the want of variety, and grew
tired of it. It was like the life of the cloister, cut short
before it had well begun. He drifted on till he reached a
crisis, which is neither spleen nor disgust, but combines all
the symptoms of both. When a human being is transplanted
into an uncongenial soil, to lead a starved, stunted existence,
there is always a little discomfort over the transition. Then,
gradually, if nothing removes him from his surroundings, he
grows accustomed to them, and adapts himself to the vacuity
which grows upon him and renders him powerless. Even
now, Gaston's lungs were accustomed to the air ; and he was
willing to discern a kind of vegetable happiness in days that
brought no mental exertion and no responsibilities. The
constant stirring of the sap of life, the fertilizing influences
of mind on mind, after which he had sought so eagerly in
Paris, were beginning to fade from his memory, and he was
in a fair way of becoming a fossil with these fossils, and ending his days among them, content, like the companions of
Ulysses, in his gross envelope.

One evening Gaston de Nueil was seated between a dowager
and one of the vicars-general of the diocese, in a gray-paneled
drawing-room, floored with large, white tiles. The family
portraits which adorned the walls looked down upon four
card-tables, and some sixteen persons gathered about them,
chattering over their whist. Gaston, thinking of nothing,
digesting one of those exquisite dinners to which the provincial looks forward all through the day, found himself justifying the customs of the country.

He began to understand why these good folk continued to
play with yesterday's pack of cards and shuffled them on a
threadbare tablecloth, and how it was that they had ceased to
dress for themselves or others. He saw the glimmerings of
something like a philosophy in the even tenor of their perpetual round, in the calm of their methodical monotony, in

their ignorance of the refinements of luxury. Indeed, he almost came to think that luxury profited nothing; and even now, the city of Paris, with its passions, storms, and pleasures, was scarcely more than a memory of childhood.

He admired in all sincerity the red hands and shy, bashful manner of some young lady who at first struck him as an awkward simpleton, unattractive to the last degree, and surpassingly ridiculous. His doom was sealed. He had gone from the provinces to Paris; he had led the feverish life of Paris; and now he would have sunk back into the lifeless life of the provinces, but for a chance remark which reached his ear—a few words that called up a swift rush of such emotions as he might have felt when a strain of really great music mingles with the accompaniment of some tedious opera.

"You went to call on Mme. de Beauséant yesterday, did you not?" The speaker was an elderly lady, and she addressed the head of the local royal family.

"I went this morning. She was so poorly and depressed that I could not persuade her to dine with us to-morrow."

"With Mme. de Champignelles?" exclaimed the dowager, with something like astonishment in her manner.

"With my wife," calmly assented the noble. "Mme. de Beauséant is descended from the House of Burgundy, on the spindle side, 'tis true, but the name atones for everything. My wife is very much attached to the Vicomtesse, and the poor lady has lived alone for such a long while, that——"

The Marquis de Champignelles looked round about him while he spoke with an air of cool unconcern, so that it was almost impossible to guess whether he made a concession to Mme. de Beauséant's misfortunes or paid homage to her noble birth; whether he felt flattered to receive her in his house, or, on the contrary, sheer pride was the motive that led him to try to force the country families to meet the Vicomtesse.

The women appeared to take counsel of each other by a

glance; there was a sudden silence in the room, and it was felt that their attitude was one of disapproval.

"Does this Mme. de Beauséant happen to be the lady whose adventure with M. d'Ajuda-Pinto made so much noise?" asked Gaston of his neighbor.

"The very same," he was told. "She came to Courcelles after the marriage of the Marquis d'Ajuda; nobody visits her. She has, besides, too much sense not to see that she is in a false position, so she has made no attempt to see any one. M. de Champignelles and a few gentlemen went to call upon her, but she would see none but M. de Champignelles, perhaps because he is a connection of the family. They are related through the Beauséants; the father of the present Vicomte married a Mlle. de Champignelles of the older branch. But though the Vicomtesse de Beauséant is supposed to be a descendant of the House of Burgundy, you can understand that we could not admit a wife separated from her husband into our society here. We are foolish enough still to cling to these old-fashioned ideas. There was the less excuse for the Vicomtesse, because M. de Beauséant is a well-bred man of the world, who would have been quite ready to listen to reason. But his wife is quite mad——" and so forth and so forth.

M. de Nueil, still listening to the speaker's voice, gathered nothing of the sense of the words; his brain was too full of thick-coming fancies. Fancies? What other name can you give to the alluring charms of an adventure that tempts the imagination and sets vague hopes springing up in the soul; to the sense of coming events and mysterious felicity and fear at hand, while as yet there is no substance of fact on which these phantoms of caprice can fix and feed? Over these fancies thought hovers, conceiving impossible projects, giving in the germ all the joys of love. Perhaps, indeed, all passion is contained in that thought-germ, as the beauty, and fragrance, and rich color of the flower are all packed in the seed.

M. de Nueil did not know that Mme. de Beauséant had taken refuge in Normandy, after a notoriety which women for the most part envy and condemn, especially when youth and beauty in some way excuse the transgression. Any sort of celebrity bestows an inconceivable prestige. Apparently for women, as for families, the glory of the crime effaces the stain ; and if such and such a noble house is proud of its tale of heads that have fallen on the scaffold, a young and pretty woman becomes more interesting for the dubious renown of a happy love or a scandalous desertion, and the more she is to be pitied, the more she excites our sympathies. We are only pitiless to the commonplace. If, moreover, we attract all eyes, we are to all intents and purposes great ; how, indeed, are we to be seen unless we raise ourselves above other people's heads ? The common herd of humanity feels an involuntary respect for any person who can rise above it, and is not over particular as to the means by which they rise.

It may have been that some such motives influenced Gaston de Nueil at unawares, or perhaps it was curiosity, or a craving for some interest in his life ; or, in a word, that crowd of inexplicable impulses which, for want of a better name, we are wont to call " fatality," that drew him to Mme. de Beauséant.

The figure of the Vicomtesse de Beauséant rose up suddenly before him with gracious thronging associations. She was a new world for him, a world of fears and hopes, a world to fight for and to conquer. Inevitably he felt the contrast between this vision and the human beings in the shabby room ; and then, in truth, she was a woman ; what woman had he seen so far in this dull, little world, where calculation replaced thought and feeling, where courtesy was a cut-and-dried formality, and ideas of the very simplest were too alarming to be received or to pass current ? The sound of Mme. de Beauséant's name revived a young man's dreams and wakened urgent desires that had lain dormant for a little.

Gaston de Nueil was absent-minded and preoccupied for the

19

rest of that evening. He was pondering how he might gain
access to Mme. de Beauséant, and truly it was no very easy
matter. She was believed to be extremely clever. But if
men and women of parts may be captivated by something
subtle or eccentric, they are also exacting, and can read all
that lies below the surface; and after the first step has been
taken, the chances of failure and success in the difficult task
of pleasing them are about even. In this particular case,
moreover, the Vicomtesse, besides the pride of her position,
had all the dignity of her name. Her utter seclusion was the
least of the barriers raised between her and the world. For
which reasons it was well-nigh impossible that a stranger,
however well born, could hope for admittance; and yet, the
next morning found M. de Nueil taking his walks abroad in
the direction of Courcelles, a dupe of illusions natural at his
age. Several times he made the circuit of the garden walls,
looking earnestly through every gap at the closed shutters or
open windows, hoping for some romantic chance, on which
he founded schemes for introducing himself into this unknown
lady's presence, without a thought of their impracticability.
Morning after morning was spent in this way to mighty little
purpose; but with each day's walk that vision of a woman
living apart from the world, of love's martyr buried in solitude, loomed larger in his thoughts, and was enshrined in his
soul. So Gaston de Nueil walked under the walls of Courcelles, and some gardener's heavy footstep would set his heart
beating high with hope.

He thought of writing to Mme. de Beauséant, but, on
mature consideration, what can you say to a woman whom you
have never seen, a complete stranger? And Gaston had little
self-confidence. Like most young persons with a plentiful
crop of illusions still standing, he dreaded the mortifying
contempt of silence more than death itself, and shuddered at
the thought of sending his first tender epistle forth to face so
many chances of being thrown into the fire. He was dis-

tracted by innumerable conflicting ideas. But by dint of inventing chimeras, weaving romances, and cudgeling his brains, he hit at last upon one of the hopeful stratagems that are sure to occur to your mind if you persevere long enough, a stratagem which must make clear to the most inexperienced woman that here was a man who took a fervent interest in her. The caprice of social conventions puts as many barriers between lovers as any Oriental imagination can devise in the most delightfully fantastic tale; indeed, the most extravagant pictures are seldom exaggerations. In real life, as in the fairy tales, the woman belongs to him who can reach her and set her free from the position in which she languishes. The poorest of calenders that ever fell in love with the daughter of the Khalif is in truth scarcely farther from his lady than Gaston de Nueil from Mme. de Beauséant. The Vicomtesse knew absolutely nothing of M. de Nueil's wanderings round her house; Gaston de Nueil's love grew to the height of the obstacles to overleap; and the distance set between him and his extemporized lady-love produced the usual effect of distance, in lending enchantment.

One day, confident in his inspiration, he hoped everything from the love that must pour forth from his eyes. Spoken words, in his opinion, were more eloquent than the most passionate letter; and, besides, he would engage feminine curiosity to plead for him. He went, therefore, to M. de Champignelles, proposing to employ that gentleman for the better success of his enterprise. He informed the Marquis that he had been intrusted with a delicate and important commission which concerned the Vicomtesse de Beauséant, that he felt doubtful whether she would read a letter written in an unknown handwriting, or put confidence in a stranger. Would M. de Champignelles, on his next visit, ask the Vicomtesse if she would consent to receive him—Gaston de Nueil? While he asked the Marquis to keep his secret in case of a refusal, he very ingeniously insinuated sufficient reasons for his own admittance, to be duly passed on to the Vicomtesse. Was not M. de Champignelles a man of honor, a loyal gentleman incapable of lending himself to any transaction in bad taste, nay, the merest suspicion of bad taste! Love lends a young man all the self-possession and astute craft of an old ambassador; all the Marquis' harmless vanities were gratified, and the haughty grandee was completely duped. He tried hard to fathom Gaston's secret; but the latter, who would have been greatly perplexed to tell it, turned off M. de Champignelles' adroit questioning with a Norman's shrewdness, till the Marquis, as a gallant Frenchman, complimented his young visitor upon his discretion.

M. de Champignelles hurried off at once to Courcelles, with that eagerness to serve a pretty woman which belongs to his time of life. In the Vicomtesse de Beauséant's position such a message was likely to arouse keen curiosity; so although her memory supplied no reason at all that could bring M. de Nueil to her house, she saw no objection to his visit—after some prudent inquiries as to his family and condition. At the same time, she began by a refusal. Then she discussed the propriety of the matter with M. de Champignelles, directing her questions so as to discover, if possible, whether he knew the motives for the visit, and finally revoked her negative answer. The careful discussion and the extreme discretion shown perforce by the Marquis had seriously piqued her curiosity.

M. de Champignelles had no mind to cut a ridiculous figure. He said, with the air of a man who can keep another's counsel, that the Vicomtesse must know the purpose of this visit perfectly well; while the Vicomtesse, in all sincerity, had no notion what it could be. Mme. de Beauséant, in perplexity, connected Gaston with people whom he had never met, went astray after various wild conjectures, and asked herself if she had seen this M. de Nueil before. In truth, no love letter, however sincere or skillfully indited, could have produced so much effect as this riddle. Again and again Mme. de Beauséant puzzled over it.

When Gaston heard that he might call upon the Vicomtesse, his rapture at so soon obtaining the ardently longed-for good fortune was mingled with singular embarrassment. How was he to contrive a suitable sequel to this stratagem?

"Bah! I shall see *her*," he said over and over again to himself as he dressed. "See her, and that is everything!"

He fell to hoping that once across the threshold of Courcelles he should find an expedient for unfastening this Gordian knot of his own tying. There are believers in the omnipotence of necessity who never turn back; the close presence of danger is an inspiration that calls out all their powers for victory. Gaston de Nueil was one of these.

He took particular pains with his dress, imagining, as youth is apt to imagine, that success or failure hangs on the position of a curl, and ignorant of the fact that anything is charming in youth. And, in any case, such women as Mme. de Beauséant are only attracted by the charms of wit or character of an unusual order. Greatness of character flatters their vanity, promises a great passion, seems to imply a comprehension of the requirements of their hearts. Wit amuses them, responds to the subtlety of their natures, and they think that they are understood. And what do all women wish but to be amused, understood, or adored? It is only after much reflection on the things of life that we understand the consummate coquetry of neglect of dress and reserve at a first interview; and by the time we have gained sufficient astuteness for successful strategy, we are too old to profit by our experience.

While Gaston's lack of confidence in his mental equipment drove him to borrow charms from his clothes, Mme. de Beauséant herself was instinctively giving more attention to her toilet.

"I would rather not frighten people, at all events," she said to herself as she arranged her hair.

In M. de Nueil's character, person, and manner there was that touch of unconscious originality which gives a kind of flavor to things that any one might say or do, and absolves everything that they may choose to do or say. He was highly cultivated, he had a keen brain, and a face, mobile as his own nature, which won the good-will of others. The promise of passion and tenderness in the bright eyes was fulfilled by an essentially kind heart. The resolution which he made as he entered the house at Courcelles was in keeping with his frank nature and ardent imagination. But, bold as he was with love, his heart beat violently when he had crossed the great court, laid out like an English garden, and the manservant, who had taken his name to the Vicomtesse, returned to say that she would receive him.

"M. le Baron de Nueil."

Gaston came in slowly, but with sufficient ease of manner; and it is a more difficult thing, be it said, to enter a room where there is but one woman than a room that holds a score.

A great fire was burning on the hearth in spite of the mild weather, and by the soft light of the candles in the sconces he saw a young woman sitting on a high-backed *bergère* in the angle by the hearth. The seat was so low that she could move her head freely; every turn of it was full of grace and delicate charm, whether she bent, leaning forward, or raised and held it erect, slowly and languidly, as though it were a heavy burden, so low that she could cross her feet and let them appear, or draw them back under the folds of a long, black dress.

The Vicomtesse made as if she would lay the book that she was reading on a small, round stand; but as she did so she turned towards M. de Nueil, and the volume, insecurely laid upon the edge, fell to the floor between the stand and the sofa. This did not seem to disconcert her. She looked up, bowing almost imperceptibly in response to his greeting, without rising from the depths of the low chair in which she lay. Bending forwards, she stirred the fire briskly, and stooped to pick up a fallen glove, drawing it mechanically over her left hand, while her eyes wandered in search of its fellow. The glance was instantly checked, however, for she stretched out a thin, white, all-but-transparent right hand, with flawless ovals of rose-colored nail at the tips of the slender, ringless fingers, and pointed to a chair as if to bid Gaston be seated. He sat down, and she turned her face questioningly towards him. Words cannot describe the subtlety of the winning charm and inquiry in that gesture; deliberate in its kindliness, gracious yet accurate in expression, it was the outcome of early education and of a constant use and wont · of the graciousness of life. Those movements of hers, so swift, so deft, succeeded each other so smoothly that Gaston de Nueil was fascinated by the blending of a pretty woman's fastidious carelessness with the high-bred manner of a great lady.

Mme. de Beauséant stood out in such strong contrast against the automatons among whom he had spent two months of exile in that out-of-the-world district of Normandy that he could not but find in her the realization of his romantic dreams; and, on the other hand, he could not compare her perfections with those of other women whom he had formerly admired. Here in her presence, in a drawing-room like some salon in the Faubourg Saint-Germain, full of costly trifles lying about upon the tables, and flowers and books, he felt as if he were back in Paris. It was a real Parisian carpet beneath his feet; he saw once more the high-bred type of Parisienne, the fragile outlines of her form, her exquisite charm, her disdain of the studied effects which do so much to spoil provincial women.

Mme. de Beauséant had fair hair and dark eyes, and the pale complexion that belongs to fair hair. She held up her brow nobly like some fallen angel, grown proud through the fall, disdainful of pardon. Her way of gathering her thick hair into a crown of plaits above the broad, curving lines of the bandeaux upon her forehead, added to the queenliness of her face. Imagination could discover the ducal coronet of Burgundy in the spiral threads of her golden hair; all the courage of her house seemed to gleam from the great lady's brilliant eyes, such courage as women use to repel audacity or scorn, for they were full of tenderness and gentleness. The outline of that little head, so admirably poised above the long, white throat, the delicate, fine features, the subtle curves of the lips, the mobile face itself, wore an expression of delicate discretion, a faint semblance of irony suggestive of craft and insolence. Yet it would have been difficult to refuse forgiveness to those two feminine failings in her; for the lines that came out in her forehead whenever her face was not in repose, like her upward glances (that pathetic trick of manner), told unmistakably of unhappiness, of a passion that had all but cost her her life. A woman, sitting in the great, silent salon, a woman cut off from the rest of the world in this remote little valley, alone, with the memories of her brilliant, happy, and impassioned youth, of continual gaiety and homage paid on all sides, now replaced by the horrors of the void—was there not something in the sight to strike awe that deepened with reflection? Consciousness of her own value lurked in her smile. She was neither wife nor mother, she was an outlaw; she had lost the one heart that could set her pulses beating without shame; she had nothing from without to support her reeling soul; she must even look for strength from within, live her own life, cherish no hope save that of forsaken love, which looks forward to death's coming, and hastens his lagging footsteps. And this while life was in its prime. Oh! to feel destined for happiness and to die—never having given nor received it! A woman too! What pain was this! These thoughts, flashing across M. de Nueil's mind like lightning, left him very humble in the presence of the greatest charm with which woman can be invested. The triple aureole of beauty, nobleness, and misfortune dazzled him ; he stood in dreamy, almost open-mouthed admiration of the Vicomtesse. But he found nothing to say to her.

Mme. de Beauséant, by no means displeased, no doubt, by his surprise, held out her hand with a kindly but imperious gesture ; then, summoning a smile to her pale lips, as if obeying, even yet, the woman's impulse to be gracious—

"I have heard from M. de Champignelles of a message which you have kindly undertaken to deliver, monsieur," she said. "Can it be from——"

With that terrible phrase Gaston understood, even more clearly than before, his own ridiculous position, the bad taste and bad faith of his behavior towards a woman so noble and so unfortunate. He reddened. The thoughts that crowded in upon him could be read in his troubled eyes ; but suddenly, with the courage which youth draws from a sense of its own wrong-doing, he gained confidence, and very humbly interrupted Mme. de Beauséant.

"Madame," he faltered out, "I do not deserve the happiness of seeing you. I have deceived you basely. However strong the motive may have been, it can never excuse the pitiful subterfuge which I used to gain my end. But, madame, if your goodness will permit me to tell you——"

The Vicomtesse glanced at M. de Nueil, haughty disdain in her whole manner. She stretched her hand to the bell and rang it.

"Jacques," she said, "light this gentleman to the door," and she looked with dignity at the visitor.

She rose proudly, bowed to Gaston, and then stooped for the fallen volume. If all her movements on his entrance had been caressingly dainty and gracious, her every gesture now was no less severely frigid. M. de Nueil rose to his feet, but he stood waiting. Mme. de Beauséant flung another glance at him. "Well, why do you not go ?" she seemed to say.

There was such cutting irony in that glance that Gaston

grew white as if he were about to faint.   Tears came into his eyes, but he would not let them fall, and scorching shame and despair dried them.   He looked back at Mme. de Beauséant, and a certain pride and consciousness of his own worth was mingled with his humility ; the Vicomtesse had a right to punish him, but ought she to use her right ?   Then he went out.

As he crossed the ante-chamber, a clear head and wits sharpened by passion were not slow to grasp the danger of his situation.

" If I leave this house, I can never come back to it again," he said to himself.   " The Vicomtesse will always think of me as a fool.   It is impossible that a woman, and such a woman, should not guess the love that she has called forth. Perhaps she feels a little, vague, involuntary regret for dismissing me so abruptly.   But she could not do otherwise, and she cannot recall her sentence.   It rests with me to understand her."

At that thought Gaston stopped short on the flight of steps with an exclamation ; he turned sharply, saying, "I have forgotten something," and went back to the salon.   The lackey, all respect for a baron and the rights of property, was completely deceived by the natural utterance, and followed him.   Gaston returned quietly and unannounced. The Vicomtesse, thinking that the intruder was the servant, looked up and beheld M. de Nucil.

" Jacques lighted me to the door," he said, with a half-sad smile which dispelled any suspicion of jest in those words, while the tone in which they were spoken went to the heart. Mme. de Beauséant was disarmed.

" Very well, take a seat," she said.

Gaston eagerly took possession of a chair.   His eyes were shining with happiness ; the Vicomtesse, unable to endure the brilliant light in them, looked down at the book.   She was enjoying a delicious, ever-new sensation ; the sense of a man's delight in her presence is an unfailing feminine instinct. And then, besides, he had divined her, and a woman is so grateful to the man who has mastered the apparently capricious, yet logical, reasoning of her heart; who can track her thought through the seemingly contradictory workings of her mind, and read the sensations, or shy or bold, written in fleeting red, a bewildering maze of coquetry and self-revelation.

"Madame," Gaston exclaimed in a low voice, "my blunder you know, but you do not know how much I am to blame. If you only knew what joy it was to——"

"Ah! take care," she said, holding up one finger with an air of mystery, as she put out her hand towards the bell.

The charming gesture, the gracious threat, no doubt, called up some sad thought, some memory of the old happy time when she could be wholly charming and gentle without an after-thought; when the gladness of her heart justified every caprice, and put charm into every least movement. The lines in her forehead gathered between her brows, and the expression of her face grew dark in the soft candle-light. Then looking across at M. de Nueil gravely but not unkindly, she spoke like a woman who deeply feels the meaning of every word.

"This is all very ridiculous! Once upon a time, monsieur, when thoughtless high spirits were my privilege, I should have laughed fearlessly over your visit with you. But now my life is very much changed. I cannot do as I like, I am obliged to think. What brings you here? Is it curiosity? In that case I am paying dearly for a little fleeting pleasure. Have you fallen *passionately* in love already with a woman whom you have never seen, a woman with whose name slander has, of course, been busy? If so, your motive in making this visit is based on disrespect, on an error which accident brought into notoriety."

She flung her book down scornfully upon the table, then,

with a terrible look at Gaston, she went on : " Because I once was weak, must it be supposed that I am always weak? This is horrible, degrading. Or have you come here to pity me? You are very young to offer sympathy with heart troubles. Understand this clearly, sir, that I would rather have scorn than pity. I will not endure compassion from any one."

There was a brief pause.

" Well, sir," she continued (and the face that she turned to him was gentle and sad), " whatever motive induced this rash intrusion upon my solitude, it is very painful to me, you see. You are too young to be totally without good feeling, so surely you will feel that this behavior of yours is improper. I forgive you for it, and, as you see, I am speaking of it to you without bitterness. You will not come here again, will you? I am entreating when I might command. If you come to see me again, neither you nor I can prevent the whole place from believing that you are my lover, and you would cause me great additional annoyance. You do not mean to do that, I think."

She said no more, but looked at him with a great dignity which abashed him.

" I have done wrong, madame," he said, with deep feeling in his voice, " but it was through enthusiasm and thoughtlessness and eager desire of happiness, the qualities and defects of my age. Now, I understand that I ought not to have tried to see you," he added ; " but, at the same time, the desire was a very natural one "—and making an appeal to feeling rather than to the intellect, he described the weariness of his enforced exile. He drew a portrait of a young man in whom the fires of life were burning themselves out, conveying the impression that here was a heart worthy of tender love, a heart which, notwithstanding, had never known the joys of love for a young and beautiful woman of refinement and taste. He explained, without attempting to justify, his

unusual conduct. He flattered Mme. de Beauséant by showing that she had realized for him the ideal lady of a young
man's dream, the ideal sought by so many, and so often
sought in vain. Then he touched upon his morning prowl-
ings under the walls of Courcelles, and his wild thoughts at
the first sight of the house, till he excited that vague feeling
of indulgence which a woman can find in her heart for the
follies committed for her sake.

An impassioned voice was speaking in the chill solitude ;
the speaker brought with him a warm breath of youth and the
charms of a carefully cultivated mind. It was so long since
Mme. de Beauséant had felt stirred by real feeling delicately
expressed, that it affected her very strongly now. In spite of
herself, she watched M. de Nueil's expressive face, and admired the noble confidence of a soul, unbroken as yet by the
cruel discipline of the life of the world, unfretted by continual scheming to gratify personal ambition and vanity.
Gaston was in the flower of his youth, he impressed her as a
man with something in him, unaware as yet of the great
career that lay before him. So both these two made reflections most dangerous for their peace of mind, and both strove
to conceal their thoughts. M. de Nueil saw in the Vicomtesse a rare type of woman, always the victim of her perfection and tenderness ; her graceful beauty is the least of her
charms for those who are privileged to know the infinite of
feeling and thought and goodness in the soul within ; a
woman, whose instinctive feeling for beauty runs through all
the most varied expressions of love, purifying its transports,
turning them to something almost holy ; wonderful secret of
womanhood, the exquisite gift that nature so seldom bestows.
And the Vicomtesse, on her side, listening to the ring of
sincerity in Gaston's voice, while he told of his youthful
troubles, began to understand all that grown children of five-
and-twenty suffer from diffidence, when hard work has kept
them alike from corrupting influences and intercourse with

men and women of the world whose sophistical reasoning and
experience destroy the fair qualities of youth.   Here was the
ideal of women's dreams, a man unspoiled as yet by the
egoism of family or success, or by that narrow selfishness
which blights the first impulses of honor, devotion, self-sacrifice, and high demands of self; all the flowers so soon wither
that enrich at first the life of delicate but strong emotions,
and keep alive the loyalty of the heart.

But these two, once launched forth on the vast sea of sentiment, went far indeed in theory, sounding the depths in
either soul, testing the sincerity of their expressions; only,
whereas Gaston's experiments were made unconsciously, Mme.
de Beauséant had a purpose in all that she said.   Bringing
her natural and acquired subtlety to the work, she sought to
learn M. de Nueil's opinions by advancing, as far as she
could do so, views diametrically opposed to her own.   So witty
and so gracious was she, so much herself with this stranger,
with whom she felt completely at ease, because she felt sure
that they should never meet again, that, after some delicious
epigram of hers, Gaston exclaimed unthinkingly—

"Oh ! madame, how could any man have left you?"

The Vicomtesse was silent.   Gaston reddened, he thought
that he had offended her ; but she was not angry.   The first
deep thrill of delight since the day of her calamity had taken
her by surprise.   The skill of the cleverest *roué* could not
have made the impression that M. de Nueil made with that
cry from the heart.   That verdict wrung from a young man's
candor gave her back innocence in her own eyes, condemned
the world, laid the blame upon the lover who had left her,
and justified her subsequent solitary drooping life.   The
world's absolution, the heartfelt sympathy, the social esteem
so longed for, and so harshly refused, nay, all her secret
desires were given her to the full in that exclamation, made
fairer yet by the heart's sweetest flatteries and the admiration
that women always relish eagerly.   He understood her, un-

derstood all, and he had given her, as if it were the most natural thing in the world, the opportunity of rising higher through her fall. She looked at the clock.

"Ah! madame, do not punish me for my heedlessness. If you grant me but one evening, vouchsafe not to shorten it, I pray you."

She smiled at the pretty speech.

"Well, as we must never meet again," she said, "what signifies a moment more or less? If you were to care for me, it would be a pity."

"It is too late now," he said.

"Do not tell me that," she answered gravely. "Under any other circumstances I should be very glad to see you. I will speak frankly, and you will understand how it is that I do not choose to see you again, and ought not to do so. You have too much magnanimity not to feel that if I were so much as suspected of a second trespass, every one would think of me as a contemptible and vulgar woman; I should be like other women. A pure and blameless life will bring my character into relief. I am too proud not to endeavor to live like one apart in the world, a victim of the law through my marriage, man's victim through my love. If I were not faithful to the position which I have taken up, then I should deserve all the reproach that is heaped upon me; I should be lowered in my own eyes. I had not enough lofty social virtue to remain with a man whom I did not love. I have snapped the bonds of marriage in spite of the law; it was wrong, it was a crime, it was anything you like, but for me the bonds meant death. I meant to live. Perhaps if I had been a mother I could have endured the torture of a forced marriage of suitability. At eighteen we scarcely know what is done with us, poor girls that we are! I have broken the laws of the world, and the world has punished me; we both did rightly. I sought happiness. Is it not a law of our nature to seek for happiness? I was young, I was beautiful. I thought that I had found a nature as loving, as apparently passionate. I was loved indeed ; for a little while——"

She paused.

" I used to think," she said, " that no one could leave a woman in such a position as mine. I have been forsaken ; I must have offended in some way. Yes, in some way, no doubt, I failed to keep some law of our nature, was too loving, too devoted, too exacting—I do not know. Evil days have brought light with them? For a long while I blamed another, now I am content to bear the whole blame. At my own expense, I have absolved that other of whom I once thought I had a right to complain. I had not the art to keep him ; fate has punished me heavily for my lack of skill. I only knew how to love ; how can one keep one's self in mind when one loves ? So I was a slave when I should have sought to be a tyrant. Those who know me may condemn me, but they will respect me too, Pain has taught me that I must not lay myself open to this a second time. I cannot understand how it is that I am living yet, after the anguish of that first week of the most fearful crisis in a woman's life. Only from three years of loneliness would it be possible to draw strength to speak of that time as I am speaking now. Such agony, monsieur, usually ends in death ; but this—well, it was the agony of death with no tomb to end it. Oh ! I have known pain indeed ! "

The Vicomtesse raised her beautiful eyes to the ceiling ; and the cornice, no doubt, received all the confidences which a stranger might not hear. When a woman is afraid to look at her interlocutor, there is in truth no gentler, meeker, more accommodating confidante than the cornice. The cornice is quite an institution in the boudoir; what is it but the confessional, *minus* the priest ?

Mme. de Beauséant was eloquent and beautiful at that moment ; nay, " coquettish," if the word were not too heavy. By justifying herself, by raising insurmountable barriers be-

tween herself and love, she was stimulating every sentiment
in the man before her; nay, more, the higher she set the
goal, the more conspicuous it grew. At last, when her eyes
had lost the too eloquent expression given to them by painful
memories, she let them fall on Gaston.

"You acknowledge, do you not, that I am bound to find a
solitary, self-contained life ?" she said quietly.

So sublime was she in her reasoning and her madness that
M. de Nueil felt a wild longing to throw himself at her feet;
but he was afraid of making himself ridiculous, so he held his
enthusiasm and his thoughts in check. He was afraid, too,
that he might totally fail to express them, and in no less terror
of some awful rejection on her part, or of her mockery, an apprehension which strikes like ice to the most fervid soul.
The revulsion which led him to crush down every feeling
as it sprang up in his heart cost him the intense pain that
diffident and ambitious natures experience in the frequent
crises when they are compelled to stifle their longings. And
yet, in spite of himself, he broke the silence to say in a falter-
ing voice—

"Madame, permit me to give way to one of the strongest
emotions of my life, and own to all that you have made me
feel. You set the heart in me swelling high! I feel within
me a longing to make you forget your mortifications, to devote my life to this, to give you love for all who have ever
given you wounds or hate. But this is a very sudden out-
pouring of the heart, nothing can justify it to-day, and I
ought not——"

"Enough, monsieur," said Mme. de Beauséant; "we have
both of us gone too far. By giving you the sad reasons for a
refusal which I am compelled to give, I meant to soften it and
not to elicit homage. Coquetry only suits a happy woman.
Believe me, we must remain strangers to each other. At a
later day you will know that ties which must inevitably be
broken ought not to be formed at all."

20

She sighed lightly, and her brows contracted, but almost immediately grew clear again.

"How painful it is for a woman to be powerless to follow the man she loves through all the phases of his life! And if . that man loves her truly, his heart must surely vibrate with pain to the deep trouble in hers. Are they not twice unhappy?"

There was a short pause. Then she rose smiling.

"You little suspected, when you came to Courcelles, that you were to hear a sermon, did you?"

. Gaston felt even farther than at first from this extraordinary woman. Was the charm of that delightful hour due after all to the coquetry of the mistress of the house? She had been anxious to display her wit. He bowed stiffly to the Vicomtesse, and went away in desperation.

On the way home he tried to detect the real character of a creature supple and hard as a steel spring; but he had seen her pass through so many phases, that he could not make up his mind about her. The tones of her voice, too, were ringing in his ears; her gestures, the little movements of her head, and the varying expression of her eyes grew more gracious in memory, more fascinating as he thought of them. The Vicomtesse's beauty shone out again for him in the darkness; his reviving impressions called up yet others, and he was enthralled anew by womanly charm and wit, which at first he had not perceived. He fell to wandering musings, in which the most lucid thoughts grow refractory and flatly contradict each other, and the soul passes through a brief frenzy fit. Youth only can understand all that lies in the dithyrambic outpourings of youth when, after a stormy siege of the most frantic folly and coolest commonsense, the heart finally yields to the assault of the latest comer, be it hope or despair, as some mysterious power determines.

At three-and-twenty, diffidence nearly always rules a man's conduct; he is perplexed with a young girl's shyness, a girl's trouble ; he is afraid lest he should illy express his love, sees nothing but difficulties, and takes alarm at them ; he would be bolder if he loved less, for he has no confidence in himself, and with a growing sense of the cost of happiness comes a conviction that the woman he loves cannot easily be won ; perhaps, too, he is giving himself up too entirely to his own pleasure, and fears that he can give none ; and when, for his misfortune, his idol inspires him with awe, he worships in secret and afar, and, unless his love is guessed, it dies away. Then it often happens that one of these dead early loves lingers on, bright with illusions in many a young heart. What man is there but keeps within him these virgin memories that grow fairer every time they rise before him, memories that hold up to him the ideal of perfect bliss ? Such recollections are like children who die in the flower of childhood, before their parents have known anything of them but their smiles.

So M. de Nueil came home from Courcelles, the victim of a mood fraught with desperate resolutions. Even now he felt that Mme. de Beauséant was one of the conditions of his existence, and that death would be preferable to life without her. He was still young enough to feel the tyrannous fascination which fully developed womanhood exerts over immature and impassioned natures ; and, consequently, he was to spend one of those stormy nights when a young man's thoughts travel from happiness to suicide and back again—nights in which youth rushes through a lifetime of bliss and falls asleep from sheer exhaustion. Fateful nights are they, and the worst misfortune that can happen is to awake a philosopher afterwards. M. de Nueil was far too deeply in love to sleep ; he rose and betook to inditing letters, but none of them were satisfactory, and he burned them all.

The next day he went to Courcelles to make the circuit of her garden walls, but he waited till nightfall ; he was afraid that she might see him. The instinct that led him to act in

this way arose out of so obscure a mood of the soul, that none
but a young man, or a man in like case, can fully understand
its mute ecstasies and its vagaries, matter to set those people
who are lucky enough to see life only in its matter-of-fact
aspect shrugging their shoulders.   After painful hesitation,
Gaston wrote to Mme. de Beauséant.   Here is the letter,
which may serve as a sample of the epistolary style peculiar to lovers, a performance which, like the drawings prepared
with great secrecy by children for the birthdays of father or
mother, is found to be insufferable by every mortal except the
recipients:

" MADAME:—Your power over my heart, my soul, myself,
is so great that my fate depends wholly upon you to-day.
Do not throw this letter into the fire; be so kind as to read it
through.   Perhaps you may pardon the opening sentence
when you see that it is no commonplace, selfish declaration,
but that it expresses a simple fact.   Perhaps you may feel
moved, because I ask for so little, by the submission of one
who feels himself so much beneath you, by the influence that
your decision will exercise upon my life.   At my age, madame,
I only know how to love, I am utterly ignorant of ways of
attracting and winning a woman's love, but in my own heart
I know raptures of adoration of her.   I am irresistibly drawn
to you by the great happiness that I feel through you; my
thoughts turn to you with the selfish instinct which bids us
draw nearer to the fire of life when we find it.   I do not
imagine that I am worthy of you; it seems impossible that I,
young, ignorant, and shy, could bring you one-thousandth
part of the happiness that I drink in at the sound of your
voice and the sight of you.   For me you are the only woman
in the world.   I cannot imagine life without you, so I have
made up my mind to leave France, and to risk my life till I
lose it in some desperate enterprise, in the Indies, in Africa, I
care not where.   How can I quell a love that knows no limits

save by opposing to it something as infinite? Yet, if you
will allow me to hope, not to be yours, but to win your friendship, I will stay. Let me come, not so very often, if you
require it, to spend a few such hours with you as those stolen
hours of yesterday. The keen delight of that brief happiness,
to be cut short at the least over-ardent word from me, will
suffice to enable me to endure the boiling torrent in my veins.
Have I presumed too much upon your generosity by this
entreaty to suffer an intercourse in which all the gain is mine
alone? You could find ways of showing the world, to which
you sacrifice so much, that I am nothing to you; you are so
clever and so proud! What have you to fear? If I could
only lay bare my heart to you at this moment, to convince
you that it is with no lurking after-thought that I make this
humble request! Should I have told you that my love was
boundless, while I prayed you to grant me friendship, if I
had any hope of your sharing this feeling in the depths of
my soul? No, while I am with you, I will be whatever you
will, if only I may be with you. If you refuse (as you have
the power to refuse), I will not utter one murmur, I will go.
And if, at a later day, any other woman should enter into
my life, you will have proof that you were right; but if I
am faithful till death, you may feel some regret perhaps. The
hope of causing you a regret will soothe my agony, and that
thought shall be the sole revenge of a slighted heart."

Only those who have passed through all the exceeding tribu-
lations of youth, who have seized on all the chimeras with two
white pinions, the nightmare fancies at the disposal of a fervid
imagination, can realize the horrors that seized upon Gaston
de Nueil when he had reason to suppose that his ultimatum
was in Mme. de Beauséant's hands. He saw the Vicomtesse,
wholly untouched, laughing at his letter and his love, as those
can laugh who have ceased to believe in love. He could
have wished to have his letter back again. It was an absurd

letter.   There were a thousand and one things, now that he came to think of it, that he might have said, things infinitely better and more moving than those stilted phrases of his, those accursed, sophisticated, pretentious, fine-spun phrases, though, luckily, the punctuation had been pretty bad, and the lines shockingly crooked.   He tried not to think, not to feel ; but he felt and thought, and was wretched.   If he had been thirty years old, he might have gotten drunk, but the innocent of three-and-twenty knew nothing of the resources of opium nor of the expedients of advanced civilization.   Nor had he at hand one of those good friends of the Parisian pattern who understand so well how to say *Pæte, non dolet !* by producing a bottle of champagne, or alleviate the agony of suspense by carrying you off somewhere to make a night of it.   Capital fellows are they, always in low water when you are in funds, always off to some watering-place when you go to look them up, always with some bad bargain in horseflesh to sell you ; it is true, that when you want to borrow of them, they have always just lost their last louis at play ; but in all other re-spects they are the best fellows on earth, always ready to embark with you on one of the steep down-grades where you lose your time, your soul and your life !

At length M. de Nueil received a missive through the instru-mentality of Jacques, a letter that bore the arms of Burgundy on the scented seal, a letter written on vellum note-paper.

He rushed away at once to lock himself in, and read and re-read *her* letter.

"You are punishing me very severely, monsieur, both for the friendliness of my effort to spare you a rebuff, and for the attraction which intellect always has for me.   I put confidence in the generosity of youth, and you have disappointed me. And yet, if I did not speak unreservedly (which would have been perfectly ridiculous), at any rate I spoke frankly of my position, so that you might imagine that I was not to be touched by a young soul. My distress is the keener for my interest in you. I am naturally tender-hearted and kindly, but circumstances force me to act unkindly. Another woman would have flung your letter, unread, in the fire; I read it, and I am answering it. My answer will make it clear to you that while I am not untouched by the expression of this feeling which I have inspired, albeit unconsciously, I am still far from sharing it, and the step which I am about to take will show you still more plainly that I mean what I say. I wish, besides, to use, for your welfare, that authority, as it were, which you give me over your life; and I desire to exercise it this once to draw aside the veil from your eyes.

"I am nearly thirty years old, monsieur; you are barely two-and-twenty. You yourself cannot know what your thoughts will be at my age. The vows that you make so lightly to-day may seem a very heavy burden to you then. I am quite willing to believe that at this moment you would give me your whole life without a regret, you would even be ready to die for a little brief happiness; but at the age of thirty experience will take from you the very power of making daily sacrifices for my sake, and I myself should feel deeply humiliated if I accepted them. A day would come when everything, even nature, would bid you leave me, and I have already told you that death is preferable to desertion. Misfortune has taught me to calculate; as you see, I am arguing perfectly dispassionately. You force me to tell you that I have no love for you; I ought not to love, I cannot, and I will not. It is too late to yield, as women yield, to a blind unreasoning impulse of the heart, too late to be the mistress whom you seek. My consolations spring from God, not from earth. Ah, and besides, with the melancholy insight of disappointed love, I read hearts too clearly to accept your proffered friendship. It is only instinct. I forgive the boyish ruse, for which you are not responsible as yet. In the name of this passing fancy of yours, for the sake of your career and my own peace of mind, I bid you stay in your own country; you must not spoil a fair and honorable life for an illusion which, by its very nature, cannot last.   At a later day, when you have accomplished your real destiny, in the fully developed manhood that awaits you, you will appreciate this answer of mine, though to-day it may be that you blame its hardness. You will turn with pleasure to an old woman whose friendship will certainly be sweet and precious to you then; a friendship untried by the extremes of fashion and the disenchanting processes of life; a friendship which noble thoughts and thoughts of religion will keep pure and sacred. Farewell; do my bidding with the thought that your success will bring a gleam of pleasure into my solitude, and only think of me as we think of absent friends.''

Gaston de Nueil read the letter, and wrote the following lines:

"MADAME:—If I could cease to love you, to take the chances of becoming an ordinary man which you hold out to me, you must admit that I should thoroughly deserve my fate. No, I shall not do as you bid me; the oath of fidelity which I swear to you shall only be absolved by death. Ah! take my life, unless indeed you do not fear to carry a remorse all through your own——''

When the man returned from his errand, M. de Nueil asked him with whom he left the note?

"I gave it to Mme. le Vicomtesse herself, sir; she was in her carriage and just about to start.''

"For the town?''

"I don't think so, sir. Mme. la Vicomtesse had post-horses.''

"Ah! then she is going away,'' said the Baron.

"Yes, sir," the man answered.

Gaston de Nueil at once prepared to follow Mme. de Beau-séant. She led the way as far as Geneva, without a suspicion that he followed. And he? Amid the many thoughts that assailed him during that journey, one all-absorbing problem filled his mind—"Why did she go away?" Theories grew thickly on such ground for supposition, and naturally he inclined to the one that flattered his hopes—"If the Vicomtesse cares for me, a clever woman would, of course, choose Switzerland, where nobody knows either of us, in preference to France, where she would find censorious critics."

An impassioned lover of a certain stamp would not feel attracted to a woman clever enough to choose her own ground; such women are too clever. However, there is nothing to prove that there was any truth in Gaston's supposition.

The Vicomtesse took a small house by the side of the lake. As soon as she was installed in it, Gaston came one summer evening in the twilight. Jacques, that flunkey in grain, showed no sign of surprise, and announced "M. le Baron de Nueil" like a discreet domestic well acquainted with good society. At the sound of the name, at the sight of its owner, Mme. de Beauséant let her book fall from her hands; her surprise gave him time to come close to her, and to say in tones that sounded like music in her ears—

"What joy it was to me to take the horses that brought you on this journey!"

To have the inmost desires of the heart so fulfilled! Where is the woman who could resist such happiness as this? An Italian woman, one of those divine creatures who, psychologically, are as far removed from the Parisian as if they lived at the Antipodes, a being who would be regarded as profoundly immoral on this side the Alps, an Italian (to resume) made the following comment on some French novels which she had been reading: "I cannot see," she remarked, "why these poor lovers take such a time over coming to an arrange-

ment which ought to be the affair of a single morning."
Why should not the novelist take a hint from this worthy
lady, and refrain from exhausting the theme and the reader?
Some few passages of coquetry it would certainly be pleasant
to give in outline; the story of Mme. de Beauséant's demurs
and sweet delayings, that, like the vestal virgins of antiquity,
she might fall gracefully, and by lingering over the innocent
raptures of first love draw from it its utmost strength and
sweetness. M. de Nueil was at an age when a man is the
dupe of these caprices, of the fence which women delight to
prolong; either to dictate their own terms, or to enjoy the
sense of their power yet longer, knowing instinctively as they
do that it must soon grow less. But, after all, these little
boudoir protocols, less numerous than those of the Congress
of London, are too small to be worth mentioning in the history of this passion.

For three years Mme. de Beauséant and M. de Nueil lived
in the villa on the lake of Geneva. They lived quite alone,
received no visitors, caused no talk, rose late, went out together upon the lake, knew, in short, the happiness of which
we all of us dream. It was a simple little house, with green
shutters, and broad balconies shaded with awnings, a house
contrived of set purpose for lovers, with its white couches,
soundless carpets, and fresh hangings, everything within it
reflecting their joy. Every window looked out on some new
view of the lake; in the far distance lay the mountains, fantastic visions of changing color and evanescent cloud; above
them spread the sunny sky, before them stretched the broad
sheet of water, never the same in its fitful changes. All their
surroundings seemed to dream for them, all things smiled
upon them.

Then weighty matters recalled M. de Nueil to France.
His father and brother died, and he was obliged to leave
Geneva. The lovers bought the house; and, if they could
have had their way, they would have removed the hills piece-

meal, drawn off the lake with a siphon, and taken everything away with them.

Mme. de Beauséant followed M. de Nueil. She realized her property, and bought a considerable estate near Manerville, adjoining Gaston's lands, and here they lived together; Gaston very graciously giving up Manerville to his mother for the present in consideration of the bachelor freedom in which she left him.

Mme. de Beauséant's estate was close to a little town in one of the most picturesque spots in the valley of the Auge. Here the lovers raised barriers between themselves and social intercourse, barriers which no creature could overleap, and here the happy days of Switzerland were lived over again. For nine whole years they knew happiness which it serves no purpose to describe; happiness which may be divined from the outcome of the story by those whose souls can comprehend poetry and prayer in their infinite manifestations.

All this time Mme. de Beauséant's husband, the present Marquis (his father and elder brother having died), enjoyed the soundest health. There is no better aid to life than a certain knowledge that our demise would confer a benefit on some fellow-creature. M. de Beauséant was one of those ironical and wayward beings who, like holders of life-annuities, wake with an additional sense of relish every morning to a consciousness of good health. For the rest, he was a man of the world, somewhat methodical and ceremonious, and a calculator of consequences, who could make a declaration of love as quietly as a lackey announces that "Madame is served."

This brief biographical notice of his lordship the Marquis de Beauséant is given to explain the reasons why it was impossible for the Marquise to marry M. de Nueil.

So, after a nine years' lease of happiness, the sweetest agreement to which a woman ever put her hand, M. de Nueil and Mme. de Beauséant were still in a position quite

as natural and quite as false as at the beginning of their adventure.   And yet they had reached a fatal crisis, which may
be stated as clearly as any problem in mathematics.

Mme. le Comtesse de Nueil, Gaston's mother, a straight-
laced and virtuous person, who had made the late Baron happy
in strictly legal fashion, would never consent to meet Mme.
de Beauséant.   Mme. de Beauséant quite understood that the
worthy dowager must of necessity be her enemy, and that she
would try to draw Gaston from his unhallowed and immoral
way of life.   The Marquise de Beauséant would willingly have
sold her property and gone back to Geneva, but she could
not bring herself to do it; it would mean that she distrusted
M. de Nueil.   Moreover, he had taken a great fancy to this
very Valleroy estate, where he was making plantations and
improvements.   She would not deprive him of a piece of
pleasurable routine-work, such as women always wish for their
husbands, and even for their lovers.

A Mlle. de Rodière, twenty-two years of age, an heiress
with a rent-roll of forty thousand livres, had come to live in
the neighborhood.   Gaston always met her at Manerville
whenever he was obliged to go thither.   These various personages being to each other as the terms of a proportion
sum, the following letter will throw light on the appalling
problem which Mme. de Beauséant had been trying for the
past month to solve:

"My beloved angel, it seems like nonsense, does it not, to
write to you when there is nothing to keep us apart, when a
caress so often takes the place of words, and words too are
caresses?   Ah, well, my love.   There are some things that a
woman cannot say when she is face to face with the man she
loves; at the bare thought of them her voice fails her, and
the blood goes back to her heart; she has no strength, no
intelligence left.   It hurts me to feel like this when you are
near me, and it happens often.   I feel that my heart should

be wholly sincere for you ; that I should disguise no thought, however transient, in my heart ; and I love the sweet carelessness, which suits me so well, too much to endure this embarrassment and constraint any longer. So I will tell you about my anguish—yes, it is anguish. Listen to me ! do not begin with the little ' Tut, tut, tut,' that you use to silence me, an impertinence that I love, because anything from you pleases me. Dear soul from heaven, wedded to mine, let me first tell you that you have effaced all memory of the pain that once was crushing the life out of me. I did not know what love was before I knew you. Only the candor of your beautiful young life, only the purity of that great soul of yours, could satisfy the requirements of an exacting woman's heart. Dear love, how very often I have thrilled with joy to think that in these nine long, swift years, my jealousy has not been once awakened. All the flowers of your soul have been mine, all your thoughts. There has not been the faintest cloud in our heaven ; we have not known what sacrifice is ; we have always acted on the impulses of our hearts. I have known happiness, infinite for a woman. Will the tears that drench this sheet tell you all my gratitude? I could wish that I had knelt to write the words ! Well, out of this felicity has arisen torture more terrible than the pain of desertion. Dear, there are very deep recesses in a woman's heart ; how deep in my own heart, I did not know myself until to-day, as I did not know the whole extent of love. The greatest misery which could overwhelm us is a light burden compared with the mere thought of harm for him whom we love. And how if we cause the harm, is it not enough to make one die?—— This is the thought that is weighing upon me. But it brings in its train another thought that is heavier far, a thought that tarnishes the glory of love, and slays it, and turns it into a humiliation which sullies life as long as it lasts. You are thirty years old ; I am forty. What dread this difference in age calls up in a woman who loves ! It is possible that, first

of all unconsciously, afterwards in earnest, you have felt the
sacrifices that you have made by renouncing all in the world
for me.   Perhaps you have thought of your future from the
social point of view, of the marriage which would, of course,
increase your fortune, and give you avowed happiness and
children who would inherit your wealth; perhaps you have
thought of reappearing in the world, and filling your place
there honorably.   And then, if so, you must have repressed
those thoughts, and felt glad to sacrifice heiress and fortune
and a fair future to me without my knowledge.   In your young
man's generosity, you must have resolved to be faithful to the
vows which bind us each to each in the sight of God.   My
past pain has risen up before your mind, and the misery from
which you rescued me has been my protection.   To owe
your love to your pity !   The thought is even more painful to
me than the fear of spoiling your life for you.   The man who
can bring himself to stab his mistress is very charitable if he
gives her her death-blow while she is happy and ignorant of
evil, while illusions are in full blossom—— Yes, death is
preferable to the two thoughts which have secretly saddened
the hours for several days.   To-day, when you asked 'What
ails you?' so tenderly, the sound of your voice made me
shiver.   I thought that, after your wont, you were reading my
very soul, and I waited for your confidence to come, thinking
that my presentiments had come true, and that I had guessed
at all that was going on in your mind.   Then I began to think
over certain little things that you always do for me, and I
thought I could see in you the sort of affectation by which a
man betrays a consciousness that his loyalty is becoming a
burden.   And in that moment I paid very dear for my happiness.   I felt that nature always demands the price for the
treasure called love.   Briefly, has not fate separated us?   Can
you have said, 'Sooner or later I must leave poor Claire;
why not separate in time?'   I read that thought in the
depths of your eyes, and went away to cry by myself.

Hiding my tears from you! the first tears that I have shed for sorrow for these ten years; I am too proud to let you see them, but I did not reproach you in the least.

"Yes, you are right. I ought not to be so selfish as to bind your long and brilliant career to my so-soon worn-out life. And yet—how if I have been mistaken? How if I have taken your love melancholy for a deliberation? Oh, my love, do not leave me in suspense; punish this jealous wife of yours, but give her back the sense of her love and yours; the whole woman lies in that—that consciousness sanctifies everything.

"Since your mother came, since you paid a visit to Mlle. de Rodière, I have been gnawed by doubts dishonoring to us both. Make me suffer for this, but do not deceive me; I want to know everything that your mother said and what you think! If you have hesitated between some alternative and me, I give you back your liberty. I will not let you know what happens to me; I will not shed tears for you to see; only—I will not see you again. Ah! I cannot go on, my heart is breaking——

"I have been sitting benumbed and stupid for some moments. Dear love, I do not find that any feeling of pride rises against you; you are so kind-hearted, so open; you would find it impossible to hurt me or to deceive me; and you will tell me the truth, however cruel it may be. Do you wish me to encourage your confession? Well, then, heart of mine, I shall find comfort in a woman's thought. Has not the youth of your being been mine, your sensitive, wholly gracious, beautiful, and delicate youth? No woman shall find henceforth the Gaston whom I have known, nor the delicious happiness that he has given me—— No; you will never love again as you have loved, as you love me now; no, I shall never have a rival, it is impossible. There will be no bitterness in my memories of our love, and I shall think of nothing else. It is out of your power to enchant any woman henceforth by the childish provocations, the charming ways of a

young heart, the soul's winning charm, the body's grace, the
swift communion of rapture, the whole divine cortège of
young love, in fine.

"Oh, you are a man now, you will obey your destiny,
weighing and considering all things. You will have cares,
and anxieties, and ambitions, and concerns that will rob *her*
of the unchanging smile that made your lips fair for me.
The tones that were always so sweet for me will be troubled
at times; and your eyes that lighted up with radiance from
heaven at the sight of me will often be lustreless for *her*.
And besides, as it is impossible to love you as I love you, you
will never care for that woman as you have cared for me.
She will never keep a constant watch over herself as I have
done; she will never study your happiness at every moment
with an intuition which has never failed me. Ah, yes, the
man, the heart and soul, which I shall have known will exist
no longer. I shall bury him deep in my memory, that I may
have the joy of him still; I shall live happy in that fair past
life of ours, a life hidden from all but our inmost selves.

"Dear treasure of mine, if all the while no least thought
of liberty has risen in your mind, if my love is no burden on
you, if my fears are chimerical, if I am still your Eve—the
one woman in the world for you—come to me as soon as you
have read this letter; come quickly! Ah! in one moment I
will love you more than I have ever loved you, I think, in
these nine years. After enduring the needless torture of these
doubts of which I am accusing myself, every added day of
love, yes, every single day, will be a whole lifetime of bliss.
So speak, and speak openly; do not deceive me, it would be
a crime. Tell me, do you wish for your liberty? Have you
thought of all that a man's life means? Is there any regret
in your mind? That *I* should cause you a regret! I should
die of it. I have said it: I love you enough to set your
happiness above mine, your life before my own. Leave on
one side, if you can, the wealth of memories of our nine

years' happiness, that they may not influence your decision,
but speak! I submit myself to you as to God, the one Con-
soler who remains if you forsake me."

When Mme. de Beauséant knew that her letter was in M.
de Nueil's hands, she sank in such utter prostration, the over-
pressure of many thoughts so numbed her faculties that she
seemed almost drowsy. At any rate, she was suffering from
a pain not always proportioned in its intensity to a woman's
strength; pain which women alone know. And while the
unhappy Marquise awaited her doom, M. de Nueil, reading
her letter, felt that he was "in a very difficult position," to
use the expression that young men apply to a crisis of this
kind.

By this time he had all but yielded to his mother's impor-
tunities and to the attractions of Mlle. de la Rodière, a somewhat insignificant, pink-and-white young person, as straight as
a poplar. It is true that, in accordance with the rules laid
down for marriageable young ladies, she scarcely opened her
mouth, but her rent-roll of forty thousand livres spoke quite
sufficiently for her. Mme. de Nueil, with a mother's sincere
affection, tried to entangle her son in virtuous courses. She
called his attention to the fact that it was a flattering distinction to be preferred by Mlle. de la Rodière, who had refused
so many great matches; it was quite time, she urged, that he
should think of his future, such a good opportunity might not
repeat itself, some day he would have eighty thousand livres of
income from land; money made anything bearable; if Mme.
de Beauséant loved him for his own sake, she ought to be the
first to urge him to marry. In short, the well-intentioned
mother forgot no arguments which the feminine intellect can
bring to bear upon the masculine mind, and by these means
she had brought her son into a wavering condition.

Mme. de Beauséant's letter arrived just as Gaston's love of
her was holding out against the temptations of a settled life

21

conformable to received ideas.   That letter decided the day.
He made up his mind to break off with the Marquise and to
marry.

" One must live a man's life," said he to himself.

Then followed some inkling of the pain that this decision
would give to Mme. de Beauséant.   The man's vanity and the
lover's conscience further exaggerated this pain, and a sincere
pity for her seized upon him.   All at once the immensity of
the misery became apparent to him, and he thought it necessary and charitable to deaden the deadly blow.   He hoped to
bring Mme. de Beauséant to a calm frame of mind by gradually reconciling her to the idea of separation ; while Mlle.
de la Rodière, always like a shadowy third between them,
should be sacrificed to her at first, only to be imposed upon
her later.   His marriage should take place later, in obedience
to Mme. de Beauséant's expressed wish.   He went so far as
to enlist the Marquise's nobleness and pride and all the great
qualities of her nature to help him to succeed in this com-
passionate design.   He would write a letter at once to allay
her suspicions.   *A letter !* For a woman with the most exquisite feminine perception, as well as the intuition of passionate love, a letter in itself was a sentence of death.

So when Jacques came and brought Mme. de Beauséant
a sheet of paper folded in a triangle, she trembled, poor
woman, like a snared swallow.   A mysterious sensation of
physical cold spread from head to foot, wrapping her about
in an icy winding-sheet.   If he did not rush to her feet, if
he did not come to her in tears, and pale, and like a lover,
she knew that all was lost.   And yet, so many hopes are
there in the heart of a woman who loves, that she is only
slain by stab after stab, and loves on till the last drop of
life-blood drains away.

"Does madame need anything?" Jacques asked gently, as
he went away.

"No," she said.

"Poor fellow!" she thought, brushing a tear from her eyes, "he guesses my feelings, servant though he is!"

She read: "My beloved, you are inventing idle terrors for yourself——" The Marquise gazed at the words, and a thick mist spread before her eyes. A voice in her heart cried, "He lies!" Then she glanced down the page with the clairvoyant eagerness of passion, and read these words at the foot, "*Nothing has been decided as yet*——" Turning to the other side with convulsive quickness, she saw the mind of the writer distinctly through the intricacies of the wording; this was no spontaneous outburst of love. She crushed it in her fingers, twisted it, tore it with her teeth, flung it in the fire, and cried aloud, "Ah! base that he is! I was his, and he has ceased to love me!"

She sank half-dead upon the couch.

M. de Nueil went out as soon as he had written his letter. When he came back, Jacques met him on the threshold with a note. "Madame la Marquise has left the château," said the man.

M. de Nueil, in amazement, broke the seal and read:

"MADAME:—If I could cease to love you, to take the chances of becoming an ordinary man which you hold out to me, you must admit that I should thoroughly deserve my fate. No, I shall not do as you bid me; the oath of fidelity which I swear to you shall only be absolved by death. Ah! take my life, unless indeed you do not fear to carry a remorse all through your own——"

It was his own letter, written to the Marquise as she set out for Geneva nine years before. At the foot of it Claire de Bourgogne had written, "Monsieur, you are free."

M. de Nueil went to his mother at Manerville. In less than three weeks he married Mlle. Stéphanie de la Rodière.

If this commonplace story of real life ended here, it would

be to some extent a sort of mystification.   The first man you
meet can tell you a better.   But the widespread fame of the
catastrophe (for, unhappily, this is a true tale), and all the
memories which it may arouse in those who have known the
divine delights of infinite passion, and lost them by their own
deed, or through the cruelty of fate—these things may perhaps
shelter the story from criticism.

Mme. la Marquise de Beauséant never left Valleroy after
her parting from M. de Nueil.   After his marriage she still
continued to live there, for some inscrutable woman's reason ;
any woman is at liberty to assign the one which most appeals
to her.   Claire de Bourgogne lived in such complete retirement that none of the servants, save Jacques and her own
woman, ever saw their mistress.   She required absolute silence
all about her, and only left her room to go to the chapel on
the Valleroy estate, whither a neighboring priest came to say
mass every morning.

The Comte de Nueil sank a few days after his marriage into
something like conjugal apathy, which might be interpreted
to mean either happiness or unhappiness.

" My son is perfectly happy," his mother said everywhere.

Mme. Gaston de Nueil, like a great many young women,
was a rather colorless character, sweet and passive.   A month
after her marriage she had expectations of becoming a mother.
All this was quite in accordance with ordinary views.   M. de
Nueil was very nice to her ; but two months after his separation
from the Marquise, he grew notably thoughtful and abstracted.
But then he always had been serious, his mother said.

After seven months of this tepid happiness, a little thing
occurred, one of those seemingly small matters which imply
such great development of thought and such widespread
trouble of soul, that only the bare fact can be recorded ;
the interpretation of it must be left to the fancy of each
individual mind.   One day, when M. de Nueil had been
shooting over the lands of Manerville and Valleroy, he crossed

Mme. de Beauséant's park on his way home, summoned Jacques, and when the man came, asked him, "Whether the Marquise was as fond of game as ever?"

Jacques, answering in the affirmative, Gaston offered him a good round sum (accompanied by plenty of specious reasoning) for a very little service. Would he set aside for the Marquise the game that the Count would bring? It seemed to Jacques to be a matter of no great importance whether the partridge on which his mistress dined had been shot by her keeper or by M. de Nueil, especially since the latter particularly wished that the Marquise should know nothing about it.

"It was killed on her land," said the Count, and for some days Jacques lent himself to the harmless deceit. Day after day M. de Nueil went shooting, and came back at dinnertime with an empty bag. A whole week went by in this way. Gaston grew bold enough to write a long letter to the Marquise, and had it conveyed to her. It was returned to him unopened. The Marquise's servant brought it back about nightfall. The Count, sitting in the drawing-room listening, while his wife at the piano mangled a *Caprice* of Hérold's, suddenly sprang up and rushed to the Marquise, as if he were flying to an assignation. He dashed through a well-known gap into the park, and went slowly along the avenues, stopping now and again for a little to still the rapid beatings of his heart. Smothered sounds as he came nearer the château told him that the servants must be at supper, and he went straight to Mme. de Beauséant's room.

Mme. de Beauséant never left her bedroom. M. de Nueil could gain the doorway without making the slightest sound. There, by the light of two wax-candles, he saw the thin, white Marquise in a great armchair; her head was bowed, her hands hung listlessly, her eyes gazing fixedly at some object which she did not seem to see. Her whole attitude spoke of hopeless pain. There was a vague something like hope in her bearing, but it was impossible to say whither

Claire de Bourgogne was looking—forwards to the tomb or backwards into the past. Perhaps M. de Nueil's tears glittered in the deep shadows; perhaps his breathing sounded faintly; perhaps unconsciously he trembled, or again it may have been impossible that he should stand there, his presence unfelt by that quick sense which grows to be an instinct, the glory, the delight, the proof of perfect love. However it was, Mme. de Beauséant slowly turned her face towards the doorway, and beheld her lover of bygone days. Then Gaston de Nueil came forward a few paces.

"If you come any farther, sir," exclaimed the Marquise, growing paler, " I shall fling myself out of the window! "

She sprang to the window, flung it open, and stood with one foot on the ledge, her hand upon the iron balustrade, her face turned towards Gaston.

"Go out! go out!" she cried, "or I will throw myself over."

At that dreadful cry the servants began to stir, and M. de Nueil fled like a criminal.

When he reached his home again he wrote a few lines and gave them to his own man, telling him to give the letter himself into Mme. de Beauséant's hands, and to say that it was a matter of life and death for his master. The messenger went. M. de Nueil went back to the drawing-room where his wife was still murdering the *Caprice*, and sat down to wait until the answer came. An hour later, when the *Caprice* had come to an end, and the husband and wife sat in silence on opposite sides of the hearth, the man came back from Valleroy and gave his master his own letter, unopened.

M. de Nueil then arose, went into a small room beyond the drawing-room, where he had left his rifle, and shot himself.

The swift and fatal ending of the drama, contrary as it is to all the habits of young France, is only what might have been expected. Those who have closely observed, or known

for themselves by delicious experience, all that is meant by
the perfect union of two beings, will understand Gaston de
Nueil's suicide perfectly well. A woman does not bend and
form herself in a day to the caprices of passion. The pleasure
of loving, like some rare flower, needs the most careful ingenuity of culture. Time alone, and two souls attuned each to
each, can discover all its resources, and call into being all
the tender and delicate delights for which we are steeped in a
thousand superstitions, imagining them to be inherent in the
heart that lavishes them upon us. It is this wonderful response of one nature to another, this religious belief, this
certainty of finding peculiar or excessive happiness in the
presence of one we love, that accounts in part for perdurable
attachments and long-lived passion. If a woman possesses
the genius of her sex, love never comes to be a matter of use
and wont. She brings all her heart and brain to love, clothes
her tenderness in forms so varied, there is such art in her
most natural movements, or so much nature in her art, that in
absence her memory is almost as potent as her presence. All
other women are as shadows compared with her. Not until
we have lost or known the dread of losing a love so vast and
glorious, do we prize it at its just worth. And if a man who
has once possessed this love shuts himself out from it by his
own act and deed, and sinks to some loveless marriage; if,
by some incident, hidden in the obscurity of married life, the
woman with whom he hoped to know the same felicity makes
it clear that it will never be revived for him; if, with the
sweetness of divine love still on his lips, he has dealt a deadly
wound to *her*, his wife in truth, whom he forsook for a social
chimera—then he must either die or take refuge in a material-
istic, selfish, and heartless philosophy, from which impassioned
souls shrink in horror.

As for Mme. de Beauséant, she doubtless did not imagine
that her friend's despair could drive him to suicide, when he

had drunk deep of love for nine years. Possibly she may have thought that she alone was to suffer. At any rate, she did quite rightly to refuse the most humiliating of all positions; a wife may stoop for weighty social reasons to a kind of compromise which a mistress is bound to hold in abhorrence, for in the purity of her passion lies all its justification.

ANGOULÊME, *September,* 1832.

THE IMAGINARY MISTRESS.

(La Fausse Maîtresse.)

Dedicated to the Comtesse Clara Maffei.

In the month of September, 1835, one of the richest heiresses of the Faubourg Saint-Germain, Mademoiselle du Rouvre, the only child of the Marquis du Rouvre, married Count Adam Mitgislas Laginski, a young Polish exile.

I allow myself to spell the names as they are pronounced, to spare the reader the sight of the fortifications of consonants by which, in the Slav languages, the vowels are protected, no doubt to secure them against loss, seeing how few they are.

The Marquis du Rouvre had dissipated almost the whole of one of the finest fortunes of the nobility, to which he had formerly owed his alliance with a Mademoiselle de Ronquerolles. Hence Clémentine had for her uncle, on her mother's side, the Marquis de Ronquerolles, and for her aunt Madame de Sérizy. On her father's side she possessed another uncle in the eccentric person of the Chevalier du Rouvre, the younger son of the house, an old bachelor who had grown rich by speculations in land and houses.

The Marquis de Ronquerolles was so unhappy as to lose both his children during the visitation of cholera. Madame de Sérizy's only son, a young officer of the highest promise, was killed in Africa at the fight by the Macta. In these days rich families run the risk of ruining their children if they have too many, or of becoming extinct if they have but one or two, a singular result of the Civil Code not foreseen by Napoleon. Thus, by accident, and in spite of Monsieur du

(329)

Rouvre's reckless extravagances for Florine, one of the most charming of Paris actresses, Clémentine had become an heiress. The Marquis de Ronquerolles, one of the most accomplished diplomats of the new dynasty, his sister, Madame de Sérizy, and the Chevalier du Rouvre agreed that, to rescue their fortunes from the Marquis' clutches, they would leave them to their niece, to whom they each promised ten thousand francs a year on her marriage.

It is quite unnecessary to say that the Pole, though a refugee, cost the French government absolutely nothing. Count Adam belonged to one of the oldest and most illustrious families of Poland, connected with most of the princely houses of Germany, with the Sapiéhas, the Radziwills, the Mniszechs, the Rzewuskis, the Czartoryskis, the Leszinskis, the Lubomirskis; in short, all the great Sarmatian *skis*. But a knowledge of heraldry is not a strong point in France under Louis Philippe, and such nobility could be no recommendation to the *bourgeoisie* then in power. Besides, when, in 1833, Adam made his appearance on the Boulevard des Italiens, at Frascati's, at the Jockey Club, he led the life of a man who, having lost his political prospects, falls back on his vices and his love of pleasure. He was taken for a student.

The Polish nationality, as the result of an odious government reaction, had fallen as low as the Republicans had tried to think it high. The strange struggle of *movement* against *resistance*—two words which thirty years hence will be inexplicable—made a farce of what ought to have been so worthy : the name, that is, of a vanquished nation to which France gave hospitality, for which entertainments were devised, for which every one danced or sang by subscription ; a nation, in short, which at the time when, in 1796, Europe was fighting France, had offered her six thousand men, and such men !

Do not conclude from this that I mean to represent the Emperor Nicholas as being in the wrong as regards Poland, or Poland as regards the Emperor Nicholas. In the first place, it would be a silly thing enough to slip a political discussion into a tale which ought to interest or to amuse. Besides, Russia and Poland were equally right : one for aiming at unity of empire, the other for desiring to be free again. It may be said, in passing, that Poland might have conquered Russia by the influence of manners instead of beating her with weapons; thus imitating the Chinese, who at last Chinesified the Tartars, and who, it is to be hoped, will do the same by the English. Poland ought to have *polished* the Russians ; Poniatowski had tried it in the least temperate district of the empire. But that gentleman was a misunderstood king—all the more so because he did not, perhaps, understand himself.

How was it possible not to hate the poor people who were the cause of the horrible deceit committed on the occasion of the review when all Paris was eager to rescue Poland ? People affected to regard the Poles as allies of the Republican party, forgetting that Poland was an aristocratic republic. Thenceforth the party of wealth poured ignoble contempt on the Pole, who had been deified but a few days since. The wind of a riot has always blown the Parisians round from north to south under every form of government. This weathercock temper of Paris opinion must be remembered if we would understand how, in 1835, the name of Pole was a word of ridicule among the race who believe themselves to be the wittiest and politest in the world, and its central luminary, in a city which, at this day, wields the sceptre of art and literature.

There are, alas ! two types of Polish refugees—the republican Pole, the son of Lelewel, and the noble Pole of the party led by Prince Czartoryski. These two kinds of Pole are as fire and water, but why blame them ? Are not such divisions always to be observed among refugees whatever nation they belong to, and no matter what country they go to ? They carry their country and their hatreds with them. At Brussels two French emigrant priests expressed the greatest

aversion for each other ; and when one of them was asked his
reasons, he replied, pointing to his companion in misery, " He
is a Jansenist ! "   Dante, in his exile, would gladly have
stabbed any adversary of the "Bianchi." In this lies the reason of the attacks made on the venerable Prince Adam Czartoryski by the French radicals, and that of the disapproval
shown to a section of the Polish emigrants by the Cæsars of
the counter and the Alexanders by letters patent.

In 1834 Adam Mitgislas Laginski was the butt of Parisian
witticisms. " He is a nice fellow though he is a Pole," said
Rastignac. " All the Poles are great lords," said Maxime de
Trailles, "but this one pays his gambling debts ; I begin to
think that he must have had an estate."

And without offense to the exiles, it may be remarked that
the levity, the recklessness, the fluidity of the Sarmatian character justified the calumnies of the Parisians, who, indeed,
in similar circumstances, would be exactly like the Poles.
The French aristocracy, so admirably supported by the Polish
aristocracy during the Revolution, certainly made no equivalent return to those who were forced to emigrate in 1832.
We must have the melancholy courage to say that, in this, the
Faubourg Saint-Germain remains Poland's debtor.

Was Count Adam rich, was he poor, was he an adventurer ?
The problem long remained unsolved. Diplomatic circles,
faithful to their instructions, imitated the silence observed by
the Emperor Nicholas, who at that time counted every Polish
emigrant as dead. The Tuileries, and most of those who
took their cue from thence, gave an odious proof of this characteristic policy dignified by the name of prudence. A
Russian prince, with whom they had smoked many cigars at
the time of the emigration, was ignored because, as it seemed,
he had fallen into disgrace with the Emperor Nicholas.

Thus placed between the prudence of the court and that of
diplomatic circles, Poles of good family lived in the Biblical
solitude of *Super flumina Babylonis,* or frequented certain

drawing-rooms which served as neutral territory for every variety of opinion. In a city of pleasure like Paris, where amusement is to be had in every rank, Polish recklessness found twice as many pretexts as it needed for leading a dissipated bachelor life. Besides, it must be said that Count Adam Laginski had against him at first both his appearance and his manners.

There are two types of Pole, as there are two types of Englishwoman. When an Englishwoman is not a beauty, she is horribly ugly—and Count Adam belongs to the second category. His face is small, somewhat sour, and looks as if it had been squeezed in a vise. His short nose, fair hair, red mustache and beard give him the expression of a goat; all the more so because he is short and thin, and his eyes, tinged with dingy yellow, startle you by the oblique leer which Virgil's line has made famous. How is it that, in spite of such unfavorable conditions, he has such exquisite manners and style? The solution of this mystery is given by his dress, that of a finished dandy, and by the education he owes to his mother, a Radziwill. If his courage carries him to the point of rashness, his mind is not above the current and trivial pleasantries of Paris conversation; still, he does not often find a young fellow who is his superior among men of fashion. These young men nowadays talk far too much of horses, income, taxes, and deputies, for French conversation to be what it once was. Wit needs leisure, and certain inequalities of position. Conversation is better perhaps at St. Petersburg and Vienna than it is in Paris. Equals need no subtleties; they tell each other everything straight out, just as it is. Hence the ironical laughters of Paris could scarcely discern a man of family in a light-hearted student, as he seemed, who in talking passed carelessly from one subject to another, who pursued amusement with all the more frenzy because he had just escaped from great perils, and who, having left the country where his family was known, thought himself at liberty to lead an irresponsible life without risking a loss of consideration.

One fine day in 1834, Adam bought a large house in the Rue de la Pépinière. Six months later it was on as handsome a footing as the richest houses in Paris. Just at the time when Laginski was beginning to be taken seriously he saw Clémentine at the Italian opera, and fell in love with her. A year later he married her. Madame d'Espard's circle set the fashion of approval. Mothers of families then learned, too late, that ever since the year 900, the Laginskis had ranked with the most illustrious families of the north. By a stroke of prudence, most unlike a Pole, the young Count's mother had, at the beginning of the rebellion, mortgaged her estates for an immense sum advanced by two Jewish houses, and invested in the French funds. Count Adam Laginski had an income of more than eighty thousand francs. This put an end to the astonishment expressed in some drawing-rooms at the rashness of Madame de Sérizy, of old de Ronquerolles, and of the Chevalier du Rouvre in yielding to their niece's mad passion.

As usual, the world rushed from one extreme to the other. During the winter of 1836, Count Adam became the fashion, and Clémentine Laginski one of the queens of Paris. Madame de Laginski, at the present time, is one of the charming group of young married women among whom shine Mesdames de Lestorade, de Portenduère, Marie de Vandenesse, du Guénic, and de Maufrigneuse, the very flower of Paris society, who live high above the parvenus, bourgeois, and wire-pullers of recent politics.

This preamble was needful to define the sphere in which was carried through one of those sublime efforts, less rare than the detractors of the present time imagine—pearls hidden in rough shells, and lost in the depths of that abyss, that ocean, that never-resting tide called the world—the age—Paris, London, or St. Petersburg—whichever you will.

If ever the truth that architecture is the expression of the manners of a race was fully demonstrated, is it not since the revolution of 1830, under the reign of the House of Orleans? Great fortunes have shrunk in France, and majestic mansions of our fathers are constantly being demolished and replaced by a sort of tenement-houses, in which a peer of France of July dwells on the third floor, over some newly enriched empiric. Styles are mingled in confusion. As there is no longer any court, any nobility to set a "tone," no harmony is to be seen in the productions of art. On the other hand, architecture has never found more economical tricks for imitating what is genuine and thorough, never displayed more ingenuity and resource in arrangement. Ask an artist to deal with a strip of the garden of an old "hôtel" now destroyed, and he will build you a little Louvre crushed under its ornamentation; he will give you a courtyard, stables, and, if you insist, a garden; inside he contrives such a number of little rooms and corridors, and cheats the eye so effectually, that you fancy yourself comfortable; in fact, there are so many bedrooms that a ducal retinue can live and move in what was only the bake-house of a president of a law court.

The Comtesse Laginski's house is one of these modern structures, with a courtyard in front and a garden behind. To the right of the courtyard are the servants' quarters, balanced on the left by the stables and coach-houses. The porter's lodge stands between two handsome gates. The chief luxury of this house consists in a delightful conservatory at the end of a boudoir on the ground-floor, where all the beautiful reception-rooms are. It was a philanthropist driven out of England who built this architectural gem, constructed the conservatory, planned the garden, varnished the doors, paved the out-buildings with brick, filled the windows with green glass, and realized a vision like that—in due proportion —of George IV. at Brighton. The inventive, industrious, and ready Paris artisan had carved his doors and window-

frames; his ceilings were imitated from those of the middle
ages or of Venetian palaces, and there was a lavish outlay of
marble slabs in external paneling. Steinbock and François
Souchet had carved the cornices of the doors and chimney-
shelves; Schinner had painted the ceilings with the brush of
a master. The wonders of the stairs—marble as white as a
woman's arm—successfully defied those of the famous Hôtel
Rothschild.

In consequence of the disturbances, the price of this folly
was not more than eleven hundred thousand francs. For an
Englishman this was giving it away. All this splendor, called
princely by people who do not know what a real prince is,
stood in the garden of a contractor—a Crœsus of the Revolution, who had died at Brussels a bankrupt after a sudden con-
vulsion of the Bourse. The Englishman died at Paris—died
of Paris—for to many people Paris is a disease; sometimes it
is several diseases. His widow, a Methodist, had a perfect
horror of the nabob's little house—this philanthropist had
been a dealer in opium. The virtuous widow ordered that
the scandalous property should be sold just at the time when
the disturbances made peace doubtful on any terms. Count
Adam took advantage of the opportunity; and you shall be
told how it happened, for nothing could be less consonant
with his lordly habits.

Behind this house, built of stone fretted like a melon,
spreads the green velvet of an English lawn, shaded at the
farther end by an elegant clump of exotic trees, among which
rises a Chinese pavilion with its mute bells and pendent gilt
eggs. The greenhouse and its fantastic decorations screen
the outer wall on the south side. The other wall, opposite
the greenhouse, is hung with creepers grown in arcades over
poles and cross-beams painted green. This meadow, this
realm of flowers, these graveled paths, this mimic forest, these
aerial trellises cover an area of about twenty-five square
perches, of which the present value would be four hundred

thousand francs, as much as a real forest. In the heart of
this silence won from Paris birds sing; there are blackbirds,
nightingales, bullfinches, chaffinches, and numbers of spar-
rows. The conservatory is a vast flower-bed, where the air
is loaded with perfume, and where you may walk in winter as
though summer was blazing with all its fires. The means by
which an atmosphere is produced at will of the tropics, China
or Italy, are ingeniously concealed from view. The pipes in
which the boiling water circulates—the steam, hot air, what-
not—are covered with soil, and look like garlands of growing
flowers.

The boudoir is spacious. On a small plot of ground the
miracle wrought by the Paris fairy called Architecture is to
produce everything on a large scale. The young Countess'
boudoir was the pride of the artist to whom Count Adam intrusted the task of redecorating the house. To sin there
would be impossible, there are too many pretty trifles. Love
would not know where to alight amid work-tables of Chinese
carving, where the eye can find thousands of droll little figures
wrought in the ivory—the outcome of the toil of two families
of Chinese artists; vases of burnt topaz mounted on filigree
stands; mosaics that invite to theft; Dutch pictures, such as
Schinner now paints again; angels imagined as Steinbock
conceives of them (but does not always work them out himself); statuettes executed by geniuses pursued by creditors
(the true interpretation of the Arab myths); sublime first
sketches by our greatest artists; fronts of carved chests let
into the wainscot, and alternating with the inventions of
India embroidery; gold-colored curtains draped over the
doors from an architrave of black oak wrought with the
swarming figures of a hunting scene; chairs and tables
worthy of Madame de Pompadour; a Persian carpet, and
so forth. And finally, as a crowning touch, all this splendor,
seen under a softened light filtering in through lace curtains,
looks all the more beautiful. On a marble slab, among some

22

antiques, a lady's whip, with a handle carved by Mademoiselle de Fauveau, shows that the Countess is fond of riding.

Such is a boudoir in 1837, a display of property to divert the eye, as though ennui threatened to invade the most restless and unresting society in the world. Why is there nothing individual, intimate, nothing to invite reverie and repose? Why? Because no one is sure of the morrow, and every one enjoys life as a prodigal spends a life-interest.

One morning Clémentine affected a meditative air, as she lounged on one of those deep siesta chairs from which we cannot bear to rise, so cleverly has the upholsterer who invented them contrived to fit them to the curves of laziness and the comfort of the *Dolce far niente.* The doors to the conservatory were open, admitting the scent of vegetation and the perfumes of the tropics. The young wife watched Adam, who was smoking an elegant narghileh, the only form of pipe she allowed in this room. Over the other door, curtains, caught back by handsome ropes, showed two magnificent rooms beyond: one in white and gold, resembling that of the Hôtel Forbin-Janson, the other in the taste of the Renaissance. The dining-room, unrivaled in Paris by any but that of the Baron de Nucingen, is at the end of a corridor, with a ceiling and walls decorated in a mediæval style. This corridor is reached, on the courtyard front, through a large anteroom, through whose glass door the splendor of the stairs is seen.

The Count and Countess had just breakfasted; the sky was a sheet of blue without a cloud; the month of April was drawing to a close. The household had already known two years of happiness, and now, only two days since, Clémentine had discovered in her home something resembling a secret, a mystery. A Pole, let it be repeated to his honor, is generally weak in the presence of a woman; he is so full of tenderness that, in Poland, he becomes her inferior; and though Polish women are admirable creatures, a Pole is even more quickly

routed by a Parisienne. Hence, Count Adam, pressed hard
with questions, had not enough artless cunning to sell his
secret dear to his wife. With a woman there is always something to be got for a secret ; and she likes you the better for
it, as a rogue respects an honest man whom he has failed to
take in. The Count, more ready with his sword than with
his tongue, only stipulated that he should not be required to
answer till he had finished his narghileh full of *tombaki*.

"When we were traveling," said she, "you replied to
every difficulty by saying, 'Paz will see to that!' You
never wrote to anybody but Paz. On my return, every one
refers me to *the captain*. I want to go out. The captain!
Is there a bill to be paid! The captain. If my horse's
pace is rough, they will speak to Captain Paz. In short,
here I feel as if it were a game of dominoes; everywhere
Paz! I hear no one talked of but Paz, but I can never see
Paz. What is Paz? Let our Paz be brought to see me."

"Then is not everything as it ought to be?" said the
Count, relinquishing the mouthpiece of his narghileh.

"Everything is so quite what it ought to be, that if we
had two hundred thousand francs a year, we should be ruined
by living in the way we do with a hundred and ten thousand," said she. She pulled the bell-handle embroidered in
tent-stitch, a marvel of skill. A manservant dressed like a
Minister at once appeared.

"Tell Monsieur le Capitaine Paz that I wish to speak to
him," said she.

"If you fancy you will find anything out in that way——"
said Count Adam with a smile.

It may be useful to say that Adam and Clémentine, married
in December, 1835, after spending the winter in Paris, had
during 1836 traveled in Italy, Switzerland, and Germany.
They returned home in November, and during the winter just
past the Countess had for the first time received her friends,
and then had discovered the existence—the almost speechless

and unacknowledged, but most useful presence—of a factotum whose person seemed to be invisible—this Captain Paz or Paç.

"Monsieur le Capitaine Paz begs Madame la Comtesse to excuse him; he is round at the stables, and in a dress which does not allow of his coming at this minute. But as soon as he is dressed Count Paz will come," said the manservant deferentially.

"Why, what was he doing?"

"He was showing Constantine how to groom the Countess' horse; the man did not do it to his mind," replied the servant.

The Countess looked at the man; he was quite serious, and took good care not to imply by a smile the comment which inferiors so often allow themselves on a superior who seems to have descended to their level.

"Ah, he was brushing down Cora?"

"You are not riding out this morning, madame?" said the servant; but he got no answer, and went.

"Is he a Pole?" asked Clémentine of her husband, who bowed affirmatively.

Clémentine lay silent, examining Adam. Her feet, almost at full length on a cushion, her head in the attitude of a bird listening on the edge of its nest to the sounds of the grove, she would have seemed charming to the most blasé of men. Fair and slight, her hair curled English fashion, she looked like one of the almost fabulous figures in "Keepsakes," especially as she was wrapped in a morning gown of Persian silk, of which the thick folds did not so effectually disguise the graces of her figure and the slenderness of her waist, as that they could not be admired through the thick covering of flowers and embroidery. As she crossed the brightly colored stuff over her chest, the hollow of her throat remained visible, the white skin contrasting in tone with the handsome lace trimming over the shoulders. Her eyes, fringed with black lashes, emphasized the expression of curiosity that puckered a pretty mouth. On her well-formed brow were traced the characteristic curves of the Paris woman, willful, light-hearted, well-educated, but invulnerable to vulgar temptations. Her hands, almost transparent, hung from each arm of her deep chair; the taper fingers, curved at the tips, showed nails like pink almonds that caught the light.

Adam smiled at his wife's impatience, gazing at her with a look which conjugal satiety had not yet made lukewarm. This slim little Countess had known how to be mistress in her own house, for she scarcely acknowledged Adam's admiration. In the glances she stole at him there was perhaps a dawning consciousness of the superiority of a Parisienne to this spruce, lean, and red-haired Pole.

"Here comes Paz," said the Count, hearing a step that rang in the corridor.

The Countess saw a tall, handsome man come in, well-built, bearing in his features the marks of the grief which comes of strength and misfortune. Paz had dressed hastily in one of those tightly fitting coats, fastened by braid straps and oval buttons, which used to be called *polonaises*. Thick, black hair, but ill-kempt, covered his squarely-shaped head, and Clémentine could see his broad forehead as shiny as a piece of marble, for he held his peaked cap in his hand. That hand was like the hand of the Hercules carrying the infant Mercury. Robust health bloomed in a face equally divided by a large Roman nose, which reminded Clémentine of the handsome Trasteverini. A black silk stock put a finishing touch of martial appearance to this mystery of nearly six feet high, with jet-black eyes as lustrous as an Italian's. The width of his full trousers, hiding all but the toes of his boots, showed that Paz still was faithful to the fashions of Poland. Certainly, to a romantic woman, there must have been something burlesque in the violent contrast observable between the captain and the Count, between the little Pole with his narrow frame and this fine soldier, between the carpet-knight and the knight servitor.

"Good-morning, Adam," he said to the Count with familiarity.

Then he bowed gracefully, asking Clémentine in what way he could serve her.

"Then you are Laginski's friend?" asked the lady.

"For life and death," replied Paz, on whom the young Count shed his most affectionate smile, as he exhaled his last fragrant puff of smoke.

"Well, then, why do you not eat with us? Why did you not accompany us to Italy and to Switzerland? Why do you hide yourself so as to avoid the thanks I owe you for the constant services you do us?" said the young Countess, with a sort of irritation, but without the slightest feeling.

In fact, she detected a kind of volunteer slavery on the part of Paz. At that time such an idea was inseparable from a certain disdain for a socially amphibious creature, a being at once secretary and bailiff, neither wholly bailiff nor wholly secretary, some poor relation—inconvenient as a friend.

"The fact is, Countess," he replied with some freedom, "that no thanks are owing to me. I am Adam's friend, and I find my pleasure in taking charge of his interests."

"And is it for your pleasure too that you remain standing?" said Count Adam.

Paz sat down in an armchair near the doorway.

"I remember having seen you on the occasion of our marriage, and sometimes in the courtyard," said the lady; "but why do you, a friend of Adam's, place yourself in a position of inferiority?"

"The opinion of the Paris world is to me a matter of indifference," said he. "I live for myself, or, if you choose, for you two."

"But the opinion of the world as regards my husband's friend cannot be a matter of indifference to me——"

"Oh, madame, the world is easily satisfied by one word: Eccentric—say that."

After a short pause he asked, "Do you propose going out?"

"Will you come to the Bois?" said the Countess.

"With pleasure," and so saying Paz bowed and went out.

"What a good soul! He is as simple as a child," said Adam.

"Tell me now how you became friends," said Clémentine.

"Paz, my dearest, is of a family as old, as noble, and as illustrious as our own. At the time of the fall of the Pazzi a member of the family escaped from Florence into Poland, where he settled with some little fortune, and founded the family of the Paz, on which the title of Count was conferred.

"This family, having distinguished itself in the days of our royal republic, grew rich. The cutting from the tree felled in Italy grew with such vigor that there are several branches of the house of the Counts Paz. It will not, therefore, surprise you to be told that there are rich and poor members of the family. Our Paz is the son of a poor branch. As an orphan, with no fortune but his sword, he served under the Grand Duke Constantine at the time of our Revolution. Carried away by the Polish party, he fought like a Pole, like a patriot, like a man who has nothing—three reasons for fighting well. In the last skirmish, believing his men were following him, he rushed on a Russian battery, and was taken prisoner. I was there. This feat of courage roused my blood. 'Let us go and fetch him!' cried I to my horsemen. We charged the battery like freebooters, and I rescued Paz, I being the seventh. We were twenty when we set out, and eight when we came back, including Paz.

"When Warsaw was betrayed we had to think of escaping from the Russians. By a singular chance Paz and I found ourselves together at the same hour and in the same place on the other side of the Vistula. I saw the poor captain arrested by some Prussians, who at that time had made themselves blood-hounds for the Russians. When one has fished a man out of the Styx, one gets attached to him. This new danger threatening Paz distressed me so much that I allowed myself to be taken with him, intending to be of service to him. Two men can sometimes escape when one alone is lost. Thanks to my name and some family connection with those on whom our fate depended—for we were then in the power of the Prussians—my flight was winked at. I got my dear captain through as a common soldier and a servant of my house, and we succeeded in reaching Dantzic. We stowed ourselves in a Dutch vessel sailing for England, where we landed two months later.

"My mother had fallen ill in England, and awaited me there; Paz and I nursed her till her death, which was accelerated by the disasters to our cause.

"We then left England, and I brought Paz to France; in such adversities two men become brothers. When I found myself in Paris with sixty-odd thousand francs a year, not to mention the remains of a sum derived from the sale of my mother's diamonds and the family pictures, I wished to secure a living to Paz before giving myself up to the dissipations of Paris life. I had discerned some sadness in the captain's eyes, sometimes even a suppressed tear floated there. I had had opportunities of appreciating his soul, which is thoroughly noble, lofty, and generous. Perhaps it was painful to him to find himself bound by benefits to a man six years younger than himself without being able to repay him. I, careless and light-hearted as a boy, might ruin myself at play, or let myself be ensnared by some woman; Paz and I might some day be sundered. Though I promised myself that I would always provide for all his needs, I foresaw many chances of forgetting, or being unable to pay Paz an allowance. In short, my angel, I wished to spare him the discomfort, the humiliation, the shame of having to ask me for money, or of seeking

in vain for his comrade in some day of necessity. *Dunque,*
one morning after breakfast, with our feet on the fire-dogs,
each smoking his pipe, after many blushes, and with many
precautions, till I saw he was looking at me quite anxiously, I
held out to him a bond to bearer producing two thousand four
hundred francs interest yearly——''

Clémentine quickly rose, seated herself on Adam's knees,
and putting her arm round his neck, kissed him on the brow,
saying—

"Dear heart, how noble I think you! And what did Paz
say?"

"Thaddeus?" said the Count; "he turned pale and said
nothing."

"Thaddeus—is that his name?"

"Yes. Thaddeus folded up the paper and returned it to
me, saying, 'I thought, Adam, that we were as one in life and
death, and that we should never part; do you wish to see no
more of me.' 'Oh,' said I, 'is that the way you take it?
Well, then, say no more about it. If I am ruined, you will
be ruined.' Said he, 'You are not rich enough to live as a
Laginski should; and do you not need a friend to take care
of your concerns, who will be father and brother to you, and
a trusted confidant?' My dear girl, Paz, as he uttered the
words, spoke with a calmness of tone and look which covered a
motherly feeling, but which betrayed the gratitude of an Arab,
the devotion of a dog, and the friendship of a savage, always
ready and always unassuming. On my honor! I took him
in our Polish fashion, laying my hand on his shoulder, and I
kissed him on the lips. 'For life and death then,' said I.
'All I have is yours, do just as you will.'

"It was he who found me this house for almost nothing.
He sold my shares when they were high, and bought when
they were low, and we purchased this hovel out of the difference. He is a connoisseur in horses, and deals in them so
well that my stable has cost me very little, and yet I have the

finest beasts and the prettiest turn-out in Paris. Our servants, old Polish soldiers whom he found, would pass through the fire for us. While I seem to be ruining myself, Paz keeps my house with such perfect order and economy that he has even made good some losses at play, the follies of a young man. My Thaddeus is as cunning as two Genoese, as keen for profit as a Polish Jew, as cautious as a good housekeeper. I have never been able to persuade him to live as I did when I was a bachelor. Sometimes it has needed the gentle violence of friendship to induce him to come to the play when I was going alone, or to one of the dinners I was giving at an eating-house to a party of congenial companions. He does not like the life of drawing-rooms.''

"Then what does he like?" asked Clémentine.

"He loves Poland, and weeps over her. His only extravagance has been money sent, more in my name than in his own, to some of our poor exiles."

"Dear, how fond I shall be of that good fellow," said the Countess. "He seems to me as simple as everything that is truly great."

"All the pretty things you see here," said Adam, praising his friend with the most generous security, "have been found by Paz; he has bought them at sales, or by some chance. Oh! he is keener at a bargain than a trader. If you see him rubbing his hands in the courtyard, it is because he has exchanged a good horse for a better. He lives in me; his delight is to see me well-dressed, in a dazzlingly smart carriage. He performs all the duties he imposes on himself without fuss or display. One night I had lost twenty thousand francs at whist. 'What will Paz say?' thought I to myself as I reached home. Paz gave me the sum, not without a sigh; but he did not blame me even by a look. This sigh checked me more than all the remonstrances of uncles, wives, or mothers in similar circumstances. 'You regret the money?' I asked him. 'Oh, not for you, nor for myself; no, I was only thinking that twenty poor relations of mine could have lived on it for a year.'

"The family of Paz, you understand, is quite equal to that of Laginski, and I have never regarded my dear Paz as an inferior. I have tried to be as magnanimous in my degree as he in his. I never go out or come in without going to Paz, as if he were my father. My fortune is his. In short, Thaddeus knows that at this day I would rush into danger to rescue him, as I have done twice before."

"That is not a small thing to say, my dear," remarked the Countess. "Devotion is a lightning-flash. Men devote themselves in war, but they no longer devote themselves in Paris."

"Well, then," said Adam, "for Paz I am always in war. Our two natures have preserved their asperities and their faults, but the mutual intimacy of our souls has tightened the bonds, already so close, of our friendship. A man may save his comrade's life, and kill him afterwards if he finds him a bad companion; but we have gone through what makes friendship indissoluble. There is between us that constant exchange of pleasing impressions on both sides which makes friendship, from that point of view, a richer joy, perhaps, than love."

A pretty little hand shut the Count's mouth so suddenly that the movement was almost a blow.

"Yes, indeed, my darling," said he. "Friendship knows nothing of the bankruptcy of sentiment, the insolvency of pleasures. Love, after giving more than it has, ends by giving less than it receives?"

"On both sides alike then," said Clémentine, smiling.

"Yes," said Adam. "While friendship can but increase. You need not pout. We, my angel, are as much friends as lovers; we, at least, I hope, have combined the two feelings in our happy marriage."

"I will explain to you what has made you two such good friends," said Clémentine. "The difference in your lives arises from a difference in your tastes, and not from compulsory choice; from preference, and not from the necessity of position. So far as a man can be judged from a glimpse, and from what you tell me, in this instance the subaltern may at times be the superior."

"Oh! Paz is really my superior," replied Adam simply. "I have no advantage over him but that of luck."

His wife kissed him for this generous avowal.

"The perfect skill with which he conceals the loftiness of his soul is an immense superiority," the Count went on. "I say to him, 'You are a sly fellow; you have vast domains in your mind to which you retire.' He has a right to the title of Count Paz; in Paris he will only be called captain."

"In short, a Florentine of the middle ages has resuscitated after three centuries," said the Countess. "There is something of Dante in him, and something of Michael Angelo."

"Indeed, you are right; he is at heart a poet," replied Adam.

"And so I am married to two Poles," said the young Countess, with a gesture resembling that of a genius on the stage.

"Darling child!" said Adam, clasping Clémentine to him, "you would have distressed me very much if you had not liked my friend. We were both afraid of that, though he was delighted at my marrying. You will make him very happy by telling him that you love him—oh! as an old friend."

"Then I will go to dress; it is fine, we will all three go out," said Clémentine, ringing for her maid.

Paz led such an underground life that all the fashion of Paris wondered who it was that accompanied Clémentine Laginski when they saw her driving to the Bois and back between him and her husband. During the drive Clémentine had insisted that Thaddeus was to dine with her. This whim of a despotic sovereign compelled the captain to make an unwonted toilet. On returning from her drive Clémentine dressed with some coquettish care, in such a way as to produce an effect even on Adam as she entered the room where the two friends were awaiting her.

"Count Paz," said she, "we will go to the opera together."

It was said in the tone which from a woman conveys, "If you refuse, we shall quarrel."

"With pleasure, madame," replied the captain. "But as I have not a count's fortune, call me captain."

"Well, then, captain, give me your arm," said she, taking it and leading him into the dining-room with a suggestion of the caressing familiarity which usually so greatly enraptures a lover.

The Countess placed the captain next her, and he sat like a poor sub-lieutenant dining with a wealthy general. Paz left it to Clémentine to talk, listening to her with all the air of deference to a superior, contradicting her in nothing, and waiting for a positive question before making any reply. In short, to the Countess he seemed almost stupid, and her graces all fell flat before this icy gravity and diplomatic dignity. In vain did Adam try to rouse him by saying, "Come, cheer up, captain. It might be supposed that you were not at home. You must have laid a bet that you would disconcert Clémentine?" Thaddeus remained heavy and half-asleep.

When the three were alone at dessert the captain explained that his life was planned diametrically unlike that of other people; he went to bed at eight o'clock, and rose at daybreak; and he thus excused himself, saying he was very sleepy.

"My intention in taking you to the opera was only to amuse you, Captain Paz; but do just as you please," said Clémentine, a little nettled.

"I will go," said Paz.

"Duprez is singing in *William Tell*," said Adam. "Would you prefer the *Variétés?*"

The captain smiled and rang the bell; the manservant appeared. "Tell Constantine," said Paz, "to take out the large carriage instead of the coupé. We cannot sit comfortably in it," he added, turning to the Count.

"A Frenchman would not have thought of that," said Clémentine, smiling.

"Ah, but we are Florentines transplanted to the north," replied Thaddeus, with a meaning and an expression which showed that his dullness at dinner had been assumed.

But by a very conceivable want of judgment, there was too great a contrast between the involuntary self-betrayal of this speech and the captain's attitude during dinner. Clémentine examined him with one of those keen flashes by which a woman reveals at once her surprise and her observancy. Thus, during the few minutes while they were taking their coffee in the drawing-room, silence reigned—an uncomfortable silence for Adam, who could not divine its cause. Clémentine no longer disturbed Thaddeus. The captain, for his part, retired again into military rigidity, and came out of it no more, either on the way, or in the box, where he affected to be asleep.

"You see, madame, that I am very dull company," said he, during the ballet in the last act of *William Tell*. "Was I not right to 'stick to my last,' as the proverb says?"

"On my word, my dear captain, you are neither a coxcomb nor a chatterbox; you are perhaps a Pole."

"Leave me then to watch over your pleasures," he replied, "to take care of your fortune and your house; that is all I am good for."

"Tartufe! begone!" cried Adam, smiling. "My dear, he is full of heart, well informed—he could, if he chose, hold his own in any drawing-room. Clémentine, do not believe what his modesty tells you."

"Good-night, Countess. I have proved my willingness, and now will avail myself of your carriage to go to bed at once. I will send it back for you."

Clémentine bowed slightly, and let him go without replying.

"What a bear!" said she to the Count. "You are much, much nicer."

Adam pressed his wife's hand unseen.

"Poor, dear Thaddeus, he has endeavored to be a foil when many men would have tried to seem more attractive than I."

"Oh!" said she, "I am not sure that was not intentional; his behavior would have mystified an ordinary woman."

Half an hour later, while Boleslas the groom was calling "Gate," and the coachman, having turned the carriage to drive in, was waiting for the gates to be opened, Clémentine said to the Count—

"Where does the captain roost?"

"Up there," said Adam, pointing to an elegantly constructed attic extending on both sides of the gateway with a window looking on to the street. "His rooms are over the coach-houses."

"And who lives in the other half?"

"No one as yet," replied Adam. "The other little suite, over the stables, will do for our children and their tutor."

"He is not in bed," said the Countess, seeing a light in the captain's room when the carriage was under the pillared portico—copied from that at the Tuileries, and taking the place of the ordinary zinc awning painted to imitate striped ticking.

Paz, in his dressing-gown, and pipe in hand, was watching Clémentine as she disappeared into the hall. The day had been a cruel one to him. And this is the reason: Thaddeus had felt a fearful shock to his heart on the day when, Adam having taken him to the opera to pronounce his opinion, he first saw Mademoiselle du Rouvre; and again, when he saw her in the mayor's office and at Saint-Thomas d'Aquin, and recognized in her the woman whom a man must love to the exclusion of all others—for Don Juan himself preferred one among the *mille e tre!*

Hence Paz had strongly advocated the classical bridal tour after the wedding. Fairly easy all the time while Clémentine was absent, his tortures began again on the return of the happy couple. And this was what he was thinking as he inhaled his latakia from a cherry-stem pipe, six feet long, a gift from Adam: "Only I and God, who will reward me for suffering in silence, may ever know how I love her! But how can I manage to avoid alike her love or her hatred?"

And he sat thinking, thinking, over this problem of the strategy of love.

It must not be supposed that Thaddeus lived bereft of all joy in the midst of his pain. The triumphant cunning of this day was a source of secret satisfaction. Since the Count's return with his wife, day by day he felt ineffable happiness in seeing that he was necessary to the couple, who, but for him, would have rushed inevitably into ruin. What fortune can hold out against the extravagance of Paris life? Clémentine, brought up by a reckless father, knew nothing of household management, which nowadays the richest women and the highest in rank are obliged to undertake themselves. Who in these days can afford to keep a steward? Adam, on his part, as the son of one of the great Polish nobles who allowed themselves to be devoured by the Jews, and who was incapable of husbanding the remains of one of the most enormous fortunes in Poland—where fortunes were enormous—was not of a temper to restrict either his own fancies or his wife's. If he had been alone, he would probably have ruined himself before his marriage. Paz had kept him from gambling on the Bourse, and does not that say all?

Consequently, when he found that, in spite of himself, he was in love with Clémentine, Paz had not the choice of leaving the house and traveling to forget his passion. Gratitude, the clue to the mystery of his life, held him to the house where he alone could act as man of business to this heedless couple. Their long absence made him hope for a calmer spirit: but the Countess came back more than ever lovely, having acquired that freedom of thought which marriage confers on the Paris woman, and displaying all the charms of a young wife, with the indefinable something which comes of happiness, or of the independence allowed her by a man as trusting, as chivalrous, and as much in love as Adam was.

The consciousness of being the working hub of this magnificent house, the sight of Clémentine stepping out of her carriage on her return from a party, or setting out in the morning for the Bois de Boulogne, a glimpse of her on the Boulevards in her pretty carriage, like a flower in its nest of leaves, filled poor Thaddeus with deep, mysterious ecstasies which blossomed at the bottom of his heart without the slightest trace appearing in his features. How, during these five months, should the Countess ever have seen the captain? He hid from her, concealing the care he took to keep out of her way.

Nothing is so near divine love as a hopeless love. Must not a man have some depth of soul thus to devote himself in silence and obscurity? This depth, where lurks the pride of a father—or of God—enshrines the worship of love for love's sake, as power for power's sake was the watchword of the Jesuits; a sublime kind of avarice, since it is perennially generous, and modeled indeed on the mysterious Being of the first principles of the world. Is not their result nature? And nature is an enchantress; she belongs to man, to the poet, the painter, the lover; but is not the cause superior to nature in the sight of certain privileged souls, and some stupendous thinkers? The cause is God. In that sphere of causes dwelt

23

the spirits of Newton, of Laplace, of Kepler, of Descartes, Malebranche, Spinoza, Buffon, of the true poets and saints of the second century of our era, of Saint Theresa of Spain and the sublime mystics.   Every human emotion contains some analogy with the frame of mind in which the effect is neglected in favor of the cause, and Thaddeus has risen to the height whence all things look different.   Abandoned to the unspeakable joys of creative energy, Thaddeus was, in love, what we recognize as greatest in the records of genius.

"No, she is not altogether deceived," thought he, as he watched the smoke curl from his pipe. "She might involve me in an irremediable quarrel with Adam if she spited me; and if she should flirt to torment me, what would become of me?"

The fatuity of this hypothesis was so unlike the captain's modest nature, and his somewhat German shyness, that he was vexed with himself for its having occurred to him, and went to bed determined to await events before taking any decisive steps.

Next morning Clémentine breakfasted very well without Thaddeus, and made no remark on his disobedience.   That day, as it happened, was her day for being "at home," and this, with her, demanded a royal display.   She did not observe the absence of Captain Paz, on whom devolved all the arrangements for these great occasions.

"Well and good!" said Paz to himself, as he heard the carriages rumble out at two in the morning; "the Countess was only prompted by a Parisian's whim or curiosity."

So the captain fell back into his regular routine, disturbed for a day by this incident.   Clémentine, diverted by the details of life in Paris, seemed to have forgotten Paz.   For do you suppose that it is a mere trifle to reign over this inconstant city?   Do you imagine, by any means, that a woman risks nothing but her fortune playing at that absorbing game?

The winter is to a woman of fashion what, of yore, a campaign was to the soldiers of the empire. What a work of art —of genius—is a costume or a head-dress created to make a sensation! A fragile, delicate woman wears her hard and dazzling armor of flowers and diamonds, silk and steel, from nine in the evening till two or often three in the morning. She eats little, to attract the eye by her slender shape; she cheats the hunger that attacks her during the evening with debilitating cups of tea, sweet cakes, heating ices, or heavy slices of pastry. The stomach must submit to the commands of vanity. She awakes late, and thus everything is in contradiction to the laws of nature, and nature is ruthless.

No sooner is she up than the woman of fashion begins to dress for the morning, planning her dress for the afternoon. Must she not receive and pay visits, and go to the Bois on horseback or in her carriage? Must she not always be practicing the drill of smiles, and fatigue her brain in inventing compliments which shall seem neither stale nor studied? And it is not every woman who succeeds. And then you are surprised, when you see a young woman, whom the world has welcomed in her freshness, faded and blighted at the end of three years. Six months spent in the country are barely enough to heal the wounds inflicted by the winter. We hear nothing talked of but dyspepsia and strange maladies, unknown to women who devote themselves to their household. Formerly a woman was sometimes seen; now she is perpetually on the stage.

Clémentine had to fight her way; she was beginning to be quoted, and amid the cares of this struggle between her and her rivals there was hardly a place for love of her husband! Thaddeus might well be forgotten. However, a month later, in May, a few days before her departure to stay at Ronquerolles in Burgundy, as she was returning from her drive she saw Thaddeus in a side alley of the Champs-Élysées—Thaddeus, carefully dressed, and in raptures at seeing his Countess so beautiful in her phaeton, with champing horses, splendid liveries ; in short, the dear people he admired so much.

" There is the captain," said she to Adam.

" Happy fellow !" said the Count. " These are his great treats ! There is not a smarter turn-out than ours, and he delights in seeing everybody envying us our happiness. You have never noticed him before, but he is there almost every day."

" What can he be thinking of?" said Clémentine.

" He is thinking at this moment that the winter has cost a great deal, and that we shall save a little by staying with your old uncle Ronquerolles," said Adam.

The Countess had the carriage stopped in front of Paz, and desired him to take the seat by her side in the carriage. Thaddeus turned as red as a cherry.

" I shall poison you," he said ; " I have just been smoking cigars."

" And does not Adam poison me ?" she replied quickly.

" Yes, but he is Adam," replied the captain.

" And why should not Thaddeus enjoy the same privilege ? " said the Countess with a smile.

This heavenly smile had a power which was too much for his heroic resolutions ; he gazed at Clémentine with all the fire of his soul in his eyes, but tempered by the angelic expression of his gratitude—that of a man who lived solely by gratitude. The Countess folded her arms in her shawl, leaned back pensively against the cushions, crumpling the feathers of her handsome bonnet, and gazed out at the passers-by. This flash from a soul so noble, and hitherto so resigned, appealed to her feelings. What, after all, was Adam's great merit ? Was it not natural that he should be brave and generous ? But the captain ! Thaddeus possessed, or seemed to possess, an immense superiority over Adam. What sinister thoughts distressed the Countess when she once more observed the contrast between the fine, complete physical nature which distinguished Thaddeus and the frail constitution which, in her husband, betrayed the inevitable degeneration of aristo-cratic families which are so mad as to persist in intermarrying! But the devil alone knew these thoughts, for the young wife sat with vague meditation in her eyes, saying nothing till they reached home.

"You must dine with us, or I shall be angry with you for having disobeyed me," said she as she went in. "You are Thaddeus to me, as you are to Adam. I know the obliga-tions you feel to him, but I also know all we owe to you. In return for two impulses of generosity which are so natural, you are generous at all hours and day after day. My father is coming to dine with us, as well as my uncle Ronquerolles and my aunt de Sérizy; dress at·once," she said, pressing the hand he offered to help her out of the carriage.

Thaddeus went to his room to dress, his heart at once re-joicing and oppressed by an agonizing flutter. He came down at the last moment, and all through dinner played his part of a soldier fit for nothing but to fulfill the duties of a steward. But this time Clémentine was not his dupe. His look had enlightened her. Ronquerolles, the cleverest of ambassadors next to Talleyrand, and who served de Marsay so well during his short ministry, was informed by his niece of the high merits of Count Paz, who had so modestly made himself his friend's steward.

"And how is it that this·is the first time I have ever seen Count Paz?" asked the Marquis de Ronquerolles.

"Eh! he is very sly and underhand," replied Clémentine, with a look at Paz to desire him to change his demeanor.

Alas! it must be owned, at the risk of making the captain less interesting to the reader, Paz, though superior to his friend Adam, was not a man of strong temper. He owed his appar-ent superiority to his misfortunes. In his days of poverty and isolation at Warsaw he had read and educated himself, had compared and thought much; but the creative power which

makes a great man he did not possess—can it ever be acquired? Paz was great only through his feelings, and there
could rise to the sublime; but in the sphere of sentiment, being a man of action rather than of ideas, he kept his thoughts
to himself. His thoughts, then, did nothing but eat his heart
out.

And what, after all, is an unuttered thought?

At Clémentine's speech the Marquis de Ronquerolles and
his sister exchanged glances, with a side-look at their niece,
Count Adam, and Paz. It was one of those swift dramas
which are played only in Italy or in Paris. Only in these two
parts of the world—excepting at all courts—can the eyes say
as much. To infuse into the eye all the power of the soul,
to give it the full value of speech and throw a poem or a drama
into a single flash, excessive servitude or excessive liberty is
needed.

Adam, the Marquis du Rouvre, and the Countess did not
perceive this flash of observation between a past coquette and
an old diplomat; but Paz, like a faithful dog, understood
its forecast. It was, you must remember, an affair of two
seconds. To describe the hurricane that ravaged the captain's
heart would be too elaborate for these days.

"What! the uncle and aunt already fancy that she perhaps
loves me?" said he to himself. "My happiness then depends
only on my own audacity. And Adam!——"

Ideal love and mere desire, both quite as potent as friendship and gratitude, rent his soul, and for a moment love had
the upper hand. This poor heroic lover longed to have his
day! Paz became witty; he intended to please, and in answer to some question from Monsieur de Ronquerolles he
sketched in grand outlines the Polish rebellion. Thus, at
dessert, Paz saw Clémentine drinking in every word, regarding
him as a hero, and forgetting that Adam, after sacrificing a
third of his immense fortune, had taken the risks of exile.
At nine o'clock, having taken coffee, Madame de Sérizy kissed

her niece on the forehead and took leave, carrying off Count Adam with an assertion of authority, and leaving the Marquis du Rouvre and M. de Ronquerolles, who withdrew ten min-/ utes later. Paz and Clémentine were left together.

"I will bid you good-night, madame," said Thaddeus; "you will join them at the opera."

"No," replied she. "I do not care for dancing, and they are giving an odious ballet this evening, 'The Revolt of the Seraglio.'"

There was a moment's silence.

"Two years ago Adam would not have gone without me," she went on, without looking at Paz.

"He loves you to distraction——" Thaddeus began.

"Oh! it is because he loves me to distraction that by to-morrow he will perhaps have ceased to love me!" exclaimed the Countess.

"The women of Paris are inexplicable," said Thaddeus. "When they are loved to distraction, they want to be loved rationally; when they are loved rationally, they accuse a man of not knowing how to love."

"And they are always right, Thaddeus," she replied with a smile. "I know Adam well; I owe him no grudge for it; he is fickle, and, above all, a great gentleman; he will always be pleased to have me for his wife, and will never thwart me in any of my tastes; but——"

"What marriage was ever without a but?" said Thaddeus gently, trying to give the Countess' thoughts another direction.

The least conceited man would perhaps have had the thought which nearly drove this lover mad: "If I do not tell her that I love her," said he to himself, "I am an idiot!"

There was silence between these two, one of those terrible pauses which seem bursting with thoughts. The Countess fixed a covert gaze on Paz, and Paz watched her in a mirror.

Sitting back in his armchair, like a man given up to digestion, in the attitude of an old man or an indifferent husband, the captain clasped his hands over his stomach, and mechanically twirled his thumbs, looking stupidly at their rapid movement.

"But say something good about Adam!" exclaimed Clémentine. "Tell me that he is not fickle, you who know him so well."

The appeal was sublime.

"This is the opportunity for raising an insurmountable barrier between us," thought the unhappy Paz, devising a heroic lie. "Something good," he said aloud. "I love him too well, you would not believe me. I am incapable of telling you any evil of him. And so, madame, I have a hard part to play between you two."

Clémentine looked down, fixing her eyes on his patent-leather shoes.

"You northerners have mere physical courage, you have no constancy in your decisions," said she in a low tone.

"What are you going to do alone, madame?" replied Paz, with a perfectly ingenuous expression.

"You are not going to keep me company?"

"Forgive me for leaving you."

"Why! where are you going?"

"I am going to the circus; it is the first night, in the Champs-Élysées, and I must not fail to be there ——"

"Why not?" asked Clémentine, with a half-angry flash.

"Must I lay bare my heart?" he replied coloring, "and confide to you what I conceal from my dear Adam, who believes that I love Poland alone?"

"What! our dear noble captain has a secret?"

"A disgrace which you will understand, and for which you can comfort me."

"A disgrace! You?——"

"Yes, I—Count Paz—am madly in love with a girl who was touring round France with the Bouthor family, people who have a circus after the pattern of Franconi's, but who only perform at fairs! I got her an engagement from the manager of the Cirque-Olympique."

"Is she handsome?" asked the Countess.

"In my eyes," he replied sadly. "Malaga, that is her name to the public, is strong, nimble, and supple. Why do I prefer her to every other woman in the world? Indeed, I cannot tell you. When I see her with her black hair tied back with blue ribbons that float over her bare, olive-tinted shoulders, dressed in a white tunic with a gilt border, and silk tights which make her appear a living Greek statue, her feet in frayed satin slippers, flourishing flags in her hand to the sound of a military band, and flying through an enormous hoop covered with paper which crashes in the air—when her horse rushes round at a gallop, and she gracefully drops on to him again, applauded, honestly applauded, by a whole people —well, it excites me."

"More than a woman at a ball?" said Clémentine, with insinuating surprise.

"Yes," said Paz in a choked voice. "This splendid agility, this unfailing grace in constant peril, seem to me the greatest triumph of woman. Yes, madame, Cinti and Mali-bran, Grisi and Taglioni, Pasta and Elsler, all who reign or ever reigned on the boards, seem to me unworthy to untie Malaga's shoe-strings—Malaga, who can mount or dismount a horse at a mad gallop, who slips under him from the left to reappear on the right, who flutters about the most fiery steed like a white will-o'-the-wisp, who can stand on the tip of one toe and then drop, sitting with her feet hanging, on a horse still galloping round, and who finally stands on his back without any reins, knitting a stocking, beating eggs, or stirring an omelette, to the intense admiration of the people, the true people, the peasantry and soldiers. During the walk round, madame, that enchanting Columbine used to carry chairs balanced on the tip of her nose, the prettiest Greek nose I

ever saw.   Malaga is dexterity personified.   Her strength is
Herculean ; with her tiny fist or her little foot she can shake
off three or four men.   She is the goddess of the athletes."

"She must be stupid."

"Oh!" cried Paz, "she is as amusing as the heroine of
'Peveril of the Peak.'   As heedless as a gypsy, she says
everything that comes into her head ; she cares no more for
the future than you care for the halfpence you throw to a
beggar, and she lets out really sublime things.   Nothing will
ever convince her that an old diplomat is a handsome young
man, and a million of francs would not make her change her
opinion.   Her love for a man is a perpetual flattery.   Enjoying really insolent health, her teeth are two-and-thirty Oriental pearls set in coral.   Her ' snout '—so she calls the lower
part of her face—is, as Shakespeare has it, as fresh and sweet
as a heifer's muzzle.   And it can give bitter pain!   She respects fine men, strong men—an Adolphus, an Augustus, an
Alexander—acrobats and tumblers.   Her teacher, a horrible
Cassandro, thrashed her unmercifully ; it costs thousands of
blows to give her such agility, grace, and intrepidity."

"You are drunk with Malaga!" said the Countess.

"Her name is Malaga only on the posters," said Paz, with
a look of annoyance.   "She lives in the Rue Saint-Lazare,
in a little apartment on the third floor, in velvet and silk, like
a princess.   She leads two lives—one as a dancer, and one as
a pretty woman."

"And does she love you?"

"She loves me—you will laugh—solely because I am a
Pole.   She sees in every Pole a Poniatowski, as he is shown
in the print, jumping into the Elster ; for to every Frenchman the Elster, in which it is impossible to drown, is a
foaming torrent which swallowed up Poniatowski.   And with
all this I am very unhappy, madame——"

Clémentine was touched by a tear of rage in the captain's
eye.

" You love the extraordinary, you men," said she.

" And you ? " asked Thaddeus.

" I know Adam so well that I know he could forget me for some acrobatic tumbler like your Malaga. But where did you find her ? "

" At Saint-Cloud, last September, at the fair. She was standing in a corner of the platform covered with canvas where the performers walk round. Her comrades, all dressed as Poles, were making a terrific Babel. I saw her silent and dreamy, and fancied I could guess that her thoughts were melancholy. Was there not enough to make her so—a girl of twenty ? That was what touched me."

The Countess was leaning in a bewitching attitude, pensive, almost sad.

" Poor, poor Thaddeus ! " she exclaimed. And with the good-fellowship of a really great lady, she added, not without a meaning smile, " Go ; go to the circus ! "

Thaddeus took her hand and kissed it, dropping a hot tear, and then went out. After having invented a passion for a circus-rider, he must give it some reality. Of his whole story nothing had been true but the minute attention he had given to the famous Malaga, the rider of the Bouthor troupe at Saint-Cloud ; her name had just caught his eye on an advertisement of the circus. The clown, bribed by a single five-franc piece, had told Paz that the girl was a foundling, or had perhaps been stolen.

Thaddeus now went to the circus and saw the handsome horsewoman again. For ten francs, a groom—they fill the place of dressers at a circus—informed him that Malaga's name was Marguerite Turquet, and that she lived in the Rue des Fossés-de-Temple, on a fifth floor.

Next day, with death in his soul, Paz found his way to that quarter, and asked for Mademoiselle Turquet, in summer the understudy of the principal rider at the cirque, and in winter " a super" in a Boulevard theatre.

"Malaga!" shouted the doorkeeper, rushing into the attic, "here is a fine gentleman for you! He is asking Chapuzot all about you; and Chapuzot is cramming him to give me time to let you know."

"Thank you, Madame Chapuzot; but what will he say to find me ironing my gown?"

"Pooh, stuff! When a man is in love, he loves everything about you."

"Is he an Englishman? They are fond of horses."

"No. He looks to me like a Spaniard."

"So much the worse. The Spaniards are down in the market they say. Stay here, Madame Chapuzot, I shall not look so left to myself."

"Who were you wanting, monsieur?" said the woman, opening the door to Thaddeus.

"Mademoiselle Turquet."

"My child," said the porter's wife, wrapping her shawl round her, "here is somebody asking for you."

A rope on which some linen was airing knocked off the captain's hat.

"What is your business, monsieur?" asked Malaga, picking it up.

"I saw you at the circus; you remind me, mademoiselle, of a daughter I lost; and out of affection for my Héloïse, whom you are so wonderfully like, I should wish to be of use to you, if you will allow me."

"Well, to be sure! But sit down, Monsieur le Général," said Madame Chapuzot. "You cannot say fairer—nor handsomer."

"I am not by way of love-making, my good lady," said Paz. "I am a father in deep distress, eager to be cheated by a likeness."

"And so I am to pass as your daughter?" said Malaga, very roguishly, and without suspecting the absolute truth of the statement.

"Yes," said Paz. "I will come sometimes to see you; and that the illusion may be perfect, I will place you in handsome lodgings, nicely furnished——"

"I shall have furniture of my own?" said Malaga, looking at Madame Chapuzot.

"And servants," Paz went on; "and live quite at your ease."

Malaga looked at the stranger from under her brow.

"From what country are you, monsieur?"

"I am a Pole."

"Then I accept," said she.

Paz went away, promising to call again.

"That is a tough one!" said Marguerite Turquet, looking at Madame Chapuzot. "But I am afraid this man is wheedling me to humor some fancy. Well, I will risk it."

A month after this whimsical scene, the fair circus-rider was established in rooms charmingly furnished by Count Adam's upholsterer, for Paz wished that his folly should be talked about in the Laginski household. Malaga, to whom the adventure was like an Arabian Night's dream, was waited on by the Chapuzot couple—at once her servants and her confidants. The Chapuzots and Marguerite Turquet expected some startling climax; but at the end of three months, neither Malaga nor the Chapuzots could account for the Polish Count's fancy. Paz would spend about an hour there once a week, during which he sat in the drawing-room, never choosing to go either into Malaga's boudoir nor into her bedroom, which, in fact, he never entered in spite of the cleverest manœuvring on her part and on that of the Chapuzots. The Count inquired about the little incidents that varied the horsewoman's life, and on going away he always left two forty-franc pieces on the chimney-shelf.

"He looks dreadfully bored," said Madame Chapuzot.

"Yes," replied Malaga, "that man is as cold as frost after a thaw."

"He is a jolly good fellow, all the same," cried Chapuzot, delighted to see himself dressed in blue Elbeuf cloth, and as smart as a minister's office-messenger.

Paz, by his periodical tribute, made Marguerite Turquet an allowance of three hundred and twenty francs a month. This sum, added to her small earnings at the circus, secured her a splendid existence as compared with her past squalor. Strange tales were current among the performers at the circus as to Malaga's good fortune. The girl's vanity allowed her rent to be stated at sixty thousand francs, instead of the modest six thousand which her rooms cost the prudent captain. According to the clowns and supers, Malaga ate off silver plate; and she certainly came to the circus in pretty burnouses, in shawls, and elegant scarfs. And, to crown all, the Pole was the best fellow a circus-rider could come across; never tiresome, never jealous, leaving Malaga perfect freedom.

"Some women are so lucky!" said Malaga's rival. "Such a thing would never happen to me, though I bring in a third of the receipts."

Malaga wore smart "coal-scuttles," and sometimes gave herself airs in a carriage in the Bois de Boulogne, where the youth of fashion began to observe her. In short, Malaga was talked about in the flash world of equivocal women, and her good fortune was attacked by calumny. She was reported to be a somnambulist, and the Pole was said to be a magnetizer in search of the philosopher's stone. Other comments of a far more venomous taint made Malaga more inquisitive than Psyche; she reported them, with tears, to Paz.

"When I owe a woman a grudge," said she to conclude, "I do not calumniate her, I do not say that a man magnetizes her to find stones. I say that she is a bad lot, and I prove it. Why do you get me into trouble?"

Paz was cruelly speechless.

Madame Chapuzot succeeded at last in discovering his name and title. Then, at the Hôtel Laginski, she ascertained

some positive facts: Thaddeus was unmarried; he was not
known to have a dead daughter either in Poland or France.
Malaga could not help feeling a thrill of terror.

"My dear child," exclaimed Madame Chapuzot, "that
monster——"

A man who was satisfied with gazing at a beautiful creature
like Malaga—gazing at her by stealth—from under his brows
—not daring to come to any decision—without any confidence; such a man, in Madame Chapuzot's mind, must be a
monster. "That monster is breaking you in, to lead you on
to something illegal or criminal. God above us! if you were
to be brought up at the assizes—and it makes me shudder
from head to foot to think of it, I quake only to speak of it
—or in the criminal court, and your name was in the newspapers!—— Do you know what I should do in your place?
Well, in your place, to make all safe, I should warn the
police."

One day, when mad notions were fermenting in Malaga's
brain, Paz having laid his gold-pieces on the velvet chimney-
shelf, she snatched up the money and flung it in his face, saying, "I will not take stolen money!"

The captain gave the gold to the Chapuzots, and came no
more.

Clémentine was spending the summer on the estate of her
uncle, the Marquis de Ronquerolles, in Burgundy.

When the troupe at the circus no longer saw Thaddeus in
his seat, there was a great talk among the artists. Malaga's
magnanimity was regarded as folly by some, as cunning by
others. The Pole's behavior, as explained to the most experienced of the women, seemed inexplicable. In the course
of a single week, Thaddeus received thirty-seven letters from
women of the town. Happily for him, his singular reserve
gave rise to no curiosity in fashionable circles, and remained
the subject of discussion in the flash set only.

Two months later, the handsome rider, swamped in debt,

wrote to Count Paz the following letter, which the dandies of the day regarded as a masterpiece:

" You, whom I still venture to call my friend, will you not take pity on me after what passed between us, which you took so ill? My heart disowns everything that could hurt your feelings. If I was so happy as to make you feel some charm when you sat near me, as you used to do, come again—— otherwise, I shall sink into despair. Poverty has come upon me already, and you do not know what stupid things it brings with it. Yesterday I lived on a herring for two sous and one sou's worth of bread. Is that a breakfast for the woman you love? The Chapuzots have left me after seeming so devoted to me. Your absence has shown me the shallowness of human attachment. A bailiff, who turned a deaf ear to me, has seized everything on behalf of the landlord, who has no pity, and of the jeweler, who will not wait even ten days; for with you men, credit vanishes with confidence. What a position for a woman who has nothing to reproach herself for but a little amusement! My dear friend, I have taken everything of any value to my uncle's; I have nothing left but my memory of you, and the hard weather is coming on. All through the winter I shall have no fire, since nothing but melodrama is played at the Boulevard, in which I have nothing to do but tiny parts, which do not show a woman off. How could you misunderstand my noble feelings towards you, for, after all, we have not two ways of expressing our gratitude? How is it that you, who seemed so pleased to see me comfortable, could leave me in misery? Oh, my only friend on earth, before I go back to travel from fair to fair with the Bouthors—for so, at any rate, I can make my living—forgive me for wanting to know if I have really lost you for ever. If I should happen to think of you just as I was jumping through the hoop, I might break my legs by missing time. Come what may, I am yours for life.   MARGUERITE TURQUET."

"This letter," exclaimed Thaddeus, shouting with laughter, "is well worth my ten thousand francs."

Clémentine came home on the following day, and Paz saw her once more, lovelier and more gracious than ever. During dinner the Countess preserved an air of perfect indifference towards Thaddeus, but a scene took place between the Count and his wife after their friend had left. Thaddeus, with an affectation of asking Adam's advice, had left Malaga's letter in his hands, as if by accident.

"Poor Thaddeus!" said Adam to his wife, after seeing Paz make his escape. "What a misfortune for a man of his superior stamp to be the plaything of a ballet-girl of the lowest class! He will love anything; he will degrade himself; he will be unrecognizable before long. Here, my dear, read that," and he handed her Malaga's letter.

Clémentine read the note, which smelt of tobacco, and tossed it away with disgust.

"However thick the bandage over his eyes may be, he must have found something out. Malaga must have played him some faithless trick."

"And he is going back to her!" cried Clémentine. "He will forgive her! You men can have no pity for any but those horrible women!"

"They need it so badly!" said Adam.

"Thaddeus did himself justice—by keeping to himself!" said she.

"Oh, my dearest, you go too far," said the Count, who, though he was at first delighted to lower his friend in his wife's eyes, would not be the death of the sinner.

Thaddeus, who knew Adam well, had begged for absolute secrecy; he had only spoken, he said, as an excuse for his dissipations, and to beg his friend to allow him to have a thousand crowns for Malaga.

"He is a man of great pride," Adam went on.

"What do you mean?"

24

"Well, to have spent no more than ten thousand francs on her, and to wait for such a letter as that to rouse him before taking her the money to pay her debts! For a Pole, on my honor!"

"But he may ruin you!" said Clémentine in the acrid tone of a Parisian woman when she expresses her cat-like distrustfulness.

"Oh! I understand him," said Adam. "He would sacrifice Malaga to us."

"We shall see," replied the Countess.

"If it were needful for his happiness, I should not hesitate to ask him to give her up. Constantine tells me that during the time when he was seeing her, Paz, usually so sober, sometimes came in quite fuddled. If he allowed himself to take to drink, I should be as much grieved as if he were my son."

"Do not tell me any more!" cried the Countess with another gesture of disgust.

Two days later the captain could see in her manner, in the tone of her voice, in her eyes, the terrible results of Adam's betrayal. Scorn had opened gulfs between him and this charming woman. And he fell forthwith into deep melancholy, devoured by this thought, "You have made yourself unworthy of her." Life became a burden to him; the bright sunshine was gloomy in his eyes. Nevertheless, under these floods of bitter thought, he had some happy moments: he could now give himself up without danger to his admiration for the Countess, who never paid him the slightest attention when, at a party, hidden in a corner, mute, all eyes and all heart, he did not lose one of her movements, not a note of her song when she sang. He lived in this enchanting life: he might himself groom the horse that she was to ride, and devote himself to the management of her splendid house with redoubled care for its interests.

These unspoken joys were buried in his heart like those of a mother, whose child never knows anything of his mother's heart: for is it knowledge so long as even one thing remains unknown? Was not this finer than Petrarch's chaste passion for Laura, which, after all, was well repaid by a wealth of glory, and by the triumph of the poetry she had inspired? Was not the emotion which Assas felt in dying, in truth a whole life? This emotion Paz felt every day without dying, but also without the guerdon of immortality.

What is there in love that Paz, notwithstanding these secret delights, was consumed by sorrow? The Catholic religion has so elevated love that she has married it inseparably, so to speak, to esteem and generosity. Love does not exist apart from the fine qualities of which man is proud, and so rarely are we loved if we are contemned, that Thaddeus was perishing of his self-inflicted wounds. Only to hear her say that she could have loved him, and then to die! The hapless lover would have thought his life well paid for. The torments of his previous position seemed to him preferable to living close to her, loading her with his generosity without being appreciated or understood. In short, he wanted the price of his virtue.

He grew thin and yellow, and fell so thoroughly ill, consumed by low fever, that during the month of January he kept his bed, though refusing to see a physician. Count Adam grew extremely uneasy about his poor Thaddeus. The Countess then was so cruel as to say, when they were together one day, "Let him alone; do you not see that he has some Olympian remorse?"

This speech stung Thaddeus to the verge of despair; he got up, went out, tried some amusement, and recovered his health.

In the month of February, Adam lost a rather considerable sum at the Jockey Club, and, being afraid of his wife, he begged Thaddeus to place this sum to the account of his extravagance for Malaga.

"What is there strange in the notion that the ballet-girl

should have cost you twenty thousand francs? It concerns no one but me. Whereas, if the Countess should know that I had lost it at play, I should fall in her esteem, and she would be in alarm for the future."

"This to crown all!" cried Thaddeus, with a deep sigh.

"Ah! Thaddeus, this service would make us quits if I were not already the debtor."

"Adam, you may have children. Give up gambling," said his friend.

"And twenty thousand francs more that Malaga has cost us!" exclaimed the Countess some days after, on discovering Adam's generosity to Paz. "And ten thousand before —that is thirty thousand in all! Fifteen hundred francs a year, the price of my box at the Italian opera, a whole fortune to many people. Oh! you Poles are incomprehensible!" cried she, as she picked some flowers in her beautiful conservatory. "You care no more than that!"

"Poor Paz——"

"Poor Paz, poor Paz!" she echoed, interrupting him. "What good does he do us? I will manage the house myself! Give him the hundred louis a year that he refused, and let him make his own arrangements with the Olympic Circus."

"He is of the greatest use to us; he has saved us at least forty thousand francs this year. In short, my dearest, he has placed a hundred thousand francs for us in Nucingen's bank, and a steward would have netted them."

Clémentine was softened, but she was not the less hard on Thaddeus.

Some days after she desired Paz to come to her in her boudoir, where, a year since, she had been startled by comparing him with the Count. This time she received him alone, without any suspicion of danger.

"My dear Paz," said she, with the careless familiarity of fine folks to their inferiors, "if you love Adam as you say you do, you will do one thing which he will never ask, but which I, as his wife, do not hesitate to require of you——"

"It is about Malaga," said Thaddeus with deep irony.

"Well, yes, it is," she said. "If you want to end your days with us, if you wish that we should remain friends, give her up. How can an old soldier——"

"I am but five-and-thirty, and have not a gray hair!"

"You look as if you had," said she, "and that is the same thing. How can a man so capable of putting two and two together, so superior——"

What was horrible was that she spoke the word with such an evident intention of rousing in him the nobleness of soul which she believed to be dead.

"So superior as you are," she went on, after a little pause, which a gesture from Paz forced upon her, "allow yourself to be entrapped like a boy. Your affair with her has made Malaga famous. Well! My uncle wanted to see her, and he saw her. My uncle is not the only one; Malaga is very ready to receive all these gentlemen. I believed you to be high-minded. Take shame to yourself! Come, would she be an irreparable loss to you?"

"Madame, if I knew of any sacrifice by which I might recover your esteem, it would soon be made; but to give up Malaga is not a sacrifice——"

"In your place that is what I should say if I were a man," replied Clémentine. "Well, but if I take it as a great sacrifice, there is nothing to be angry at."

Paz went away, fearing he might do some mad act; he felt his brain invaded by crazy notions. He went out for a walk, lightly dressed in spite of the cold, but failed to cool the burning of his face and brow. "I believed you to be high-minded!" He heard the words again and again. "And scarcely a year ago," said he to himself, "to hear Clémentine, I had beaten the Russians single-handed!" He thought of quitting the Laginski household, of asking to be sent on service in the Spahi Regiment, and getting himself killed in Africa; but a dreadful fear checked him: "What would become of them without me? They would soon be ruined. Poor Countess, what a horrible life it would be for her to be reduced even to thirty thousand francs a year! Come," said he to himself, "since she can never be yours, courage, finish your work!"

As all the world knows, since 1830 the Carnival in Paris has grown to prodigious proportions, making it European, and burlesque, and animated to a far greater degree than the departed carnivals of Venice. Is this because, since fortunes have so enormously diminished, Parisians have thought of amusing themselves collectively, just as in their clubs they have a drawing-room without any mistress of the house, without politeness, and quite cheap? Be this as it may, the month of March was prodigal of those balls, where dancing, farce, coarse fun, delirium, grotesque figures, and banter made keen by Paris wit, achieved gigantic results. This madness had its pandemonium at that time in the Rue Saint-Honoré, and its Napoleon in Musard, a little man born to rule an orchestra as tremendous as the rampant mob, and to conduct a galop— that whirl of witches at their Sabbath, and one of Auber's triumphs, for the galop derived its form and its poetry from the famous galop in *Gustavus*. May not this vehement finale serve as a symbol of an age when, for fifty years, everything has rushed on with the swiftness of a dream?

Now, our grave Thaddeus, bearing an immaculate image in his heart, went to Malaga to invite her, the queen of carnival dancing, to spend an evening at Musard's as soon as he learned that the Countess, disguised to the teeth, was intending to come with two other young ladies, escorted by their husbands, to see the curious spectacle of one of these monster balls. On Shrove Tuesday night, in the year of grace 1838, at four o'clock in the morning, the Countess, wrapped in a black domino, and seated on a bench of one of the amphitheatres of the Babylonian hall where Valentino has since given his concerts, saw Thaddeus, dressed as Robert Macaire, leading the circus-rider in the costume of a savage, her head dressed with nodding plumes like a horse at a coronation, and leaping among the groups like a perfect Jack-o'-lantern.

"Oh!" exclaimed Clémentine to her husband, " you Poles are not men of character. Who would not have felt sure of Thaddeus? He gave me his word, not knowing that I should be here and see all without being seen."

Some days after this she invited Paz to dinner. After dinner, Adam left them together, and Clémentine scolded Thaddeus in such a way as to make him feel that she would no longer have him about the house.

"Indeed, madame," said Thaddeus, humbly, "you are quite right. I am a wretch; I had pledged my word. But what can I do? I put off the parting with Malaga till after the Carnival. And I will be honest with you; the woman has so much power over me."

"A woman who gets herself turned out of Musard's by the police, and for such dancing?"

"I admit it; I sit condemned; I will quit your house. But you know Adam. If I hand over to you the conduct of your affairs, you will have to exert great energy. Though I have the vice of Malaga, I know how to keep an eye on your concerns, how to manage your household, and superintend the smallest details. Allow me then to remain until I have seen you qualified to continue my system of management. You have now been married three years, and are safe from the first follies consequent on the honeymoon. The ladies of Paris society, even with the highest titles, understand very well in these days how to control a fortune and a household. Well, as soon as I am assured, not of your capacity, but of your firmness, I will leave Paris."

"It is Thaddeus of Warsaw that speaks, not Thaddeus of the circus. Come back to us cured."

" Cured ? Never ! " said Paz, his eye fixed on Clémentine's pretty feet. " You cannot know, Countess, all the spice, the unexpectedness there is in that woman's wit."   And feeling his courage fail him, he added : " There is not a single woman of fashion, with her prim airs, who is worth that frank young animal nature."

" In fact, I should not choose to have anything in me of the animal ! " said the Countess, with a flashing look like an adder in a rage.

After that day Count Paz explained to Clémentine all her affairs, made himself her tutor, taught her the difficulties of managing her property, the real cost of things, and the way to avoid being too extensively robbed by her people. She might trust Constantine, and make him her major-domo. Thaddeus had trained Constantine. By the month of May he thought the Countess perfectly capable of administering her fortune ; for Clémentine was one of those clear-sighted women whose instincts are alert, with an inborn genius for household rule.

The situation thus naturally brought about by Thaddeus took a sudden turn most distressing for him, for his sufferings were not so light as he made them seem. The hapless lover had not reckoned with accident. Adam fell very seriously ill. Thaddeus, instead of leaving, installed himself as his friend's sick-nurse. His devotedness was indefatigable. A woman who had had an interest in looking through the telescope of fore-sight would have seen in the captain's heroism the sort of punishment which noble souls inflict on themselves to subdue their involuntary thoughts of sin ; but women see everything or nothing, according to their frame of mind ; love is their sole luminary.

For forty-five days Paz watched and nursed Mitgislas with-out seeming to have a thought of Malaga, for the excellent reason that he never did think of her. Clémentine, seeing

Adam at death's door, and yet not dead, had a consultation of the most famous doctors.

"If he gets through this," said the most learned of the physicians, "it can only be by an effort of nature. It lies with those who nurse him to watch for the moment and aid nature. The Count's life is in the hands of his attendants."

Thaddeus went to communicate this verdict to Clémentine, who was sitting in the Chinese pavilion, as much to rest after her fatigues as to leave the field free for the doctors, and not to be in their way. As he trod the graveled paths leading from the boudoir to the rockery on which the Chinese summer-house was built, Clémentine's lover felt as though he were in one of the gulfs described by Alighieri. The unhappy man had never foreseen the chance of becoming Clémentine's husband, and he had bogged himself in a swamp of mud. When he reached her his face was set, sublime in its despair. Like Medusa's head, it communicated terror.

"He is dead?" said Clémentine.

"They have given no hope; at least, they leave it to nature. Do not go in just yet. They are still there, and Bianchon himself is examining him."

"Poor fellow! I wonder whether I have ever worried him," she said.

"You have made him very happy; be quite easy on that point," said Thaddeus; "and you have been indulgent to him——"

"The loss will be irreparable."

"But, dear lady, supposing the Count should die, had you not formed your opinion of him?"

"I do not love him blindly," she said; "but I loved as a wife ought to love her husband."

"Then," said Thaddeus, in a voice new to Clémentine's experience of him, "you ought to feel less regret than if you were losing one of those men who are a woman's pride, her love, her whole life! You may be frank with such a friend as

I am—— I shall regret him—I! Long before your marriage I had made him my child, and I have devoted my life to him. I shall have no interest left on earth. But life still has charms for a widow of four-and-twenty."

"Why, you know very well that I love no one," said she, with the roughness of sorrow.

"You do not know yet what it is to love," said Thaddeus.

"Oh! husband for husband, I have sense enough to prefer a child like my poor Adam to a superior man. For nearly a month now we have been asking ourselves, 'Will he live?' These fluctuations have prepared me, as they have you, for this end. I may be frank with you? Well, then, I would give part of my life to save Adam. Does not independence for a woman, here in Paris, mean liberty to be gulled by the pretense of love in men who are ruined or profligate? I have prayed God to spare me my husband—so gentle, such a good fellow, so little fractious, and who was beginning to be a little afraid of me."

"You are honest, and I like you the better for it," said Thaddeus, taking Clémentine's hands, which she allowed him to kiss. "In such a solemn moment there is indescribable satisfaction in finding a woman devoid of hypocrisy. It is possible to talk to you. Consider the future; supposing God should not listen to you—and I am one of those who are most ready to cry to Him: Spare my friend!—for these fifty nights past have not made my eyes heavy, and if thirty days and thirty nights more care are needed, you, madame, may sleep while I watch. I will snatch him from death, if, as they say, he can be saved by care. But if, in spite of you, in spite of me, the Count is dead. Well, then, if you were loved, or worshiped, by a man whose heart and character were worthy of yours——"

"I have perhaps madly wished to be loved, but I have never met——"

"Supposing you were mistaken."

Clémentine looked steadily at Thaddeus, suspecting him less of loving her than of a covetous dream; she poured contempt on him by a glance, measuring him from head to foot, and crushed him with two words, "Poor Malaga!" pronounced in those tones such as fine ladies alone can find in the gamut of their contempt.

She rose and left Thaddeus fainting, for she did not turn round, but walked with great dignity back to her boudoir, and thence up to her husband's room.

An hour later Paz returned to the sick man's bedside, and gave all his care to the Count, as though he had not received his own death-blow.

From that dreadful moment he became silent; he had a duel to fight with disease, and he carried it through in a way that excited the admiration of the doctors. At any hour his eyes were always beaming like two lamps. Without showing the slightest resentment towards Clémentine, he listened to her thanks without accepting them; he seemed deaf. He had said to himself, "She shall owe Adam's life to me!" and these words he had, as it were, written in letters of fire in the sick man's room.

At the end of a fortnight Clémentine was obliged to give up some of the nursing, or risk falling ill from so much fatigue. Paz was inexhaustible. At last, about the end of August, Bianchon, the family doctor, answered for the Count's life—

"Ah, madame," said he to Clémentine, "you are under not the slightest obligation to me. But for his friend we could not have saved him!"

On the day after the terrible scene in the Chinese pavilion, the Marquis de Ronquerolles had come to see his nephew, for he was setting out for Russia with a secret mission; and Paz, overwhelmed by the previous evening, had spoken a few words to the diplomat.

On the very day when Count Adam and his wife went out
for the first time for a drive, at the moment when the carriage
was turning from the steps, an orderly came into the courtyard and asked for Count Paz. Thaddeus, who was sitting
with his back to the horses, turned round to take a letter
bearing the stamp of the minister for foreign affairs, and put
it into the side-pocket of his coat, with a decision which
precluded any questions on the part of Clémentine or Adam.
It cannot be denied that persons of good breeding are masters
of the language that uses no speech. Nevertheless, as they
reached the Porte Maillot, Adam, assuming the privilege of a
convalescent whose every whim must be indulged, said to
Thaddeus—

"There can be no indiscretions between two brothers
who love each other as you and I do; you know what is in
that letter; tell me, I am in a fever of curiosity to know it
also."

Clémentine looked at Thaddeus as an angry woman can,
and said to her husband, "He has been so sulky with me
these two months that I shall take good care not to press
him."

"Oh dear me!" replied Thaddeus, "as I cannot hinder
the newspapers from publishing it, I may very well reveal the
secret. The Emperor Nicholas does me the favor of appoint-
ing me captain on service in a regiment starting with the
Khiva Expedition."

"And you are going?" cried Adam.

"I shall go, my dear fellow. I came as captain, and as
captain I return. Malaga might lead me to make a fool of
myself. We shall dine together to-morrow for the last time.
If I did not set out in September for St. Petersburg, I should
have to travel overland, and I am not rich. I must leave
Malaga her little independence. How can I fail to provide
for the future of the only woman who has understood me?
Malaga thinks me a great man? Malaga thinks me hand-

some ! Malaga may perhaps be faithless, but she would go through——''

"Through a hoop for you, and fall on her feet on horseback!" said Clémentine, sharply.

"Oh, you do not know Malaga," said the captain, with deep bitterness, and an ironical look which made Clémentine uneasy and silent.

"Farewell to the young trees of this lovely Bois de Boulogne, where Parisian ladies drive, and the exiles wander who have found a home here. I know that my eyes will never again see the green trees of the Allée de Mademoiselle, or of the Route des Dames, nor the acacias, nor the cedar at the Ronds-points.

"On the Asiatic frontier, obedient to the schemes of the great Emperor I have chosen to be my master, promoted perhaps to command an army, for sheer courage, for constantly risking my life, I may indeed regret the Champs-Élysées where you, once, made me take a place in the carriage, by your side. Finally, I shall never cease to regret the severity of Malaga—of the Malaga I am at this moment thinking of."

This was said in a tone that made Clémentine shiver.

"Then you love Malaga very truly?" she said.

"I have sacrificed for her the honor we never sacrifice——"

"Which?"

"That which we would fain preserve at any cost in the eyes of the idol we worship."

After this speech Thaddeus kept an impenetrable silence; he broke it only when, as they drove down the Champs-Élysées, he pointed to a wooden structure and said, "There is the circus!"

Before their last dinner he went to the Russian embassy for a few minutes, and thence to the minister for foreign affairs, and he started for Havre next morning before the Countess and Adam were up.

"I have lost a friend," said Adam, with tears in his eyes, when he learned that Count Paz was gone, "a friend in the truest sense of the word, and I cannot think what has made him flee from my house as if it were the plague.   We are not the sort of friends to quarrel over a woman," he went on, looking full at Clémentine, "and yet all he said yesterday was about Malaga.   But he never laid the tip of his finger on the girl."

"How do you know?" asked Clémentine.

"Well, I was naturally curious to see Mademoiselle Turquet, and the poor girl cannot account for Thaddeus' extraordinary reserve——"

"That is enough," said the Countess, going off to her own room, and saying to herself, "I have surely been the victim of some sublime hoax."

She had scarcely made the reflection, when Constantine placed in her hands the following letter, which Thaddeus had scrawled in the night:

"COUNTESS:—To go to be killed in the Caucasus, and to bear the burden of your scorn, is too much; a man should die unmutilated.   I loved you from the first time I saw you, as a man loves the woman he will love for ever, even when she is faithless—I, under obligations to Adam, whom you chose and married—I, so poor, the volunteer steward, devoted to your household.   In this dreadful catastrophe I found a delightful existence.   To be an indispensable wheel in the machine, to know myself useful to your luxury and comfort, was a source of joy to me; and if that joy had been keen when Adam alone was my care, think what it must have been when the woman I worshiped was at once the cause and the effect!   I have known all the joys of motherhood in my love; and I accepted life on those terms.   Like the beggars on the high-roads, I built myself a hut of stones on the skirts of your beautiful home, but without hold-

ing out my hand for alms. I, poor and unhappy, but blinded
by Adam's happiness, I was the donor. Yes, you were hedged
in by a love as pure as that of a guardian angel; it watched
while you slept; it caressed you with a look as you passed by;
it was glad merely to exist; in short, you were the sunshine
of home to the hapless exile who is now writing to you, with
tears in his eyes, as he recalls the happiness of those early
days.

"At the age of eighteen, with no one to love me, I had
chosen as an ideal mistress a charming woman at Warsaw, to
whom I referred all my thoughts and my wishes, the queen
of my days and nights. This woman knew nothing of it, but
why inform her? For my part, what I loved was love.

"You may fancy, from this adventure of my boyhood, how
happy I was, living within the sphere of your influence,
grooming your horse, picking out new gold-pieces for your
purse, superintending the splendor of your table and your entertainments, seeing you eclipse fortunes greater than your
own by my good management. With what zeal did I not
rush round Paris when Adam said to me, 'Thaddeus, *she*
wants this or that!' It was one of those joys for which there
are no words. You have now and again wished for some trifle
within a certain time which has compelled me to feats of
expedition, driving for six or seven hours in a cab; and what
happiness it has been to walk in your service. When I have
watched you smiling in the midst of your flowers without
being seen by you, I have forgotten that no one loved me—
in short, at such moments I was but eighteen again.

"Sometimes, when my happiness turned my brain, I would
go at night and kiss the spot where your feet had left, for me,
a luminous trace, just as of old I had stolen, with a thief's
miraculous skill, to kiss a key which Countess Ladislas had
touched on opening a door. The air you breathed was em-
balmed; to me it was fresh life to breathe it; and I felt, as
they say is the case in the tropics, overwhelmed by an atmo-

sphere surcharged with creative elements. I must tell you all these things to account for the strange fatuity of my involuntary thoughts. I would have died sooner than divulge my secret.

"You may remember those few days when you were curious, when you wanted to see the worker of the wonders which had at last struck you with surprise. I believed—forgive me, madame—I believed that you would love me. Your kindliness, your looks—interpreted by a lover—seemed fraught with so much danger to me that I took up Malaga, knowing that there are *liaisons* which no woman can forgive; I took the girl up at the moment when I saw that my love was inevitably infectious. Overwhelm me now with the scorn which you poured upon me so freely when I did not deserve it; but I think I may be quite sure that if, on the evening when your aunt took the Count out, I had said what I have here written, having once said it I should have been like the tame tiger who has at last set his teeth in living flesh, and who scents warm blood——

.   "*Midnight.*

"I could write no more, the memory of that evening was too vivid! Yes, I was then in a delirium! I saw expectancy in your eyes; victory and its crimson banners may have burned in mine and fascinated yours. My crime was to think such things—and perhaps wrongly. You alone can be judge of that fearful scene when I succeeded in crushing love, desire, the most stupendous forces of manhood under the icy hand of gratitude which must be eternal. Your terrible scorn punished me. You have showed me that neither disgust nor contempt can ever be gotten over. I love you like a madman. I must have gone away if Adam had died. There is all the more reason since Adam is saved. I did not snatch my friend from the grave to betray him. And, indeed, my departure is the due punishment for the thought that came to me that I would let him die when the physicians said his life depended on his attendants.

"Farewell, madame; in leaving Paris I lose everything, but you lose nothing in parting with yours most faithfully,

"THADDEUS PAZ."

"If my poor Adam says he has lost a friend, what have I lost?" thought Clémentine, sitting dejected, with her eyes fixed on a flower in the carpet.

This is the note which Constantine delivered privately to his master—

"MY DEAR MITGISLAS:—Malaga has told me all. For the sake of your happiness, never let a word escape you in Clémentine's presence as to your visits to the circus-rider; let her still believe that Malaga costs me a hundred thousand francs. With the Countess' character she will not forgive you either your losses at play or your visits to Malaga. I am not going to Khiva, but to the Caucasus. I have a fit of spleen, and at the pace I mean to go, in three months I shall be Prince Paz, or dead. Farewell; though I have drawn sixty thousand francs out of Nucingen's, we are quits.

"THADDEUS."

"Idiot that I am! I very nearly betrayed myself just now by speaking of the circus-rider!" said Adam to himself.

Thaddeus has been gone three years, and the papers do not as yet mention any Prince Paz. Countess Laginski takes a keen interest in the Emperor Nicholas' expeditions; she is a Russian at heart, and reads with avidity all the news from that country. Once or twice a year she says to the ambassador, with an affectation of indifference, "Do you know what has become of our poor friend Paz?"

Alas! most Parisian women, keen-eyed and subtle as they

25

are supposed to be, pass by—and always will pass by—such an one as Paz without observing him. Yes, more than one Paz remains misunderstood; but, fearful thought! some are misunderstood even when they are loved. The simplest woman in the world requires some little coxcombry in the greatest man; and the most heroic love counts for nothing if it is uncut; it needs the arts of the polisher and the jeweler.

In the month of January, 1842, Countess Laginski, beautified by gentle melancholy, inspired a mad passion in the Comte de la Palférine, one of the most audacious bucks of Paris at this day. La Palférine understood the difficulty of conquering a woman guarded by a chimera; to triumph over this bewitching woman, he trusted to a surprise, and to the assistance of a woman who, being a little jealous of Clémentine, would lend herself to plot the chances of the adventure.

Clémentine, incapable with all her wit of suspecting such treachery, was so imprudent as to go with this false friend to the masked ball at the opera. At about three in the morning, carried away by the excitement of the ball, Clémentine, for whom La Palférine had exhausted himself in attentions, consented to sup with him, and was getting into the lady's carriage. At this critical moment she was seized by a strong arm, and in spite of her cries placed in her own carriage, which was standing with the door open, though she did not know that it was waiting.

"He has not left Paris!" she exclaimed, recognizing Thaddeus, who ran off when he saw the carriage drive away with the Countess.

Had ever another woman such a romance in her life?

Clémentine is always hoping to see Paz again.

PARIS, *January*, 1842.

www.ingramcontent.com/pod-product-compliance
Lightning Source LLC
Chambersburg PA
CBHW032314280326
41932CB00009B/812